THE ENGLAND FOOTBALL FACT BOOK

THE ENGLAND FOOTBALL FACT BOOK

Cris Freddi

GUINNESS PUBLISHING

THE AUTHOR

Cris Freddi is the leading authority on matches played by
the England team. His articles appear regularly in the
national press, specialist magazines and fanzine annuals.
Educated at Oxford, the author of two published novels,
he now lives in London.
A depressingly average footballer and tennis player, he's
one of the best armchair sportsmen in the country,
appearing on BBC Radio's *Brain of Sport* and twice reaching
the final of ITV's *Sportsmasters*.

Editor: Charles Richards
Text design and layout: Steve Leaning
Cover design: Ad Vantage Studios

Published in Great Britain by Guinness Publishing Ltd,
33 London Road, Enfield, Middlesex

Front cover, from top: Alf Ramsey, Bobby Moore,
Nat Lofthouse, David Platt

Typeset in Baskerville and Helvetica by
Ace Filmsetting Ltd, Frome, Somerset

Printed and bound in Great Britain by
The Bath Press, Bath

British Library Cataloguing in Publication Data
Freddi, Cris, *1955–*
   The England football fact book
   1. Association football: Matches (Competitions):
   History
   I. Title
   796.33466
ISBN 0–85112–991–9

CONTENTS

ACKNOWLEDGEMENTS

A number of football books start their thank-you page with a word for David Barber, who has the key to the FA library. Add this one to the list. David has football in his veins and the patience of Job in the rest of him, sorely tested by my constant knocking on his door. I've never been turned away yet, or charged for photocopying. A veritable prince, and I doff my cap.

Special mentions too for Douglas Lamming's patient correspondence and remarkable generosity in making his collection of photographs available to us – and for Simon Duncan and Charles Richards, my editors at Guinness.

The rest – the other side of the coin from the Federations (mainly South American) who don't reply to letters, the clubs who don't return SAEs, the statisticians who guess some of their facts – go something like this (no sliding scale of actual help received): Gunther Nagy; Dave Allan; Andrzej Markowski; Vincenc Chysky; Len & Elsie Mellowship; Lars-Olof Wendler; Per Persson; Gareth Davies, Ceri Stennett and especially Ian Garland; Mike Gibson; Ted Green; Jon Silk; Michel Oreggia; the amazing Ron Templeton; Everton FC; QPR FC; Nottm Forest FC; Coventry City FC; Wade Martin (Stoke City); Matthew Chiles at West Brom; Graham Hughes at Wolves; Derek at Aston Villa; the Football Associations of Austria, Denmark, Malaysia, Romania, West Germany and the USSR; the staff at Colindale for their good humour and above all lightning speed; Ray Spiller; Kim Baratt; JH Macias; Andy Porter; John Cross; John Helliar; Bert Nicholson; David Toole; George Church; Roger Titford. There are others, but 12 years is a long time and I never thought I'd need to keep names for a page like this and . . . anyway, if you're not on this list and should be, consider yourself on it.

Above all, thanks and the best of everything to Brian Mellowship, who knows how much he's contributed and how little he's been repaid. This book wouldn't have been the same without him and is therefore dedicated to him, except for any errors, which are all my own work.

Last but not really, thanks to Christopher Rowe, for all the means to the end.

INTRODUCTION

I always knew it was impossible to put together a 'definitive work' on this subject. Here it is.

The first thing you realise is that delving into pre-war football is like digging among the remains of a lost civilisation; they didn't always write everything down. This means two things: a) you have to do much more reading to find what you're looking for, and b) you don't find it anyway. Bear with this one example: Bob Howarth was chosen as captain of the England team to play Ireland in 1890; he dropped out on the morning of the match and someone else tossed the coin. A someone not worth mentioning, it seems, because no-one does! National press, local press, Ulster papers – you name it, they don't. They can tell you who captained the amateur team that played Wales on the very same day, but Southern editors were never terribly interested in Northern professionals, rarely even listing their initials. Doubtless they thought them *frightfully* difficult to tell apart.

It gets worse. You read a dozen reports, and it becomes clear that not only did the substitute captain escape attention, just about everything else was missed too. Understandably so, to be fair, given the conditions: after the 'almost incessant rain of the past week', the pitch was a 'quagmire', even 'a veritable bog'; players slipped and fell until it was 'almost impossible to distinguish the players, so black an appearance did they present'. As a result, each England goal (there were nine) is credited to at least two different players. In the next match, at Hampden Park, Scotland's goal was scored by 'M'Pherson, I think'. You see the problem. The bottom line is that in the absence of film, there are times when we'll *never know for sure*. Cut out the last line and use it as a bookmark.

What it all means is that a book like this can't make any guarantees. Too many facts are missing, albeit a relative handful out of thousands and thousands, and sources tend to disagree about others. Every effort has been made, as they say, but there are still gaps in the jigsaw: a referee here, an England captain there (six in all), the occasional attendance figure, I've missed a penalty or two. It adds up to very, very little, given that so much has been unearthed – but it pays to remember it's not all here. I'd have written everything down if only *they* had.

Much the same goes for the players' individual biographies. Again, it's no-one's fault. In 1972, Douglas Lamming and Morley Farror brought out a book with pen portraits of all the players who'd won England caps till then. Doug Lamming's updated edition (1990) referred to it as a seminal work on British soccer, which is immodest but absolutely right – so much so that no-one could write a book about England players without drawing on it, or the revised version, and I've done both. But again, a word of caution. Several years ago, Jim Creasy did some exhaustive work in the newspaper library at Colindale that uncovered the christian names and dates of birth of hundreds of Football League players, including a great many who played for England; quite a number of these appear to have gone straight into the new Lamming book. There are two problems with this. First, you wonder about the sources for the first book, and second, the new ones may not all be reliable. Most of them are, no doubt, but if, say, Raich Carter's date of birth is correct, he would have been 20 when he played for England Schools. No fault of Jim's, of course. It's just that printing errors exist, mistakes are made, newspapers don't claim to be infallible. Even when they do write it down, they don't always write it right.

Of course, Doug Lamming will have checked the Colindale input against his own sources (Barry Hugman's excellent League Players' Records, for instance) but nevertheless, where there's more than one version, I've thought it best to say so, even where one looks less plausible than the other. I've taken the same approach with the lists of records, pointing out alternatives where they exist. The point is, they do exist – and, even in a football fact book, a fact is sometimes just a consensus of opinion. (Actually, after 12 years' tearing hair out in libraries, it's often a four-letter word, but let that pass.)

So beware (a little). Understand that a list of Oldest Players depends on a list of available dates of birth, and some of them aren't available yet. The same goes for penalty saves, first-minute goals, attendances – but, in all honesty, not too much else. Mistakes may have been made in adding up days and years to arrive at a player's age, but these should be obvious and forgiveable, as should any printing errors. Research has been done, collation has gone on, facts have been checked. Above all, there's been no guesswork. That's one guarantee this book does make.

We been working nights. Be sceptical, but enjoy.

BIBLIOGRAPHY

Anyone writing a reference book has to read hundreds of others. Some useful, some very useful, some downright confusing, all grist to the mill. Of the hundreds, the following have produced the best grist:

The two Lamming books of course, the first in collaboration with the late Morley Farror: *A Century of English International Football* (1972) and *An English Internationalists' Who's Who* (1990). Without them, the biography section here would have been possible but even more incomplete. Two tremendous pieces of research. (Incidentally, if Doug's books are as good as I say they are, should you be buying this one? Well, apart from the obvious difference of this including a records section, it's also more recent – the latest if not the greatest – and another 29 players have won England caps since Doug's latest book. But it also has a different emphasis, highlighting the players as *England* players, leaving aside their club careers to concentrate on the international goals they scored, the exact dates of their first and last caps, how often they captained England and so on – I think it's the first of *that* kind. The Lamming volumes spread their net wider. If you want to know where an England player was born, his life after football, even the school he went to, that's where to look.)

Who's Who of Scottish Internationalists Douglas Lamming. Just as good as his English version.
Rothmans Book of Football League Records 1888–89 to 1978–79 Ian Laschke.
Rothmans Football League Players Records 1946–81 Barry Hugman.
Rothmans Yearbooks various. Fine for dates of birth, some mistakes in international line-ups.
The Football Encyclopaedia 1934.
The Football Annual various; soccer editor, Charles Alcock.
Athletic News Annual various.
Gamage's Annuals various again.
Leng's Football Handbook not so various; just 1903.
100 Years of Scottish Football John Rafferty. Variable.
England v Scotland Brian James. Many errors but very good in parts.
A Lifetime in Football Charles Buchan.
40 Years in Football Ivan Sharpe.
50 Years of Football Frederick Wall.
Association Football & the Men who Made it Gibson & Pickford.
Refereeing Round the World Arthur Ellis.
Soccer: a Panorama Brian Glanville.
Captain of Hungary Ferenc Puskas.

History of Queen's Park FC 1867–1917 Richard Robinson.
The Book of Football 1906.
Wisden Book of Obituaries.
Who's Who of Test Cricketers Christopher Martin-Jenkins.
Against the World Kevin Keegan. Very good (yes, honestly).
Sporting Days and Sporting Ways NL Jackson.
Association Football NL Jackson.
Annals of the Corinthians BO Corbett.
The Guinness Book of Athletics Facts and Feats Peter Matthews.
5000 Goles Blancos History of Real Madrid.
Boys of '66 Martin Tyler.
Cup Final Extra Martin Tyler.
Forward Arsenal! Bernard Joy.
Bobby Moore Jeff Powell.
Alf Ramsey: Anatomy of a Football Manager Max Marquis.
Sheffield Wednesday: a Complete Record Keith Farnsworth.
L–Equipe Guide 1984–85.

And look out for the *Welsh International Who's Who* by Ian Garland & Gareth Davies.

On top of the hundreds of books, there are newspapers by the thousand. All the national press of course, nowadays especially *The Guardian*, *The Independent* and *The Times*. Before 1940, and especially last century, *The Sporting Life*, *Sportsman*, *Sporting Chronicle*, *Athletic News*, *The Field*, *Glasgow Evening News*, *Glasgow Herald*, *Scottish Referee*, *Belfast Evening Telegraph*, *Ulster Football & Cycling News*, *Ireland's Saturday Night*, *Northern Whig* (Belfast), *Irish Times*, *Wrexham Advertiser*, *Le Figaro*, *ABC* (Madrid), *L'Independance Belge*, *France Foorball*, *El Mercurio* (Santiago, Chile), *Excelsior* (Mexico City), *Clarin*, *La Nacion* (Buenos Aires), *El Comercio* (Quito), *Accrington Times*, *Preston Herald*, *Blackburn Standard* . . .

In the end, though, however much you read and double-check, you're at the mercy of your sources. If they're at fault, I can only refer you back to them and say they were reproduced in good faith and of course I'm utterly blameless and was only following orders. Where faults show up, tell me and not the publishers. But not *too* harshly please – and, where possible, quote your own sources.

CMG Freddi
Shepherd's Bush
June 1991

8

PART ONE
THE ENGLAND RECORDS

Figures given throughout the book are correct up to and including the match against Malaysia on 12 June 1991

MOST CAPS

125	Peter Shilton	1970–90
108	Bobby Moore	1962–73
106	Bobby Charlton	1958–70
105	Billy Wright	1946–59
89	Bryan Robson	1980–91
86	Kenny Sansom	1979–88
84	Ray Wilkins	1976–86
77	Terry Butcher	1980–90
76	Tom Finney	1946–58
73	Gordon Banks	1963–72
72	Alan Ball	1965–75
68	Gary Lineker	1984–91
67	Martin Peters	1966–74
65	Dave V Watson	1974–82
65	John Barnes	1983–91
63	Ray Wilson	1960–68
63	Kevin Keegan	1972–82
62	Emlyn Hughes	1969–80
61	Ray Clemence	1972–83
61	Chris Waddle	1985–90
57	Jimmy Greaves	1959–67
56	Johnny Haynes	1954–62
54	Stanley Matthews	1934–57
53	Glenn Hoddle	1979–88
52	Trevor Francis	1977–86
50	Phil Neal	1976–83
49	Ron Flowers	1955–66
49	Geoff Hurst	1966–72
49	Peter Beardsley	1986–91

All four century totals have been European records in their day, generally accepted as world bests.

No other country has produced so many centurions. Poland and East Germany come closest, with two each: Grzegorz Lato (103) and Kaziu Deyna (102); Joachim Streich (102) and Hans-Jurgen Dorner (100) respectively. If matches against club sides and regional selections are included, Pele and Gylmar of Brazil also won more than 100 each.

Wright won all his caps while Walter Winterbottom was manager, Moore exactly 100 under Alf Ramsey. He broke Charlton's record in Turin in 1973 – and wasn't best pleased that the Italian FA didn't make a presentation!

MOST CONSECUTIVE CAPS

70	Billy Wright	1951–59
40	Ron Flowers	1958–63
37	Kenny Sansom	1984–87
33	Billy Wright	1946–50
33	Roger Byrne	1954–57
33	Dave V Watson	1977–80
31	Jimmy Armfield	1960–63
29	Alf Ramsey	1949–53
29	Des Walker	1989–91
27	Neil Franklin	1946–50
27	Bobby Moore	1966–68
26	Ernie Blenkinsop	1928–33
25	Billy Wedlock	1907–12
25	Jimmy Dickinson	1951–54
25	Bobby Charlton	1960–62
25	Martin Peters	1969–71
25	Mick Channon	1973–76
25	Stuart Pearce	1989–90

Wright's total is still easily the world record. The figures for Blenkinsop, Franklin and Byrne constitute their entire England careers. Byrne's was ended only by his death in the Munich air disaster.

Walker's run ended when he was rested after the FA Cup Final and did not play against the Soviet Union.

In a time when fewer internationals were played, Billy Wedlock's 25 were spread over six seasons (1907–12).

GAPS BETWEEN CAPS

Yrs	Days		
11	59	Ian Callaghan	1966–77
9	347	Andy Ducat	1910–20
9	164	Raich Carter	1937–46
8	10	Arthur Dunn	1884–92
7	359	Larry Lloyd	1972–80
7	343	Fanny Walden	1914–22
7	329	Stanley Matthews	1939–47
7	213	Frank Lampard	1972–80
7	129	Tommy Lawton	1939–46
7	28	Charlie Buchan	1913–20
6	356	Vic Watson	1923–30
6	204	Mike O'Grady	1962–69
6	203	Joe Hodkinson	1913–19
6	56	Charlie Wallace	1914–20
6	56	Bill Watson	1914–20
6	29	George Elliott	1914–20
6	6	Joe McCall	1914–20

Walden, O'Grady and Lampard won only two caps each.

Even Callaghan couldn't quite match Irishman **Billy McCracken's** feat, which was surely a record for all international football: due to the First World War and a much-publicised altercation with the selectors, he didn't play for Ireland between the England matches of 1907 and 1919, a gap of **12 years 251 days**.

Wor Bobby's 100th cap was won against Northern Ireland in 1970. Made captain for the day, he celebrated by scoring England's third in a 3–1 win (Bob Thomas)

MOST APPEARANCES AGAINST ONE COUNTRY

13	Billy Wright	v Scotland	1947–59
13	Billy Wright	v N Ireland	1946–58
12	Bob Crompton	v Scotland	1902–14
12	Bob Crompton	v Wales	1902–14
12	Billy Wright	v Wales	1946–58
12	Bobby Charlton	v Scotland	1958–69
12	Bobby Moore	v Scotland	1963–73
11	Tom Finney	v Wales	1946–57
11	Bobby Moore	v Wales	1962–73
11	Peter Shilton	v N Ireland	1972–87
10	Norman C Bailey	v Scotland	1878–87
10	Steve Bloomer	v Scotland	1895–1907
10	Bob Crompton	v Ireland	1902–14
10	Tom Finney	v Scotland	1948–58
10	Bobby Charlton	v Wales	1958–70
10	Bobby Charlton	v N Ireland	1958–70
10	Gordon Banks	v Scotland	1963–72
10	Bobby Moore	v N Ireland	1962–73
10	Alan Ball	v Scotland	1966–75
10	Peter Shilton	v Scotland	1973–89

MOST APPEARANCES AGAINST ONE COUNTRY (non-British)

8	Alan Ball	v West Germany	1965–75
7	Bobby Moore	v W Germany	1965–72
6	Bobby Charlton	v Portugal	1958–69
6	Bobby Charlton	v Brazil	1959–70
6	Gordon Banks	v W Germany	1965–72
6	Peter Shilton	v Italy	1973–90
5	Billy Wright	v France	1947–57
5	Bobby Charlton	v Spain	1960–68
5	Bobby Moore	v Brazil	1962–70
5	Geoff Hurst	v W Germany	1966–72
5	Colin Bell	v W Germany	1968–75
5	Peter Shilton	v Poland	1973–89
5	Peter Shilton	v Denmark	1982–90
5	Peter Shilton	v W Germany	1982–90
5	Gary Lineker	v Eire	1985–91

When Hurst played his first game for England, and his last, and scored the only hat-trick in a World Cup Final, the opposition was West Germany on each occasion.

Left *Andrew Ducat, Aston Villa, Surrey and England. Waited nearly ten years for his fifth cap at football, then only another 15 months for his first at cricket* (Lamming)

MOST APPEARANCES AGAINST ENGLAND

20	Billy Meredith	Wales	1895–1920
20	Pat Jennings	N Ireland	1964–85
15	Sammy McIlroy	N Ireland	1974–86
14	Ivor Allchurch	Wales	1950–65
13	Billy Bingham	N Ireland	1951–63
13	Jimmy McIlroy	N Ireland	1951–65
12	Bill Lewis	Wales	1885–97
12	Danny Blanchflower	N Ireland	1950–62
11	Olphie Stanfield	Ireland	1887–97
11	Bobby Walker	Scotland	1900–13
11	Billy Gillespie	Ireland	1913–30
11	Alan Morton	Scotland	1921–32
11	Elisha Scott	Ireland	1920–35
11	Rod Thomas	Wales	1969–77
11	Leighton James	Wales	1973–83
11	John Mahoney	Wales	1967–83
10	Charles Campbell	Scotland	1874–86
10	Watty Arnott	Scotland	1884–93
10	Bob Milne	Ireland	1894–1906
10	Andrew Aitken	Scotland	1901–11
10	Grenville Morris	Wales	1896–1912
10	Billy Scott	Ireland	1903–13
10	Fred Keenor	Wales	1920–30
10	Alf Sherwood	Wales	1946–56
10	Cliff Jones	Wales	1955–67
10	Denis Law	Scotland/Rest of the World	1960–72
10	Terry Neill	N Ireland	1961–73
10	Mike England	Wales	1963–73
10	Pat Rice	N Ireland	1971–79
10	Terry Yorath	Wales	1971–80
10	Kenny Dalglish	Scotland	1973–82
10	Bryan Flynn	Wales	1975–83

The Scotts were brothers, and both captained Ireland against England.

Mahoney won his first and last caps in matches against England.

Danny Blanchflower, Jimmy McIlroy and Billy Bingham all played against England for the 10th time in the Northern Ireland match of 1960.

MOST APPEARANCES AGAINST ENGLAND (non-British)

7	Gylmar	Brazil	1956–69
7	Franz Beckenbauer	W Germany	1966–75
6	Armand Swartenbroeks	Belgium	1921–27
6	Jan Debie	Belgium	1921–29
6	Florimond van Halme	Belgium	1923–29
6	Francisco (Paco) Gento	Spain/Rest of World	1955–68
6	Mario Coluna	Portugal	1958–66
6	Dino Zoff	Italy	1973–80
6	Romeo Benetti	Italy	1973–80
6	Imre Garaba	Hungary	1981–90
6	David O'Leary	Eire	1976–91
5	Pierre Braine	Belgium	1924–29
5	Raymond Braine	Belgium/Rest of Europe	1926–38
5	Vladimir Beara	Yugoslavia/FIFA	1950–58
5	Jose Travacos	Portugal	1947–58
5	Branko Zebec	Yugoslavia/FIFA	1953–60
5	Gerhard Hanappi	Austria/FIFA	1951–61
5	Jose Augusto	Portugal	1958–66
5	Eusebio	Portugal/Rest of the World	1961–66
5	Horst-Dieter Hottges	W Germany	1965–72
5	Dragan Dzajic	Yugoslavia	1965–74
5	Ivo Viktor	Czechoslovakia	1966–75
5	Giacinto Facchetti	Italy	1973–77
5	Sepp Maier	W Germany	1970–78
5	Pat Bonner	Eire	1985–91
5	Paul McGrath	Eire	1985–91

The Braines were brothers.

WON 50th CAP IN A MATCH AGAINST ENGLAND

Branko Stankovic	Yugoslavia	1954
Jacques (Jacky) Fatton	Switzerland	1954
Danny Blanchflower	N Ireland	1961
Billy Bingham	N Ireland	1962
Janos Gorocs	Hungary	1965
Horst-Dieter Hottges	W Germany	1972
Robert Sara	Austria	1979
Leighton James	Wales	1982
John Kosmina	Australia	1983
Liam Brady	Eire	1985
Zlatko Vujovic	Yugoslavia	1987
Alain Geiger	Switzerland	1988
Mick McCarthy	Eire	1990

Brady celebrated with a goal, McCarthy with a near miss from inside his own half. His free-kick, taken by the wind, clipped the top of Chris Woods' crossbar.

There may well be others, but *not* Terry Neill of Northern Ireland in 1972, despite what some reference books say. It was his 51st cap.

Two players won their 100th cap in a match against England: **Gylmar** of Brazil in 1969 (a total that included matches against club teams, as does Kosmina's) and **Joachim Streich** of East Germany in 1984.

The most capped player to appear against England was **Pat Jennings**, who won his 113th cap for Northern Ireland at Wembley in 1985.

Mike Summerbee leaves empty-handed as big Pat collects at Wembley in 1972, the only time he was on the winning side against England (Popperfoto)

LONGEST ENGLAND CAREERS

Yrs	days		
22	228	Stanley Matthews	1934–57
19	224	Peter Shilton	1970–90
13	54	Sam Hardy	1907–20
13	34	Raich Carter	1934–47
13	23	Jesse Pennington	1907–20
12	242	Billy Wright	1946–59
12	56	Bobby Charlton	1958–70
12	45	Billy Walker	1920–32
12	32	Bob Crompton	1902–14
12	28	Steve Bloomer	1895–1907
12	24	Tom Finney	1946–58
11	178	Bobby Moore	1962–73
11	108	Ian Callaghan	1966–77
11	57	Charlie Buchan	1913–24
11	49	Bryan Robson	1980–91
11	45	Ron Flowers	1955–66
11	01	Ray Clemence	1972–83
10	254	Andy Ducat	1910–20
10	191	Emlyn Hughes	1969–80
10	168	Ray Wilkins	1976–86
10	52	John Goodall	1888–98
10	34	Terry Butcher	1980–90
10	15	Alan Ball	1965–75
10	2	Johnny Holt	1890–1900

LONGEST CAREERS AGAINST ENGLAND

BRITISH PLAYERS

Yrs	days			
24	363	Billy Meredith	Wales	1895–1920
21	11	Pat Jennings	N Ireland	1964–85
19	233	Billy McCracken	Ireland	1902–21
17	247	Billy Gillespie	Ireland	1913–30
15	361	Grenville Morris	Wales	1896–1912
15	252	Bill Lacey	Ireland	1909–24
15	125	John Mahoney	Wales	1967–83
14	361	Elisha Scott	Ireland	1920–35
14	354	Lot Jones	Wales	1905–20
14	353	Ted Vizard	Wales	1911–26
14	321	Ivor Allchurch	Wales	1950–65
14	246	Moses Russell	Wales	1914–28
13	361	Jimmy McIlroy	N Ireland	1951–65
13	261	Albert (Bert) Gray	Wales	1924–37

NON-BRITISH PLAYERS

Yrs	days			
15	195	Uwe Seeler	W Germany	1954–70
14	200	David O'Leary	Eire	1976–91
13	236	Robert Sara	Austria	1965–79
13	205	Silvio Piola	Rest of Europe/ Italy	1938–52
13	34	Gylmar	Brazil	1956–69
12	356	Francisco Gento	Spain	1955–68
12	289	Oleg Blokhin	USSR	1973–86
12	201	Ruud Krol	Holland	1969–82
12	155	Raymond Braine	Belgium/ Rest of Europe	1926–38

Below *Veteran captains Arthur Knight (left) and Billy Meredith before the England–Wales Victory international in 1919. The following season they appeared in official England matches, Knight for the first and only time, Meredith for the 20th and last* (Hulton)

66 British and 24 foreign players have appeared in England matches at least 10 years apart, the most recent from outside the British Isles being **Eric Gerets** and **Jan Ceulemans** of Belgium in the 1990 World Cup.

The England players who started the match in Tunis with a mere 534 caps behind them. Back row, left to right: Gascoigne, Pearce, Lineker, Walker, Waddle, Shilton. Front: Butcher, Hodge, Stevens, Robson, Barnes (Allsport/ Ben Radford)

THE MOST EXPERIENCED TEAM

The 15 who drew 1–1 with Tunisia in 1990 went into the match with a total of 606 caps behind them. However, the most experienced *starting line-up* (total 563) played in the very next match, against Eire in Cagliari.

v Tunisia 1990		v Eire 1990	
Peter Shilton	117	Peter Shilton	118
M Gary Stevens	38	M Gary Stevens	39
Stuart Pearce	23	Stuart Pearce	24
Bryan Robson (capt)	84	Bryan Robson (capt)	85
Des Walker	17	Des Walker	18
Terry Butcher	71	Terry Butcher	72
Chris Waddle	51	Chris Waddle	52
Paul Gascoigne	10	Paul Gascoigne	11
Gary Lineker	50	Gary Lineker	51
John Barnes	52	John Barnes	53
Steve Hodge	21	Peter Beardsley	40
Peter Beardsley	39		
Mark Wright	23		
David Platt	4		
Steve Bull	6		

The most experienced opposition may well have been the Northern Ireland 13 who went into the 1985 World Cup qualifier at Wembley with exactly 500 caps behind them. Experience told, as a goalless draw saw both countries through to the finals.

The 16 players who made up the Rest of the World team at Wembley in 1963 had more than 650 previous caps between them. Puskas, di Stefano and Kopa had finished playing for their countries.

THE LEAST EXPERIENCED TEAM

Besides the very first England team (1872), which of course had no previous official international experience, there were several others in the early years with just a handful of caps behind them: 1873 v Scotland (only 2 previous appearances among the entire XI), 1876 v Scotland and 1892 v Wales (only 4), and so on.

The least experienced England team this century beat Sweden 4–2 in 1923 with 7 new caps, and 7 previous appearances between the other four. The least experienced since the last war (v Ireland in the first peacetime international) had 16 caps behind them. Since the arrival of Ramsey, numbers have gone up dramatically, and only one England team has gone into a match with fewer than 50 past appearances: in the second Wales match of 1976. There were just 3 new caps, but only 47 previous appearances between the rest.

Three England teams (all v Scotland, 1872–76–79) featured six players who won just one cap each. Every one of the first six England teams had at least five such players. The most since World War II is a relatively sober four in the Northern Ireland game in 1954: Ray Barlow, Bill Foulkes, Brian Pilkington and Johnny Wheeler.

In Lisbon in 1974, in his very last match in charge, as if trying to show that he *could* make changes, Ramsey picked a team with 145 caps behind it, of which Martin Peters and Alan Ball were responsible for 128. The other nine players had collected only 17 between them.

MOST NEW CAPS IN A TEAM

11	1872 v Scotland
9	1873 v Scotland
9	1876 v Scotland
9	1889 v Ireland
9	1946 v Ireland

The most in recent years has been 8 in the Welsh centenary match of **1976**, when Phil Boyer, Dave Clement, Mick Doyle, Trevor Cherry, Phil Neal, Peter Taylor, Ray Kennedy and Phil Thompson made their debuts.

MOST LAST CAPS IN A TEAM

10	1939 v Romania
9	1890 v Ireland
8	1874 v Scotland
8	1875 v Scotland
8	1925 v France

The most in recent years has been 5, in two virtual B matches: **Australia** in **1980** (Brian Greenhoff, Frank Lampard, Alan Sunderland, Brian Talbot and Peter Ward) and **Iceland** in **1982** (Joe Corrigan, Paul Goddard, Terry McDermott, Steve Perryman and Dave V Watson).

MOST NEW CAPS IN AN OPPOSING TEAM

11	Scotland	1872
11	Ireland	1882
10	Wales	1885
8	Ireland	1887
8	Ireland	1919
8	Ireland	1946

Scotland and Ireland played their very first international matches against England. The 1919 and 1946 games were Ireland's first after the two World Wars.

In recent years, the most has been the **6** in the **Brazilian** team that drew 1–1 at Wembley in **1987**. Mirandinha, who scored the equaliser, was one of them, the captain Geraldao another.

MOST LAST CAPS IN AN OPPOSING TEAM

11	Bohemia	1908
11	Scotland	1939
7	Scotland	1914

These were Scotland's last matches before the two World Wars.

The match in Prague was the last ever played by **Bohemia**.

The first Welsh team to play England (1879) included five players who won only the one cap.

ONE-CAP WONDERS

No fewer than 316 players (nearly one in three) have played for England just the once.

GOALSCORERS

33 in all, including **5 who scored hat-tricks**:

1888	Albert Allen	v Ireland
1889	Jack Yates	v Ireland
1893	Walter Gilliat	v Ireland
1894	John Veitch	v Wales
1908	Frank Bradshaw	v Austria

Several scored twice, including William Kenyon Slaney (scorer of England's first ever goal), Harold Halse, Joe Payne of 10-goal fame, and Jack Haines.

Others include journalist Norman Creek, Bill Nicholson, Tony Kay, Paul Goddard, and Danny Wallace.

GOALKEEPERS WHO DIDN'T CONCEDE A GOAL

1872	Robert Barker	v Scotland
1882	JFP Rawlinson	v Ireland
1897	Willie Foulke	v Wales
1901	Matt Kingsley	v Wales
1920	Jack Mew	v Ireland
1921	Ernest ('Tim') Coleman	v Wales
1922	Teddy Davison	v Wales
1924	Harry Hardy	v Belgium
1932	Harold Pearson	v Scotland
1974	Phil Parkes	v Portugal
1983	Nigel Spink	v Australia

Barker was England's first goalkeeper; he changed places with WJ Maynard during the second half and therefore, like Spink, played only half a match as an international goalkeeper.

ONE-CAP CAPTAINS

1873	Alexander Morten	v Scotland
1875	Charles Alcock	v Scotland
1883	Jack Hudson	v Ireland
1919	Arthur Knight	v Ireland
1922	Max Woosnam	v Wales
1923	Graham Doggart	v Belgium
1925	Claude Ashton	v Ireland

BROTHERS

Two sets of brothers won only one cap each: Alfred and Edward **Lyttleton**, Rex and Bertie **Corbett**.

DOUBLE INTERNATIONALS

1877	Alfred Lyttleton	Cricket
1879	Reginald Birkett	Rugby Union
1901	Charles (CB) Fry	Cricket
1910	Wally Hardinge	Cricket
1933	John Arnold	Cricket
1951	Arthur Milton	Cricket

Arnold won only one cap at both sports.
Fry also equalled an unofficial world long jump record.

OTHERS

Frank Barson, Clem Stephenson, Herbie Roberts (the prototype stopper centre-half), Arthur Rowe, George Eastham senior, Bernard Joy (the last amateur to play for England), Jimmy Hagan, Jesse Pye, Ernie Taylor, Bill Foulkes, Brian Miller, Ron Henry, Ken Shellito, Derek Temple, John Hollins, Alex Stepney, Ian Storey-Moore, Colin Harvey, Jeff Blockley, Phil Boyer, John Gidman.

SHORTEST ENGLAND CAREERS

Mins		
8	Jimmy Barrrett	1928
8	Peter Ward	1980
9	Brian Marwood	1988
17	Peter Davenport	1985
18	Kevin Hector*	1973
19	Brian Little	1975
20	Steve Perryman	1982
23	Nigel Winterburn	1989
26	Trevor Whymark	1977
45	Frank Hartley	1923
45	Jimmy Rimmer	1976
45	Nigel Spink	1983
45	Michael Phelan	1989
45	Lee Sharpe	1991
49	Steve Hunt*	1984
50	Paul Goddard	1982
65	Charlie George	1976
70	Mark Walters	1991
74	Tony Brown	1971
75	WH Carr	1875
76	Fred Fox	1925
78	Brian Stein	1984
82	Alan Sunderland	1980

*from 2 appearances

One source says Barrett went off injured after only 4 minutes of the match against Ireland, but that may have been the time he was actually injured.

Paul Goddard came on for Cyrille Regis and scored England's equaliser in Rekyjavik – but won no further caps, making him the only England goal-scorer with an international career of less than 90 minutes (Bob Thomas)

Ward came on as substitute for Sunderland against Australia in Sydney.

Carr missed a train from Sheffield and arrived late for the match against Scotland in 1875, leaving England with only 10 men (and a substitute goalkeeper) for the first quarter of an hour or so.

Because the pitch was covered in snow before the England–Wales match of **1879**, the captains agreed to play for only an hour instead of an hour and a half – so **RD Anderson**, **Tom Sorby** and **Herbert Whitfeld** played only **60** minutes for England.

No England player has had an international career as short as that of **Beat Reider**, who played only **5** minutes for Switzerland in total, at Wembley in 1977, the same stadium where fellow

Swiss **Peter Meier** played his **30** minutes of international football in 1971.

After Renzo Buffon, Italy's goalkeeper and captain, had broken his nose on Johnny Haynes' knee in **1961**, **Giuseppe Vavassori** came on for his first cap and let in two goals, including a shot that went between his legs; he never played for Italy again – an international career of **34** minutes.

John Cowan won his only cap as substitute for Northern Ireland at Wembley in 1970.

No player has had a more fleeting acquaintance with the England team than **Semir Tuce** of Yugoslavia, who came on as substitute at Wembley in 1986, was injured and himself substituted after less than **2** minutes.

SUBSTITUTES

The first substitute in an England match (indeed, in any international) appeared way back in 1908, when Dai Davies came on for Wales just after half-time, taking over in goal from Charlie Morris who'd replaced the injured Dickie Roose. Davies was the only player to win senior caps at both football and rugby league. Incidentally, it must have taken a pretty bad injury to force Roose to leave the pitch as he'd played almost the entire match against England in 1904 with a fractured little finger of the left hand.

There was nearly a substitution in the match against Ireland in 1892, after John Peden had to leave the field with an injured knee – but it was decided that no-one could come on to replace him because he went off as the result of a foul!

The first player to make his England debut as a substitute was Norman Hunter against Spain in 1965.

MOST TIMES A SUBSTITUTE

14	Chris Waddle
13	John Barnes
12	Tony Woodcock
12	Mark Hateley
11	Peter Beardsley
10	Trevor Francis
10	Glenn Hoddle
9	Chris Woods
8	Steve Bull
8	Trevor Steven
7	David Platt

MOST TIMES SUBSTITUTED

20	Chris Waddle
19	Bryan Robson
16	Peter Beardsley
16	Gary Lineker
15	Peter Shilton
12	John Barnes
10	Tony Woodcock
9	Trevor Brooking
8	Paul Mariner
8	Trevor Francis
8	Trevor Steven

GOALSCORING SUBSTITUTES

1950	Jimmy Mullen	v Belgium
1956	Nat Lofthouse (2)	v Finland
1956	Tommy Taylor (2)	v Yugoslavia
1964	Bobby Charlton	v USA
1970	Brian Kidd	v Ecuador
1976	Peter Taylor	v Wales
1978	Tony Currie	v Wales
1978	Tony Currie	v Hungary
1981	Terry McDermott	v Switzerland
1982	Paul Goddard	v Iceland
1982	Tony Woodcock	v W Germany
1982	Mark Chamberlain	v Luxembourg
1982	Glenn Hoddle	v Luxembourg
1985	Trevor Steven	v USA
1989	Paul Gascoigne	v Albania
1989	Steve Bull	v Scotland
1990	Steve Bull	v Tunisia
1990	David Platt	v Belgium
1990	Peter Beardsley	v Poland
1991	David Hirst	v N Zealand

Mullen was England's first ever substitute. He came on for Jackie Milburn after 10 minutes and scored in the first minute of the second half.

Peter Taylor and Chamberlain scored on their England debuts, Kidd in his last England match, Goddard in his only one.

Lofthouse came on for Tommy Taylor, injured in a collision with goalkeeper Keijo Hurri who also had to leave the pitch; Aare Klinga replaced him.

GOALSCORING SUBSTITUTES AGAINST ENGLAND

1953	Otto Decker (2)	USA		1987	Wolfram Wuttke	W Germany
1968	Rolf Andersson	Sweden		1988	Viktor Pasulko	USSR
1976	Roberto	Brazil		1990	Eugene Ekeke	Cameroon
1978	Ronnie Worm	W Germany		1990	Tony Cascarino	Eire
1980	Terry Cochrane	N Ireland				
1980	Dani (pen)	Spain				
1984	Sergei Gotsmanov	USSR				
1984	Oleg Protasov	USSR				

Gotsmanov and Protasov scored in the same game, Protasov in the last minute.

Worm had scored v England B the previous evening.

Right *Jimmy Mullen, who set England on the way to a 4–1 win in Brussels with the equaliser after coming on as substitute* (Popperfoto)

The Daddy Of Them All

Saturday 30 November 1872
West of Scotland Cricket Ground, Hamilton Crescent, Partick, Glasgow 3500

SCOTLAND 0   ENGLAND 0

Referee: William Keay (Scotland)
Umpires: Charles Alcock (England) & H Smith (Scotland)

SCOTLAND

Bob Gardner (capt)
William Ker
Joseph Taylor
James Thompson
James Smith
Robert Smith
Robert Leckie
Alexander Rhind
Willie M MacKinnon
Jamie ('Jerry') Weir
David Wotherspoon

ENGLAND

Robert Barker	Hertfordshire Rangers
Ernest Greenhalgh	Notts County
Reginald Welch	Wanderers
Frederick Chappell	Oxford University
William John Maynard	1st Surrey Rifles
John Brockbank	Cambridge University
Charles Clegg	Sheffield Wednesday
Arnold Kirke Smith	Oxford University
Cuthbert Ottaway (capt)	Oxford University & Old Etonians
Charles John Chenery	Crystal Palace
Charles John Morice	Barnes

The general consensus is that every player was affiliated to Queen's Park: the Smiths attended the club's meetings even though they had moved to London and were playing for South Norwood. But Ker had apparently left for Granville FC in the same month that the international was played, and Alcock's football annual lists Thompson as also playing for Granville.

The players refused to guarantee to buy prints, so there are no photographs of the first official international match (which was arguably just a continuation of the Wanderers – Queen's Park rivalry). There was no crossbar at the time; a late shot by Leckie landed on top of the tape.

The scoreline gives a clue as to the style of the times. Both sides played with eight forwards, but each player was expected to dribble past opponent after opponent before inevitably losing the ball. Scotland's famous, radical, method of actually passing it was obviously still in its infancy. Anyway, who knows? Perhaps the end product wasn't considered as important as the do-or-die dribble against impossible odds. The past is another country, alright.

The Smiths were the first brothers to play international football. Clegg's brother William appeared in the next match, later in the same season.

Barker played in goal until the second half, when he changed places with Maynard, who's listed as England's first goalkeeper in most reference books. Gardner too played outfield during the second half, changing positions with R Smith.

Ottaway, at 22 years 133 days, was England's youngest captain before Bobby Moore in 1963.

Maynard, aged 19 years 257 days, was the first teenager to play in an official international.

Nine players won just this one cap: Barker, Brockbank, Chappell, Clegg, Kirke Smith, Morice; Leckie, Rhind and J Smith.

Crystal Palace was a different club from the current one.

Chappell later changed his name to Maddison and is usually listed as such in record books. Kirke Smith is usually listed under Smith, but contemporary match reports show Kirke as part of his surname. Gardner apparently once signed himself RW Gardiner.

Alcock, the FA Secretary, helped pick himself to play, but couldn't take his place in the team. He finally played against Scotland in 1875. Tom Lawrie, who refereed later England matches, was selected by Scotland, but he too cried off, and never did play international football. Nor did Archibald Rae, who was originally selected but replaced by Weir; he refereed the 1874 England–Scotland match.

GOALSCORERS

MOST GOALS

49	Bobby Charlton***	1958–70	14	George Hilsdon**	1908–09
45	Gary Lineker****	1985–91	13	Bobby Smith	1960–63
44	Jimmy Greaves	1959–67	13	Martin Chivers	1971–73
30	Tom Finney***	1946–58	13	Paul Mariner	1977–83
30	Nat Lofthouse	1950–58	12	Fred Dewhurst	1886–89
29	Vivian Woodward	1903–11	12	Cliff Bastin**	1933–38
28	Steve Bloomer	1895–1907	12	Trevor Francis	1978–83
26	Bryan Robson*	1981–89	11	Charlie Bambridge	1879–85
24	Geoff Hurst****	1966–71	11	John Goodall	1888–96
24	Own goals	1887–1991	11	GO Smith	1893–99
23	Stan Mortensen	1947–53	11	Wilf Mannion	1946–50
22	Tommy Lawton**	1938–48	11	Stanley Matthews	1934–56
21	Mick Channon***	1973–77	11	Bryan Douglas	1958–63
21	Kevin Keegan*	1974–82	10	Eric Brook	1933–37
20	Martin Peters	1966–73	10	Jackie Milburn	1948–51
18	George Camsell	1929–36	10	Dennis Wilshaw	1953–56
18	Dixie Dean	1927–31	10	Ron Flowers******	1959–62
18	Johnny Haynes	1954–61	10	Francis Lee	1969–72
18	Roger Hunt	1962–67	10	Allan Clarke***	1970–73
16	Tommy Taylor	1953–57	10	John Barnes	1984–90
16	Tony Woodcock	1979–84		*penalties	
14	Tinsley Lindley	1886–91			

One of Woodward's goals was deflected in by Janos Weinber of Hungary in 1909. *The Sporting Life* doesn't even mention Woodward, and says the last touch was by a Hungarian defender. Official Hungarian records list it as a Weinber own goal.

Similarly, Bobby Charlton's goal against Wales in 1966 needed some generous assistance from goalkeeper Tony Millington. That 49 is a sacrosanct total by now, but . . .

Woodward and Bloomer's totals were world records at the time.

Matthews scored his 10th goal in the Northern Ireland match of 1948, and his 11th against the same country eight years later.

The penultimate. Bobby Charlton moves in on a fumble by Pat Jennings to score his 48th goal for England in his 100th international (Hulton)

GOALSCORERS

MOST GOALS AGAINST

8	John Smith	Scotland	1879–84
7	Geordie Ker	Scotland	1880–82
7	Billy Gillespie	Ireland	1913–26
6	Laurie Reilly	Scotland	1949–55
4	Harry McNiel	Scotland	1875–78
4	Willie M Mackinnon	Scotland	1876–79
4	John McDougall	Scotland	1878–79
4	Andy N Wilson	Scotland	1920–23
4	Jules Dewaquez	France	1923–29
4	Alec Jackson	Scotland	1926–28
4	Dai Astley	Wales	1933–38

4	Trevor Ford	Wales	1950–52
4	Nandor Hidegkuti	Hungary	1953–54
4	Ferenc Puskas	Hungary	1953–54
4	Denis Law	Rest of the World/Scotland	1963–67

Smith also had a goal disallowed in 1879, Law in 1961.

Gillespie was the only player to score in six separate matches against England, Dewaquez the only foreign player to score in four.

MOST GOALS IN A GAME

5	Howard Vaughton	1882	v Ireland
5	Steve Bloomer	1896	v Wales
5	Willie Hall	1938	v Ireland
5	Malcolm Macdonald	1975	v Cyprus
4	Arthur Brown	1882	v Ireland
4	Ben Spilsbury	1886	v Ireland
4	GO Smith	1899	v Ireland
4	Steve Bloomer	1901	v Wales
4	Vivian Woodward	1908	v Austria
4	George Hilsdon	1908	v Hungary
4	Vivian Woodward	1909	v Hungary
4	George Camsell	1929	v Belgium
4	Tommy Lawton	1946	v Holland
4	Tommy Lawton	1947	v Portugal
4	Stan Mortensen	1947	v Portugal
4	Jack Rowley	1949	v N Ireland
4	Tom Finney**	1950	v Portugal
4	Dennis Wilshaw	1955	v Scotland
4	Jimmy Greaves	1963	v N Ireland
4	Roger Hunt	1964	v USA
4	Jimmy Greaves	1966	v Norway
4	Gary Lineker	1987	v Spain
4	Gary Lineker	1991	v Malaysia

Sources vary. Some (a small minority) credit Bloomer with only 4 (or even fewer) in the 1896 match, GO Smith with 5 or only 3 in 1899 (4 is commonly agreed upon, perhaps splitting the difference!). **Fred Geary** is variously credited with 2, 3, 4, even 5 goals against **Ireland** in **1890**, although **Bill Townley** may just possibly have scored 4 in the same game!

Vaughton, Brown and Mortensen scored 5 or 4 on debut, Vaughton setting a world record for a new cap broken only by **Chacho** of Spain who scored **6** against Bulgaria (in another 13–0 win) in **1933**.

Hall's 5 included 3 in 3½ minutes, probably the fastest hat-trick in all international football.

Macdonald scored the second goal against West Germany then all 5 against Cyprus in the next game, a record 6 consecutive England goals. He may well have been the only player to head 4 goals in an England match.

*penalties

The rabbit killer waits till he sees the whites of their eyes. All of Malcolm Macdonald's goals against Cyprus at Wembley in 1975 were scored from close range (Hulton)

SEASON'S LEADING SCORERS

Season		Scorer
1872–73	2	Kenyon Slaney
1873–74	1	Kingsford
1974–75	1	Wollaston, Alcock
1875–76	–	
1876–77	1	A Lyttleton
1877–78	1	Wylie, A Cursham
1878–79	2	C Bambridge
1879–80	3	Sparks
1880–81	1	C Bambridge
1881–82	6	Vaughton
1882–83	4	C Mitchell
1883–84	3	H Cursham
1884–85	2	C Bambridge
1885–86	4	Spilsbury
1886–87	6	Lindley
1887–88	5	F Dewhurst
1888–89	3	Yates
1889–90	3	Geary
1890–91	2	J Goodall, E Chadwick Lindley
1891–92	2	J Goodall, Daft
1892–93	4	Spiksley
1893–94	3	J Veitch
1894–95	3	Bloomer
1895–96	6	Bloomer
1896–97	4	Bloomer
1897–98	3	Wheldon
1898–99	5	GO Smith
1899–00	1	H Johnson C Sagar GP Wilson Bloomer
1900–01	5	Bloomer
1901–02	2	Settle
1902–03	4	Woodward
1903–04	2	Common, Bache
1904–05	2	Woodward
1905–06	2	Bond
1906–07	1	Hardman Stewart Bloomer
1907–08	12	Hilsdon*
1908–09	11	Woodward
1909–10	1	Fleming Ducat
1910–11	2	Woodward
1911–12	3	Holley Fleming
1912–13	2	Hampton
1913–14	1	J Smith, Wedlock, Fleming
1919–20	2	Kelly, Cock
1920–21	1	Kelly, W Walker Buchan, Chambers
1921–22	1	Kelly Kirton
1922–23	4	Chambers Hegan
1923–24	2	T Roberts Gibbins
1924–25	3	W Walker
1925–26	3	F Osborne
1926–27	12	Dean
1927–28	4	Dean
1928–29	6	Camsell
1929–30	5	Camsell
1930–31	4	Burgess
1931–32	4	JW Smith, Crooks
1932–33	3	Bastin
1933–34	4	Brook
1934–35	3	Brook
1935–36	5	Camsell
1936–37	8	Steele
1937–38	5	S Matthews
1938–39	7	W Hall
1946–47	10	Lawton
1947–48	7	Mortensen
1948–49	3	Mortensen, J Morris, Finney
1949–50	6	Mortensen
1950–51	4	Baily, Milburn
1951–52	7	Lofthouse
1952–53	8	Lofthouse
1953–54	6	Lofthouse
1954–55	6	Bentley
1955–56	4	Lofthouse
1956–57	10	T Taylor
1957–58	5	Kevan
1958–59	8	R Charlton*
1959–60	2	R Charlton* Greaves
1960–61	13	Greaves
1961–62	5	Flowers****
1962–63	5	R Charlton
1963–64	8	Greaves
1964–65	6	Greaves
1965–66	8	Hunt
1966–67	3	Hurst
1967–68	5	R Charlton, Peters
1968–69	8	Hurst****
1969–70	4	Peters
1970–71	5	Chivers
1971–72	2	Chivers, Hurst
1972–73	5	Chivers
1973–74	5	Channon
1974–75	6	Macdonald
1975–76	9	Channon*
1976–77	4	Channon**
1977–78	2	Keegan, P Barnes, Currie, Neal*
1978–79	4	Keegan
1979–80	4	Keegan, Woodcock
1980–81	3	McDermott*
1981–82	6	Robson, Mariner
1982–83	4	T Francis, Woodcock
1983–84	2	Robson, Mariner, Woodcock
1984–85	6	Robson
1985–86	9	Lineker
1986–87	7	Lineker
1987–88	7	Lineker
1988–89	3	Lineker, J Barnes
1989–90	6	Lineker**
1990–91	10	Lineker**

* penalties

The team that drew 0–0 with Wales in 1921. The middle seats are occupied by three of England's joint top scorers that season, Bob Kelly, captain Charlie Buchan and Harry Chambers (Hulton)

GOALSCORERS

MOST GOALS IN A SEASON

13	Jimmy Greaves	1960–61		8	Nat Lofthouse	1952–53
12	George Hilsdon*	1907–08		8	Bobby Charlton	1958–59
12	Dixie Dean	1926–27		8	Jimmy Greaves	1963–64
11	Vivian Woodward	1908–09		8	Roger Hunt	1965–66
10	Tommy Lawton	1946–47		8	Geoff Hurst****	1968–69
10	Tommy Taylor	1956–57		* penalties		
10	Gary Lineker**	1990–91				
9	Vivian Woodward	1907–08				
9	Mick Channon*	1975–76				
9	Gary Lineker	1985–86				
8	Freddie Steele	1936–37				

All of Lineker's goals in 1986 came in World Cup matches: a hat-trick in a qualifier against Turkey at Wembley, and six in the finals in Mexico.

SEASON'S LEADING SCORER MOST TIMES

6	Steve Bloomer
6	Gary Lineker
4	Vivian Woodward
4	Nat Lofthouse
4	Bobby Charlton
4	Jimmy Greaves

Lineker achieved this in successive seasons, 1985–86 to 1990–91

GOALS IN CONSECUTIVE SEASONS

		From	To
13	Bobby Charlton	1957–58	1969–70
9	Jimmy Greaves	1958–59	1966–67
9	Kevin Keegan	1973–74	1981–82
9	Bryan Robson	1981–82	1989–90
8	Charlie Bambridge	1878–79	1885–86
7	Steve Bloomer	1894–95	1900–01
7	Johnny Haynes	1954–55	1960–61
7	Geoff Hurst	1965–66	1971–72
7	Gary Lineker	1984–85	1990–91
6	John Goodall	1890–91	1895–96
6	Nat Lofthouse	1950–51	1955–56
6	Tony Woodcock	1979–80	1984–85

Charlton's only goal of 1966–67, against Wales at Wembley, was helped in by Tony Millington and might just as easily have been listed as the goalkeeper's own goal, in which case Charlton's sequence would have ended after 9 successive seasons . . .

GOALS IN CONSECUTIVE MATCHES

10	Steve Bloomer	1895–99
9	George Camsell	1929–36
7	Tinsley Lindley	1886–88
6	John Goodall	1891–95
6	Jimmy Windridge	1908
6	Tommy Lawton	1938–39
5	Fred Dewhurst	1887–89
5	Dixie Dean	1927
5	Tom Finney	1946–47
5	Tommy Lawton	1947
5	Nat Lofthouse	1952
5	Jimmy Greaves	1960–61
5	Bobby Smith	1960–61
5	Paul Mariner	1981–82

Bloomer (who scored in his *first* 10 internationals), Camsell, Goodall and Finney missed one or more England matches on the way. Mariner 'missed' what was effectively a kind of 'B' match against Iceland, played the day before he scored against Finland in 1982. Later, in the World Cup match against Czechoslovakia, he made a half serious attempt to claim Jozef Barmos' own goal as his own; it would have given him a goal in 6 successive games.

Lindley is usually credited with goals in 9 successive games, but it now seems unlikely that he scored in his third match, against Wales in 1886.

Camsell scored in every England game he played, Lawton in his first six, Dean at least 2 goals in each of his first five.

One source (a distinct minority) mentions John Goodall scoring against Scotland in 1889, which would mean he scored in 10 successive matches.

SCORED IN MOST MATCHES

37	Bobby Charlton
28	Gary Lineker
27	Jimmy Greaves
24	Tom Finney
24	Own goal
19	Bryan Robson
18	Nat Lofthouse
18	Geoff Hurst
18	Martin Peters
18	Kevin Keegan

Lineker has scored against 19 different countries, Charlton 18, Greaves 16 as well as the Rest of the World.

SCORED IN EVERY MATCH

9	George Camsell	1929–36
4	Fred Tilson	1934–35
3	Jack Southworth	1889–92
3	Joe Carter	1926–29
3	Jack Smith	1931
3	Jimmy Hampson	1930–32
3	Fred Pickering	1964

The fastest left foot in World Cup finals history – Bryan Robson scores against France in Bilbao (Bob Thomas)

FIRST-MINUTE GOALS

Secs

17	Tommy Lawton	1947	v Portugal
27	Bryan Robson	1982	v France
30	Jack Cock	1919	v Ireland
30	Bill Nicholson	1951	v Portugal
34	Tommy Lawton	1947	v Belgium
35	Edgar Chadwick	1892	v Scotland
38	Bryan Robson	1989	v Yugoslavia
42	Gary Lineker	1991	v Malaysia
55	Geoff Hurst	1971	v Switzerland

The following, timed rather more approximately, were scored in or around the first minute:

WS Kenyon Slaney	1873	v Scotland
Raich Carter	1946	v Ireland
Tommy Lawton	1947	v Ireland
Harold Hassall	1953	v N Ireland
Dennis Wilshaw	1955	v Scotland
Jimmy Greaves	1960	v Spain
Bryan Robson	1982	v N Ireland
John Barnes	1987	v Turkey

Robson scored (v France) the fastest reliably-timed goal in the history of the World Cup finals, and (v Yugoslavia) the fastest ever scored in a senior match at Wembley, undercutting Jackie Milburn's 45 seconds in the 1955 FA Cup Final.

Lawton scored first-minute goals in consecutive matches, against Portugal and Belgium.

Cock and Nicholson scored on debut, Hassall (twice) in his last international.

Kenyon Slaney's was the first goal ever scored in an England match.

Carter, making up for lost time, scored England's first goal after the Second World War. Cock had scored England's first after World War I.

Lineker's goal, appropriately enough, was his 42nd for England.

FIRST-MINUTE GOALS AGAINST ENGLAND

Seconds

28	Georges Moreel	1949	France

Others were scored after approximately one minute:

Bob McColl	1900	Scotland
Charlie Thomson	1914	Scotland
Patalino	1951	Portugal
Nandor Hidegkuti	1953	Hungary
Erich Hof	1961	Austria
Dimitris Saravakos (pen)	1989	Greece

Bob Crompton scored an own goal in the first minute of the match against Scotland in 1907.

Nicholson and Patalino scored within the first minute (or so) of the same match.

Moreel won only the one cap.

LAST-MINUTE GOALS

1880	Charlie Bambridge	v Scotland
1899	Charlie Athersmith	v Ireland
1905	Vivian Woodward	v Wales
1906	Dickie Bond	v Ireland
1928	Bob Kelly	v Scotland
1928	Dixie Dean	v Ireland
1930	David Jack	v Germany
1950	Jackie Milburn	v Wales
1951	Harold Hassall	v Portugal
1952	Nat Lofthouse	v Switzerland
1953	Alf Ramsey (pen)	v FIFA
1956	Johnny Haynes	v Scotland
1956	Tommy Taylor	v Yugoslavia
1957	John Atyeo	v Eire
1957	John Atyeo	v Eire
1959	Ray Parry	v N Ireland
1960	Johnny Haynes	v Yugoslavia
1961	Bryan Douglas	v Mexico
1963	Bobby Charlton	v Switzerland
1965	Alan Peacock	v N Ireland
1966	Geoff Hurst	v W Germany (aet)
1967	Geoff Hurst	v Scotland
1970	Alan Ball	v Colombia
1971	Martin Chivers	v Greece
1973	Allan Clarke	v Czechoslovakia
1977	Paul Mariner	v Luxembourg
1978	Peter Barnes	v Wales
1982	Phil Neal	v Luxembourg
1989	Paul Gascoigne	v Albania
1990	Paul Gascoigne	v Czechoslovakia
1990	Steve Bull	v Tunisia
1990	David Platt	v Belgium (aet)
1990	Peter Beardsley	v Poland
1991	Gary Lineker	v N Zealand

One source (a distinct minority) says Ball scored after 84 minutes.

Atyeo scored at Wembley in a 5-2 win, then in Dublin headed the equaliser that sent England to the 1958 World Cup finals – and was never selected again!

Kelly and Peacock scored in the last minute of their last international, Parry in the last minute of his first.

Against Yugoslavia, Haynes emulated Jack in scoring the equaliser in a 3-3 draw.

Platt and Lineker scored the only goal of the match.

Charlton and Hurst (v West Germany) brought up their hat-tricks.

Neal was England's seventh scorer in the match, a record.

Ramsey's penalty preserved (for one more match) England's unbeaten home record against foreign opposition.

Taylor was the last substitute to score twice in a game for England.

Against Holland at Wembley in 1970, Bobby Charlton put the ball in the net just after the final whistle, one of the ways he missed out on a 50th goal in internationals.

LAST-MINUTE GOALS AGAINST

1883	John Smith	Scotland
1908	Bill Davies	Wales
1923	Jules Dewaquez	France
1929	Alex Cheyne	Scotland
1929	Jacques Moeschal	Belgium
1931	Jamie Kelly	Ireland
1947	Peter Doherty	Ireland
1948	Davie Walsh	Ireland
1953	Laurie Reilly	Scotland
1954	Willie Ormond	Scotland
1959	Graham Moore	Wales
1964	Dejalma Dias	Brazil
1966	Wolfgang Weber	W Germany
1968	Rolf Andersson	Sweden
1974	Mario Kempes*	Argentina
1976	Alan Curtis	Wales
1976	Roberto	Brazil
1982	Jesper Olsen	Denmark
1984	Oleg Protasov	USSR
1985	Alessandro Altobelli*	Italy

* penalties

Most reports say the final whistle went almost immediately after Dr Smith's goal; one says four minutes later. Either way, it made him the only man to score two hat-tricks against England, whose players protested that the ball hadn't crossed the line before goalkeeper Harry Swepstone knocked it away.

Cheyne scored in his first game for Scotland. It was apparently the first goal scored direct from a corner in international football.

Moeschal's goal is usually credited to the more famous Raymond Braine by English sources – but L'Independance Belge is quite clear about it: he pushed Braine off the ball and scored!

Doherty was knocked out in the act of heading the equaliser.

Ormond's goal is sometimes listed as a Roger Byrne own goal.

Moore, who scored for Cardiff against Brighton in 1958, is the only man to score a last-minute equaliser on his debut in League as well as international football.

Curtis' goal was also in his first international.

The 1966 World Cup Final is the only England match to feature goals in the last minute of normal and extra time.

Kempes scored the equaliser from a penalty awarded by referee Arturo Ithurralde, who was also Argentinian. It was the first match between the two sides since the notorious World Cup quarter-final of 1966, and it was a condition of the game being played at Wembley that the officials be from Argentina.

Protasov had come on just three minutes earlier. Andersson was also a sub.

SCORED ON DEBUT

No fewer than **172 players** have achieved this, including 14 who scored a hat-trick (see HAT-TRICKS) and 33 who scored twice, a list which includes Steve Bloomer, Vivian Woodward, Dixie Dean, George Camsell, Joe Payne, Nat Lofthouse, Bobby Robson and Mike O'Grady.

Those who scored once include GO Smith, Alf Common, Pongo Waring, Ted Drake, Len Goulden, Tom Finney, Jackie Milburn, Johnny Haynes, Don Revie, Bobby Charlton, Jimmy Greaves, Gerry Hitchens, Bobby Smith and Roger Hunt.

SINCE 1970

1970	Allan Clarke*	v Czechoslovakia
1971	Chris Lawler	v Malta
1975	David Johnson (2)	v Wales
1976	Ray Kennedy	v Wales
1976	Peter Taylor	v Wales
1979	Glenn Hoddle	v Bulgaria
1982	Paul Goddard	v Iceland
1982	Sammy Lee	v Greece
1982	Mark Chamberlain	v Luxembourg
1986	Danny Wallace	v Egypt
1989	Steve Bull	v Scotland
1991	Dennis Wise	v Turkey

*penalty

Kennedy and Taylor scored in the same match. Taylor, Goddard, Chamberlain and Bull came on as substitutes.

Lawler lived up to his reputation as one of the great goalscoring defenders.

Tommy Lawton (v Wales 1938) and Clarke are the only players to score from the penalty spot on their England debut. Clarke scored on his wife's birthday, which was also their wedding anniversary and the anniversary of his transfer from Fulham to Leicester!

More than **60** opposition players have scored against England on their international debut, including Geordie Ker of Scotland, who scored a hat-trick; Billy Gillespie and Joe Bambrick of Ireland; Bobby Templeton, Bobby Johnstone, Graham Leggat and Jim McCalliog of Scotland; Alan Curtis and Mark Hughes of Wales; and Mirandinha of Brazil.

FASTEST DEBUT GOALS

Time	Player	Year	Opponent
30 sec	Jack Cock	1919	v Ireland
30 sec	Bill Nicholson	1951	v Portugal
1 min	WS Kenyon Slaney	1873	v Scotland
2	Gerry Hitchens	1961	v Mexico
3	Geoffrey Wilson	1900	v Wales
c.4	Howard Vaughton	1882	v Ireland
5	Jack Haines	1948	v Switzerland
5	Colin Grainger	1956	v Brazil
6	Fred Pickering	1964	v USA
7	Stan Mortensen	1947	v Portugal
7	Mark Chamberlain	1982	v Luxembourg
10	AG Bonsor	1873	v Scotland
10	Charlie Buchan	1913	v Ireland
10	Jack Smith	1931	v Ireland
10	David Johnson	1975	v Wales
11	John Atyeo	1955	v Spain

Atyeo also scored in the last minute of his last international, against Eire in 1957.

Cock, probably the first Cornishman to play for England, scored England's first goal after the First World War.

Chamberlain scored after coming on as substitute.

The goals by Kenyon Slaney and Bonsor were the first ever scored by England.

Fastest of all debutants was **Georges Moreel** of **France**, who scored against England in **1949** after just **28** seconds of his only international. Billy Foulkes scored for **Wales** against England after **3** minutes of the **1951** match, with supposedly his first touch in international football. **Abdelkader Firoud** scored an own goal after **4** minutes of his debut for **France**, at Highbury in **1951**.

SCORED IN LAST MATCH

123 players have achieved this, including 7 who scored hat-tricks and another 25 who scored twice, the last being Tommy Taylor against France in 1957.

Those who scored once include Charles Alcock, Billy Mosforth, Billy Bassett, Steve Bloomer, Vivian Woodward, Pongo Waring, George Camsell, Ted Drake, Cliff Bastin (pen), Stan Mortensen, Alf Ramsey (pen), Len Shackleton and Roy Bentley.

SINCE 1960

1961	Dennis Viollet	v Luxembourg
1961	Ray Pointer	v Portugal
1962	Ray Crawford	v Austria
1962	Gerry Hitchens	v Brazil
1963	Tony Kay	v Switzerland
1963	Jimmy Melia	v Switzerland
1963	Bryan Douglas	v Switzerland
1963	Bobby Smith	v N Ireland
1964	Fred Pickering	v Belgium
1965	Alan Peacock	v N Ireland
1966	George Eastham	v Denmark
1969	Mike O'Grady	v France
1972	Francis Lee	v W Germany
1982	Paul Goddard	v Iceland
1986	Danny Wallace	v Egypt

Kay, Goddard and Wallace won only one cap each.

Leslie Compton (v Yugoslavia 1950) and **Mike Pejic** (v Scotland 1974) scored **own goals** in their last internationals.

More than **40** opposition players have scored against England in their last international match, including Scots Dr John Smith (his 8th goal against England), Charlie Thomson, Ian St John and Mark McGhee; Hughie Barr of Northern Ireland; and, it seems, Obdulio Varela, Uruguay's famous captain in the 1950 and 1954 World Cups.

OLDEST GOALSCORERS

Yrs	days			
41	248	Stanley Matthews	1956	v N Ireland
36	182	Tom Finney	1958	v N Ireland
36	58	Tom Finney (pen)	1958	v USSR
35	197	Tom Finney	1957	v Wales
34	223	Tom Finney	1956	v Wales
34	216	Jack Charlton	1969	v Portugal
34	136	Bob Kelly	1928	v Scotland
34	10	Jimmy Moore	1923	v Sweden
33	252	Jack Charlton	1969	v Romania
33	251	Stanley Matthews	1948	v N Ireland
33	239	Tom Finney	1955	v N Ireland
33	211	Tom Finney	1955	v Spain
33	186	Bob Kelly	1927	v Luxembourg
33	163	George Camsell	1936	v Belgium
33	160	George Camsell	1936	v Austria
33	139	Billy Wedlock	1914	v Wales
33	133	Raich Carter	1947	v France
33	128	George Camsell	1936	v Scotland
33	112	Raich Carter	1947	v Scotland
33	81	Stan Pearson (2)	1952	v Scotland
33	76	Steve Bloomer	1907	v Scotland
33	56	Nat Lofthouse	1958	v USSR
33	53	Jack Smith (2)	1931	v Spain
33	48	Dave V Watson	1979	v Bulgaria
33	7	George Camsell	1935	v Germany
OWN GOAL				
38	71	Leslie Compton	1950	v Yugoslavia

YOUNGEST GOALSCORERS

Yrs	days			
19	16	Tommy Lawton	1938	v Wales
19	20	Tommy Lawton	1938	v Rest of Europe
19	34	Tommy Lawton	1938	v Norway
19	41	Tommy Lawton	1938	v Ireland
19	86	Jimmy Greaves	1959	v Peru
19	123	Joe Baker	1959	v N Ireland
19	150	Tommy Lawton	1939	v Scotland
19	172	Jimmy Brown (2)	1882	v Ireland
19	178	Tommy Lawton	1939	v Italy
19	238	Jackie Robinson	1937	v Finland
19	238	Duncan Edwards	1956	v W Germany
19	239	Jimmy Greaves	1959	v Wales
19	240	Stanley Matthews	1934	v Wales
19	283	Tom Galley	1937	v Norway
19	320	Joe Lofthouse	1885	v Ireland
19	358	Johnny Haynes	1954	v N Ireland
19/20		Billy Mosforth	1879	v Scotland

Lawton scored in his first six internationals. His first goal was a penalty; he was the youngest player to take one for England.

Tommy Walker was also only 19 when he scored the equaliser for Scotland at Wembley in 1936, keeping his nerve as the wind twice blew the ball off the penalty spot.

The youngest to score a hat-trick was Dixie Dean, against Belgium in 1927, at 20yr 109d. He scored another ten days later. The oldest was Gary Lineker, who scored four against Malaysia in 1991 at 30yr 194d.

SCORERS OF LANDMARK GOALS

Number			
1	WS Kenyon Slaney	1873	v Scotland
50	Nevill Cobbold	1883	v Ireland
100	George Woodhall	1888	v Wales
500	Joe Carter	1929	v Belgium
1000	Jimmy Greaves	1960	v Wales
1500	Trevor Steven	1986	v Egypt

SCORERS OF LANDMARK GOALS AGAINST ENGLAND

Number			
1	Henry Renny-Tailyour	1873	Scotland
50	John Smith	1883	Scotland
100	Bob McColl	1900	Scotland
500	Peter Ducke	1963	E Germany

GOALS DIRECT FROM CORNERS

Alex Cheyne was reputedly the first to achieve this in international football. He scored in the last minute of his first game for Scotland, at Hampden in 1929, the only goal of the game.

Seymour Morris also scored on debut, in 1936 as Wales beat England at home for the first time since 1882.

Pierre Littbarski scored for West Germany in 1987, the ball brushing Viv Anderson's head on the way.

As far as match reports show, no-one has managed the feat for England.

HANDS OF GOD

Maradona's for Argentina in 1986 wasn't the first. In 1939, Silvio Piola's fist put Italy ahead in the San Siro, the follow-through giving George Male a black eye. Justice was done when Willie Hall equalised in a 2–2 draw.

Either Percy Walters or Harry Allen ('Allen, I believe,' said The Athletic News) handled to prevent a certain goal 30 seconds from the end of the drawn match against Scotland in 1890. The Scots took several bites at the free-kick (penalties weren't yet awarded) but it came to nothing.

The Hand of Pearce kept out Muller's goal-bound shot as England beat Brazil 1–0 at Wembley in 1990.

When Dennis Wise scored the only goal of his first game against Turkey in 1991, the ball seemed to hit his hand on the way in.

HAT-TRICKS

MOST HAT-TRICKS

6	Jimmy Greaves
5	Gary Lineker
4	Vivian Woodward
4	Bobby Charlton
3	Stan Mortensen
2	Steve Bloomer
2	Dixie Dean
2	George Camsell
2	Tommy Lawton
2	Tommy Taylor
2	Geoff Hurst

HAT-TRICK ON DEBUT

1882	Howard Vaughton (5)	v Ireland
1882	Arthur Brown (4)	v Ireland
1888	Albert Allen	v Ireland
1889	Jack Yates	v Ireland
1890	Fred Geary	v Ireland
1893	Walter Gilliat	v Ireland
1894	John Veitch	v Wales
1897	Fred Wheldon	v Ireland
1899	Jimmy Settle	v Ireland
1908	Frank Bradshaw	v Austria
1937	George Mills	v Ireland
1946	Wilf Mannion	v N Ireland
1947	Stan Mortensen (4)	v Portugal
1964	Fred Pickering	v USA

Note that **Luther Blissett** scored his hat-trick against **Luxembourg** in **1982** in his *second* international; he'd come on as substitute against West Germany two months earlier.

One report credits debutant **Fred Spiksley** with three goals against **Wales** in **1893**. Several others don't.

The only player to score *against* England on his international debut was Geordie Ker of Scotland in 1880.

HAT-TRICK IN LAST MATCH

1884	Harry Cursham	v Ireland
1888	Albert Allen	v Ireland
1889	Jack Yates	v Ireland
1893	Walter Gilliat	v Ireland
1894	John Veitch	v Wales
1908	Frank Bradshaw	v Austria
1926	Frank Osborne	v Belgium

Notice that all except Cursham and Osborne won only one cap each.

HAT-TRICKS AGAINST ENGLAND

1878	John McDougall	Scotland
1880	Geordie Ker	Scotland
1881	John Smith	Scotland
1883	John Smith	Scotland
1900	Bob McColl	Scotland
1928	Alec Jackson	Scotland
1930	Richard Hofmann	Germany
1953	Nandor Hidegkuti	Hungary
1958	Aleksandar Petakovic	Yugoslavia
1959	Juan Seminario	Peru
1988	Marco van Basten	Holland

McColl scored all three in the first half, Petakovic all three in the second, Hofmann two while England were down to 10 men, McColl his second and third while England were virtually down to nine (Jimmy Crabtree limping, Wliiam Oakley concussed after breaking his nose while Jack Bell scored Scotland's second).

England's first hat-trick against Scotland didn't arrive until 1955, in the 72nd match between the two countries, when Dennis Wilshaw scored four at Wembley (no-one else on either side has ever scored more than three in an England–Scotland match). Since then, the only hat-trick in matches between the two countries has been scored by Jimmy Greaves in 1961.

The *Athletic News* match report credits **Willie M MacKinnon** with three goals in the 1879 Scotland match, but the second came out of a confusing scrimmage in front of goal and is usually attributed to John McDougall.

Against England in 1882, Ker scored twice after hitting the bar with only the goalkeeper to beat.

While Alec Jackson was scoring his three at Wembley, **Alex James** was scoring twice as well hitting the bar, inches away from the only instance of two hat-tricks against England in the same match.

HAT-TRICKS IN THE SAME MATCH

1882	v Ireland	Vaughton (5)	A Brown (4)
1908	v Austria	Woodward (4)	Bradshaw (3)
1947	v Portugal	Lawton (4)	Mortensen (4)
1960	v Luxembourg	Greaves	R Charlton
1963	v N Ireland	Greaves (4)	Paine
1964	v USA	Hunt (4)	Pickering

Because it's proved impossible, so far, to find a full report of the match against Ireland in 1882, there's no knowing whether Vaughton or Brown scored England's first ever hat-trick. Vaughton, who scored in the first few minutes, must be favourite.

As we've seen, out of all the confusion surrounding the match comes the possibility that both Fred Geary and Bill Townley (or Nat Walton!) scored hat-tricks against Ireland in 1890.

Against Ireland in 1897, when **Fred Wheldon** scored three, **Steve Bloomer** got two and had a goal disallowed.

ALL 3 GOALS IN A GAME

1954	Roy Bentley	v Wales	3-2
1975	Malcolm Macdonald (5)	v Cyprus	5-0
1986	Gary Lineker	v Poland	3-0
1987	Gary Lineker (4)	v Spain	4-2
1991	Gary Lineker (4)	v Malaysia	4-2

ALL 3 OPPOSITION GOALS

1883	John Smith	Scotland	3-2
1930	Richard Hofmann	Germany	3-3
1988	Marco van Basten	Holland	3-1

Van Basten spoiled Shilton's 100th game for England.

Below *Spain's keeper Andoni Zubizarreta couldn't stop club colleague Gary Lineker from scoring four times in Madrid* (Bob Thomas)

PENALTIES

SCORED

6	Ron Flowers
4	Geoff Hurst
4	Gary Lineker
3	Alf Ramsey
3	Tom Finney
3	Bobby Charlton
3	Allan Clarke
3	Mick Channon
2	George Hilsdon
2	Cliff Bastin
2	Tommy Lawton
2	Phil Neal

Hurst converted all four in a single season, 1968–69.

Those who scored once include Ernest Needham, Don Revie, Kevin Keegan, Terry McDermott, Bryan Robson and David Platt.

Finney's penalty against the USSR in the 1958 World Cup was his 29th goal for England, equalling Vivian Woodward's record.

Lineker is the only player to score from the penalty spot three times (and in two separate matches) against the same country, Cameroon in 1990 and 1991.

MISSED

2	Ernest Needham	2	Roger Byrne
2	Tom Finney	2	Francis Lee

MISSED – and never scored for England at all

Jimmy Crabtree	1899
Roy Goodall	1927
Alf Strange	1930
George Hardwick	1946
Roger Byrne (2)	1956
Jimmy Langley	1958

The Sporting Life claims Crabtree scored twice (and had two other goals disallowed) against Wales in 1896, but the report is remarkably muddled and the writer seems to have had a very poor vantage point, mentioning only six of the nine England scorers and crediting Bloomer with only one goal. More coherent sources say Bloomer scored at least four, and Crabtree none at all.

England seem to have missed a penalty against **Wales** in **1896** and **Belgium** in **1921**. Culprits unknown.

TWO SUCCESSFUL PENALTIES IN A MATCH

1950	Tom Finney	v Portugal	5-3
1969	Geoff Hurst	v France	5-0
1990	Gary Lineker	v Cameroon	3-2 (aet)

ONE SCORED, ONE MISSED IN SAME MATCH

1960	Bobby Charlton	v Scotland	1-1
1971	Allan Clarke	v Malta	5-0

Against England

1980	Dani	Spain	2-1

Charlton missed the same penalty twice, the only England player to take three spot-kicks in the same international – a performance matched by Dani, who scored with his first attempt, and with his second, which he was ordered to retake for halting in his approach run; Clemence then saved his third kick.

Before the game against Wales in 1902, England hadn't failed to score in 52 matches since 1884. Nudger Needham missed a penalty and the game was drawn 0–0, whereupon England went another 32 matches before failing to score – but for Needham's miss (and Steve Bloomer's disallowed goal), an incredible world record total of 85 consecutive matches. As it was, the 52 was a European record before Puskas' Hungarians overhauled it.

You can't fool all of them all of the time. The referee orders a retake for ungentlemanly conduct, Clemence goes the right way at the third attempt, Dani misses in Naples (Colorsport)

Kempes beats Shilton from the spot to score his second goal of the match in 1974. Seventeen years later, Argentina again recovered from 2–0 down to force a draw at Wembley (Colorsport)

Jimmy Crabtree seems to have been the first to take (and miss) a penalty while playing for England. Had he scored, England would have put 14 past Ireland in 1899, a new record for a single match that would still stand today. Joe McAllen, the Irish captain, scored one of his team's two goals that day – from the penalty spot.

Only one England match, against Brazil at Wembley in 1956, has featured two missed penalties, Gylmar saving first from John Atyeo then from Roger Byrne. Both were awarded for handball by Zozino.

England were awarded a penalty in each of four consecutive matches in 1969. Geoff Hurst scored with three, Francis Lee missed the other.

Glenn Hoddle was the last to miss a penalty while playing for England, in the match against the USA in 1985. Arnie Mausser, who saved it, was making a record-breaking 35th appearance for the States. He was the first player since 1892 to play against England without belonging to a recognised club.

Trevor Francis scored a goal, scored from a penalty, had to retake it because the referee hadn't blown, put the retake over the bar, and was booked – all in the same game, the third in the series against Australia on the summer tour of 1983.

Two players missed out on a hat-trick by missing a penalty: Billy Walker against Belgium in 1924, and Eric Brook against Italy in 1934 (the only player to miss a first-minute penalty in an England match). Brook scored his 2 goals within the first 10 minutes.

England's penalty takers in the 1990 World Cup semi-final shoot-out were Gary Lineker, Peter Beardsley, David Platt, and the two who missed: Stuart Pearce and Chris Waddle. The four German takers (and scorers) were Andreas Brehme, Lothar Matthaus, Karl-Heinz Riedle and Olaf Thon.

PENALTIES AGAINST ENGLAND

Only one player, **Allan Simonsen** of **Denmark**, has scored twice from the penalty spot against England: in **1978** and **1983**.

Those who scored once include Gunnar Gren, Ladislav Kubala, Raymond Kopa, Gunter Netzer, Mario Kempes, Daniel Passarella, Alessandro Altobelli, Graeme Souness and Salvatore Schillaci.

MISSED AGAINST ENGLAND

1892	Sam Torrans	Ireland
1897	Bob Milne	Ireland
1902	Bob Milne	Ireland
1908	Billy Meredith	Wales
1909	James Stark	Scotland
1930	Fred Keenor	Wales
1934	Billy Evans	Wales
1935	Jackie Coulter	Ireland
1959	Jimmy McIlroy	N Ireland
1962	Oscar Montalvo	Peru
1969	Carlos Alberto	Brazil
1980	Dani	Spain
1985	Andreas Brehme	W Germany
1986	Aleksandr Chivadze	USSR

Stark, who never played for Scotland again, was the captain. The referee who awarded the penalty was also Scottish – and also called James Stark!

PENALTY AWARDED TO EACH SIDE

1899	v Ireland	Jimmy Crabtree	Joe McAllen
1938	v Switzerland	Cliff Bastin	Andre ('Trello') Abegglen
1947	v Sweden	Tommy Lawton	Gunnar Gren
1951	v Austria	Alf Ramsey	Ernst Stojaspal
1953	v FIFA	Alf Ramsey	Ladislav Kubala
1990	v Cameroon	Gary Lineker (2)	Emmanuel Kunde

Only Crabtree missed.

MATCHES DECIDED BY A SINGLE PENALTY

1955	v France	0–1	Raymond Kopa
1970	v Czechoslovakia	1–0	Allan Clarke
1977	v Wales	0–1	Leighton James
1981	v Scotland	0–1	John Robertson
1983	v Denmark	0–1	Allan Simonsen

PENALTY IN 3 SUCCESSIVE MATCHES

1902	Ernest Needham
1962	Ron Flowers
1969	Geoff Hurst

Needham missed the last two.

OWN GOALS

This is a vexed one. For a start, there's the problem of interpretation (what exactly constitutes an own goal?) and national associations prefer to credit the last of their own players to touch the ball, awarding own goals grudgingly when there's very little alternative. The following, in England matches, had fewer credible alternatives than most.

FOR ENGLAND

1887	Jack Powell	Wales
1894	Charlie Parry	Wales
1895	Sam Torrans	Ireland
1895	Neil Gibson	Scotland
1924	Edouard Baumann	France
1925	Philippe Bonnardel	France
1927	Andre Rollet	France
1927	Fred Keenor	Wales
1937	Oivind Holmsen	Norway
1949	Bjorn Spydevold	Norway
1951	Abdelkader Firoud	France
1955	John Charles	Wales
1957	Mel Hopkins	Wales
1964	Laurent Verbiest	Belgium
1966	Terry Hennessey	Wales
1971	Anton Weibel	Switzerland
1973	Peter Lorimer	Scotland
1973	Murtaz Khurtsilava	USSR
1979	Jimmy Nicholl	N Ireland
1980	Markus Tanner	Switzerland
1982	Jozef Barmos	Czechosolvakia
1982	Marcel Bossi	Luxembourg
1986	Mohammed Omar	Egypt
1991	Ian Gray	Australia

Keenor and Khurtsilava were captains.

Verbiest's goal is occasionally (but not usually) credited to Alan Hinton. It would have been his only goal for England.

Firoud scored after just four minutes of his first international.

French sources list one of Jackie Hegan's goals against **France** in **1923** as a **Pierre Mony** own goal – and 'credit' goalkeeper **Alex Thepot** with Rollet's own goal of **1927**.

Bobby Charlton's goal against **Wales** in **1966** was arguably a **Millington** own goal, which would mean there were two in the same game . . .

David Johnson's goal against **Northern Ireland** in **1980** seemed, on television, to go in off **Noel Brotherston's** foot. Indeed, some sources do list it as a Brotherston own goal.

In the World Cup match against **France** in **1966**, Roger Hunt headed straight at goalkeeper **Marcel Aubour**, who palmed it firmly into the net.

French players scored own goals in each of three successive matches against England 1924–27 – though Baumann's has been credited to Harry Storer in the past. However, most sources (English as well as French) give it to the defender. Sorry, Harry.

When John Barnes took his equalising free-kick against **Greece** in **1989**, the ball came back off the bar and away from the goal before going in off the goalkeeper, without whose touch it would certainly not have crossed the line. The goal remains JB's property in the record books, but should really be listed as a **Spiros Economopoulos** own goal. Space permitting.

Lee Dixon's scoring shot against Eire at Wembley in 1991 took a critical deflection off Steve Staunton.

According to *The Sporting Life*, one of Vivian Woodward's goals against Hungary in 1908 was scored by a defender. Indeed, official Hungarian sources list it as a **Janos Weinber** own goal.

Fred Keenor and John Charles, both of Wales, are the only two opposition players to score for and against England.

Playing as an inside-forward, Sam Torrans missed a penalty for Ireland against England in 1892. Three seasons later, as a full back, he scored an own goal in the same fixture, the only such double in matches involving England.

GOALSCORERS

AGAINST ENGLAND

1882	Alf Jones	v Wales
1889	Harry Allen	v Scotland
1905	Reg ('Tim') Williamson	v Ireland
1907	Bob Crompton	v Scotland
1924	Teddy Taylor	v Scotland
1927	Herbert Jones	v Ireland
1927	Jack Hill	v Wales
1950	Leslie Compton	v Yugoslavia
1954	Jimmy Dickinson	v Belgium (aet)
1973	Bobby Moore	v Poland
1974	Mike Pejic	v Scotland
1974	Colin Todd	v Scotland
1980	Phil Thompson	v Wales
1983	Phil Neal	v Australia
1988	Tony Adams	v Holland

Crompton, Hill and Moore were captains. **'Baishe' Bower**, captain against **Wales** in **1925**, is occasionally awarded the goal scored by the Welsh captain Fred Keenor.

Williamson and Taylor were goalkeepers. Taylor's goal marked the first international ever played at Wembley..Williamson 'scored' in his first international, Compton and Pejic in their last.

Adams is the only player to score for both sides in an England match – and he may even have done it twice. He also scored at the right end against the Dutch, at Wembley, and later in that same season, after heading the equaliser against the **USSR** in the European Championship finals, he challenged for a low cross in his own penalty area. Film of the incident doesn't prove conclusively that Viktor Pasulko did get the final touch . . .

Moore's own goal is credited to Robert Gadocha by the Polish FA, but the angle of deflection and the England captain's movement towards the ball make it clearly his. In his biography, Mooro himself admits to it!

The 1974 Scotland match was the only one in which two own goals have been scored by one side in any England match. The goals have sometimes been credited to Dalglish and Jordan, but again the angles of deflection . . .

The only time both sides benefited from an own goal was the 1927 Wales match when the captains were the culprits. The match was played on Hill's home club ground, Turf Moor.

Andreas Brehme's free-kick for **West Germany** in the **1990** World Cup semi-final took a huge, looping deflection off **Paul Parker** . . .

Willie Ormond's last-minute lob at Hampden in **1954** has sometimes been called an own goal by **Roger Byrne**, who never scored *for* England despite taking two penalties and also deflected Paulinho's odd-looking goal for **Brazil** in **1956**. If these *were* own goals, he was the only player to score an own goal and miss a penalty (let alone two of each) while playing for England.

John Smith of **Scotland** is the only player to score two hat-tricks against England – but one of his three goals in the **1881** match has been attributed (by two contemporary football annuals) to defender **Edgar Field**.

Own goals featured in three consecutive England matches in 1927, against France, Ireland and Wales.

When **West Germany** finally beat England for the first time (1–0 in **1968**), Beckenbauer's shot was deflected heavily enough to send Banks the wrong way; indeed, one or two sources have called it a **Brian Labone** own goal, but the German's have always credited it to the Kaiser.

Neal scored Australia's only goal of the match; it prevented Peter Shilton from equalling Gordon Banks' record of 7 successive clean sheets. In the very next match, against Denmark at Wembley, Neal's handball gave away the penalty that put England out of the European Championship finals – and ended his international career.

Left *Leslie Compton isn't about to commit hari-kiri after scoring an own goal in his last international. Believe it or not, this is the Olympic torch* (Popperfoto)

The Country that Never Was

Saturday 13 June 1908
Letna stadium, Prague 12 000

BOHEMIA (0) 0   ENGLAND (1) 4

Hilsdon 2 (1 pen)
Windridge
Rutherford

Referee: John Lewis (England)

BOHEMIA	ENGLAND	
Miroslav Jenik	HP (Horace Peter) Bailey	Leicester Fosse
Rudolf Krummer	Bob Crompton	Blackburn Rovers
Richard Vesely	Water Corbett	Birmingham FC
Emanuel Benda (capt)	Ben Warren	Derby County
Karel Kotouc	Billy Wedlock	Bristol City
Josef (Jan?) Jirkovsky	Bob Hawkes	Luton Town
Vaclav Lomoz (Siroky?)	Jock Rutherford	Newcastle Utd
Josef Belka	Vivian Woodward (capt)	Tottenham Hotspur
Jan ('Jenny') Stary	George Hilsdon	Chelsea
Ctibor Maly*	Jimmy Windridge	Chelsea
Miroslav ('Milda') Macoun	Arthur Bridgett	Sunderland

Coach: John Madden (Scotland)
First caps: Krummer, Lomoz
* Apparently known as Ctibor in Bohemia, Otibor in Moravia.

Coach: –
First caps: 0
Last caps: Bailey, Corbett, Hawkes, Rutherford.

Of all the 676 matches involving England, this was perhaps the quirkiest, played against a country that not only doesn't exist now but never existed at all; England's only official international against a club side.

In 1908 there was a Bohemian FA but no actual country called Bohemia, which was a province of the giant Austro-Hungarian empire – and, after World War I, part of Czechoslovakia. Looking back, it's hard to understand how this match ever came to be regarded as a full, *bona fide* international – because it certainly wasn't at the time. Indeed, *The Sporting Life* classified it as 'versus Prague'. Contrast this with what's happened to the England–Canada match of 1891, which was definitely seen as a full international at the time it was played.

The 1908 match came at the end of England's first official foreign tour, enthusiastic crowds having already flocked to Crompton's hefty full-back play, Hilsdon's shooting, the 'rubberman' centre-half Wedlock, and above all the ball control and goals of the amateur centre-forward and captain Woodward. He and Hilsdon had scored 12 between them as Austria were beaten 6–1 and 11–1, Hungary 7–0. It was a strong and skilful England team, dominant in Britain as well as abroad, and Bohemia's task looked well beyond them.

It was – eventually. Coached by a former Scotland international and playing with the cohesion of the club side they were, they trailed only 1–0 at half-time, and the match was only turned decisively away from them by the penalty awarded by a referee from Blackburn. Hilsdon scored his second goal from the spot, and the strength of the English professionals seems to have told in the end.

The statistics here, especially the Bohemian team, appear in complete form for the first time, as far as I'm aware, in any British publication. All the home players were members of the Slavia club in Prague. This was the last of the six international matches played by Bohemia, and the only one in which Hungary weren't the opposition. It was the 98th played by England, the first with an unchanged team.

CLEAN SHEETS

66	Peter Shilton
35	Gordon Banks
27	Ray Clemence
19	Chris Woods
10	Harry Hibbs
9	Frank Swift
7	Sam Hardy
7	Vic Woodley
7	Ron Springett

Only 11 of Woods' total have been in complete matches; he was regularly Shilton's substitute.

CONSECUTIVE CLEAN SHEETS

7	Gordon Banks	1966
6	Peter Shilton	1983
6	Peter Shilton	1984–85
6	Chris Woods	1987–88
5	Ray Clemence	1974–75
5	Chris Woods	1985–86
5	Peter Shilton	1989
5	Chris Woods	1988–90

It took Eusebio's second-half penalty to stop Banks – and a Phil Neal own goal to beat Shilton in 1983:

MINUTES WITHOUT CONCEDING A GOAL

707	Banks, Bonetti	1966
642	Shilton	1983
635	Clemence, Shilton	1974–75
594	Shilton	1989
560	Shilton	1984–85
526	Clemence, Shilton, Corrigan	1981–82
523	Shilton, Banks	1970–71

Between Harald Sunde's 4th-minute goal for Norway (6–1) and Eusebio's penalty for Portugal after 82 minutes (2–1), Banks and Bonetti kept out Denmark (2–0), Poland (1–0), Uruguay (0–0), Mexico (2–0), France (2–0) and Argentina (1–0).

PENALTY SAVES

1892	Bill Rowley	from Sam Torrans	Ireland
1902	Bill George	from Bob Milne	Ireland
1909	Sam Hardy	from James Stark	Scotland
1930	Harry Hibbs	from Fred Keenor	Wales
1959	Ron Springett	from Jimmy McIlroy	N Ireland
1962	Ron Springett	from Oscar Montalvo	Peru
1969	Gordon Banks	from Carlos Alberto	Brazil
1980	Ray Clemence	from Dani	Spain
1985	Peter Shilton	from Andreas Brehme	W Germany

Springett saved a penalty in his first international, Rowley in his last.

Dani had beaten Clemence from the spot earlier in the same match.

Shilton couldn't quite reach any of the four West German shots in the 1990 World Cup penalty shoot-out though he went the right way each time.

Peter Shilton faced 15 penalties while playing for England, saving only this one from Andreas Brehme in Mexico City (Colorsport)

GOALKEEPER CAPTAINS

1873	Alexander Morten
1891	Billy Moon
1896	George Raikes
1948	Frank Swift (2)
1981	Ray Clemence
1982–90	Peter Shilton (15)

So there were at least two before Big Swifty. *The Sporting Life* and *The Sportsman* both confirm that Morten replaced Charles Alcock in the team (and as captain) in only the second official match played by England. The match report in *The Times* lists GO Smith as captain against Ireland in 1896, but *The Irish Times* and a leading Ulster sports paper, *Ireland's Saturday Night*, are quite categorical about Raikes, although (who'd be a researcher?) Belfast's *Northern Whig* suggests Lodge . . . !

Billy Walker was England's captain when he went in goal for the last quarter of an hour after Fred Fox was injured in Paris in 1925.

Shilton also took over as captain when Ray Wilkins was substituted against Scotland in 1986, and collected the Rous Cup.

Other countries have had fewer qualms about making their 'keepers captains. Several have done so against England, including Scotland (Bob Gardner 1872–73, Jimmy McAuley 1887); Wales (Jimmy Trainer 1895–97) and Ireland (Billy Scott a record four times 1908–12), his brother Elisha three times 1929–33, Pat Jennings 1979).

Others (there are over 25) include Ricardo Zamora of Spain (1929–31); Frantisek Planicka (1934–37) and Ivo Viktor (1970) of Czechoslovakia; Antonio Carbajal of Mexico (1959); Gyula Grosics of Hungary (1960–62); Gylmar of Brazil (1963); Dino Zoff of Italy (1980); Luis Arconada of Spain (1981–82) and Harald Schumacher of West Germany (1985).

The first time both goalkeepers captained their teams in any international was back in 1873, in only the second one ever played, Alexander Morten and Bob Gardner doing the honours. The second and last time it happened in an England match was 110 years later, when Hungary were beaten at Wembley in 1983. Peter Shilton and Bela Katzirz led the sides.

MOST CAPPED GOALKEEPERS

		Goals Conceded	Average
125	Peter Shilton	80	0.64
73	Gordon Banks	57	0.78
61	Ray Clemence	51	0.84
33	Ron Springett	48	1.45
25	Harry Hibbs	26	1.04
24	Bert Williams	34	1.42
24	Chris Woods	8	0.33
23	Gil Merrick	45	1.96
21	Sam Hardy	25	1.19
19	Vic Woodley	26	1.37

Shilts stopped Clem winning at least 100 caps, Clem stopped Shilts short of at least 150. For a while it was hard to choose between them and Ron Greenwood didn't try. At the end of the 1979 summer tour, he took Shilton off at half-time in Vienna, replacing him with Clemence; England, 3–1 down at the interval, lost 4–3.

For the next few years, neither won more than three caps in succession, an arrangement which looks even more unsatisfactory in retrospect. They even alternated, to no good effect, during the 1980 European Championship finals. By the time the 1982 World Cup came round, Greenwood had changed his mind and Shilton played throughout the finals. When Bobby Robson made it clear that he had the same Number One in mind, Clemence retired from international football, too early even at 35.

IN GOAL AND OUT

In England's first ever match, against Scotland in 1872, WJ Maynard changed places with Robert Barker during the second half; they both played in goal and up front.

Reginald Welch played at half-back in that match – and in goal against Scotland in 1874.

When William Carr missed a train and arrived late for the match against Scotland in 1879, Charles Alcock decided to start with only ten men – and put AG Bonsor in goal for the first quarter of an hour before Carr arrived.

Billy Walker took over in goal when Fred Fox (in his only international) was injured while conceding the second French goal in 1925. Walker kept a clean sheet for 14 minutes as England won 3–2.

When Ted Hufton stayed off at half-time against Ireland in 1927, Jack Ball took his place and conceded only one goal.

After Vic Woodley was injured against Norway during the 1937 summer tour, Eddie Hapgood was selected as goalkeeper in the next match, against Sweden. Woodley made a speedy recovery.

After Jimmy Mullen's boot broke Billy Smyth's nose in the Northern Ireland match of 1953, Billy Dickson took over in goal and kept a clean sheet for the last 10 minutes or so.

When Jack Kelsey was injured during the England–Wales match in 1956, Alf Sherwood went in goal, and conceded all three goals as England won 3–1. Kelsey came back on after half-time and stayed out on the left wing.

It seems that Jimmy McAulay ('the ablest goalkeeper the world has ever seen'), who appeared five times against England (1883–87), won his first cap for Scotland as a forward against Wales in 1882.

An Arsenal For A Battle

Wednesday 14 November 1934
Arsenal Stadium, Highbury 56 044

ENGLAND (3) 3   ITALY (0) 2
Brook 8, 10   Meazza 58, 62
Drake 15

Referee: Otto Olsson (Sweden)

ENGLAND		ITALY	
Frank Moss	Arsenal	Carlo Ceresoli	Ambrosiana-Inter
George Male	Arsenal	Eraldo Monzeglio	Bologna
Eddie Hapgood (capt)	Arsenal	Luigi Allemandi	Ambrosiana-Inter
Cliff Britton	Everton	Attilio Ferraris (capt)	Lazio
Jack Barker	Derby Co	Luisito Monti	Juventus
Wilf Copping	Arsenal	Luigi Bertolini	Juventus
Stanley Matthews	Stoke City	Enrique (Enrico) Guaita	Roma
Ray Bowden	Arsenal	Pietro Serantoni	Juventus
Ted Drake	Arsenal	Giuseppe (Peppino) Meazza	Ambrosiana-Inter
Cliff Bastin	Arsenal	Giovanni (Gioanin) Ferrari	Juventus
Eric Brook	Man City	Raimundo (Mumo) Orsi	Juventus

Manager: –
First Caps: Drake, Male
Last Cap: Moss

Manager: Vittorio Pozzo
First/Last caps: 0

Italy were the world champions and England were taking no chances, staging the match on the ground of the most successful team in the country, picking seven players from the club (though Male and Drake weren't first choices) and making Hapgood captain for the first time.

They had reason to be wary. Of the leading European teams, only Germany were already playing with a stopper centre-half, the big gun against England's main strengths: fast direct wingers, a powerful centre-forward, shoulder charges in midfield, and a little rough stuff on the goalkeeper (mainly at home; they were more gentle, and far less successful, abroad). Italy didn't have a stopper as such, but there was a pretty good approximation in the fearsome Monti, runner-up in the World Cup and Olympic Games with Argentina, World Cup winner with Italy, a brutal tackler who could hit the important long passes out to the wings. Above all, the Italians were professional and fit, one of the very few sides who could slog it out in English mud. A battle royal was in prospect.

It very quickly turned into a *slugfest*, and very quickly an unequal one: within five minutes Monti had broken a toe. It may have been an accident; the Italians didn't think so and rolled up their sleeves. Hapgood had his nose broken, Drake was injured. Meanwhile Copping was putting his shoulder about; the referee was seeing no evil. Brook, fast and aggressive and revelling in the whole thing, had his penalty saved in the first minute but scored with a header and then smashed in a free-kick after Ceresoli decided he could do without a wall. England went 3-0 up after 15 minutes with a goal by Drake. Italy, reshuffling, brought a man into defence at the expense of attack.

In the second half, they made a better fist (!) of it. Allemandi marked the young Matthews out of the game; Meazza scored with a shot then a header; Moss kept out the rest. In Italy the result was proclaimed a moral victory, and certainly the loss of Monti had been crucial – Pozzo claimed as much when he

The moment when it was still a friendly. Hapgood (right) and Ferraris are captaining their countries for the first time (Hulton)

paraded the injured centre-half in a wheelchair at the railway station; then put his finger on the real reason behind the Battle of Highbury. England were excellent, he said (ever the anglophile); the power of the shoulder charge takes the breath away. Quite.

This was England's first match against reigning world champions – and the only time seven players from one club have appeared in an England team.

The story goes that the original choice of referee, Peco Bauwens of Germany, had been vetoed by the visitors because he spoke English but no Italian – but this seems to be something passed on by old wives. The Italians had been happy enough to invite Bauwens to referee their match against England in Rome in 1933, and were to do so again in Milan in 1939.

CAPTAINS

MOST TIMES CAPTAIN

90	Billy Wright	1948–59
90	Bobby Moore	1963–73
65	Bryan Robson	1982–91
29	Kevin Keegan	1976–82
23	Bob Crompton	1903–14
23	Emlyn Hughes	1974–80
22	Johnny Haynes	1960–62
21	Eddie Hapgood	1934–39
15	Norman C Bailey	1881–87
15	Jimmy Armfield	1962–66
15	Peter Shilton	1982–90

GO Smith was captain **14** (possibly **16**) times between 1896 and 1901.

CAPTAIN ON DEBUT

1872	Cuthbert Ottaway
1873	Alexander Morten
1875	Charles Alcock
1883	Jack Hudson
1889	Jack Brodie
1919	Arthur Knight
1922	Max Woosnam
1923	BCA Patchitt
1923	Graham Doggart
1925	Claude Ashton
1946	George Hardwick

Amateurs to a man – except Hardwick, who was captain in the first match after the Second World War.

CAPTAIN IN LAST MATCH

50 players have achieved this, including Charles Alcock, GO Smith, fullback partners Bob Crompton and Jesse Pennington, Billy Walker, Sam Barkas, Eddie Hapgood, Stan Cullis.

SINCE 1945

1948	George Hardwick
1959	Billy Wright
1960	Ronnie Clayton
1962	Johnny Haynes
1966	Jimmy Armfield
1973	Bobby Moore
1975	Alan Ball
1976	Gerry Francis
1982	Mick Mills
1990	Peter Shilton
1990	Terry Butcher
1991	Bryan Robson

MOST GOALS SCORED WHILE CAPTAIN

21	Vivian Woodward	1908–09
19	Bryan Robson*	1983–89
11	Kevin Keegan*	1977–81
8	Gary Lineker*	1990–91
7	GO Smith	1898–99
5	Tinsley Lindley	1888–91

* penalty

It's possible that GO Smith was captain against **Ireland** and **Wales** in **1896**; if so, his total stands at **10**.

Only three England matches have featured goals by both captains: against Ireland in 1899, when GO Smith scored four and Joe McAllen once; in 1980, when Kevin Keegan scored after Daniel Passarella had pulled a goal back for Argentina; and against Greece in 1989, when Bryan Robson answered Dimitris Saravakos' first-minute strike. In each case, the opposition goal came from a penalty.

Billy Gillespie of Ireland scored in four different matches as captain against England (1921–26). **Fred Keenor** scored in three, and an own goal in another.

Most of VJ Woodward's goals for England were scored against fellow amateurs (Colorsport)

Derek Kevan equalises against Scotland at Wembley in 1957, watched by big Geordie Young (far right), captain against England for the eighth and last time (Popperfoto)

HAT-TRICKS BY CAPTAINS

1899	GO Smith (4)	v Ireland
1908	Vivian Woodward (4)	v Austria
1909	Vivian Woodward (4)	v Hungary
1909	Vivian Woodward	v Austria
1984	Bryan Robson	v Turkey
1991	Gary Lineker (4)	v Malaysia

Robson won the race with Tony Woodcock to reach the rebound after Steve Williams had hit a post. Woodcock scored twice that day; he never scored an international hat-trick. Williams hasn't played for England since.

Lineker scored all of England's goals in the game.

No opposition captain has scored a hat-trick against England.

YOUNGEST CAPTAINS

Yrs	days		
22	47	Bobby Moore	1963
22	133	Cuthbert Ottaway	1872
22	140	William Rawson	1877
22	211	Stan Cullis	1939
22	281	William Moon	1891
22	282	BCA Patchitt	1923
22	358	George Raikes	1896

There's still the slight possibility that **Tinsley Lindley** captained England on his debut, against Ireland in 1886, when aged 20yr 137d; though one source nominates Shutt, and at least three others PM Walters!

Ottaway was England's first ever captain.

Moon and Raikes were goalkeepers.

OLDEST CAPTAINS

Yrs	days		
40	292	Peter Shilton	1990
36	230	Jesse Pennington	1920
35	111	Billy Wright	1959
35	39	Billy Walker	1932
34	277	Frank Swift	1948
34	229	Dave V Watson	1981
34	190	Bob Crompton	1914
34	95	Joe McCall	1920
34	75	Bryan Robson	1991

Again, it's quite possible that **Alexander Morten** was 40 or even 42 when he was captain against Scotland in 1873: England's oldest ever debutant, goalkeeper, and captain.

MOST TIMES CAPTAIN AGAINST ENGLAND

8	Fred Keenor	Wales	1923–29
8	George Young	Scotland	1948–57
8	Danny Blanchflower	N Ireland	1955–62
7	Billy Gillespie	Ireland	1921–30
7	Terry Neill	N Ireland	1964–73
6	Mike England	Wales	1964–73
6	Terry Yorath	Wales	1976–80

The most by a non-British player is **5**, by **Armand Swartenbroeks** of **Belgium** (1923–27) and Italy's **Giacinto Facchetti** (1973–77).

No-one captained England either side of a World War. Alec McNair captained Scotland against England in 1912 and, in his last international, 1920.

States of Shock

Thursday 29 June 1950
Estadio Independencia, Belo Horizonte, Brazil 10 151

World Cup Group 2

UNITED STATES (1) 1   ENGLAND (0) 0
Gaetjens 38

Referee: Generoso Dattilo (Italy)

UNITED STATES		ENGLAND	
Frank Borghi	Simpkins FC, St Louis	Bert Williams	Wolves
Harry Keough	McMahon, St Louis	Alf Ramsey	Tottenham
Joe Maca	Brooklyn Hispaniola	Johnny Aston	Manchester United
Eddie McIlvenny (capt)	Philadelphia Nationals	Billy Wright (capt)	Wolves
Charlie Colombo	Simpkins FC, St Louis	Laurie Hughes	Liverpool
Walter Bahr	Philadelphia Nationals	Jimmy Dickinson	Portsmough
Frank Wallace	Simpkins FC, St Louis	Tom Finney	Preston
Gino Pariani	Simpkins FC, St Louis	Wilf Mannion	Middlesbrough
Joe Gaetjens	Brookhattan	Roy Bentley	Chelsea
John Souza	Ponta Delgada	Stan Mortensen	Blackpool
Ed Souza	Ponta Delgada	Jimmy Mullen	Wolves

Manager: Chubby Lyons
Coach: Bill Jeffrey

Selector: Arthur Drewry
Manager: Walter Winterbottom

Hindsight's a fine thing, but it really is odd that the Americans were taken so lightly. Just two weeks earlier, they'd lost only 1–0 to an FA XI in New York, and in the first group match led Spain 1–0 before conceding three in the last quarter of an hour; this while England were struggling in the heat against Chile. Admittedly even the Americans talked about expecting a heavy defeat, but perhaps it was just talk . . .

English reports of the match have usually tended to be little more than a list of missed chances, Borghi acrobatics, terrible refereeing – possibly because the writers thought this was what *must* have happened, still believing that the Americans were very small fry. In fact there was much more cut and thrust than that. Yes, England had more of the ball, but that may not have been all that significant; all three of the other countries in their group fell back to the edge of their area, where the English attacks would often break down.

Not so one of the USA's, towards the end of the first half. A throw-in from McIlvenny to Bahr, a hopeful cross, or shot, a glancing header by Gaetjens . . . shock horror. Actually it was a strange goal; one photograph shows keeper Bert Williams with his toes fractionally *behind* the line, with Gaetjens just a yard or so in front of him. What was he doing, waiting for the ball to float into his hands? Didn't he see Gaetjens coming? Or perhaps he did, and took his eye off the ball. Curiouser and curiouser, and what looks like a bad mistake by the goalkeeper.

In the second half, England switched their attack, but made little headway. Again, match reports recount chances missed, often unluckily – but it's usually the same three that get mentioned: Mortensen's effort possibly crossing the line, Mullen's header from Ramsey's free-kick doing the same, Morty breaking through to be rugby-tackled by the Italian Colombo under the nose of a smiling Italian referee. Ho hum. The truth seems to be that England made relatively few chances for all the possession they had, while the States, with much less of the ball, went on causing trouble, forcing Ramsey to kick off the line and drawing two good saves from Williams.

Afterwards, while McIlvenny and Gaetjens were chaired off the pitch, Wright and Winterbottom admitted that the Americans had been stronger, fitter and had fought harder; and an editor in London thought the 1–0 scoreline must have been a misprint for 1–10. A remarkable match. Not quite the great upset it appeared, but an upset all the same – and England were glad to host Italy–North Korea in 1966.

OLDEST & YOUNGEST

THE OLDEST

Yrs	days		
42	103	Stanley Matthews	1957
40	292	Peter Shilton	1990
38	71	Leslie Compton	1950
36	230	Jesse Pennington	1920
36	228	Sam Hardy	1920
36	200	Tom Finney	1958
36	171	Ted Hufton	1929
35	268	Sam Chedgzoy	1924
35	264	Bert Williams	1955
35	240	Dave V Watson	1982
35	195	Eph Longworth	1923
35	187	Frank Hudspeth	1925
35	145	Frank Swift	1949
35	111	Billy Wright	1959
35	103	Ray Clemence	1983
35	80	Charlie Wallace	1920
35	50/51	Harry Healless	1928
35	42	Ted Ditchburn	1956
35	41	Teddy Taylor	1926
35	39	Billy Walker	1932
35	34	Jack Charlton	1970

As mentioned elsewhere, it's quite possible that **Alexander Morten** was **40**, or even **42**, when he won his only cap in **1873**.

One newspaper report claimed Taylor was **39yr 91d** when he last played for England. There's also doubt about Pennington, Hufton and Chedgzoy. But in general the list is pretty reliable.

THE OLDEST OPPOSITION PLAYERS

Yrs	days			
45	230	Billy Meredith	Wales	1920
41	209	Elisha Scott	Ireland	1935
40	155	Pat Jennings	N Ireland	1985
38/39		Silvio Piola	Italy	1952
38	351	Alan Morton	Scotland	1932
38	308	Gylmar	Brazil	1969
38	266	Billy McCracken	Ireland	1922
38	108	Dino Zoff	Italy	1980
38	76	Billy Gillespie	Ireland	1930
38	37	Roger Miller (Milla)	Cameroon)	1990

According to official Brazilian sources (which include matches against club sides and regional select teams) Gylmar was winning his 100th and last cap.

Piola was called out of international retirement to captain Italy against England in Florence. It was his last cap.

One source claims Elisha Scott was **42yr 56d**.

Lot Jones may have been **38** when he played for **Wales** against England in **1920**. Chile's goalkeeper and captain **Sergio Livingstone** may have been as old as **43** when he played against England in **1953**.

OLDEST DEBUTANTS

Yrs	days		
38	64	Leslie Compton	1950
35	187	Frank Hudspeth	1925
34	227	Jackie Bestall	1935
34	192	Teddy Davison	1922
34	183	Jack Crawford	1931
34	71	Dicky Downs	1920
34	13	Jack Harrow	1922
34	10	Jimmy Moore	1923
33/34		Fred Bullock	1920
33	304	Jimmy Bagshaw	1919
33	218	Jerry Dawson	1921
33	185	Jim Taylor	1951
33	48	Arthur Knight	1919
33	36	Jack Fort	1921
33	26	Clem Stephenson	1924

Again, **Morten** in **1873** may have been **40** or **42**, the oldest ever. Stephenson may have been **34yr 26d**. **Teddy Taylor** may have been as old as **35yr 228d** when he won his first cap in **1922**.

Compton (or Morten) seems to have been the oldest for any country.

Bullock and Downs made their debuts in the same match, as did Teddy Taylor and Harrow.

It was once thought that **Arthur Chadwick** was born in 1866, which would have made him **33** or **34** when he was capped in **1900**. It now seems much more likely that he was born in 1875.

The oldest opposition new boy was very probably **Ronnie Simpson** in **1967**. At **36yr 196d**, he was Scotland's oldest ever debutant. Back in 1945, at **14yr 304d**, he'd been the youngest player in any first class match.

Scotland's oldest debutant earns his cap the hard way. Geoff Hurst puts the full force of his 25 years into a close-range shot and 36-year-old Ronnie Simpson bears the brunt (Hulton)

THE YOUNGEST

Yrs days

Yrs	days	Name	Year
17	252	JFM Prinsep	1879
17	311	Tot Rostron	1881
18	23	Clem Mitchell	1880
18	183	Duncan Edwards	1955
18	210	Jimmy Brown	1881
18	328	Arthur Brown	1904
18/19		Billy Mosforth	1877
18/19		Tom Brindle	1880
18/19		Harry Lilley	1892
19	16	Tommy Lawton	1938
19	32	Albert Geldard	1933
19	70	Billy Bassett	1888
19	86	Jimmy Greaves	1959
19	123	Joe Baker	1959
19	146	TM Pike	1886
19	179	Jock Rutherford	1904
19	186	Robert Vidal	1873
19	222	Billy Moon	1888
19	222	John Barnes	1983
19	237	Lindsay Bury	1877
19	238	Jackie Robinson	1937
19	240	Stanley Matthews	1934
19	249	Cliff Bastin	1931
19	256	Ray Wilkins	1976
19	257	WJ Maynard	1872
19	264	RD Anderson	1879
19	265	Arthur Bambridge	1881
19	267	Jimmy Forest	1884
19	283	Tom Galley	1937
19	300	Charlie Athersmith	1892
19	304	Lee Sharpe	1991
19	309	Nick Pickering	1983
19	320	Robert S King	1882
19	320	Joe Lofthouse	1885
19	324	Tony Allen	1959
19	350	Johnny Haynes	1954
19	350	Bobby Thomson	1963
19	351	Jimmy Ward	1885
19	362	Alan Hinton	1962
19	362	Alan Ball	1965

Pike may have been a year, Galley two years, older. **Harold Morse** may have been **19** when he was capped in **1879**. **Edward Johnson** may have been **19**, even as young as **17**, in **1880**.

James Frederick McLeod Prinsep was born on 27 July 1861 and won his only cap on 5 April 1879.

Moon was England's youngest ever goalkeeper.

It used to be said that Jackie Robinson was 17 years 9 months when he first played for England – but it now transpires that he was rather economical with the truth about his age while signing for Sunderland in 1946. When it came out that he was two years older than he claimed, the club succeeded in having the transfer fee reduced!

Vidal was only **16yr 183d** when he played against **Scotland** in **1870**. The match is now classed as unofficial, but at the time was given the same status as the games of 1872–73–74 . . .

YOUNGEST OPPOSITION PLAYERS

Several 18-year-olds have appeared against England, but it's hard to find any who were definitely younger than that. The only certainty seems to have been the schoolboy goalkeeper **Blendi Nallbani**, who was called up at the eleventh hour to play for **Albania** at Wembley in **1989**, aged **17yr 19d**. He wasn't disgraced in a 5–0 defeat.

Others who may have been 17 when they played against England:

Bob Davies	Wales	1892
Willie K Gibson	Ireland	1894
Grenville Morris	Wales	1896
Alex King	Scotland	1896

THE OLDEST TEAM

This would appear to be the band of First World War survivors who outlasted Scotland 5–4 in 1920, after being 4–2 down at half-time, despite an average age of **30yr 251d**:

	Yrs	days
Sam Hardy	36	227
Eph Longworth	32	190
Jesse Pennington (capt)	36	230
Andy Ducat	34	54
Joe McCall	33	265
Arthur Grimsdell	26	18
Charlie Wallace	35	80
Bob Kelly	26	146
Jack Cock	26	148
Fred Morris	26	227
Alf Quantrill	23	29

It's possible that Pennington may have been 35, not 36.

Perhaps only the Brazilians of 1962 had a higher average age (over 32). They beat England 3–1 on the way to retaining the World Cup.

THE YOUNGEST TEAM

The eleven that played against Wales in 1959 were all aged under 26 (an England record), with an average of 22yr 254d – but younger still were the players who beat Wales 3–2 in 1880. Although Hunter may have been as old as 28, the average was between **21** and **22**:

	Yrs	days
John Sands	20/21	
Edwin Luntley	22/23	
Tom Brindle	18/19	
Jack Hunter	27/28	
Fred Hargreaves	21	212
Tom Marshall	21	185
Harry Cursham	20	109
FJ Sparks (capt)	24	255
Clem Mitchell	18	23
Edward Johnson	19/20	
Billy Mosforth	21/22	

THE YOUNGEST AGAINST

This may well have been the Hungarians of 1908, who had an average age of under **21**, perhaps even under **20**. They were no match for a battle-hardened England team who won 7–0, Hungary's greatest ever margin of defeat.

	Yrs
Laszlo Domonkos	19/20
Gyula Rumbold	20/21
Ferenc Csudor	21/22
Peter Ficzere	22/23
Sandor Brody	23/24
Ferenc Simon	21/22
Zoltan Ronay	19/20
Ferenc Weisz	22/23
Karoly Korody	20/21
Imre Schlosser	18/19
Gaspar Borbas (capt)	23/24

Schlosser had already won eight previous caps. Hungary's first famous player, good enough to score against England, his international career lasted from 1906 to 1921.

THE LONGEST-LIVED

Nearly **50** England players lived to be over 80. Records are still sketchy in places, but these seem to be the most senior citizens:

Yrs	days		Died
95	238	Dick Pym	1988
95	209	Ben Howard Baker	1987
94	45	Henry Wace	1947
93	279	George Raikes	1966
93	164	Walter Gilliat	1963
92	201	Bertie Corbett	1967
91	331	Albert Gosnell	1972
91	246	Thelwell Mather Pike	1957
91	146	Frank Osborne	1988
91	3	Doc Greenwood	1951
90	30	Kelly Houlker	1956
89	352	Tom Parker	1987
89	267	Vic Watson	1988
89	141	Percy Fairclough	1947
89	52	George Brann	1954
89	28	Jimmy Ruffell	1989
87	88	Jackie Hegan	1989
88	147	Bob Holmes	1955
88	46–76	Jack Southworth	1956
88	9	Joe Reader	1954
87/88		Rex Corbett	1967
87	334	Robert Stuart King	1950
87	333	Tommy Crawshaw	1960
87	272	Eddie Mosscrop	1980
87	241	George Thornewell	1986
87		Reginald Welch	1939
87	13	Jesse Pennington	1970
87	11	Charles Clegg	1937

Jack D Cox was somewhere between **86yr 150d** and **87yr 181d** when he died in **1957**.

Watson may have been a year older, Pennington a year younger.

Clegg and Welch were the last survivors of the very first England team.

The Corbetts were brothers. Clegg's brother William also lived to be 80, dying in 1932.

Several players born between 1891 and 1904 may still be alive:
Harry Jones (b 1891)
Albert Read (b 1899)
Jack Ball (b 1899 or 1900)
BCA Patchitt (b 1900)
Albert Barratt (b 1901)
George Waterfield (b 1901)
Harold Miller (b 1902)
Harry Burgess (b 1904)
Hugh Turner (b 1904)

THE SHORTEST-LIVED

Yrs	days		Died
21	143	Duncan Edwards	1958
22	139	David Pegg	1958
22/23		George Tait	1882
23	25	AG Goodwyn	1874
23	26	CW Wilson	1881
26	08	Tommy Taylor	1958
26	123	Harry Bradshaw	1899
27	18–48	Albert Aldridge	1891
27	256	Cuthbert Ottaway	1878
27/28		Tom Meehan	1924
28	73	Tot Rostron	1891
28		Joe Marsden	1897
28	363	Roger Byrne	1958
29	35	Harry Allen	1895
29	209	Jeff Hall	1959

Eric Stephenson may still have been **29** when he was killed in action in 1944.

Edwards, Pegg, Taylor and Byrne died in the Munich air crash; Meehan of sleeping sickness; Hall of polio while still in the England squad.

TALLEST & SHORTEST

THE TALLEST

Ft	ins		
6	4½	Billy Gunn	1884
6	4½	Joe Corrigan*	1976–82
6	4	Bob Roberts*	1887–90
6	4	Terry Butcher	1980–90
6	4	Gary Pallister	1988
6	4	Dave Beasant*	1989
6	3	George Cotterill	1891–93
6	3	Jack Hill	1925–29
6	3	Harry Clarke	1954
6	3	Mark Wright	1984–90
6	3	David Seaman*	1988–90
6	3	Brian Deane	1991
6	2½	Larry Lloyd	1971–80

* goalkeepers

Willie Foulke (1897) and Frank Swift (1946–49), both goalkeepers, were each variously described as being 6ft 2in and 6ft 4in. Charlie Buchan claimed Herbert Morley (1910) was 6ft 3in. Alan Smith is either 6ft 2¾ or 6ft 3in.

Only Gunn (whose long reach made him a formidable Test batsman) and Cotterill were forwards.

Roberts took size 13 in boots.

THE SHORTEST

Ft	ins		
5	2⅛	Fanny Walden	1914–22
5	3	Tommy Magee	1923–25
5	3	Jackie Bestall	1935
5	4	Harry Davis	1903
5	4	Jimmy Conlin	1906
5	4	Steve Smith	1895
5	4	Johnny Hancocks	1948–50
5	4	Warren Bradley	1959
5	4¼	Danny Wallace	1986
5	4½	Johnny Holt	1890–1900
5	4½	Billy Wedlock	1907–14
5	4¾	Herbert Burgess	1904–6
5	4¾	Norman Deeley	1959

Others under 5ft 6in include Jack Reynolds, Joe Beresford, Wally Boyes, Johnny Berry, Bryan Douglas, Wilf Mannion, Nobby Stiles and Derek Statham. It's possible that Jack Crawford was only 5ft 2in.

Wallace's height is variously listed as 5ft 4in and 5ft 4½in; here the difference is split!

At one time, Sheffield Utd had an entire half-back line made up of England players who were 5ft 6in or less: Rabbi Howell, Ernest Needham, Tommy Morren.

Hancocks took size 2 in boots.

England's shortest ever goalkeeper was Teddy Davison (1922) at 5ft 7in.

THE TALLEST OPPOSITION

Ft	ins			
6	4½	Ludek Miklosko*	Czechoslovakia	1990
6	4	Ivan Horvat	Yugoslavia	1950–56
6	4	Jose Torres	Portugal	1964–66
6	4	Roman Wojcicki	Poland	1986–89
6	4	Niall Quinn	Eire	1988
6	4	Bela Katzirz*	Hungary	1981–83
6	3½	Gordon McQueen	Scotland	1975–79
6	3	John Smith	Scotland	1877–84
6	3	Derek Dougan	N Ireland	1960–72
6	3	Jari Rantanen	Finland	1985
6	3	Rodger Gray	N Zealand	1991

* goalkeeper

Beware: this is a very badly documented subject, prone to all kinds of exaggeration. For instance, Stan Cullis claimed that Silvio Piola, Italy's World Cup centre-forward of the thirties, was 6ft 3in, and one (admittedly unreliable) source refers to the famous Spanish goalkeeper Ricardo Zamora as being 6ft 5in, which can only have been true if every other team-mate and opponent was at least 6ft 2in. See photographs for evidence.

Grimsby Town's Craven, Glover and (left) Jackie Bestall, one of the smallest (and oldest) inside-forwards to win an England cap (Hulton)

THE SHORTEST OPPOSITION

Ft	ins			
5	2	Manuel Grimaldo	Peru	1962
5	4	Bobby Collins	Scotland	1957–65
5	4	Jimmy Johnstone	Scotland	1966–74
5	4	Brian Flynn	Wales	1975–83
5	5	Rees Williams	Wales	1921
5	5	Alan Morton	Scotland	1921–32
5	5	Jimmy Dunn	Scotland	1928
5	5	Wilbur Cush	N Ireland	1950–59
5	5	Francisco Gento	Spain	1955–68
5	5	Enrique Collar	Spain	1955
5	5	Archie Gemmill	Scotland	1972–80
5	5½	Hughie Gallacher	Scotland	1925–35
5	5½	Alex James	Scotland	1928–30
5	5½	Luigi (Lou) Macari	Scotland	1972–77

Flynn was only **5ft 2in** in 1973. He weighed 8st 7lb. By 1984 this had gone up to 12 stone!

Grimaldo was the first player to be sent off in an England match – not for fighting.

Valter, who never played against England but was in Brazil's 1956 squad at Wembley, was only **5ft 3in**.

The Wembley Wizards of 1928, who beat England 5–1, had 4 'five-fivers' in their forward line alone, in Morton, James, Gallacher and Dunn. Only Alec Jackson was taller.

Again, bear in mind: this is a very badly documented subject.

HEAVIEST & LIGHTEST

THE HEAVIEST

St	lb	
17	0	Willie Foulke*
15	0	Fred Pelly
14	12	Joe Corrigan*
14	7	Harry Thickett
14	6	Nigel Spink*
14	5	Terry Butcher
14	4	Larry Lloyd
14	2	Jimmy Barrett
14	0	William Oakley
14	0	Jack Hillman*
14	0	Bobby Benson
14	0	Frank Swift*
14	0	Gordon West*
14	0	Peter Shilton*
14	0	Phil Parkes*

* goalkeepers

Foulke's weight is an estimate. So many stories have been told about him – how he weighed over 20 stone while playing in the First Division, over 24 while stopping penalties for pennies in retirement, as much as both full backs put together while he was at Chelsea – that it's hard to separate fact from fun. He may even have been quite trim in his England days; say, 16 stone . . .

Barrett weighed as much as 15 stone according to Bernard Joy, Pelly 16 stone according to BO Corbett.

Oakley apparently put on more than two stone during his England career; he weighed less than 12 stone when winning the AAA long jump title.

Not the least of big Joe Corrigan's feats was victory in the fight against the flab. In 1973, before he won his first cap, he was recorded as 15st 11½lb.

Parkes was exactly 14 stone when he won his only cap; by 1986 he was a stone heavier. **Matt Kingsley**, another goalkeeper, was capped in 1903; two years later he was **14st 4lb**. According to *The Book Of Football*, **Bill George** (yet another) was **16 stone** in 1906, four years after his last cap. **Steve Foster** weighed less than 13 stone when he was capped in 1982; by 1990, he was **14 stone**.

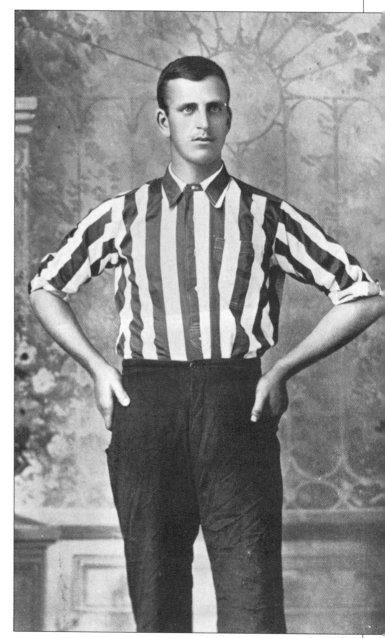

Never mind the quality . . . William Henry Foulke wears the trousers (Bob Thomas)

THE LIGHTEST

St	lb		
8	9	Fanny Walden	1914–22
9	2	Dicky Spence	1936
9	4	Jackie Hegan	1923
9	5	Johnny Hancocks	1948–50
9	5	Dennis Wise	1991
9	6	Jimmy Conlin	1906
9	8	Rabbi Howell	1895–99
9	8	Frank Broome	1938–39
9	9	Johnny Berry	1953–56
9	10	Eddie Mosscrop	1914
9	10	Bryan Douglas	1958–63
9	10	Warren Bradley	1959
9	10	Alan Ball	1965–75
9	10	Danny Wallace	1986
9	12	Steve Hodge	1986–91
9	13	Harold Hardman	1905–08

Ball's weight is correct for 1967 and 1968; by 1984 it had risen to 10st 5lb.

Jimmy Conlin may have weighed only **9st 1lb**.

It's possible that **Jack Crawford** (1931) weighed as little as 8st 6lb, making him the smallest player to have represented England (see TALLEST AND SHORTEST).

THE LIGHTEST OPPOSITION

St	lb			
9	4	Eric McMordie	N Ireland	1969–72
9	7	David McCreery	N Ireland	1976–87
9	9	Gil Reece	Wales	1965–74
9	10	Osvaldo Ardiles	Argentina	1977
9	10	Tony Villars	Wales	1974
9	11	Trevor Anderson	N Ireland	1973–77
9	13	Archie Gemmill	Scotland	1972–80

McMordie's weight is correct for 1973; he may have been even lighter in 1969. Similarly, Ardiles was 9st 10lb in 1984; he may have weighed even less when he played against England.

Gemmill's weight fluctuated from 11st 2lb in 1973 to, unusually, under 10 stone by 1984.

Yet again, this isn't exactly an exhaustive list . . .

THE HEAVIEST OPPPOSITION

Again a very badly researched subject (at least by this writer!). Frederick Wall, the old FA Secretary, claimed Dr John Smith of Scotland (who scored 8 goals against England) weighed 15 stone. It's quite possible that Jock Hutton, Scotland's full back against England (1923–26), weighed the same. Jan Molby (Denmark, 1983–88) has apparently reached 14st 7lb at times, teammate Kent Nielsen (1988–90) 14st 1 lb. John Hughes, Scotland's Yogi Bear (1968), was 14st 2lb, Ludek Miklosko (Czechoslovakia, 1990), now in goal for West Ham, 14st 3lb.

The biggest man to have played against England may have been **Jari Rantanen**, who scored Finland's goal in 1985 when they avoided defeat for the first time against England. He was 6ft 3in and (in 1990, by which time he was on Leicester City's books) weighed **15st 2lb**.

Right *Jan Molby playing for Denmark at Wembley in 1988. Neil Webb (only a stone lighter) scored the only goal of the game* (Bob Thomas)

The Home Truth

Wednesday 25 November 1953
Empire Stadium, Wembley 100 000

ENGLAND (2) 3   HUNGARY (4) 6
Sewell 15   Hidegkuti 1, 20, 56
Mortensen 37   Puskas 22, 29
Ramsey (pen) 61   Bozsik 54

Referee: Leo Horn (Holland)

ENGLAND

Gil Merrick	Birmingham City
Alf Ramsey	Tottenham Hotspur
Bill Eckersley	Blackburn Rovers
Billy Wright (capt)	Wolves
Harry Johnston	Blackpool
Jimmy Dickinson	Portsmouth
Stanley Matthews	Blackpool
Ernie Taylor	Blackpool
Stan Mortensen	Blackpool
Jackie Sewell	Sheffield Wednesday
George Robb	Tottenham Hotspur

Manager: Walter Winterbottom
New caps: Robb, Taylor
Last caps: Robb, Taylor, Ramsey, Eckersley, Johnston, Mortensen

HUNGARY

Gyula Grosics*	Honved
Jeno Buzanszky	Banyasz Dorog
Mihaly Lantos	Voros Lobogo
Jozsef Bozsik	Honved
Gyula Lorant	Honved
Jozsef Zakarias	Voros Lobogo
Laszlo Budai	Honved
Sandor Kocsis	Honved
Nandor Hidegkuti	Voros Lobogo
Ferenc Puskas (capt)	Honved
Zoltan Czibor	Honved

*sub (80m in)
Sandor Geller   Voros Lobogo

Manager: Gusztav Sebes
Coach: Gyula Mandi/Mandl*
* Mandi in most sources, Mandl in a 1926
Hungarian almanack (possibly a misprint)

Below *While Puskas, Groscis, Lorant and Hidegkuti seem tense, Wright looks confident* (Hulton)

Above *Graphic illustration of the confusion in England's defence. As Hidegkuti comes from deep to score his third and Hungary's sixth, his expected marker Johnston is at the far end of the picture* (Hulton)

Hungary arrived with 21 unbeaten matches and the Olympic title under their belts, but most of the smart sterling was on another home win. Not so smart. Knowing smiles all round when the tubby little Hungarian captain juggled the ball in the centre circle before the kick-off; smiles wiped off faces when Hidegkuti made space for a long cross-shot in the first minute: 1–0, and at last a continental team that could shoot as well as pussyfoot.

They went on shooting and heading throughout, hitting a post through Kocsis, having a goal disallowed. They were 6–2 ahead after less than an hour and seem to have coasted the rest. England for their part had chosen a hotchpotch forward line: Ernie Taylor, expected to direct the play although this was his first international and Hungary were a great team; Robb, hyped by the London press, replacing the brilliant Finney;

Mortensen slightly out of position. But none of this should detract; Hungary were much too good.

There were exceptional players up front (Puskas, Kocsis, Czibor) and in midfield (Hidegkuti, Bozsik), a no-prisoners defence, a world-class goalkeeper. There were tactical innovations: the deep-lying centre forward leaving Johnston in no man's land; the keeper who swept the entire penalty area; a style of play based on moving triangles. Above all, perhaps, there was Puskas. His drag-back that left Billy Wright on his backside, his two goals, his personality (and belly), all personified a kind of football that was soon about to die away. He, possibly more than the match itself, was a kind of watershed.

England had been playing against foreign opposition at home since 1923. This was the first defeat.

It was Hungary's 22nd successive match without losing, on the way to a European record 32 which was ended by the 1954 World Cup Final. They were the reigning Olympic and Central European Champions.

Hidegkuti's hat-trick was the last conceded by England at home.

Ramsey's successful penalty was his third for England, which was then a record.

This was Wright's 40th international as captain, also a record at the time.

Puskas scored his 61st and 62nd goals for Hungary, on his way to an eventual world record of 83 that still stands.

Voros Lobogo means Red Banner/Red Flag. The club had once been (and would be again) MTK of Budapest.

MANAGERS & COACHES

CLUB LEVEL

A great many England players went into coaching and management when their playing careers were over, with varying degrees of success; among them Ronnie Allen, Jimmy Armfield, Alan Ball, Cliff Britton, Frank Broome, Major Frank Buckley, Bobby and Jack Charlton, Allan Clarke, Brian Clough, Stan Cullis, Ted Drake, Jimmy Hagan, Colin Harvey, Eric Houghton, Don Howe, Wilf McGuinness, Stanley Matthews, Joe Mercer, Brian Miller, Alan Mullery, Bill Nicholson, Steve Perryman, Don Revie, Arthur Rowe, Jimmy Seed, Ken Shellito and Billy Wright.

Officials:
Jem Bayliss was later chairman at West Brom, Phil Bach at Middlesbrough, Harold Hardman at Manchester United.

Dennis Hodgetts became vice-president of Aston Villa.

AF Hills was founder and managing director of Thames Ironworks, later West Ham United.

Elphinstone Jackson was a founder member of India's FA in 1893.

INTERNATIONAL LEVEL

Alf Ramsey	England
Joe Mercer	England
Don Revie	England & UAE
Bobby Robson	England

Ramsey was the only player to captain as well as manage England.

Ronnie Allen	Saudi Arabia
Jack Butler	Belgium
Edgar Chadwick	Holland
Jack Charlton	Eire
Billy Elliott	Libya
Bill McGarry	Saudi Arabia
Fred Pentland	Spain
Jackie Sewell	Zambia
Tony Waiters	Canada
Ray Wood	UAE

UAE – United Arab Emirates

Butler played his only game for England against Belgium in 1924; in 1936 he coached the Belgians to their only win over England. He was born in Ceylon.

Pentland was Spain's coach when in 1929 they became the first foreign country to beat England and the first to beat England at the first attempt.

Ken Armstrong was chief coach to the New Zealand FA, **Billy Marsden** to the Dutch FA.

ENGLAND MANAGERS' COMPLETE RECORDS

	Career	P	W	D	L	F	A	Record
Walter Winterbottom	1946–62	139	78	33	28	383	196	67.99%
Alf Ramsey	1963–74	113	69	27	17	224	98	73.01%
Joe Mercer	1974	7	3	3	1	9	7	64.29%
Don Revie	1974–77	29	14	8	7	49	25	62.07%
Ron Greenwood	1977–82	55	33	12	10	93	40	70.09%
Bobby Robson	1982–90	95	47	30	18	158	60	65.26%
Graham Taylor	1990–91	12	9	3	0	21	7	87.50%

MOST MATCHES AS OPPOSITION COACH

13	Gaston Barreau	France	1923–55
13	Billy Bingham	N Ireland & Greece	1967–87
12	Dave Bowen	Wales	1964–74
10	Peter Doherty	N Ireland	1951–60
9	Helmut Schon	W Germany	1965–78
8	Jimmy Murphy	Wales	1956–63
7	Willie Maxwell	Belgium	1921–28
7	Mike Smith	Wales & Egypt	1975–86
7	Jock Stein	Scotland	1979–85

Maxwell had played for Scotland against England in 1898.

Barreau was joint manager for the last few years of his term.

Scotland's appointment of their first ever manager, Andy Beattie in 1954, was in a way a throwback to the very first international match in 1872; then Queen's Park gave their captain Bob Gardner 'full and sole power' to select the Scotland team. In contrast, the team that played England in 1892 was the brainchild of 38 selectors!

Old Stoneface? The best record of any England manager – and three nerveless penalties as an England player
(Popperfoto)

COACHED TWO DIFFERENT TEAMS AGAINST ENGLAND

Vittorio Pozzo	Italy 1933–48	Rest of Europe 1938	The last time Northern Ireland beat
Walter Nausch	Austria 1951–52	FIFA 1953	England, at Wembley in 1972, Terry
Billy Bingham	N Ireland 1967–87	Greece 1971	Neill scored the only goal of the game.
Mike Smith	Wales 1975–79	Egypt 1986	He's the only captain/player-manager
Carlos Alberto Parreira	Kuwait 1982	Saudi Arabia 1988	to score against England.
Sepp Piontek	Denmark 1979–89	Turkey 1991	

Nearly Ten Past

Saturday 15 April 1961
Empire Stadium, Wembley 97 350

Home Championship

ENGLAND (3) 9   SCOTLAND (0) 3

Robson 9	Mackay 48
Greaves 19, 29, 82	Wilson 53
Douglas 56	Quinn 75
Smith 73, 85	
Haynes 78, 80	

Referee: Marcel Lequesne (France)

ENGLAND

Ron Springett	Sheffield Wednesday
Jimmy Armfield	Blackpool
Mick McNeil	Middlesbrough
Bobby Robson	WBA
Peter Swan	Sheffield Wednesday
Ron Flowers	Wolves
Bryan Douglas	Blackburn
Jimmy Greaves	Chelsea
Bobby Smith	Tottenham Hotspur
Johnny Haynes (capt)	Fulham
Bobby Charlton	Manchester United

Manager: Walter Winterbottom
First/last caps: 0

SCOTLAND

Frank Haffey	Celtic
Bobby Shearer	Rangers
Eric Caldow (capt)	Rangers
Dave Mackay	Tottenham Hotspur
Billy McNeill	Celtic
Robert (Bert) McCann	Motherwell
Johnny MacLeod	Hibernian
Denis Law	Manchester City
Ian St John	Motherwell
Pat Quinn	Motherwell
Davie Wilson	Rangers

Manager: Ian McColl
First caps: Shearer, McNeill, MacLeod, Quinn
Last caps: Haffey, McCann

England go 2–0 ahead. Greaves times his run, the defenders just run, Haffey would like to. Story of the match
(Hulton)

Very nearly ten past. The cross is too quick for everyone, including Smith who misses it (and his hat-trick) in front of an open goal (Hulton)

This was England's fifth match of the season, and a world-class forward line had been getting its eye in: 5-2, 9-0, 4-2, 5-1. Against this, Scotland ranged a muscled defence (Shearer, Caldow, McNeill, Mackay) and a goalkeeper who'd played well against England at Hampden the year before, though oddly this would be only his second cap.

Reports of the match are usually just a catalogue of the goals (true, they don't leave much space for anything else) with a few chortles thrown in at the keeper's expense (Slap Haffey and the like), as if the whole thing had been down to him. The truth was that England's long-ball style, Haynes and Robson switching play with crossfield passes, was very effctive against anything other than a sweeper or massed defence. Scotland had neither; a goal down early on, they came out hunting the equaliser, but

their passing was too short and too intricate and England had muscles of their own in defence (Swan, McNeill, Flowers), winning enough possession to counter-attack. Nine goals on the counter? Well, things were different then.

Haffey wasn't blameless – the first goal was a long-range volley, the third a tap-in after he couldn't hold Smith's shot (not that many keepers could) – but he was often left exposed, and Scotland had little luck: Law's goal was disallowed just before half-time and they pulled back to 3-2 before Douglas scored after Greaves had taken a free-kick from the wrong place. Towards the end, yes, capitulation: it rained goals and poor Frank must have looked silly, but scorelines never tell the whole truth (nor do headlines, though one proclaimed Haffey Errors Not a Major Factor) and it's surprising that only he and McCann never played for Scot-

land again. Others may have been lucky not to join them.

England next beat Mexico 8-0 and went on to qualify for the World Cup in Chile. Scotland didn't lose 9-3 again and missed a place in the finals only after losing in extra time in a play-off against the eventual runners-up. By then Bill Brown was back, and he was a better goalkeeper – but he never featured in a football joke. What's the time at Wembley? Nearly ten past Haffey.

England scored 19 goals in the 1960–61 Home Championship, equalling the record, as did Greaves who scored seven of them. His is still the last hat-trick in an England–Scotland match.

Frank Haffey did have his moments against England, or at least against Bobby Charlton, who didn't score at Wembley and missed a penalty at Hampden.

REFEREES

MOST TIMES IN CHARGE OF AN ENGLAND MATCH

21	Tom Robertson	Scotland	1896–1908
13	Istvan Zsolt	Hungary	1954–69
11	Alex A Jackson	Scotland	1910–21
11	Willie Webb	Scotland	1935–48
10	John Langenus	Belgium	1929–39
10	Bobby Davidson	Scotland	1958–76
9	Leo Horn	Holland	1952–64
8	Mervyn Griffiths	Wales	1949–57
7	S Thompson	Ireland	1932–35
7	Peco Bauwens	Germany	1931–39
7	Albert Dusch	W Germany	1957–60

Robertson's total may have been only **20**. The situation's complicated by the fact that another Scottish Robertson, James, had charge of England's first match in 1896 – and just possibly of the second, though nearly all contemporary match reports say Tom was there.

The last English referee to take charge of an England match (v Uruguay in 1953), Arthur Ellis (Colorsport)

ENGLAND PLAYERS WHO REFEREED ENGLAND MATCHES

	Played	Refereed
RA Ogilvie	1874	1896–1908
Charles Wollaston	1874–80	1879
Charles Clegg	1872	1893
SR Bastard	1880	1879 & 1881

ENGLAND PLAYERS WHO REFEREED FA CUP FINALS

Charles Alcock	1875 & 1879
WS Buchanan	1876
William Rawson	1876 (replay)
SR Bastard	1878
Charles Clegg	1882 & 1892
Jack Pearson	1911

OPPOSITION PLAYERS WHO REFEREED ENGLAND MATCHES

		Played	Refereed
Charlie Campbell	Scotland	1874–86	1893?
John Smith	Scotland	1877–84	1892
Jack Reid	Ireland	1883	1890–95
Alfred Owen Davies	Wales	1886–90	1889
Tom Robertson	Scotland	1890	1896–1908
Heinrich Retschury	Austria	1909	1926

There's doubt as to whether John or Charlie Campbell refereed the England–Wales match of 1893.

Hugo Meisl was Austria's manager against England (1930–36), and refereed England's matches against Hungary in 1908 and 1909 and Sweden in 1923.

George Shutt (1891) and Bob Holmes (1901) were later put on the Football League list as referees, Harry Chippendale (1908) as a linesman. Fanny Walden and John Arnold later became first-class cricket umpires.

The last Englishman to referee a match involving England was Arthur Ellis, who took charge of all three matches on the South American leg of the 1953 tour, the last against Uruguay in Montevideo

The last non-neutral referee was Letchmanasamy Kathiraveloo, no less, of Malaysia.

Charles Wreford-Brown was one of the linesmen in the match against France in 1925. Bob Kelly must be the only player to act as linesman in one England game (v Belgium on the summer tour of 1927) then play in the next (v Luxembourg); he seems to have been the last England player to officiate in an England match.

England players who umpired England matches (in the days when they were as important as referees): Charles Alcock, Alexander Morten, Hubert Heron, Ernest Bambridge, Monty Betts and Sam Widdowson.

Wreford-Brown and Arthur Knight were linesmen together in two matches at the 1920 Olympics.

SR Bastard and Charlie Faultless both refereed England matches . . .

SENDINGS OFF

ENGLAND PLAYERS

1968	Alan Mullery	v Yugoslavia
1973	Alan Ball	v Poland
1977	Trevor Cherry	v Argentina
1986	Ray Wilkins	v Morocco

SENT OFF AGAINST ENGLAND

1962	Manuel Grimaldo	Peru
1964	Jose Torres	Portugal
1966	Antonio Rattin	Argentina
1966	Billy Ferguson	N Ireland
1977	Gilbert Dresch	Luxembourg
1977	Daniel Bertoni	Argentina

Mullery was sent off in the last minute of England's 424th international.

Rattin was the first player to be sent off in a senior match at Wembley, and the only captain in a game involving England (Dresch was captain against England in 1983). Both the Charlton brothers were booked in Rattin's match.

Ferguson was the first Irishman to be sent off in an international, and the first from any country in a Home Championship match.

Cherry and Bertoni were dismissed for the same incident. By all objective accounts, Cherry was an innocent victim.

Grimaldo was sent off for swearing at the referee, not for fighting. At 5ft 2in, he seems to have been the shortest man to play against England.

Alexander Vencel, Czechoslovakia's goalkeeper, was sent off from the substitutes' bench in the match against England 1975.

No England player has been sent off at home . . .

Right *Ray Wilkins wipes away the sweat of the 42 minutes he played against Morocco in Monterrey* (Colorsport)

They Was Robbed

Saturday 30 July 1966
Empire Stadium, Wembley 96 924

World Cup Final

ENGLAND (1) 4   W GERMANY (1) 2 (aet, 2–2 at 90 mins)

Hurst 19, 100, 120	Haller 13
Peters 78	Weber 90

Referee: Gottfried Dienst (Switzerland)
Linesmen: Tofik Bakhramov (USSR) & Karol Galba (Czechoslovakia)

ENGLAND		WEST GERMANY	
Gordon Banks	Leicester City	Hans Tilkowski	Borussia Dortmund
George Cohen	Fulham	Horst Dieter Hottges	Werder Bremen
Ray Wilson	Everton	Karl-Heinz Schnellinger	Milan
Nobby Stiles	Manchester United	Franz Beckenbauer	Bayern Munich
Jack Charlton	Leeds United	Wolfgang Weber	Cologne
Bobby Moore (capt)	West Ham United	Willi Schulz	Hamburg
Alan Ball	Blackpool	Sigi Held	Borussia Dortmund
Geoff Hurst	West Ham United	Helmut Haller	Bologna
Bobby Charlton	Manchester Utd	Uwe Seeler (capt)	Hamburg
Roger Hunt	Liverpool	Wolfgang Overath	Cologne
Martin Peters	West Ham United	Lothar Emmerich	Borussia Dortmund

Manager: Alf Ramsey
First/last caps: 0
Booked: Peters

Manager: Helmut Schoen
First caps: 0
Last cap: Emmerich

The shadow over England's win – when it meets the ball, they'll both be on the ground, and clearly not over the line
(Allsport)

The most televised, photographed, discussed match in English football history, played on a pitch greased by rain. It starts with a mistake or three: Ray Wilson's first, they say, of the tournament, heading the ball down weakly for Haller to shoot (none too fiercely) along the ground past Jack Charlton, who leaves it, and Banks, who might have reached it.

Six minutes later, Moore comes forward to the edge of the German penalty area, where Overath brings him down. He takes the free kick without waiting for Dienst's whistle. Hurst heads cleanly, Tilkowski doesn't move; 1–1.

For an hour neither side dominates, but it begins to look as if Schoen's use of Beckenbauer to shadow Bobby Charlton may cost Germany the match. The budding Kaiser, just 20 years old, has scored four times in the tournament; he already looks the best half back in the world. Emmerich has scored an astonishing equaliser from an impossible angle against Spain, otherwise nothing; all he offers is potential firepower and this is only his fifth cap. Schoen should perhaps have dropped him and brought in, say, Sieloff to do the midfield marking, pushing Franz further forward. But Charlton's reputation, fuelled by two goals in the semi-final, ties Beckenbauer down.

With 12 minutes left, this seems to be decisive. Following a corner, Hurst shoots, optimistically and badly, from the edge of the box. The ball balloons. When it comes down, Jack Charlton's glad Peters gets to it before he does: 2–1.

The Giraffe's relief doesn't last. Held appears to back into him, the decision goes Germany's way. Emmerich (probably scenting last-minute redemption) hits the free kick hard: pinball, finally emerging (as Moore appeals for handball by Schnellinger) for Weber to scoop it over Wilson's foot and Banks' hands. Extra time.

Schnellinger's a famous defender, but he's marking Alan Ball, and Ballie's the man of the match. He proves it by chasing to the corner flag yet again and crossing; Hurst turns his marker and shoots hard, hitting the underside of the bar; Weber gets in ahead of Hunt and heads behind for the corner. Dienst goes to Bakhramov; the much-televised nod of the head, and the most controversial goal in any World Cup Final is awarded. Justice (or someone) is blind.

In the last minute, Moore (Player of the Tournament to its very end) finds Hurst in the centre circle with a long pass. Hurst runs, Overath gives chase to the last, the cheeks puff, again Tilkowski can only stand and watch. The classic end to a match of no great quality but high, high drama.

This was England's 18th match (and 14th) win of the season; Jack Charlton played in 17 of them. All three are national records.

The Charltons were the third pair of brothers to appear in a World Cup Final, following the Evaristos in 1930 and the Walters in 1954, preceding the van de Kerkhofs in 1978 and the Forsters in 1982.

Hurst, of course, is the only player to score three times in a World Cup Final, although he needed extra time for the last two. He scored with his head and each foot.

And no, it didn't, did it? Not the whole of it over the whole of it.

Bobby Charlton (9) is ready to go down on his knees to persuade keeper Tilkowski it was a goal. A hands-on Weber tells him where to go. Referee Dienst is already on his way there (Allsport)

FOOTBALLING BACKGROUND

AMATEURS

The early years were dominated by them, so that no professional played for England until **1878 (Jack Hunter)** or **1884 (Jimmy Forrest)**, depending on definition and which sources you read.

The last amateur to play for the full England side was **Bernard Joy** of Arsenal, who won his only cap against Belgium in 1936, the only time the Belgians have ever beaten England.

The last to play exclusively for an amateur club (Joy was playing for Arsenal as well as The Casuals) was **Edgar Kail** of Dulwich Hamlet, against Spain in 1929, England's first defeat by a foreign country.

The last to captain England was **AG ('Baishe') Bower**, against Wales in 1927.

The last all-amateur England team could only manage a 1–1 draw with Wales in 1895.

No declared professionals played for Scotland against England until **1894**.

Above *Two amateurs: one ranking, one rank. Edgar Kail (left) scored twice in his first international, Claude Ashton, captain in his only England match, didn't* (Hulton)

THIRD DIVISION PLAYERS

The extra Division was added in 1920–21. Early in the same season, **Bobby McCracken** of Crystal Palace became the first Third Division player to play international football when he turned out for **Ireland** against England at Roker Park.

19 have done so for England:

1921	Jack Fort	Millwall	v Belgium
1921	Ernie Simms	Luton	v Ireland
1922	Fred Titmuss	Southampton	v Wales
1922	Bill Rawlings	Southampton	v Wales
1923	Seth Plum	Charlton	v France
1923	Harold Miller	Charlton	v Sweden
1925	Tommy Cook	Brighton	v Wales
1925	Len Graham	Millwall	v Wales
1925	Fred Fox	Millwall	v France
1925	George Armitage	Charlton	v Ireland
1926	Dick Hill	Millwall	v Belgium
1929	Len Oliver	Fulham	v Belgium
1929	Albert Barrett	Fulham	v Ireland
1937	Joe Payne	Luton	v Finland
1947	Tommy Lawton	Notts Co	v Sweden
1956	Reg Matthews	Coventry	v Scotland
1961	Johnny Byrne	Crystal Palace	v N Ireland
1976	Peter Taylor*	Crystal Palace	v Wales
1989	Steve Bull*	Wolves	v Scotland

* substitute

10 won only the one cap: Fort, Simms, Plum, Miller, Cook, Fox, Armitage, Hill, Oliver, Barrett and Payne.

Payne (2), Taylor and Bull scored on debut. Taylor scored his only two England goals in his first two matches, both against Wales. Lawton scored from a penalty against Sweden; he'd already won 19 caps while still a First Division player.

Bull played against Scotland in the close season after Wolves had won promotion to the Second Division.

MOST PLAYERS FROM ONE CLUB

7	Arsenal	1934	v Italy
6	Arsenal	1936	v Wales
6	Arsenal	1936	v Austria
6	Liverpool	1977	v Switzerland
6*	Liverpool;	1980	v Belgium

including 1 sub

England were well equipped to win the Battle of Highbury in 1934, with seven players appearing on their home club ground: Frank Moss in goal, George Male, Eddie Hapgood the captain, Wilf Copping, Ray Bowden, Ted Drake and Cliff Bastin. Male and Drake were winning their first caps, Moss his last. England won 3–2 (see MATCH FEATURE).

Liverpool very nearly matched Arsenal's seven in 1977. Impressed by World Cup rivals Italy's use of the Juventus *bloc*, manager Ron Greenwood included six players from the new European club champions in his first line-up, together with Kevin Keegan, who'd been transferred to Hamburg in the close season: Ray Clemence, Phil Neal, Terry McDermott, Emlyn Hughes as captain, Ray Kennedy – and 35-year-old Ian Callaghan, recalled after an international absence of 11 years.

The England teams against Wales in 1894 and 1895 were made up entirely of players from the **Corinthians** – but this was much more like the Barbarians rugby club than a football club in the accepted sense (at that time it didn't have its own ground, for example). Most of the players belonged to other clubs as well.

The most players from a single club to appear in any match against England is the entire eleven. The whole Scotland team which played in the very first international, in 1872, had at one time played for **Queen's Park** – but three of the players were also involved with other clubs. In the purest sense, the only 'club XI' was put out by Bohemia in 1908. The entire team played for **Slavia of Prague** (see MATCH FEATURE).

In 1904, **Sheffield United** had a complete England XI on their books, including a goalkeeper, Willie Foulke; Walter Bennett, Arthur Brown, Alf Common, Harry Johnson, Bert Lipsham, Tom Morren, Ernest Needham, Fred Priest, Harry Thickett and Bernard Wilkinson – plus Peter Boyle of Ireland.

By the end of the 1936–37 season, **Arsenal** had 12 England players in the squad: Cliff Bastin, Ray Bowden, Wilf Copping, Jack Crayston, Ted Drake, Eddie Hapgood, Joe Hulme, Bernard Joy, Alf Kirchen, George Male, Herbie Roberts and goalkeeper Frank Moss – plus Alex James of Scotland and Bob John of Wales.

Aston Villa had 10 in 1933–34: Joe Beresford, George Brown, Arthur Cunliffe, Tommy Gardner, Eric Houghton, Tommy Mort, Tommy Smart, Joe Tate, Billy Walker and Pongo Waring – as well as Danny Blair, Jimmy Gibson and Joe Nibloe of Scotland, and Dai Astley of Wales.

The match against Switzerland in 1948 was the first since 1932 without a single **Arsenal** player in the England team.

A new broom. Joe Mercer's first game in charge, against Wales in 1974, was the first without a single player from the 1966 World Cup team, an exclusive 'club' of sorts.

Greenwood's navy take on the land-locked Swiss. From left: Callaghan, McDermott, Clemence, Neal, Kennedy, cap'n Hughes, all of Liberpool. Keegan has only just gone overseas (Hulton)

PLAYED FOR TWO COUNTRIES

John Hawley Edwards played for England against Scotland in 1874, then in the first match **Wales** ever played, against Scotland in 1876.

Jack Reynolds played for **Ireland** (1890–91) and England (1892–97). He scored for Ireland in the 1890 match between the two countries, and for England in three matches (1893–94), the only player to score for and against England. He didn't score against Ireland.

Bobby Evans played for **Wales** (1906–10), including four matches against England, then for England (1911–12), including twice against Wales.

Ken Armstrong played for England (1955), then for **New Zealand** (1958–64).

Gordon Hodgson of England (1930–31) had previously won amateur caps for South Africa.

BG Jarrett, who played for England from 1876–78, was selected by **Wales** for their inaugural match of 1876, but didn't play.

Robert Topham first played for England in 1893. Back in 1885 he was picked to play for **Wales** against Scotland but didn't accept.

Three England players appeared for 'Scotland' in the unofficial matches of 1870 and 1871 (Alexander Morten, Frederick Chappell, Arnold Kirke Smith) but were all apparently born in England.

Tommy Pearson, who played for **Scotland** against England in 1947, had appeared for England in a wartime international against Scotland in 1939.

Stan Mortensen played for England from 1947–53. He'd come on as a substitute for **Wales'** Ivor Powell against England in a wartime international in 1944.

Bobby Moore and Tommy Smith played for **Team America** against England in 1976, alongside players who'd also appeared against England for their own countries: Pele, Giorgio Chinaglia, Mike England and Dave Clements. Moore would seem to be the only player to appear as captain for and against England.

The only man to play for two separate countries against England was **Jose Santamaria** (Uruguay 1954, Spain 1960), although eight players represented both Eire and Ireland either side of the Second World War: Alec Stevenson, Tom Breen, Bill Gorman, Johnny Carey, Tom ('Bud') Aherne, Con Martin and the Walsh brothers, Billy and Davie.

A number of players turned out for invitation teams as well as their own countries against England, the last occasion being 1963. Only two played for invitation teams only: full backs Juan Navarro of Spain (FIFA 1953) and Luis Eyzaguirre of Chile (Rest of the World 1963).

Denis Law is the only player to score for both his country and an invitation team against England for the Rest of the World in 1963, and Scotland (1965–66–67).

Terry Springthorpe played alongside Billy Wright in the Wolves side that won the 1949 FA Cup Final, and against him for the USA versus England in 1953.

NO CLUB

No player has ever appeared for England without belonging to a recognised football club, amateur or professional. **Edward Johnson** was still at Saltley College when he won his first cap in 1880, but he was already a member of Stoke FC.

However, several oppsition players have been 'clubless':

When **John R Morgan** of Wales played against Scotland 1877, he was a member of Cambridge University Football Club. All his subsequent caps, including 4 against England, were won while he was unaffiliated. Although most modern sources list his 'clubs' as Swansea (where he lived) or Derby School (where he worked), neither Swansea nor the school (!) had a football club at the time.

Another Welshman, goalkeeper **Bob Mills-Roberts**, was with Preston North End when he played against England 1888. Before that, according to today's record books, he was with St Thomas's Hospital, not exactly a recognised club, though he did turn out for the hospital team. Later, he was supposedly with Llanberis when he played against England 1892 – but this was simply the place where he lived; it had no football club and he came out of retirement to play!

Almost a century later, the USA team which England beat 5–0 in 1985 was made up entirely of college and Indoor League players (the NASL having collapsed) – all except goalkeeper **Arnie Mausser**, who had no club at all, was setting a new US record of 35 caps, and celebrated by saving Glenn Hoddle's penalty.

The **Canadian** team which played England in 1986 was in the same boat as the 1985 Americans. No NASL, no recognised outdoor clubs. Terry Moore was playing for Glentoran in Northern Ireland, Igor Vrablic for Seraing in Belgium – but the rest played in the Indoor League, except goalkeeper Paul Dolan, Randy Samuel, captain Bruce Wilson, Paul James, Randy Ragan, and substitute Jamie Lowery, all of whom had no club at all.

OLYMPIC GOLD MEDALS

In the early years, a great many players won amateur as well as full international caps. The following won full caps as well as Olympic gold medals at football.

1908
HP Bailey
Walter Corbett
Herbert Smith
Kenneth Hunt
Bob Hawkes
Arthur Berry
Vivian Woodward
Harold Hardman

1912
Arthur Knight
Arthur Berry
Vivian Woodward
Gordon Wright

OTHER SPORTS

COUNTY CRICKETERS

Over 70 English footballers also played county cricket, among them:

Claude Ashton	Essex	The last one-cap player to captain England	Joe Hulme	Middx	Played for the same football and cricket clubs as the Comptons
Monty Betts	Middx & Kent	Scorer of the only goal in the first FA Cup Final (1872)	Geoff Hurst	Essex	
CJ Burnup	Kent	Had a record 10 runs hit off one ball by Samuel Hill-Wood in 1900	Arthur Knight	Hampshire	England's first captain after the First World War
Raich Carter	Derbys		Jackie Lee	Leics	
Leslie Compton	Middx	Often alongside Test-playing brother Denis	Alfred & Edward Lyttleton	Middx & Worcs	Both played for both counties
Ted Drake	Hampshire		Ernest Needham	Derbys	
Willie Foulke	Derbys	A kind of Edwardian Colin Milburn, but bigger!	Cuthbert Ottaway	Kent & Middx	England's first ever football captain
John Goodall	Derbys		Harry Storer	Derbys	Later Derby County's tough-guy manager
GO Smith	Surrey		Fanny Walden	Northants	Probably the smallest ever England footballer
Mike Hellawell	Warwicks				
Eric Houghton	Warwicks				

TEST CRICKETERS

Alfred Lyttleton
Billy Gunn
Leslie Gay
Reginald ('Tip') Foster
Charles (CB) Fry
Jack Sharp
Harry Makepeace
Andy Ducat
Wally Hardinge
John Arnold
Willie Watson
Arthur Milton

Hardinge and Arnold won one cap in each sport.

Hardinge and Ducat played in only one Test match each – the same one, against Australia at Headingley. Hardinge's only football cap was also won alongside Ducat, at Hampden Park.

Watson later also became a Test selector.

Gunn's 102 not out against Australia in 1893 was the first Test century at Old Trafford.

RUGBY UNION

RH Birkett played in England's first ever rugby team, against Scotland in 1871. His son and brother also played for England, as did the football internationals **Charles P Wilson** and **John Willie Sutcliffe**. As befits a handling code, Birkett and Sutcliffe were England goalkeepers.

ATHLETICS

Most publications are happy to pass on the old chestnut about **CB Fry** setting a world long jump record that lasted 21 years. In fact, his 7.17m (23ft 6½in), set in 1893, equalled the record set by the American Charles Reber, and was broken three years later by Matthew Roseingrave of Ireland. More modest, still impressive.

Ben Howard Baker's high jump of 1.95m (6ft 5in), set in 1921, survived as the British record until 1946. He competed in the 1912 and 1920 Olympics.

Charles Clegg set a world record for 600 yards in 1873.

AAA CHAMPIONS

AF Hills	Mile	1878
RH Macaulay	High Jump	1879
William Oakley	Long Jump	1894
Ben Howard Baker	High Jump	1910–12–13–19–20–21

LAWN TENNIS

Max Woosnam captained England in his only football international, in 1922, the same year in which he reached the final of the mixed doubles at Wimbledon. The previous year, he and Randolph Lycett had won the men's doubles title. He took part in the Olympic tennis tournaments of 1920 and 1924.

OTHER

Ken Willingham was an England international at **shinty**, Louis Page at **baseball**.

Harry Daft was an England reserve at **lacrosse**.

THE OPPOSITION

Henry Renny-Tailyour, who scored Scotland's first ever goal and the first ever conceded by England, in 1873, also played rugby union for Scotland, winning a single cap (and losing to England) in each sport.

Dr Kevin O'Flanagan and his brother Michael played for Eire against England in 1946, Michael winning his only cap. They both won one cap each at rugby union, not in the same match and not against England.

Bobby Christie, who won his only Scotland cap in 1884 against England, also represented Scotland at curling.

Andrew N Wilson, who scored in each of the four matches he played for Scotland against England (1920–23), represented *England* at bowls.

Alan Hansen played golf, squash and volleyball for Scotland at Under-18 level.

OCCUPATIONS & HONOURS

DOCTORS

Unlike, say, rugby union or cricket, football has received very little medical attention. The only member of the profession to play for England seems to have been **Geoffrey Wilson** in 1884 – though Ray Wilson did become an undertaker . . .

Tinsley Lindley was awarded a doctorate in Law.

Doc Greenwood, who played for England in 1882, wasn't a medical man. He was actually christened Doctor.

Dr John Smith (1877–84) and Dr Jimmy Marshall (1932–34) played for Scotland against England; Dr John Eyton-Jones (1884), Dr Robert Mills-Roberts (1885–92) and Dr Alfred Owen Davies (1886–90) for Wales; Dr George Sheehan (1900) for Ireland; Dr Kevin O'Flanagan for Eire 1946. Socrates, Brazil's captain at Wembley in 1981, achieved a medical degree. There may well have been others.

As if to prove the point about rugby union, O'Flanagan was an Ireland international in both sports.

Two players who captained Hungary against England (Gaspar Borbas 1908, Gyorgy Sarosi 1934 and 1936) were also awarded doctorates, Sarosi for legal studies.

LEGAL EAGLES

A dozen or so England players from the early amateur days worked as solicitors and barristers, including the first captain Cuthbert Ottaway, the Clegg brothers, the Walters brothers, Tinsley Lindley (who later became a judge), Billy Moon and Harold Hardman.

VICARS

Only the **Rev Kenneth Hunt** was already ordained when he played for England. Several others joined the Squad when their international careers were over: --

Arnold Kirke Smith
Robert Sealy Vidal
Edward Lyttleton
JRB Owen
BG Jarrett
RS King
Frank Pawson
Andrew Amos
Bernard Middleditch
WE Gilliat
George Raikes

(and possibly Bernard Middleditch)

Harold Fleming and Arthur Bridgett objected to setting foot on a pitch on Christmas Day and Good Friday. Religious grounds, you might say.

The Rev W Blackmore was selected for the 1879 match against Wales, couldn't play, and never won an England cap.

William Wightman Beveridge won his first cap for Scotland in the England match of 1879 and was ordained in 1883.

BOYS IN BLUE

CC Charsley was Chief Constable, no less, of Coventry.

Tinsley Lindley was awarded the OBE for work as Chief Officer of the Nottingham Special Constabulary.

Syd Puddefoot (was there ever a better policeman's name?) was briefly with Blackpool Borough Police.

JOURNALISTS

Bernard Joy worked for the *Evening Standard* and the *Star* as well as writing a history of Arsenal.

Norman Creek worked for the *Daily Telegraph* as well as writing a history of the Corinthians.

Frank Swift wrote for the *News of the World*. He died in the Munich air crash after covering Manchester United's match in Belgrade.

Charlie Buchan edited *Football Monthly* for many years.

Others include Ivan Broadis, Jackie Milbury, Colin Veitch, Trevor Brooking. Ghosts have also been seen.

SCHOOL TEACHERS

More than 20 England players joined the profession, among them CB Fry, the Rev Kenneth Hunt, brothers Rex and Bertie Corbett, Fred Dewhurst, and Arthur Dunn who gave his name to the cup still played for by public school old boys.

The most recent have been Dennis Wilshaw, George Robb, John Atyeo and Warren Bradley.

GO Smith and William Oakley took over as joint headmasters of Ludgrove from Arthur Dunn, who founded the school.

HC Goodhart was a lecturer at Cambridge (1884–90) and Professor of Humanities at Edinburgh (1890–95).

FISH & CHIP SHOP OWNERS

Joe Beresford, Dickie Bond, Alec Lindsay – and John Connelly, who ran 'Connelly's Plaice'. Ouch.

MILITARY MEN

Try this for a game of soldiers. Many England players saw active service in the two World Wars, but a number were actually professional soldiers, in some cases rising to very high rank:

Captain Richard Lyon Geaves
Major Franklin Buckley
Lt Colonel Pelham George von Donop
Lt Colonel Kenneth Hegan
Colonel William Stanley Kenyon Slaney
Colonel Herbert Rawson
Colonel Horace Barnet
Colonel Bruce Russell
Brigadier Cecil Vernon Wingfield-Stratford
General Sir William Bromley-Davenport

Kenyon Slaney was already a captain, Goodwyn, Von Donop and Hegan lieutenants, when they played for England.

Frank Buckley and Vivian Woodward were majors in the First World War.

William John Maynard's club while he played for England was the 1st Surrey Rifles.

Reginald Welch was an army tutor.

Jack Cock won the **Military Medal** and **DCM** in the First World War, Bill H Jones in the Second. Norman Creek was in the Royal Flying Corps, and won the **Military Cross**, in the First World War. William Bromley-Davenport won the **DSO** in the Boer War. In 1884, JFM Prinsep was awarded the **Albert Medal** after saving a man in his regiment from drowning.

Herbie Roberts died while serving as a lieutenant in the Royal Fusiliers.

Among the enemy: Lieutenants (both later Colonels) Henry Renny-Tailyour and John Edward Blackburn, who both scored for Scotland in 1873; Jimmy Fitzpatrick who captained Ireland in the 1896 match; and James M Wilton (Ireland 1888–90). Ferenc Puskas of Hungary (1953–54) was known as The Galloping Major, but saw more midfields than minefields with Honved.

TALENTS

Jack Southworth was a professional violinist, good enough to play in the Hallé Orchestra. Harry Hardy was a professional oboist.

Colin Grainger sang professionally. 'Diamond Lights' by Hoddle and Waddle – or rather Glenn & Chris – reached the Top 20 in 1987. The 1970 World Cup squad's 'Back Home' reached No. 1 in the charts. Kevin Keegan's single didn't quite.

Vivian Woodward was an architect, Oliver Whateley an artist and designer, Albert Wilkes a photographer, Derek Ufton a photographer's model. Arthur Brown worked as a stonemason.

John Brockbank and John Hawtrey were actors, Colin Veitch chairman of the Newcastle People's Theatre.

Frank Bradshaw was a silversmith, as was Howard Vaughton, whose firm made 'Gothic Works' as well as the second FA Cup after the original was stolen.

Jack Cock, who had a fine tenor voice, sang in music hall. Terry Venables once sang in front of the Joe Loss orchestra. Gordon West's wife was a concert pianist.

Oh, and there was an England player called Albert Hall!

HIGH OFFICE

MPs
WS Kenyon Slaney
Alfred Lyttleton
JFP Rawlinson
William Bromley-Davenport

William Clegg was Lord Mayor of Sheffield 1893–99; CC Charsley was Deputy Mayor of Weston-super-Mare 1939–40; Cunliffe Gosling was High Sheriff of Essex 1902; Frank Burton was High Sheriff of Notts 1938–39; William Bromley-Davenport was Lord Lieutenant of Cheshire 1920–49.

Terry Paine was a Southampton town councillor 1969–71; Bill Watson was twice a councillor in Southport.

The brothers Alfred and Edward Lyttleton were Honourable; Kenyon Slaney was Right Honourable. Alfred Kinnaird, who played for Scotland against England in 1837 and was England's linesman against Scotland in 1879, was an Honourable who later became a Lord.

But tradition has it that the highest rank of all was CB Fry's for the taking. He reputedly refused the throne of Albania.

PUBLICANS

Refreshingly large numbers of England players have maintained the game's close ties with the licensing trade. Among those who ran establishments which sold intoxicating beverages:

Cliff Bastin, Fred Bullock, Alf Common, Warney Cresswell, Chris Crowe, Dixie Dean, Willie Hall, Geoff Hurst, Bedford Jezzard, Bobby Moore, Peter Osgood, Ellis Rimmer, Bill Rowley, Eddie Shimwell, Trevor Smith, Freddie Steele, Billy Wedlock, Vic Woodley.

KNIGHTHOODS

Sir Charles Clegg
Sir William Clegg
General Sir William Bromley-Davenport
Sir Stanley Matthews
Sir Alfred Ramsey
Sir Walter Winterbottom

Only Matthews was knighted for his contribution as a *player*.

CBE

Stanley Matthews
Billy Wright
Don Revie
Bobby Robson
Bobby Charlton

OBE

Rupert Anderson
William Clegg
Tinsley Lindley
KE ('Jackie') Hegan
George Eastham, jnr
Joe Mercer
Emlyn Hughes
Bobby Charlton
Gordon Banks
Bobby Moore
Tom Finney
Jack Charlton
Kevin Keegan
Peter Shilton
Bryan Robson
Brian Clough

MBE

Norman Creek	Ray Clemence
Trevor Brooking	Geoff Hurst
Jimmy Dickinson	Ian Callaghan
Terry Paine	Martin Peters
Alan Mullery	Peter Shilton
Mick Mills	Steve Perryman

PERSONAL & FAMILY

BIRTHDAYS

Edward Lyttleton and Norman C Bailey had the same birthday (23 July) and made their England debuts in the same match against Scotland 1878.

John Brockbank and Ernest Greenhalgh may have gone one better. They made their debuts together in the very first international, in Glasgow 1872 – and may have had the same date of birth (22 August 1848). Brockbank was certainly born on that date; there are doubts about Greenhalgh. At 24yr 100d, they were the oldest players in the first England team.

Mark Barham and Steve Williams had the same birthday and made their England debuts in the same match, against Australia in 1983.

Bert Mozley won his first cap on his 26th birthday (v Eire 1949), Johnny Nicholls on his 23rd (v Scotland 1954), celebrating with a goal.

Ernie ('Tim') Williamson won his last cap on his 33rd birthday, against Sweden in 1923.

Roger Hunt scored twice against France in the 1966 World Cup, the second when goalkeeper Marcel

Aubour helped his header into the net, an unexpected 28th birthday present.

Francis Lee scored England's equaliser before West Germany won 3-1 at Wembley in 1972. It was *his* 28th birthday too, and his last cap.

Paul Gascoigne came on as substitute in the 75th minute against Scotland in 1989, aged exactly 22.

Chris Woods played against Eire on his 31st birthday in 1990

Joe Mercer died aged exactly 76 in 1990.

ENGLAND'S BLACK PLAYERS

The first: Viv Anderson v Czechoslovakia 1978.

The first to score: Luther Blissett v Luxembourg 1982 (Mark Chamberlain scored later in the same game, the first to score on his debut).

The only hat trick: Blissett, in the Luxembourg match.

Most caps: John Barnes 65
Most goals: John Barnes 10

The last five players to be capped by England have all been black.

The full list
1978–88	Viv Anderson
1979–80	Laurie Cunningham
1982–87	Cyrille Regis
1982–86	Ricky Hill
1982–84	Luther Blissett
1982–84	Mark Chamberlain
1983–91	John Barnes
1983	Danny Thomas
1984	Brian Stein
1986	Danny Wallace
1988–90	David Rocastle
1988–91	Des Walker
1988–89	Michael Thomas
1989–90	Paul Parker
1989	John Fashanu
1991	Ian Wright
1991	John Salako
1991	Earl Barrett
1991	Mark Walters
1991	Brian Deane
1991	Gary Charles

BORN OUTSIDE ENGLAND

WS Kenyon Slaney	1873	India	Claude Ashton	1925	India
RL Geaves	1875	Mexico	Jack Butler	1925	Ceylon
Herbert Rawson	1875	Mauritius	Reg Osborne	1927	S Africa
William Rawson	1875–77	S Africa	Gordon Hodgson	1930–31	S Africa
Charles E Smith	1876	Ceylon	Bill Perry	1955–56	S Africa
William Lindsay	1877	India	Colin Viljoen	1975	S Africa
John Bain	1877	Scotland	Terry Butcher	1980–90	Singapore
Edward Parry	1879–82	Canada	Cyrille Regis	1982–87	French Guiana
JFM Prinsep	1879	India	Luther Blissett	1982–84	Jamaica
Stuart Macrae	1883–84	Scotland	John Barnes	1983–91	Jamaica
Elphinstone Jackson	1891	India	Brian Stein	1984	S Africa
Alf Quantrill	1920–21	India	Tony Dorigo	1989–90	Australia
Frank Osborne	1923–26	S Africa	John Salako	1991	Nigeria
Billy Bryant	1925	Belgium			

The first player to score for England (Kenyon Slaney) and the first to score against (Henry Renny-Tailyour of Scotland, in the same match) were both double-barrelled, both army officers, and both born in India.

AH Savage (1876) may have been the Arthur Henry Patrick Savage born in Australia in 1850.

The Rawsons and Osbornes were brothers.

Ceylon is now Sri Lanka of course.

Above *Despite the shirt, Tony Dorigo wasn't in the final 22 for Mexico, but had a good game in the third-place final in Italy* (Bob Thomas)
Left *Viv Anderson scores his first goal for England, the 8th against Turkey in 1984* (Bob Thomas)

CAPPED WHEN HANDICAPPED

Robert Schlienz, whose last match for West Germany was against England in 1956, had only one arm. So too did Arthur Lea, who played for Wales against England in 1889.

Like Schlienz, Holger Hieronymous won his last cap for West Germany when playing against England, at Wembley in 1982. He had only one good eye.

Rather less drastically, Raymond Kopa, who played for France and the Rest of the World against England (1955–63), had lost part of a finger in a coal-mining accident.

EYESIGHT

Jim Mitchell was almost certainly the only man to play for England while wearing spectacles. He kept goal against Ireland in 1924 – and in the 1922 FA Cup Final.

International footballers who regularly wore glasses on the field, and who played against England, include Alec Raisbeck of Scotland (1900–07) and the Belgian captain Jef Jurion (1964).

Alf Dobson didn't wear glasses on the pitch, but seems to have needed them. His poor eyesight was apparently a talking point.

Charles Crump, who umpired England's games with Wales in 1888 and 1889, wore a monocle.

The first to play for England in contact lenses was Jack Howe against Italy in 1948. Others include – famously – Nobby Stiles.

Gordon Banks lost the use of an eye in a road accident that ended his England career.

Alan Peacock is colour blind.

UNHAPPY ENDINGS

Five England players died in the Munich air disaster in 1958: Manchester United's Roger Byrne, Duncan Edwards, Tommy Taylor and David Pegg – and Frank Swift, by then a journalist travelling with the team.

Jeff Hall and Tom Meehan both died while still at their peak, of polio and sleeping sickness respectively.

Jimmy Hampson died in a fishing accident in 1938, Tommy Cooper in a motorcycling accident in 1940, Percy Fairclough in a road crash in 1947, Laurie Cunningham in a car crash in 1989, the same year that two famous players who'd both played against England died in separate road accidents on the same day: Kaziu Deyna of Poland and Italy's Gaetano Scirea *in* Poland.

Dave Clement committed suicide in 1982.

Dixie Dean had a leg amputated in 1976. Willie Hall had both legs amputated in the 1940s. Bert Lipsham lost a hand in a sawmill accident in Canada.

DIED 'IN ACTION'

Bobby Benson	Playing in a wartime match at Highbury
Arthur Chadwick	Watching from the stand at Exeter City
Andy Ducat	Batting – at Lord's, no less
Ginger Richardson	Playing in a charity match
Graham Doggart	At the FA's annual meeting
Sam Cowan	Refereeing a charity match
Dixie Dean	At Goodison Park, after watching a Merseyside derby

Jock Stein, seven times Scotland's

manager against England, died after the match against Wales that saw his team through to the 1986 World Cup finals.

Above *Butter wouldn't melt . . . Stiles, with everything still in place: teeth, specs, opponents' limbs* (Popperfoto)

NAMES

Six players in the Scotland team that played England in 1950 had the christian name William, including the entire forward line: Willie Waddell, Willie Moir, Willie Bauld, Billy Steel and Billy Liddell. They didn't score – and centre-half Willie Woodburn couldn't stop Roy Bentley scoring the only goal of the match, which won the Home Championship and deprived Scotland of a place in the World Cup finals.

Two England players had four Christian names: Albert Edward James Matthias (Jem) Bayliss and Robert Andrew Muter Macindoe Ogilvie. So too does Pat Nevin, who played for Scotland against England in 1986 and 1989: Patrick Kevin Francis Michael. All three are matched by the exotic Socrates, who captained Brazil at Wembley in 1981 and whose complete moniker reads Brazileiro Sampaio de Sousa Ferreira Oliveiro. In contrast, Francisco Sa of Argentina, who played at Wembley in 1974, had the shortest surname of any player who appeared against England!

Asa Hartford, who played against England from 1972–82, was apparently named after the singer Al Jolson, whose first name was Asa – and who died the day before Hartford was born.

CHANGE OF NAME

Frederick Patey **Chappell** played in the very first England team (v Scotland 1872) then changed his name to Frederick Brunning **Maddison** in 1873. He's listed under Maddison in most record books.

Robert Walpole Sealy **Vidal** later dropped the Vidal and called himself RW **Sealy**.

John **Hawley Edwards** is usually listed as JH Edwards, though Hawley was part of his surname. The same applies to Arnold Kirke Smith, Ben Howard Baker, and just possibly Robert Sealy Vidal and Robert Stuart King.

Reg **Smith** was born **Schmidt** but changed his name. He played for England just before the Second World War.

Similarly, **Ivan** Broadis allowed himself to be known as **Ivor**. He played during the Cold War era.

Knyvett **Crosse** played for Wales against England in 1881 under the pseudonym CK (some say CR) **Smith**.

Monty **Betts** scored the only goal of the first FA Cup Final in 1872 under the name AH **Chequer**.

Tom **Hyslop** won his first cap out of position at centre forward against England in 1896; his real name was apparently Bryce **Scouller**.

NICKNAMES

Albert Beasley	Pat
Walter Bennett	Cocky
Alfred George Bower	Baishe
Tony Brown	Bomber
Arthur Brown	Digger
Johnny Byrne	Budgie
Arthur Capes	Sailor
Allan Clarke	Sniffer
Nevill Cobbold	Nuts
John Coleman	Tim
Bill Dean	Dixie
John Thomas Downs	Dicky
Paul Goddard	Sarge
George Harrison	Jud
William Hardinge	Wally
Kenneth Hegan	Jackie
AG Henfrey	Cocky
Albert Edward Houlker	Kelly
Tom Johnson	Tosh
Ted Latheron	Pinky
Thomas Leach	Tony
Ernest Needham	Nudger
John Peacock	Joe
Thurston Rostron	Tot
Billy Richardson	Ginger
Jimmy Stewart	Tadger
Albert Sturgess	Hairpin
Fred Walden	Fanny
David Wallace	Danny
Tom Waring	Pongo

Right *The dashing Pongo. Wearing the name, and everything else, with pride* (Lamming)

Ray Wilkins	Butch
Ernie Williamson	Tim
Reg Williamson	Tim
George Woodger	Lady

There have been others: 'Fatty' for Foulke, 'Tiny' for big Jimmy Barrett, 'Supermac' etc. Weak and obvious.

RELATIVES

FATHER & SON

| Eastham | George snr | George jnr |
| Clough | Brian | Nigel |

COUSINS

Hugh Adcock	Joe Bradford
Sam Barkas	Billy Felton
George Brown	Joe Spence
Arthur Chadwick	Edgar Chadwick
Arthur Cowell	Kelly Houlker
Arthur Cunliffe	Jimmy Cunliffe
Jack Froggatt	Redfern Froggatt
Harry Hibbs	Harold Pearson
Charles E Smith	GO Smith

The Froggatts won their last caps in the same match, against the USA in 1953.

Pearson and Hibbs were goalkeepers. So too was Pearson's father Hubert, who'd been picked to play against France in 1923 but missed the match and never played for England at all. His son played against Scotland just nine years later.

Brown and Spence formed the right-wing partnership v Ireland 1926.

Jackie Milburn was a distant cousin of the Charlton brothers.

BROTHERS-IN-LAW

Charlie Bambridge	Norman C Bailey
Harry Linacre	Fred and Frank Forman
Nobby Stiles	Johnny Giles (Eire, played against England 1964–76)

FATHER & SON-IN-LAW

| Steve Bloomer | Alf Quantrill |

UNCLE & NEPHEW

| Colin Grainger | Ed Holliday |

GREAT-UNCLE & GREAT-NEPHEW

| Eric Houghton | Chris Woods |

BROTHERS

Bambridge	Ernest	Charlie	Arthur
Clegg	Charles	William	
Rawson	Herbert	William	
Heron	Hubert	Frank	
Lyttleton	Alfred	Edward	
Cursham	Arthur	Harry	
Hargreaves	Fred	Jack	
Walters	Arthur M	Percy M	
Dobson	Alf	Charlie	
Shelton	Alf	Charlie	
Topham	Robert	Arthur	
Perry	Charlie	Tom	
Forman	Frank	Fred	
Wilson	Charles P	Geoffrey P	
Corbett	Bertie	Rex	
Osborne	Frank	Reg	
Stephenson	Clem	George	
Smith	Jack	Sep	
Charlton	Bobby	Jack	

The Charltons played together 28 times, the Walters 9, the Formans 3, all three Bambridges never.

The Corbetts won only one cap each. They both became schoolteachers and both lived to be over 85. The Lyttletons also played only once each for England.

The Rawsons made their international debuts in the same match, as did the Walters, who started and finished their England careers together. They were known as Morning and Afternoon (AM and PM: geddit?)

Only three sets, A and C Bambridge (v Ireland 1884), the Formans (v Ireland 1899) and the Charltons (v Wales 1966), scored together in the same match.

The Formans were the first professional brothers to play for England.

The Osbornes were born in South Africa.

The Herons are the only brothers to play together in an international match and the FA Cup Final in the same year, 1876.

The only pairs to play in the same England team were the Curshams and two of the Bambridges. They formed the wing partnerships against Wales in 1883: the Arthurs on the right, Harry Cursham and Charlie Bam on the left.

Two England players had brothers who played against England: John Goodall (Archie, for Ireland) and John Hollins (Dave, goalkeeper for Wales).

Tom Porteous may possibly have been related to the Scottish international William Porteous.

John Barnes' father Ken played for (and captained) Jamaica.

Emlyn Hughes' father Fred played rugby league for Great Britain. His aunt played hockey for England. Bill Foulkes' grandfather was also a rugby league international, while William John Maynard's son Alfred Frederick played rugby union for England.

Eastham senior and junior played together for Ards in Northern Ireland. Harry Healless was playing minor league football alongside his son at the age of 54.

Johnny Brooks' son Shaun was an England schoolboy and youth international, as was Gary Mabbutt's brother Kevin.

Harold Miller's brother HE was an England amateur international, as was Willie Hall's nephew Harry Parr and Arthur Grimsdell's brother EF.

Graham Doggart's son Hubert played Test cricket for England, as did Teddy Taylor's cousin Charlie Hallows and Billy Moon's brother Leonard.

Leslie Compton's brother Denis was a famous Test batsman who won England caps in wartime football as well as an FA Cup winner's medal (alongside Leslie) in 1950.

Billy Gunn, a double international, had two nephews (John and the famous George) who were also England Test cricketers.

Frank Hartley's brother Ernest played hockey for England.

Brian Greenhoff's brother Jimmy was an England Under-23 international, as were Duncan Edwards' cousin Dennis Stevens, Ron Springett's brother Peter, and Johnny Aston's son John jnr.

Billy Beats' son Eddie was an England schoolboy international, as was Len Goulden's son Roy.

Danny Clapton's brother Dennis was an England youth international, as was Eric Gates' brother Bill.

Colin Grainger's father Jack played for England B. His nephew Ed Holliday won 3 full caps. His brother-in-law Jim Iley played for England Under-23.

Warney Cresswell's brother Frank was an England schoolboy international. His son Corbett was an amateur international. Jack Townrow's brother Frank also played for England Schools.

Russell Osman captained England Schools at rugby union. His father Rex was an England and youth international at football.

Reg Smith's father reputedly played senior rugby union for South Africa.

Tommy Wright's nephew Billy played for England Under-21, as have John Fashanu and Danny Wallace's brothers, Justin and Rod.

Stanley Matthews' son, Stanley junior, played tennis at Wimbledon, as did Ken Brown's daughter Amanda.

Cyrille Regis' cousin John was world indoor champion at 200 metres in 1989, won a bronze medal in the 200 metres at the 1987 World Athletics Championships, silver in the 1990 Commonwealth Games, and gold (as well as three other medals) in the 1990 European Championships.

Alfred and Edward Lyttleton had four other brothers who played first-class cricket. RE ('Tip') Foster had six, resulting in Worcestershire being nicknamed Fostershire!

William Bromley-Davenport was surely related to Hugh Richard Bromley-Davenport, the England Test cricketer. They were both at Eton in the 1880s.

RELATIVES: THE OPPOSITION

FATHER & SON

Gibson	Scotland	Neil 1895–1900	Jimmy 1926–27
Simpson	Scotland	Jimmy 1935–37	Ronnie 1967–68
Nordahl	Sweden	Gunnar 1947	Thomas 1968
Mazzola	Italy	Valentino 1948	Sandro 1973
Carlsson	Sweden	Henry ('Garvis') 1949	Bjorn 1965
Alonso	Spain	'Marquitos' 1960	'Marcos' 1981
Whelan	Eire	Ronnie snr 1964	Ronnie jnr 1985–88
Sanchis	Spain	Manuel 1965	Manuel 1987

Marcos Alonso won his first cap in the same stadium (Wembley) where his father Marcos Alonso Imaz had won his last.

BROTHERS

Smith	Scotland	Robert 1872–73	James 1872
Ker	Scotland	William 1872–73	Geordie 1880–82
McNiel	Scotland	Harry 1874–81	Moses 1880
Christie	Scotland	Robert 1884	Alex 1899
Hamilton	Scotland	Alex Jack 1885–88	James 1893
Lambie	Scotland	Johnny 1888	William 1894–97
Wilson	Scotland	Andrew 1907–13	David 1913
Shaw	Scotland	Jock 1947	Davie 1948
Gray	Scotland	Eddie 1969–76	Frank 1979–83

A third Hamilton brother, Gladstone, played against Ireland in 1906.
McNiel is the correct spelling, not McNeil as seen in yearbooks.

Davies	Wales	No fewer than four Davies brother played against England: Bob 1885, Joe 1888–93, Tommy 1903 and Lloyd 1904–14.	

As with the Christies of Scotland, note the age differences.

Owen	Wales	William P 1880–84	Elias 1884
Vaughan	Wales	Thomas 1885	John O 1892
Owen	Wales	Billy 1884–92	John 1892
Trainer	Wales	Jimmy 1889–98	Harry 1895
Pryce-Jones	Wales	Ernest 1888	Albert 1895
Meredith	Wales	Billy 1895–1920	Sam 1901–07
Morgan-Owen	Wales	Morgan 1898–1907	Hugh 1901–06
Watkins	Wales	Alfred 1898	Mart 1902–05
Morris	Wales	Charlie 1900–11	Bobby 1900–03
Parry	Wales	Tom 1900–02	Maurice 1901–09
Allchurch	Wales	Ivor 1950–65	Len 1963
Charles	Wales	John 1953–61	Mel 1955–61

Gordon	Ireland	Three Gordon brothers played against England: Willie 1892–93, Hugh 1895–96, and goalkeeper Tommy 1895.	

Most modern yearbooks don't include Willie in lists of Irish internationals at all, but at least three match reports list him in the team against England in 1892, one as captain. I haven't found one that mentions Hugh, who therefore seems to have won his first cap in the same match (v England 1895) which saw Tommy (who let in nine goals) win his last.

Pyper	Ireland	Jack 1897–1900	Jim 1898–1900
Burnison	Ireland	Joe 1901	Sam 1908–12
Scott	Ireland	Willie 1903–13	Elisha 1920–35
McCracken	Ireland	Billy 1902–21	Bobby 1920–21
Jones	Ireland	Johnny 1930–37	Sammy 1933
Blanchflower	N Ireland	Danny 1950–62	Jackie 1954–57

The Scotts were both goalkeepers, and both captained Ireland against England. Yet another goalkeeper, Tom Scott, kept goal against England (1894–98) and may have been related.

O'Flanagan	Eire	Michael 1946	Kevin 1946
O'Leary	Eire	David 1976–91	Pierse 1980

David made his international debut at Wembley. During the 1980 match at the same stadium, he was substituted by his brother.

Braine	Belgium	Pierre 1924–29	Raymond 1926–29

Raymond Braine also captained the Rest of Europe against England 1938.

Hofmann	Germany	Richard 1930	Leopold 1930	
Walter	W Germany	Fritz 1956	Ottmar 1956	
Forster	W Germany	Karlheinz 1982	Bernd 1982	
Ducke	E Germany	Peter 1963–70	Roland 1963	
Abegglen	Switzerland	Max ('Xam') 1933	Andre ('Trello') 1933–38	
Baresi	Italy	Beppe 1980	Franco 1989–90	
Kozlicek	Austria	Ernst 1958	Paul 1958	
Dahl	Sweden	Harry 1923	Albin 1923	
Nordahl	Sweden	Gunnar 1947	Knut 1947–49	Bertil 1947

The three Nordahl brothers played at Wembley in 1947, the only such instance in an England match. Gunnar's son Tom played against England in 1968. Gunnar himself also played for a FIFA XI against England in 1953.

Harry Dahl was the first foreign player to score in two matches (and three goals in all) against England.

Muhren	Holland	Gerrie 1969–70	Arnold 1982–88
van de Kerkhof	Holland	Willy 1977	Rene 1982
Koeman	Holland	Ronald 1988–90	Erwin 1988

The van de Kerkhofs were twins

| Vujovic | Yugoslavia | Zlatko 1986–87 | Zoran 1986–87 |

The Vujovics were also twins. Milos Milutinovic scored against England in 1958, and his brother Velibor (Bora) coached Mexico against England 1985–86.

| Laudrup | Denmark | Michael 1983–89 | Brian 1989 |

Their father, Finn, scored the only goal of the game against Scotland in 1971.

| de Souza | Brazil | 'Socrates' 1981 | 'Rai' 1987 |

Zico scored against England in 1981. His brother Edu (not to be confused with the Edu who played against England in 1969) coached Brazil for the first time in the match against England in 1984.

| Merry | Morocco | Mustafa 1986 | Abdelkrim ('Krimau') 1986 |
| Souza | USA | John 1950 | Ed 1950 |

| Wilim | Poland | Jan 1966 | Jerzy 1966 |
| Warzycha | Poland | Krzystof 1989–90 | Robert 1989–90 |

Jan Wilim won his first cap in the match at Goodison, Jerzy came on as substitute in the return in Chorzow. Polish yearbooks refer to them as J Wilim I and J Wilim II; Jerzy was I, Jan II!

| Hassan | Egypt | Ibrahim 1990 | Hassam 1990 |

The Hassans were twins.

| Biyik | Cameroon | Francois Omam 1990–91 | Andre Kana 1991 |
| Vidmar | Australia | Tony 1991 | Aurelio 1991 |

Sam Torrans played for Ireland against England from 1892–99. He also refereed England matches, as did John Torrans who appears to have been his brother. Tom and Stewart Lawrie, who officiated in early England matches, were certainly brothers.

There may very well be others. Lopez of Colombia, for instance; or Stylianou of Cyprus, the various Hansens and Jensens of Denmark, the Turners of Ireland and Wales, the Edges of New Zealand (Tom coming on as substitute for Declan against England in 1991).

BROTHERS-IN-LAW

Ferdinand Daucik (Czechoslovakia 1937) & Ladislao Kubala (FIFA 1953). Kubala, apart from scoring twice against England for a FIFA invitation team, was one of only two players to be capped by three different countries: Hungary, Czechoslovakia and Spain.

Ernst Kuzorra (Germany 1930) & Fritz Szepan (Germany 1933–38).

Billy Mitchell (Ireland 1931–37) & Johnny and Sammy Jones (Ireland 1930–37)

UNCLE & NEPHEW

Tommy Miller (Scotland 1920–21)
Jock Govan (Scotland 1948)

Roy Paul (Wales 1948–55)
Alan Curtis (Wales 1976–82)

GREAT-UNCLE & GREAT-NEPHEW

Willie McStay (Scotland 1925–27)
Paul McStay (Scotland 1984–89)

GRANDFATHER & GRANDSON

Patsy Gallagher (Ireland 1919–24)
Kevin Gallacher (Scotland 1988)
Note the difference in spelling.

COUSINS

Willie Cunningham (Scotland 1955)
Jim Baxter (Scotland 1962–67)

FATHER & SON-IN-LAW

George Stevenson (Scotland 1930–31)
Jimmy Forrest (Scotland 1958)

The famous Welsh players Bryn and Cliff Jones, and journalist Ken Jones, are all related.

Walter Bahr played in the USA's shock win over England in 1950, and again in 1953. His sons Chris and Matt kicked goals in various American Football Superbowls.

ODDS & ENDS

Linesmen replaced umpires in England matches in 1892.

Goal nets had first been used the year before – but don't seem to have been mandatory for some time afterwards. When Jack Barton (or someone) scored the ninth goal in Belfast in 1890, the Irish players claimed the ball had gone over the bar – and when Willie Gibson scored a very late equaliser for Ireland in 1894, England's goalkeeper Joe Reader claimed that the ball had gone past the post. It was the first time Ireland had avoided defeat against England. When Billy Bassett put England ahead against Wales in 1889, the defenders claimed that the ball had gone past the post.

Sam Widdowson, who played for England in 1880, had patented the shinguard in 1874.

Fred Blackburn was born in Blackburn and was playing for Blackburn Rovers when he was capped.

Within 15 minutes of his debut, against Scotland in 1960, Ray Wilson's nose was broken after making contact with Ian St John's knee, something which also happened to fellow left-back Mel Hopkins of Wales (he had three operations on it and says it still isn't right). No blame attached to the Saint.

The very first international, in 1872, was drawn 0–0. The next scoreless draw between England and Scotland was nearly a century later, in 1970. There was at least one goal in each of the 86 matches in between.

The England–Brazil match at Gothenburg in 1958 was the first goalless draw in any World Cup finals.

1987 saw the last Scotland–England match to be played with the old square posts. Charlie Nicholas hit the bar in a 0–0 draw.

Rabbi Howell seems to have been the only gypsy to play for England. Dragoslav Sekularac, who played against England in 1958, was also said to have Romany blood.

Dave V Watson became the first player to represent England while with his fourth different club when he played against Bulgaria 1979. Then on Southampton's books, he'd previously been with Sunderland, Manchester City and Werder Bremen. He celebrated by scoring England's first goal in a 2–0 win. Peter Shilton played for England while with five different clubs: Leicester, Stoke, Nottingham Forest, Southampton and Derby.

The German team that played England in 1935 is thought to have been the first European side to travel by air. They landed at Croydon.

Arthur Brown and Howard Vaughton became Aston Villa's first internationals against Ireland in 1882. They celebrated by scoring nine between them, including the first hat-trick by an England player.

Harry Swepstone, a founder member of the Corinthians, apparently gave the club its name.

Scotland beat England 3–2 in 1887, despite having three goals disallowed. Northern Ireland lost 5–2 to England in 1960 but hit the bar three times. Jose Aguas hit the bar and Eusebio hit a post as well as the bar as England won 2–0 and qualified for the 1962 World Cup finals.

Against Belgium in 1924, England missed a penalty, hit the post, hit the bar twice, and won 4–0.

At the Oval in 1881, Scotland played with four centre forwards: Geordie Ker, John Smith, Willie McGuire and Joe Lindsay. They scored all of Scotland's goals between them (Smith 3, McGuire, Ker 2) as England went down 6–1, still the record home defeat.

Bob Crompton played in his 10th international against Scotland in the same match (at Hampden Park in 1912) in which Bobby Walker appeared in his 10th against England.

Austria (v Germany 1908) and Hungary (v Austria 1909) both played a full international in between two matches against England; three games in three days!

England's match in Belgrade in 1939 was Yugoslavia's 100th international – and their only win in 13 matches, helped by bad injuries to Eddie Hapgood (torn ankle ligaments) and Stanley Matthews (still suffering from a hip bone chipped five days earlier against Italy).

After Stanley Matthews' goal against Wales in 1938, the *South Wales Argus*, perhaps trying to claim him as one of their own, said England's second equaliser was scored by Matt Lewis!

Before the 1938 match in Berlin's Olympic stadium, the England team were persuaded to give the Nazi salute prior to the kick-off, after which their 6–3 win ended Germany's continental record of 14 games without defeat. It was the only time Germany or West Germany conceded six goals in a home match.

Antonio Ramallets of Spain kept clean sheets against England in matches 10 years apart (1950 and 1960).

On the same day that England were beating Yugoslavia 3–0 at Wembley in 1956, another Yugoslav team was playing what their FA classifies as a full international, beating the USA 9–0 in the Melbourne Olympics.

The gate for Ireland's first international match, against England in 1882, was apparently £12 19s 7d (£12.98), less than a pound for every goal scored by England.

How many times have current Rangers and Celtic goalkeepers been in opposition in an international match? It certainly happened at Lansdowne Road in 1990: Chris Woods and Pat Bonner were in goal.

SPARE ATTIRE

Tom Priestley apparently wore a **scrum cap** when he played, to hide his baldness; he won his last cap for Ireland in the match against England in 1933.

According to Tom Finney, Dutch winger Guus Drager wore a **hairnet** when he played against England in 1946.

Charles Colombo of the USA wore **gloves** when he played against England in 1950, as did Joao Alves of Portugal in 1975 and the entire Cameroon team (as well as **John Barnes**) at a freezing Wembley in 1991.

In 1881 Llewelyn Kenrick played for Wales against England in his **suit**, or so the story goes. He came off with a wrenched knee and shattered teeth in the second half, but Wales won 1–0.

Several players (perhaps all of them) wore **knitted caps** during the first international, England–Scotland in 1872.

It's in his kit. The scoreboard at Mount Smart Stadium in Auckland displayed 'Gary Lineker, sexiest player of the match' at the first New Zealand match in 1991 . . .

LANDMARK PLAYERS

The 100th	HC Goodhart, Stuart Macrae, PJ de Paravicini, Bruce Russell	1883 v Wales
The 500th	Willis Edwards	1926 v Wales
The 1000th	Neil Webb	1987 v W Germany

The moment when Neil Webb replaced Glenn Hoddle in Dusseldorf and became the 1000th player to take his first step on England territory (Bob Thomas)

The Clowns

Wednesday 17 October 1973
Empire Stadium, Wembley 100 000

World Cup Qualifier

ENGLAND (0) 1
Clarke (pen) 63

POLAND (0) 1
Domarski 57

Referee: Vital Loraux

ENGLAND

Peter Shilton	Leicester City
Paul Madeley	Leeds United
Emlyn Hughes	Liverpool
Colin Bell	Manchester City
Roy McFarland	Derby County
Norman Hunter	Leeds United
Tony Currie	Sheffield United
Mike Channon	Southampton
Martin Chivers*	Tottenham Hotspur
Allan Clarke	Leeds United
Martin Peters (capt)	Tottenham Hotspur
* sub (88 min) Kevin Hector	Derby County

Manager: Alf Ramsey
First cap: Hector
Last cap: Chivers
Booked: McFarland

POLAND

Jan Tomaszewski	LKS Lodz
Antoni Szymanowski	Wisla Cracow
Adam Musial	Wisla Cracow
Leslaw Cmikiewicz	Legia Warsaw
Jerzy Gorgon	Gornik Zabrze
Miroslaw Bulzacki	LKS Lodz
Grzegorz Lato	Stal Mielec
Henryk Kasperczak	Stal Mielec
Jan Domarski	Stal Mielec
Kazimierz Deyna (capt)	Legia Warsaw
Robert Gadocha	Legia Warsaw

Manager: Kazimierz Gorski
Coach: Jacek Gmoch
Booked: Bulzacki

England had tuned up by beating Austria 7–0, Clarke and Channon scoring two apiece – but no-one was unduly fooled. Poland were going to be hard to beat. With players like Cmikiewicz and the hulking Gorgon (only Daniel Killer of Argentina had a better name for a stopper), hard was the operative word. But Wlodek Lubanski had been injured soon after scoring the second goal in England's visit to Chorzow; he wouldn't play at Wembley, and Poland's inspiration was supposed to have disappeared with him. Domarski had replaced him in that match, winning his first cap in the process, but Lubanski was the team's one undoubted world star, and Domarski was just Domarski . . .

England's losses weren't so serious. Alan Ball, sent off in Chorzow, was replaced by the talented Currie, another who had scored against the Austrians; Bobby Moore had given away both the Polish goals and was all too clearly in decline; Hunter was the unchallenged replacement . . .

There was a worry about the referee, who'd allowed Romania's Mocanu to cripple three England players during the previous World Cup. In the event, he wasn't a factor. Poland were defensive but there was none of the brutality they'd shown in Chorzow, especially against the Welsh. Throughout the match, needing only the draw, they didn't trust themselves to come forward in numbers, relying on the speed of their wingers in counterattacks. England began the usual Wembley bombardment.

It's passed into folklore as the match in which 30 good chances were missed, or saved by a goalkeeper who managed to perform like Yashin, Banks and Norman Wisdom rolled into one. Brian Clough called him a clown, which seems laughable after Tomaszewski's fine form in the World Cup finals the following year (he saved two penalties and almost everything else), but wasn't so far wrong on the night; he flapped at crosses, made routine saves look difficult, generally got in the way without quite looking the part, had his share of luck in his 13th international. England, as so often happened, pressed and made chances, but very few very good ones. Channon had a goal disallowed; Peters won a debatable penalty, and this time Tomaszewski went the wrong way without leaving his legs in the right place. But by then it was already getting late; it was only the equaliser . . .

Lato had challenged Hunter for a ball on the touchline. Hunter did what Moore had done with Lubanski, trying to turn inside with the ball instead of clearing; like Moore, he lost it. Lato sprinted for the penalty area, Gadocha crisscrossed on a dummy run, Lato played the ball square and Domarski got there before Hughes to shoot under Shilton, who admitted trying to make too good-looking a save. Calamity.

The last few minutes were more frenzied than ever. Hector, sent on for a ludicrous two minutes, almost bundled in the equaliser. Tomaszewski went on clowning, but when the whistle went, Hunter, Shilton and Ramsey were wearing the red noses. Not the woeful result it looked at the time – Poland were probably the third best team in the world, even (or especially) without Lubanski. But this, the night Sir Alf froze and bowed out, was the first time they believed it.

Above *On with the motley. Gorgon and Clarke (10) go into their routine, keeper Tomaszewski jingles Bell, Channon and McFarland join the chorus line* (Colorsport)

Below *The biter bit. Stormin' Norman (6) has lost the ball to Lato (7) who has passed to Domarski (9) who has just scored* (Hulton)

GROUNDS & ATTENDANCES

HOME GROUNDS

WEMBLEY

The first international at Wembley was in **1924** when England and **Scotland** drew 1–1. The last game on home territory *not* played at Wembley was in **1973** when **Northern Ireland** were beaten 2–1 at **Goodison Park** in a match designated a home tie for the Irish.

OTHER HOME STADIA

In order of first appearance:

Kennington Oval	1873	Craven Cottage	1907
Alexandra Meadows, Blackburn	1881	Valley Parade, Bradford	1909
Liverpool Cricket Club, Aigburth	1883	The City Ground, Nottingham	1909
Bramall Lane, Sheffield	1883	The Baseball Ground	1911
Whalley Range, Manchester	1885	The Den	1911
Leamington Road, Blackburn	1885	Stamford Bridge	1913
Nantwich Road, Crewe	1888	Highbury	1920
Victoria Ground, Stoke	1889	Hillsborough	1920
Anfield	1889	The Hawthorns	1922
Newcastle Road, Sunderland	1891	Selhurst Park	1926
Molineux	1891	Old Trafford	1926
Ewood Park	1891	Turf Moor	1927
Perry Barr, Birmingham	1893	Bloomfield Road, Blackpool	1932
Richmond Athletic Ground	1893	White Hart Lane	1933
County Ground, Derby	1895	Maine Road	1946
Queen's Club, London	1895	Leeds Road, Huddersfield	1946
Goodison Park	1895		
Trent Bridge	1897		
The Crystal Palace, Sydenham	1897		
Roker Park	1899		
Ashton Gate	1899		
Villa Park	1899		
The Dell	1901		
St James's Park, Newcastle	1901		
Fratton Park	1903		
Ayresome Park	1905		

Before 1913, all three matches against the other Home countries were played at home one year, all away the next.

In 1900, England played at two of the main rugby union stadia: Lansdowne Road and the Arms Park. They have never played football at Murrayfield.

FLOODLIGHTS

The first England match played under artificial light was in New York on **8 June 1953** in a match against the USA at Yankee Stadium.

The first time floodlights were switched on during an England home match was on **30 November 1955** (the anniversary of the very first international match, as it happened) for Spain's first visit to Wembley.

The first England home match played entirely under floodlights was against Northern Ireland, again at Wembley, on **20 November 1963**.

England won all three games with something to spare: 6–3, 4–1 and 8–3.

ATTENDANCES

A word of warning that probably goes without saying: no official attendance figure can ever account for every person inside a football ground. Most are underestimates. For instance, it's generally agreed that 160 000 watched the Scotland match at Hampden in 1937, and that the same number were at the Maracana in 1959.

On the other hand, some are grotesque exaggerations. Did 98 728 really watch England–Paraguay in Mexico City, 1986? It's now common knowledge that the official crowd figures for the 1990 World Cup in Italy referred to tickets bought rather than actual spectators bothering to be present. As a final example, the 1964 Scotland–England match at Hampden has at least three separate official figures: 134 146, 133 245, 133 253! Thankfully perhaps, Hampden's capacity was reduced to below 100 000 in 1972.

HIGHEST

151 000	v Brazil	Maracana	1959
149 547	v Scotland	Hampden Park	1937
149 269	v Scotland	Hampden Park	1939
137 284	v Scotland	Hampden Park	1970
136 259	v Scotland	Hampden Park	1933
135 000	v Brazil	Maracana	1969
134 544	v Scotland	Hampden Park	1954
134 504	v Scotland	Hampden Park	1952
134 146	v Scotland	Hampden Park	1964
133 426	v Scotland	Hampden Park	1948
133 300	v Scotland	Hampden Park	1950
132 441	v Scotland	Hampden Park	1962
132 437	v Scotland	Hampden Park	1956
131 215	v Scotland	Hampden Park	1931
130 711	v Scotland	Hampden Park	1968
129 693	v Scotland	Hampden Park	1935
129 183	v Scotland	Hampden Park	1960
128 000	v Spain	Chamartin	1955
127 874	v Scotland	Hampden Park	1958
127 307	v Scotland	Hampden Park	1912
123 052	v Scotland	Hampden Park	1966
121 452	v Scotland	Hampden Park	1908
120 000	v Spain	Bernabeu	1968

Chamartin was the old name for the Bernabeu, which is in the Chamartin district of Madrid.

The giant temples of Hampden Park and the Maracana dominate the list. The highest attendance from outside these two and the Bernabeu was the **105 000** who saw England draw 0–0 with Mexico at the **Azteca** in 1969. The first time 100 000 tickets were sold for an England home match was the match against Argentina 1951. Bad weather kept 60 000 at home! The first team 100 000 actually turned up to see were the Austrians of 1951.

The first **100 000** crowd for any match, anywhere, was the 102 741 that saw England lose 2–1 at Hampden in **1906**.

The 1937 crowd is still the largest for any match in Britain. The 1931 crowd was then the largest for any sporting event in history.

150 000 tickets were sold for the 1937 and 1939 matches at Hampden.

LOWEST

200	v Wales	Kennington Oval	1879
1200	v Scotland	Kennington Oval	1877
2000	v Scotland	Kennington Oval	1875
2000	v Wales	Kennington Oval	1883
2500	v Scotland	Kennington Oval	1873

The 1879 figure is no misprint; the Oval has never exactly been a hotbed of football interest, and England's first ever match against Wales, played on a snow-topped pitch, clearly failed to stir much blood. It has to be the smallest crowd to watch any international match – especially as *The Times* puts the number at around 100!

There's some suspicion that the figure for the **Ireland** match at Ballynafeigh in **1890** may have been as low as **1000**. The official estimate was six times that number.

LOWEST SINCE 1914

5000	v Romania	ANEF, Bucharest	1939
5062	v USA	Downing, Randall's Island, New York	1964
5500	v Luxembourg	Municipal, Luxembourg	1960
5700	v Bulgaria	Braden, Rancagua (Chile)	1962
6000	v Israel	Ramat Gan, Tel Aviv	1988
7271	v USA	Yankee Stadium, New York	1953
7938	v Hungary	Braden, Rancagua (Chile)	1962

England's three group matches in the 1962 World Cup finals, all at the Braden Copper Stadium, were watched by a grand total of 23 432; England's three in the triangular tournament of 1985, played at the Azteca, by less than 33 000.

LOWEST AT WEMBLEY

15 628	v Chile	1989
21 342	v Czechoslovakia	1990
23 600	v Wales	1983
23 951	v E Germany	1984
24 000	v N Ireland	1984
25 837	v Denmark	1988
27 500	v Wales	1962

A sign of how interest in the Home Championship had waned: the Northern Ireland match was England's last home game in the competition.

The Temple of the Left Foot

Saturday 6 June 1981
Nepstadion, Budapest 62–68 000

World Cup Qualifier

HUNGARY (1) 1   ENGLAND (1) 3
Garaba 44   Brooking 18, 60
                           Keegan (pen) 73

Referee: Paolo Cesarin (Italy)

HUNGARY	
Bela Katzirz	Pecsi MSC
Gyozo Martos	Waterschei (Belgium)
Laszlo Balint	Bruges (Belgium)
Jozsef Varga	Honved
Sandor Muller*	Antwerp (Belgium)
Imre Garaba	Honved
Laszlo Fazekas**	Antwerp (Belgium)
Tibor Nyilasi (capt)	Ferencvaros
Andras Torocsik	Ujpesti Dozsa
Laszlo Kiss	Vasas Budapest
Jozsef Mucha	Ferencvaros

* sub Andras Komjati   Vasas Budapest
  (54 min)
** sub Bela Bodonyi   Honved
  (61 min)

Manager: Kalman Meszoly
First cap: Komjati
Last caps: Komjati, Mucha

ENGLAND	
Ray Clemence	Liverpool
Phil Neal	Liverpool
Mick Mills	Ipswich Town
Bryan Robson	WBA
Phil Thompson	Liverpool
Dave V Watson	Southampton
Kevin Keegan (capt)	Southampton
Steve Coppell	Manchester United
Paul Mariner	Ipswich town
Trevor Brooking*	West Ham United
Terry McDermott	Liverpool
* sub Ray Wilkins (72min)	Manchester United

Manager: Ron Greenwood
First/Last caps: 0

When you're trying to win in Budapest for the first time since 1909, especially with World Cup qualification at stake, it helps if you can rustle up a good record going in to the match. England managed just the opposite.

Six matches without a win, a record sequence of four in a row without a goal, three out of four World Cup points dropped, all culminating in the fiasco in Basle: McDermott scoring that elusive goal, but only after the defence had parted like the Red Sea to concede two, followed by the usual riot on the terraces. All this and the ghosts of Puskas and Hidegkuti to come. Greenwood did what he'd done in the same situation at West Ham:

talked of resigning – then, to his credit, in front of the last ditch, picked his best team.

You could argue about individuals (Clemence, Neal, McDermott, Mariner – and Keegan and Brooking were never quite fully fit again), but, in place of Hoddle, Osman, Sansom and Peter Barnes, there was experience (381 previous caps) and a solid, tight shape, especially in midfield and central defence. And Hungary, as it quickly turned out, were no Magic Magyars. Nyilasi, for all his reputation as playmaker/striker/style guru, was anonymous in two World Cups and four matches against England. Torocsik too did little in the World Cup; he had extravagant

skills but a temper to match: both he and Nyilasi were sent off in the 1978 finals. Mucha, Muller and the opportunist Kiss frightened nobody at international level.

Somebody else once did, and the Hungarian authorities invited him back in the hope that he might once again. Not just the ghost of Puskas but his very ample corporal presence, juggling a ball in the pre-match kick-about. The last time he'd played against the same opposition for real, in this same stadium 27 years before, he'd scored twice in England's worst ever defeat (7–1). Now, just by being there, he was expected to put a hex on a team whose morale must already have been at rock-bottom.

It didn't work, partly because England, at last and for once, had their share of luck. Brooking mis-hit McDermott's cross, but the ball slipped in at the near post. Nyalisi, over-rated or not, beat Clemence, but the ball hit the bar. At one crucial stage it seemed to have run out – a one-two splitting the centre of the defence, Clemence letting the loose ball slip behind him, the hulking Garaba sweeping it in on the stroke of half-time – but it came back in the second half when Keegan ran past the same hulk to win a penalty that probably wasn't. Fortune favouring the old pro.

Anyway, by then England had scored a goal that deserved to win any match, constructed with skill and precision (Neal's neat little ball in, Keegan's exact half-volley back) and finished with an almighty thump by Brooking, of all people, he of the reputation for not being able to kick the skin off a rice pudding, though he could probably chip it into the penalty area without breaking. This one flew off his left instep to the far post, stayed on course without swerving though it was lighter than the British recipe, and lodged high up against the stanchion, where it stayed, a triumphant TV image, until Katzirz walked over to take it down. Where better to hit the perfect left-foot shot than in Puskas' home stadium, in front of the one-footed genius himself? Clever Trevor. His old club manager's international career saved by the best strike of his own.

In the very next match, the first of the following season, England's central defence self-destructed yet again, more hilariously than ever, in Oslo. But the Swiss opened the back door by winning in Romania, and perhaps that was fair as well as fortunate. This was a better England team than it sometimes looked, and it even looked pretty good when Brooking, Keegan and Trevor Francis were fit. It deserved to be in the World Cup. So too (at last and just about) did Ron Greenwood.

This and the subsequent match at Wembley were Hungary's only defeats in a sequence of 12 matches.

Keegan's goal was his 20th for England.

Meszoly, once a great centre-half, had played against England in 1962 and 1965.

Keegan (7), Robson and the scoreboard haven't caught up with Brooking, whose goal has just put Anglia 1–0 up against Magyarorszag (Colorsport)

ENGLAND: THE COMPLETE RECORD

	P	W	D	L	F	A	Record
Albania	2	2	0	0	7	0	100.00%
Argentina	10	4	4	2	15	11	60.00%
Australia	5	3	2	0	5	2	80.00%
Austria	15	8	3	4	54	25	63.33%
Belgium	18	13	4	1	67	24	83.33%
Bohemia	1	1	0	0	4	0	100.00%
Brazil	15	3	5	7	13	20	36.66%
Bulgaria	5	3	2	0	7	1	80.00%
Cameroon	2	2	0	0	5	2	100.00%
Canada	1	1	0	0	1	0	100.00%
Chile	4	2	2	0	4	1	75.00%
Colombia	2	1	1	0	5	1	75.00%
Cyprus	2	2	0	0	6	0	100.00%
Czechoslovakia	11	7	2	2	23	13	72.72%
Denmark	12	8	3	1	24	11	79.16%
Egypt	2	2	0	0	5	0	100.00%
Ecuador	1	1	0	0	2	0	100.00%
Finland	8	7	1	0	32	5	87.50%
France	20	14	2	4	60	27	75.00%
Germany (1930–38)	3	2	1	0	12	6	83.33%
E Germany	4	3	1	0	7	3	87.50%
W Germany	16	7	3	6	24	19	53.12%
Greece	5	4	1	0	10	1	90.00%
Hungary	17	11	1	5	46	27	67.65%
Iceland	1	0	1	0	1	1	50.00%
Ireland/N Ireland	96	73	17	6	319	80	84.89%
Rep of Ireland (Eire)	13	5	6	2	19	12	61.54%
Israel	2	1	1	0	2	1	75.00%
Italy	17	6	5	6	25	22	50.00%
Kuwait	1	1	0	0	1	0	100.00%
Luxembourg	7	7	0	0	38	3	100.00%
Malaysia	1	1	0	0	4	2	100.00%
Malta	2	2	0	0	6	0	100.00%
Mexico	6	3	1	2	14	3	58.33%
Morocco	1	0	1	0	0	0	50.00%
Netherlands	10	4	4	2	16	10	60.00%
New Zealand	2	2	0	0	3	0	100.00%
Norway	6	5	0	1	25	4	83.33%
Paraguay	1	1	0	0	3	0	100.00%
Peru	2	1	0	1	5	4	50.00%
Poland	8	4	3	1	11	4	68.75%
Portugal	15	8	5	2	35	17	70.00%
Romania	8	2	5	1	6	4	56.25%
Saudi Arabia	1	0	1	0	1	1	50.00%
Scotland	107	43	24	40	188	168	51.40%
Spain	16	10	2	4	37	19	68.75%
Sweden	13	6	4	3	23	14	61.54%
Switzerland	15	10	2	3	37	12	73.33%
Tunisia	1	0	1	0	1	1	50.00%
Turkey	5	4	1	0	22	0	90.00%
Uruguay	8	2	2	4	8	12	37.50%
USA	5	4	0	1	29	5	80.00%
USSR	11	5	3	3	19	13	59.09%
Wales	97	62	21	14	239	90	74.74%
Yugoslavia	14	5	5	4	23	20	53.57%
FIFA XIs	3	2	1	0	9	5	83.33%
Totals	676	391	153	132	1611	726	69.16%

Austria have conceded 7 goals in a game three times, all against England: 1908 (11–1), 1909 (8–1) and 1973 (7–0). The 1908 result was their worst ever.

England have failed to score in the last four matches against **Sweden**, a record against any country: 0–0 in 1979, 0–1 in 1986, 0–0 in 1988, 0–0 in 1989. The last goal was scored by Roger Hunt in 1968.

England lost to **Ireland** for the first time in 1913, 2–1 in Belfast. Both the Irish goals were deflected in by England defenders, and the crowd invaded the pitch three minutes from the end. As against that, Ireland played with only ten men for the last half-hour after Jim Macauley was injured. Before all this, England's record against Ireland stood at P31 W28 D3 L0 F150 A19 – 95.16%.

In recent years, **Northern Ireland** have had great trouble scoring against England, let alone winning matches, which they've done only twice since the Second World War, in 1957 and 1972, both times at Wembley. The last Irish win over England in Belfast was as long ago as 1927.

In the 24 meetings since 1964, England have conceded only 8 goals, two of them from penalties. No Irish player has scored more than once and no Irish team more than once in a game. The three goals scored in the second half of the 1964 match (England scored four in the first) and Jimmy McLaughlin's two in the same game are still landmarks.

And it's been getting worse. Only two goals in the last 12 matches, none in the last 7. Not since substitute Terry Cochrane's equaliser at Wembley in 1980 (which led to their first outright Home Championship title since 1914) have Northern Ireland scored against England.

Luxembourg have had much the same problem. England beat them four times between 1977 and 1983 without conceding a goal – no great surprise, given that Luxembourg haven't won a single international match since 1973! There have been only four draws in almost 80 matches, one of them, surprisingly (perhaps!), against Scotland in 1987.

BIGGEST WINS

13–0	v Ireland	1882
13–2	v Ireland	1899
11–1	v Austria	1908
10–0	v Portugal	1947
10–0	v USA	1964
9–0	v Ireland	1895
9–0	v Luxembourg	1960
9–0	v Luxembourg	1982
9–1	v Ireland	1890
9–1	v Wales	1896
9–1	v Belgium	1927
8–0	v Finland	1937
8–0	v Mexico	1961
8–0	v Turkey	1984
8–0	v Turkey	1987

The 1882 match was Ireland's first international. It's still their biggest defeat. 9–0 is Luxembourg's biggest.

Below *Jimmy McIlroy sets Northern Ireland on the way to the first of only two post-war wins over England, but needs a penalty that hit a post and Eddie Hopkinson's body to do it* (Popperfoto)

BIGGEST DEFEATS

1–7	v Hungary	1954
2–7	v Scotland	1878
1–6	v Scotland	1881
0–5	v Yugoslavia	1958
1–5	v Scotland	1882
1–5	v Scotland	1928
1–5	v Brazil	1964

The 1881 result is still the record home defeat.

Since 1964, only one team (**Wales** 1–4, 1980) has beaten England by more than two goals.

It could have been worse in 1958. Yugoslavia had two goals disallowed for offside, hit the bar from long range, missed at least once from close in – all with the score still 0–0!

10 GOALS IN A GAME

15	v Ireland	13–2	1899
13	v Ireland	13–0	1882
12	v Austria	11–1	1908
12	v Scotland	9–3	1961
11	v N Ireland	9–2	1949
11	v N Ireland	8–3	1963
10	v Ireland	9–1	1890
10	v Wales	9–1	1896
10	v Hungary	8–2	1909
10	v Belgium	9–1	1927
10	v Holland	8–2	1946
10	v Portugal	10–0	1947
10	v USA	10–0	1964

LONGEST UNBEATEN SEQUENCES

Games

20	1889–96
19	1965–66
18	1907–10
17	1988–90
16	1951–53
16	1955–57
14	1978–79

For the 1896 match with England, Scotland deigned to pick players with English clubs (five in all) for the first time; in front of the first 50 000 crowd to watch an international, their 2–1 win (against an England team which had lost Needham and Bloomer to injury and for which GO Smith hit a post and John Goodall had a goal disallowed) ended the Auld Enemy's record run. Their 3–2 win at Wembley in 1967 prevented the world champions from equalling it.

England's 5–0 win at Hampden in 1888 ended Scotland's world record of **22** matches without defeat.

LONGEST WINNING SEQUENCES

10	1908–09
9	1891–93
7	1898–1900
7	1949–50
7	1966

Lies, damned lies, and . . . the record was achieved against Ireland, Wales, and the embryonic, amateur Austrians and Hungarians – plus Bohemia, which wasn't even a country. There was only one win against a genuine football power: 2–0 over Scotland in 1909.

LONGEST LOSING SEQUENCES

3	1876–78	3	1959
3	1928	3	1985
3	1936	3	1988

LONGEST SEQUENCES WITHOUT A WIN

7	1958
6	1977
6	1981

The record run included three matches against the USSR, and was ended by a 5–0 win over the same country.

Below *Mick Mills (on ground) and Russell Osman are too late to stop Claudio Sulser from putting Switzerland 2–0 ahead in Basle in 1981. Terry McDermott's subsequent goal ended a record run of four scoreless matches, but England's defeat was their sixth consecutive game without a win* (Hulton)

Right *The Kaiser can only watch as Supermac scores against the world champions at Wembley in 1975* (Hulton)

ENGLAND v THE WORLD CHAMPIONS

1934	v Italy	W	3–2
1939	v Italy	D	2–2
1948	v Italy	W	4–0
1949	v Italy	W	2–0
1953	v Uruguay	L	1–2
1954	v Uruguay	L	2–4
1954	v W Germany	W	3–1
1956	v W Germany	W	3–1
1959	v Brazil	L	0–2
1962	v Brazil	L	1–3
1963	v Brazil	D	1–1
1964	v Brazil	L	1–5
1975	v W Germany	W	2–0
1978	v W Germany	L	1–2
1980	v Argentina	W	3–1
1985	v Italy	L	1–2

ENGLAND AS WORLD CHAMPIONS

The record:
P39 **W**23 **D**10 **L**6 **F**66 **A**26 71.89%

Defeats
1967	Scotland	2–3
1968	W Germany	0–1
1968	Yugoslavia	0–1
1969	Brazil	1–2
1970	Brazil	0–1
1970	W Germany	2–3(aet)

MOST ENGLAND SCORERS IN A MATCH

7	v Luxembourg	9–0	1982
6	v Ireland	9–0	1895
6	v Ireland	13–2	1899
6	v Austria	11–1	1908
6	v Finland	8–0	1937

The first two included an own goal each.

A seventh player missed a penalty in the 1899 match.

The 1982 scorers: Bossi own goal, Coppell, Woodcock, Blissett (3), Chamberlain, Hoddle and Neal.

MATCHES WON FROM 2 GOALS DOWN

1879	v Scotland	5–4 after being 4–1 down at half-time
1920	v Scotland	5–4 after being 4–2 down at half-time
1927	v Luxembourg	5–2
1976	v Italy	3–2 after being 2–0 down at half-time; all 3 England goals were scored within 7 minutes of the restart

MATCHES LOST FROM 2 GOALS UP

1882 **Wales** won **5–3** after being 2–0 and 3–1 down, with the help of an English own goal and three controversial goals allowed by the Welsh referee.

1889 **Scotland** won **3–2** with 2 goals in the last 8 minutes.

1929 **Spain** became the first foreign team to beat England (and the first to do so at the first attempt) by winning 4–3 after trailing 2–0 and 3–2.

1970 **West Germany** won a famous World Cup quarter-final by recovering from a 2–0 deficit to win **3–2** in extra time.

To the end of the 1990–91 season, England have won **48** matches that involved falling behind, the last against the USSR at Wembley in May 1991 – and lost **28** after going ahead, the last against Norway in a World Cup qualifier in 1981.

MATCHES OFF

The game against **Argentina** in **1953** was the only one to be abandoned yet still stand as an official England match. English referee Arthur Ellis called it off in a rainstorm after 23 minutes, with the score 0–0. . . . England were also drawing 0–0 with **Czechoslovakia** in **1975** when the match was abandoned. It was restarted the following day; the Czechs won 2–1 and went on to become European champions. . . . The **1902 England–Scotland** match at Ibrox was played to a finish (1–1) but declared void after a crowd disaster and replayed later in the season at Villa Park (2–2). . . . The **Switzerland** match of **1948** and the game against **Bulgaria** in **1979** were postponed for a day because of bad weather. . . . The second match against **Sweden** in **1923** isn't on the official Swedish list. It was classed as a B international to avoid paying FIFA's share of the gate! . . . Just before the abandoned match in Argentina, England lost 3–1 to a so-called **Buenos Aires XI**; Argentina class it as a full international. France and Germany include several matches against the England amateur team in their lists of full internationals.

Out of the Lions' Mouth

Sunday 1 July 1990
Stadio San Paolo, Naples 55 205

World Cup quarter-final

CAMEROON (0) 2   ENGLAND (1) 3 (aet, 2–2 at 90 mins)
Kunde (pen) 61   Platt 25
Ekeke 65   Lineker (2 pens) 83, 104

Referee: Edgardo Codesal (Mexico)

CAMEROON		ENGLAND	
Thomas N'kono	Espanol (Spain)	Peter Shilton	Derby County
Benjamin Massing	Creteil (France)	Paul Parker	QPR
Bertin Ebwelle	Tonnerre, Yaounde	Stuart Pearce	Nottm Forest
Emmanuel Kunde	Canon, Yaounde	David Platt	Aston Villa
Louis-Paul Mfede*	Canon, Yaounde	Terry Butcher (capt)**	Glasgow Rangers
Jean-Claude Pagal	La Roche sur Yon (France)	Des Walker	Nottm Forest
		Mark Wright	Derby County
Stephen Tataw (capt)	Tonnerre, Yaounde	Chris Waddle	Marseille
Thomas Libiih	Tonnerre, Yaounde	Gary Lineker	Tottenham H
Francois Omam Biyik	Laval (France)	Paul Gascoigne	Tottenham H
Kessack Maboang**	Racing Bafoussam	John Barnes*	Liverpool
Cyrille Makanaky	Toulon (France)		
		* sub Peter Beardsley (HT)	Liverpool
* sub Eugene Ekeke (62min)	Valenciennes (France)	** sub Trevor Steven (74min)	Glasgow Rangers
** sub Roger Miller (Milla) HT	Jeunesse St Pierroise (Reunion)		

Manager: Valery Nepomniachi (USSR)
Booked: Massing, N'kono, Milla

Manager: Bobby Robson
Booked: Pearce

In the World Cup, Africa had been on the move. In 1970 Morocco were the first to win a point. In 1978 Tunisia were the first to win a match – and held world champions West Germany to a draw. In 1982 Algeria *beat* West Germany and were only denied a place in the second phase by Austro-German collusion. In 1986 Morocco were the first to finish top of a group, losing to eventual finalists West Germany via a very late free-kick from Matthaus. Now the Indomitable Lions of Cameroon had become the first to reach the quarter-finals. The Africans were getting there. Step by step.

In 1986 Morocco had faltered, against a mediocre German team, through very defensive tactics probably born out of timidity. Cameroon, quite the opposite-in style, simply didn't finish what they started. Just one more goal in normal time against England and their wild tackling wouldn't have mattered.

As it happened, they were without four first choices through suspension – they'd set the tone in their opening game with two sendings-off against Argentina – and seemed to be slow learners, lunging at Lineker as they'd done with Caniggia. They were the better

side in the first half yet fell behind to Platt's header. They dominated the second when the ageless Milla came on as substitute (he was fouled for the equalising penalty and made the second), cut England's new sweeper system to shreds – and missed chances. Shilton made vital saves (one in particular when Omam Biyik was clean through), Lineker was fouled twice in the penalty area: a time-worn script.

Both England penalties look genuine enough on the screen (even if the second seems to be a foul by N'kono's head!) and Lineker took them very well in all the pressure, the goalkeeper

Lineker knows there's not long to go but controls his nerves and sends N'Kono the wrong way to force extra-time
(Colorsport)

going the wrong way each time. But this was England's second successive escape, following Platt's last-minute winner against a Belgian team which had hit the post twice. The subsequent semi-final against West Germany has gone down as a kind of coming-of-age – but this was the more vivid, more dramatic match. England were mauled but survived, the Africans went home to wait another four years. And next time? The semi-final perhaps, going out only on penalties? Or, at last, the confidence to succeed? Time to take two steps in a row.

This was the only England match to feature three successful penalties. Lineker became the first to score from two in one game since Hurst against France in 1969. He lost a stone in weight during the match.

This was Shilton's 15th match (out of a final total of 17) in the World Cup finals, a new British record.

In a poor World Cup, Cameroon were the only team to score twice in a match and lose, and needed a penalty to do it.

ENGLAND IN THE WORLD CUP FINALS

THE RECORD SO FAR

P	W	D	L	F	A	Record
41	18	12	11	55	38	58.54%

CAPTAINS & MANAGERS

Year	Captain	Manager
1950	Billy Wright	Walter Winterbottom
1954	Billy Wright	Walter Winterbottom
1958	Billy Wright	Walter Winterbottom
1962	Johnny Haynes	Walter Winterbottom
1966	Bobby Moore	Alf Ramsey
1970	Bobby Moore	Alf Ramsey
1982	Mick Mills	Ron Greenwood
1986	Bryan Robson	Bobby Robson
	Peter Shilton	
1990	Bryan Robson	Bobby Robson
	Terry Butcher	
	Peter Shilton	

No one has captained a country in more tournaments than Wright, or managed one more often than Winterbottom.

MOST TOURNAMENTS

3	Billy Wright	1950–54–58
3	Tom Finney	1950–54–58
3	Bobby Charlton	1962–66–70
3	Bobby Moore	1962–66–70
3	Terry Butcher	1982–86–90
3	Bryan Robson	1982–86–90
3	Peter Shilton	1982–86–90

Charlton was also in the 1958 squad. Had England qualified, Shilton would almost certainly have played in the **1974** and **1978** finals, equalling Antonio Carbajal's record of **5** tournaments. Shilts was also in the last 28 for the 1970 competition.

Above right *Peter Reid watches Gary Lineker score the first of his three goals against Poland in Mexico* (Bob Thomas)

Below *The USA are yet to come, and England are still happy to show their faces to the world in the Maracana, before their first match in any World Cup finals: England 2 Chile 0, 25 June 1950* (Popperfoto)

MOST MATCHES

17	Peter Shilton	1982–90
14	Bobby Charlton	1962–70
14	Bobby Moore	1962–70
14	Terry Butcher	1982–90
12	Gary Lineker	1986–90
11	Chris Waddle	1986–90
10	Billy Wright	1950–58
10	Ray Wilson	1962–66

MOST GOALS

10**	Gary Lineker	1986–90
5	Geoff Hurst	1966–70
4	Bobby Charlton	1962–66

*penalties

SEQUENCES

England played 7 successive games without defeat (1966–70), including 6 consecutive wins, just one short of Italy's record set in 1934–38.

The other side of the coin: 6 successive matches without a win (1954–62), and 4 games in a row without scoring a goal (1982–86), still the record for any country, equalling Peru's feat of 1978–82.

MOST IN ONE TOURNAMENT

6	Gary Lineker	1986
4	Geoff Hurst	1966
4**	Gary Lineker	1990
3	Nat Lofthouse	1954
3	Roger Hunt	1966
3	Bobby Charlton	1966
3	David Platt	1990

*penalties

In 1986 Lineker became the only British player to finish as top scorer in a finals tournament. He broke the British record of 5 goals scored by Peter McParland of Northern Ireland in 1958.

SCORED IN TWO TOURNAMENTS

Tom Finney	1954–58
Bobby Charlton	1962–66
Geoff Hurst	1966–70
Martin Peters	1966–70
Gary Lineker	1986–90

HAT-TRICKS

Geoff Hurst	1966	v W Germany
Gary Lineker	1986	v Poland

GOALKEEPERS: CLEAN SHEETS

Gordon Banks (1966) and Peter Shilton (1982) kept the opposition scoreless for 4 consecutive matches, still the record, first established by Gylmar of Brazil in 1958.

Shilton kept 10 clean sheets in all, surpassing the previous record of 8 first established by Sepp Maier in 1978.

Banks didn't concede a goal for 442 minutes in 1966, breaking Gylmar's record. Maier reached 476 in 1974–78, which was overhauled by Shilton in 1982–86 (499 or 500 minutes, depending on definition). Walter Zenga of Italy broke Shilton's record with 516 in 1990.

ENGLISH REFEREES IN THE WORLD CUP FINAL

1950	George Reader	
1954	Bill Ling	
1974	Jack Taylor	No other country has provided more than two.

PART TWO
THE ENGLAND PLAYERS WHO'S WHO

WALTER
ABBOTT

b 7 Dec 1877   d 1 Feb 1941   CENTRE HALF
Caps: 1   **Goals:** 0
Only cap: 3 Mar 1902 v Wales 0–0   aged 24yr 86d
England career: P1 W0 D1 L0 – 50%
Club: Everton
Started out as a very average inside left but switched to left half with great success. For some reason, chosen at centre half against Wales.

ALAN
A'COURT

b 30 Sep 1934   OUTSIDE LEFT
Caps: 5   **Goals:** 1
First cap: 6 Nov 1957 v N Ireland 2–3   aged 23yr 37d
  (1 goal)
Last cap: 26 Nov 1958 v Wales 2–2   aged 24yr 57d
England career: 1yr 20d – P5 W0 D3 L2 – 30%
Club: Liverpool
Took over when FINNEY was injured in the World Cup finals – an impossible act to follow.

TONY
ALEXANDER
ADAMS

b 10 Oct 1966   CENTRAL DEFENDER
Caps: 19   **Goals:** 4
First cap: 18 Feb 1987 v Spain 4–2   aged 20yr 131d
Last cap: 27 Mar 1991 v Eire 1–1   aged 23yr 295d
England career: 3yr 72d – P19 W6 D9 L4 – 55.26%
Club: Arsenal
Substituted: 4   **2 Goals in a Game:** 0
The first player born after the 1966 World Cup to be capped by England, big Tony was being talked about as the country's future captain – but the honeymoon didn't last long. A wretched 1990 (left out of the World Cup squad, captain of a club docked two League points for brawling, sent off and banned for three matches following a professional foul) culminated in a four-month prison sentence for drunken driving.

Before all that, his total of four goals in his first 16 internationals was already second (with DV WATSON) only to J CHARLTON's record for an England defender. The only player to score for both sides in an England match (against Holland at Wembley, 1988), he may even have done it twice (see **Own Goals**).

HUGH
ADCOCK

b 10 Apr 1903   d 16 October 1975   OUTSIDE RIGHT
Caps: 5   **Goals:** 1
First cap: 9 May 1929 v France 4–1   aged 26yr 29d

Last cap: 20 Nov 1929 v Wales 4–0   aged 26yr 221d
  (1 goal)
England career: 0yr 195d – P5 W4 D0 L1 – 80%
Club: Leicester City
Played in the same forward line as Joe BRADFORD, his cousin, in the defeat by Spain.

CHARLES
WILLIAM
ALCOCK

b 2 Dec 1842   d 26 Feb 1907   FORWARD
Caps: 1   **Goals:** 1   **Captain:** 1
Only cap: 6 Mar 1875 v Scotland 2–2   aged 32yr 94d
  (1 goal)
England career: P1 W0 D1 L0 – 50%
Club: Wanderers
One of the founding fathers. A member of the early FA Committees, Charles Alcock was the only current FA Secretary to play for England. It seems he helped select himself for each of the first five England internationals, but only played in the fourth. He was possibly the first 30-year-old to play for England (but see MORTEN) and certainly the first to score a goal while captaining England. Pretty determined to score it he was too, according to *The Sportsman*: 'There it was breasted by the England captain, and he pertinaciously adhered to it until he had got it securely over the Scottish goal-line.' Well, naturally. If there's one thing FA Secretaries need, it's pertinacious adherence.

JOHN
THOMAS
ALDERSON

b 28 Nov 1891   d 17 Feb 1972   GOALKEEPER
Caps: 1   **Goals conceded:** 1
Only cap: 10 May 1923 v France 4–1   aged 31yr 163d
England career: P1 W1 D0 L0 – 100%
Club: Crystal Palace
Jack Alderson won his cap after HF PEARSON's father Hubert dropped out. One newspaper source says he was born 23 Nov 1901, but this appears to be an error.

ALBERT
JAMES
ALDRIDGE

b 13 Apr 1864   d May 1891   RIGHT/LEFT BACK
Caps: 2   **Goals:** 0
First cap: 7 Apr 1888 v Ireland 5–1   aged 23yr 360d
Last cap: 2 Mar 1889 v Ireland 6–1   aged 24yr 323d
England career: 0yr 329d – P2 W2 D0 L0 – 100%
Clubs: West Bromwich Albion (1), Walsall Town Swifts (1)
Yearbooks list him as simply A Aldridge, his name was once thought to be Alfred; the

ALCOCK annual lists his club as still West Brom in 1889, the 1990 Lamming Who's Who says he moved to Walsall Town Swifts in July 1888. Pick the bones out of that.

ALBERT ALLEN

b April 1867   d 13 Oct 1899   INSIDE LEFT
Caps: 1   Goals: 3
Only cap: 7 Apr 1888 v Ireland 5–1
                                        aged 20yr 343d–21yr 6d
England career: P1 W1 D0 L0 – 100%
Club: Aston Villa

The first player to score a hat-trick in his only match for England.

ANTHONY ALLEN

b 27 Nov 1939   LEFT BACK
Caps: 3   Goals: 0
First cap: 17 Oct 1959 v Wales 1–1   aged 19yr 324d
Last cap: 18 Nov 1959 v N Ireland 2–1   aged 19yr 356d
England career: 0yr 32d – P3 W1 D1 L1 – 50%
Club: Stoke City

Capped too young for his own good, they said. But Tony Allen was thrown into some makeshift England teams – and anyway Ray WILSON and Mick McNEIL were just round the corner.

CLIVE DARREN ALLEN

b 20 May 1961   STRIKER
Caps: 5   Goals: 0
First cap: 10 Jun 1984 v Brazil 2–0   aged 23yr 21d
                                        (sub 76min)
Last cap: 17 Feb 1988 v Israel 0–0   aged 26yr 273d
                                        (sub'd 68min)
England career: 3yr 252d – P5 W1 D3 L1 – 50%
Clubs: Queen's Park Rangers (3), Tottenham Hotspur (2)
Substitute: 1   Substituted: 3

At the end of a very prolific but frustrating 1986–87 season, Clive Allen had what looked like a legitimate goal disallowed against Turkey as England only drew 0–0. He nearly scored for England and did score for just about everybody else, but LINEKER was around and anyway Bobby ROBSON didn't seem to rate him – the match in Istanbul was his first international for nearly three years.

HENRY ALLEN

b 19 Jan 1866   d 23 Feb 1895   CENTRE HALF

Caps: 5   Goals: 0   Own Goals: 1
First cap: 4 Feb 1888 v Wales 5–1   aged 22yr 16d
Last cap: 5 Apr 1890 v Scotland 1–1   aged 24yr 76d
England career: 2yr 60d – P5 W3 D1 L1 – 70%
Club: Wolves

Harry Allen seems to have scored Scotland's equaliser in 1889. Most yearbooks credit the goal to James Oswald, but *The Field* maintains that his shot was pushed out by MOON and came back off the centre half.

JAMES PHILLIPS ALLEN

b 16 Oct 1909   CENTRE HALF
Caps: 2   Goals: 0
First cap: 14 Oct 1933 v Ireland 3–0   aged 23yr 363d
Last cap: 15 Nov 1933 v Wales 1–2   aged 24yr 30d
England career: 0yr 32d – P2 W1 D0 L1 – 50%
Club: Portsmouth

Wales' big centre forward Dai Astley scored four goals against England; his first was a late winner at Newcastle in 1932, after Jim Allen had gone off injured, never to return.

RONALD ALLEN

b 15 Jan 1929   OUTSIDE RIGHT/CENTRE FORWARD
Caps: 5   Goals: 2
First cap: 28 May 1952 v Switzerland 3–0 aged 23yr 133d
Last cap: 1 Dec 1954 v W Germany 3–1 aged 25yr 320d
                                        (1 goal)
England career: 2yr 186d – P5 W4 D0 L1 – 80%
Club: West Bromwich Albion

Even before Hidegkuti came over to show how it was done, Ronnie Allen was a roving centre forward, dangerous and different – and misunderstood because of it. England might have built a team round him; instead, he and another free spirit, SHACKLETON, scored against the world champions at Wembley and were never picked again.

WALTER JOHN ALSFORD

b 6 Nov 1911   d 3 Jun 1968   LEFT HALF
Caps: 1   Goals: 0
Only cap: 6 Apr 1935 v Scotland 0–2   aged 23yr 151d
England career: P1 W0 D0 L1 – 0%
Club: Tottenham Hotspur

Walter Alsford was a stop-gap, COPPING and BRAY the regulars. Hampden Park in the thirties was no place for stop-gaps.

ANDREW
AMOS

b 20 Sep 1863   d 2 Oct 1931   **LEFT HALF**
Caps: 2   **Goals:** 1
First cap: 21 Mar 1885 v Scotland 1–1   aged 21yr 182d
Last cap: 29 Mar 1886 v Wales 3–1   aged 22yr 190d
     (1 goal)

England career: 1yr 8d – P2 W1 D1 L0 – 75%
Clubs: Old Carthusians, Cambridge Univ (& Corinthians)
Absent from most yearbooks' lists of international goalscorers, but it now seems likely that 'the giant Amos' and BRANN (who converted his corner kick) scored against Wales in 1886.

RUPERT DARNLEY
ANDERSON

b 29 April 1859   d 23 Dec 1944   **GOALKEEPER**
Caps: 1   **Goals conceded:** 0
Only cap: 18 Jan 1879 v Wales 2–1 aged 19yr 264d
England career: P1 W1 D0 L0 – 100%
Club: Old Etonians
One of the youngest players to keep goal for England (usually a forward in club football), he was capped when the Rev W Blackmore pulled out before the match. A snowbound pitch reduced his international career to a total of 60 minutes.

STANLEY
ANDERSON

b 27 Feb 1933   **RIGHT HALF**
Caps: 2   **Goals:** 0
First cap: 4 Apr 1962 v Austria 3–1   aged 29yr 36d
Last cap: 14 Apr 1962 v Scotland 0–2   aged 29yr 46d
England career: 0yr 10d – P2 W1 D0 L1 – 50%
Club: Sunderland
Note that the original Farror–Lamming books claimed Stan Anderson, the hard man's hard man, was born on 12 Dec 1933, while the revised Lamming edition goes along with Rothmans and their League Players' Records.

VIVIAN
ALEXANDER
ANDERSON

b 29 Aug 1956   **RIGHT BACK**
Caps: 30   **Goals:** 2
First cap: 29 Nov 1978 v Czechoslovakia 1–0
     aged 22yr 92d
Last cap: 24 May 1988 v Colombia 1–1   aged 31yr 269d
England career: 9yr 177d – P30 W16 D9 L5 – 68.33%
Clubs: Nottingham Forest (11), Arsenal (16)
     Manchester United (3)
Substituted: 1   **2 Goals in a game:** 0
Leggy and fiery, a class act, Viv Anderson suffered from that old managerial preference for

Phil NEAL. He was the first black player to win a full England cap.

JOHN
ANGUS

b 2 Sep 1938   **LEFT BACK**
Caps: 1   **Goals:** 0
Only cap: 27 May 1961 v Austria 1–3   aged 22yr 267d
England career: P1 W0 D0 L1 – 0%
Club: Burnley
Despite the scoreline, and the fact that his immediate opponent Horst Nemec scored the second, John Angus did nothing wrong in his only international, but he was never going to be anything more than Ray WILSON's stand-in.

JAMES
CHRISTOPHER
ARMFIELD

b 21 Sep 1935   **LEFT/RIGHT BACK**
Caps: 43   **Goals:** 0   **Captain:** 15
First cap: 13 May 1959 v Brazil 0–2   aged 23yr 131d
Last cap: 26 June 1966 v Finland 3–0   aged 30yr 175d
England career: 7yr 44d – P43 W23 D8 L12 – 62.79%
Club: Blackpool
Very quick, one of the first English overlappers and the best right back in the 1962 World Cup, Jimmy Armfield made his debut at the Maracana – out of position and facing the brilliant Julinho, who scored within two minutes. Things got better as he played in 31 consecutive internationals (1960–63) and became the natural leadership bridge between HAYNES and Bobby MOORE, captain in his last 14 matches.

GEORGE
HENRY
ARMITAGE

b 17 Jan 1898   d 28 Aug 1936   **CENTRE HALF**
Caps: 1   **Goals:** 0
Only cap: 24 Oct 1925 v Ireland 0–0   aged 27yr 280d
England career: P1 W0 D1 L0 – 50%
Club: Charlton Athletic
Seven players won their last England caps in Belfast: ASHTON, AUSTIN, BROMILOW, DORRELL, HOWARD BAKER, HUDSPETH – and George Armitage, whose inclusion made Charlton the first of only two Third Division clubs to provide three players for England (see RH HILL).

DAVID
ARMSTRONG

b 26 Dec 1954   **MIDFIELDER**

Caps: 3   Goals: 0
First cap: 31 May 1980 v Australia 2–1   aged 25yr 157d
                                            (sub'd 80min)
Last cap: 2 May 1984 v Wales 0–1   aged 29yr 128d
                                            (sub'd 77min)
England career: 3yr 337d – P3 W1 D0 L2 – 33.33%
Clubs: Middlesbrough (1), Southampton (2)
Substituted: 3

Has there ever been a less creative England midfield than GREGORY–WILKINS–LEE (v Denmark 1983)? How about Gregory–Wilkins–Lee–Armstrong (v Wales 1984)? Matches England never looked like saving.

KENNETH
ARMSTRONG

b 3 June 1924   **RIGHT HALF**
Caps: 1   Goals: 0
Only cap: 2 Apr 1955 v Scotland 7–2   aged 30yr 334d
England career: P1 W1 D0 L0 – 100%
Club: Chelsea

Walter Winterbottom says he wanted to give Ken Armstrong more caps but injury and the selection committee were against it. So he played 13 times for New Zealand instead. His son Ron played 27.

JOHN
ARNOLD

b 30 Nov 1907   d 3 April 1984   **OUTSIDE LEFT**
Caps: 1   Goals: 0
Only cap: 1 Apr 1933 v Scotland 1–2   aged 25yr 122d
England career: P1 W0 D0 L1 – 0%
Club: Fulham

John Arnold was a double international who was out of luck in both sports; just one cap in each, a defeat at Hampden on April Fools' Day and a duck in his first Test innings. He was later a first-class umpire.

WILLIAM JOHN
HERBERT
ARTHUR

b 14 Feb 1863   d 27 Nov 1930   **GOALKEEPER**
Caps: 7   Goals conceded: 4   Clean sheets: 3
First cap: 28 Feb 1885 v Ireland 4–0   aged 22yr 14d
Last cap: 26 Feb 1887 v Wales 4–0   aged 24yr 12d
England career: 1yr 363d – P7 W4 D3 L0 – 78.57%
Club: Blackburn Rovers

Overtook SWEPSTONE as the most capped England goalkeeper and was the first to keep three clean sheets. At one stage, he was listed as HJ Arthur, then JWH Arthur. He was known as Herbie. Or Herby. Definitely.

JAMES
ASHCROFT

b 12 Sep 1878   d 9 Apr 1943   **GOALKEEPER**
Caps: 3   Goals conceded: 2   Clean sheets: 2
First cap: 17 Feb 1906 v Ireland 5–0   aged 27yr 158d
Last cap: 7 Apr 1906 v Scotland 1–2   aged 27yr 207d
England career: 0yr 49d – P3 W2 D0 L1 – 66.66%
Club: Woolwich Arsenal

The first Arsenal player to be capped by England, Jimmy Ashcroft was dropped after conceding a controversial goal against Scotland – the force of Jimmie Howie's shot turned him round and the referee ruled that he'd carried the ball over the line.

GEORGE
SAMUEL AUSTIN
ASHMORE

b 5 May 1898   d 19 May 1973   **GOALKEEPER**
Caps: 1   Goals conceded: 3
Only cap: 24 May 1926 v Belgium 5–3   aged 28yr 19d
England career: P1 W1 D0 L0 – 100%
Club: West Bromwich Albion

It all happened to George Ashmore in May. Birth, death, international cap. Belgium weren't a strong team, but Raymond Braine was a fine player – he scored twice to force a 3–2 lead before England (and FR OSBORNE) forged ahead.

CLAUDE
THESIGER
ASHTON

b 19 Feb 1901   d 31 Oct 1942   **CENTRE FORWARD**
Caps: 1   Goals: 0   Captain: 1
Only cap: 24 Oct 1925 v Ireland 0–0   aged 24yr 247d
England career: P1 W0 D1 L0 – 50%
Club: Corinthians (& Old Wykehamists)

The last player to captain England in his only international, lucky to be capped at all ('he failed in giving cohesion to his line, and his shooting was weak'), Claude Ashton was born in Calcutta.

WILLIAM
ASHURST

b 4 May 1894   d 26 Jan 1947   **RIGHT BACK**
Caps: 5   Goals: 0
First cap: 21 May 1923 v Sweden 4–2   aged 29yr 17d
Last cap: 4 Apr 1925 v Scotland 0–2   aged 30yr 335d
England career: 1yr 318d – P5 W4 D0 L1 – 80%
Club: Notts County

Bill Ashurst was one of eight players whose international careers were ended by the result at Hampden: L GRAHAM, SEED, TUNSTALL and four Scots, Tommy Cairns, Phil McCloy, Willie

Russell and Dave Morris, the captain. Strange selectorial goings-on, not confined to south of the border.

GORDON ASTALL

b 22 Sep 1927   OUTSIDE RIGHT
Caps: 2   Goals: 1
First cap: 20 May 1956 v Finland 5–1   aged 28yr 241d
                                                  (1 goal)
Last cap: 26 May 1956 v W Germany 3–1 aged 28yr 247d
England career: 0yr 6d – P2 W2 D0 L0 – 100%
Club: Birmingham City

Chunky winger, capped when Sir Stan was unavailable for the summer tour, who put England 3–0 ahead in Helsinki.

JEFFREY ASTLE

b 13 May 1942   CENTRE FORWARD
Caps: 5   Goals: 0
First cap: 7 May 1969 v Wales 2–1   aged 26yr 359d
Last cap: 11 Jun 1970 v Czechoslovakia 1–0
                                             aged 28yr   29d
England career: 1yr 35d – P5 W3 D1 L1 – 70%
Club: West Bromwich Albion
Substitute: 1   Substituted: 1

Exceptional in the air for a man who wasn't particularly tall, Jeff made his famous televised miss against Brazil with the same foot that had blasted the only goal of the 1968 FA Cup Final.

JOHN ASTON

b 3 Sep 1921   LEFT/RIGHT BACK
Caps: 17   Goals: 0
First cap: 26 Sep 1948 v Denmark 0–0   aged 27yr 23d
Last cap: 7 Oct 1950 v N Ireland 4–1   aged 29yr 34d
England career: 2yr 11d – P17 W12 D1 L4 – 73.53%
Club: Manchester United

An inside-forward converted by Matt Busby into a cool, attacking full-back, Jack/Johnny Aston played 15 consecutive internationals (1948–50).

WILLIAM CHARLES ATHERSMITH

b 10 May 1872   d 18 Sep 1910   OUTSIDE RIGHT
Caps: 12   Goals: 3
First cap: 5 Mar 1892 v Ireland 2–0   aged 19yr 300d
Last cap: 7 Apr 1900 v Scotland 1–4   aged 27yr 333d
England career: 8yr 33d – P12 W9 D1 L2 – 79.16%
Club: Aston Villa
2 Goals in a game: 0

Charlie Athersmith, fast enough and good enough to win several caps during BASSETT's

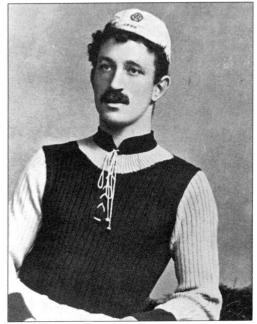

A model winger. WC Athersmith: style for the nineties
(Lamming)

reign, is generally credited with one goal out of the 13 scored against Ireland in 1899. The match report in the leading Belfast sports journal, *Ireland's Saturday Night*, credits him with two. It also goes against the majority of English Newspapers in crediting GO SMITH with only three and BLOOMER with only one.

Charlie was the most famous footballer to have once played for the Unity Gas Depot in Saltley.

PETER JOHN WALTER ATYEO

b 7 Feb 1932   INSIDE RIGHT
Caps: 6   Goals: 5
First cap: 30 Nov 1955 v Spain 4–1   aged 23yr 296d
                                                  (1 goal)
Last cap: 19 May 1957 v Eire 1–1   aged 25yr 101d
                                                  (1 goal)
England career: 1yr 170d – P6 W4 D2 L0 – 83.33%
Club: Bristol City
2 Goals in a game: 1   Penalties: 1   Missed: 1

Not a great international player, John Atyeo nevertheless brought his club scoring form to the England team. He scored after 11 minutes of his debut, and then in the last minute of both matches against Eire in 1957: at Wembley his second in a 5–1 win, and in Dublin the headed equaliser that sent England to the World Cup

Finals. After which he was dropped. Nothing new in that.

He and RW BYRNE had penalties saved by Gylmar of Brazil in 1956, the only time that has happened in an England match.

SIDNEY (SAMUEL?)
WILLIAM
AUSTIN

b 29 Apr 1900 d 2 Apr 1979 OUTSIDE RIGHT
Caps: 1 Goals: 0
Only cap: 24 Oct 1925 v Ireland 0–0 aged 25yr 178d
England career: P1 W0 D1 L0 – 50%
Club: Manchester City

Average winger, known as Sid. Or Sam.

PHILIP
BACH

b 1872 d 30 Dec 1937 FULL BACK
Caps: 1 Goals: 0
Only cap: 18 Feb 1899 v Ireland 13–2 aged 26/27
England career: P1 W1 D0 L0 – 100%
Club: Sunderland

Poacher turned gamekeeper – a player who deserved more caps, Phil Bach later became an international selector.

JOSEPH
WILLIAM
BACHE

b 8 Feb 1880 d 10 Nov 1960 INSIDE LEFT
Caps: 7 Goals: 4
First cap: 2 Mar 1903 v Wales 2–1 aged 23yr 22d
(1 goal)
Last cap: 1 Apr 1911 v Scotland 1–1 aged 31yr 52d
England career: 8yr 30d – P7 W4 D3 L0 – 78.57%
Club: Aston Villa
2 Goals in a game: 0

Joe Bache scored after 12 minutes of his debut and in each of his first four internationals, including the only goal of the game against Scotland in 1905.

THOMAS
BADDELEY

b 2 Nov 1874 d 24 Sep 1946 GOALKEEPER
Caps: 5 Goals conceded: 5 Clean sheets: 2
First cap: 14 Feb 1903 v Ireland 4–0 aged 28yr 104d
Last cap: 9 Apr 1904 v Scotland 1–0 aged 29yr 158d
England career: 1yr 54d – P5 W3 D1 L1 – 70%
Club: Wolves

Tom Baddeley was only 5ft 9in but very agile. The *Athletic News* says he was particularly brilliant against Scotland in 1903, despite the 2–1 defeat.

JOHN
JAMES
BAGSHAW

b 25 Dec 1885 d 25 Aug 1966 RIGHT HALF
Caps: 1 Goals: 0
Only cap: 25 Oct 1919 v Ireland 1–1 aged 33yr 304d
England career: P1 W0 D1 L0 – 50%
Club: Derby County

One of seven debutants in England's first match after the First World War, Jimmy Bagshaw was past his best when he had to mark tricky little Patsy Gallacher.

GARY
RICHARD
BAILEY

b 9 Aug 1958 GOALKEEPER
Caps: 2 Goals conceded: 2
First cap: 26 Mar 1985 v Eire 2–1 aged 26yr 229d
Last cap: 9 Jun 1985 v Mexico 0–1 aged 26yr 304d
England career: 0yr 75d – P2 W1 D0 L1 – 50%
Club: Manchester United

Gary Bailey's mistake allowed Liam Brady to score a late goal in his 50th international. A bad knee injury ruled out any hope of further caps.

HORACE PETER
BAILEY

b 3 Jul 1881 d 1 Aug 1960 GOALKEEPER
Caps: 5 Goals conceded: 3
First cap: 16 Mar 1908 v Wales 7–1 aged 26yr 257d
Last cap: 13 Jun 1908 v Bohemia 4–0 aged 26yr 346d
England career: 0yr 89d – P5 W5 D0 L0 – 100%
Club: Leicester Fosse
Penalties: 1 Missed: 1

Like earlier amateurs known by his initials rather than a christian name, HP came back from an easy European tour (in place of the great S HARDY) with a statistically perfect record, second only to HINE and W WILLIAMS.

MICHAEL
ALFRED
BAILEY

b 27 Feb 1942 RIGHT HALF
Caps: 2 Goals: 0
First cap: 27 May 1964 v USA 10–0 aged 22yr 90d
Last cap: 18 Nov 1964 v Wales 2–1 aged 22yr 265d
England career: 0yr 175d – P2 W2 D0 L0 – 100%
Club: Charlton Athletic

Later the driving captain of a successful Wolves team, Mike Bailey vied with MULLERY for the defensive midfield job after Sir Alf dispensed with MILNE.

NORMAN
COLES
BAILEY

b 23 Jul 1857   d 13 Jan 1923   HALF BACK
Caps: 19   Goals: 2   Captain: 15
First cap: 2 Mar 1878 v Scotland 2–7   aged 20yr 222d
Last cap: 19 Mar 1887 v Scotland 2–3   aged 29yr 239d
England career: 9yr 17d – P19 W8 D3 L8 – 50%
Club: Clapham Rovers & Old Westminsters: member of the
      Corinthians (1886–89)
Goals while captain: 1

In an age when most players won very, very few caps, Norman Bailey's run in the England team was almost freakish. He set all the main appearance and captaincy records: his 10th cap (1884) took him beyond MOSFORTH; his final total wasn't overhauled until GO SMITH was recalled for his 20th cap in 1901; he was the first to play 10 times against any one country (Scotland), the only one to do so before CROMPTON; and his total of matches as captain (his last 15 internationals) was also the record (but see GO SMITH) until the arrival of CROMPTON.

One of the original midfield workhorses, well-known for his long throws, his relatively mediocre statistical record while playing for England is explained by his 10 matches against infinitely superior Scotland teams (W1 D2 L7), which included defeats by 7–2 and 6–1.

EDWARD
FRANCIS
BAILY

b 6 Aug 1925   INSIDE LEFT
Caps: 9   Goals: 5
First cap: 2 July   1950 v Spain 0–1   aged 24yr 330d
Last cap: 4 Oct   1952 v N Ireland 2–2   aged 27yr 59d
England career: 2yr 94d – P9 W4 D4 L1 – 66.66%
Club: Tottenham Hotspur
2 Goals in a game: 2

Skilful little Eddie scored twice in each of two successive games against N Ireland and Wales immediately after the World Cup.

JOHN
BAIN

b 15 Jul 1854   d 7 Aug 1929   FORWARD
Caps: 1   Goals: 0
Only cap: 3 Mar 1877 v Scotland 1–3   aged 22yr 231d
England career: P1 W0 D0 L1 – 0%
Club: Oxford University (& probaby Old Wykehamists)

A forward in his only international, he played at right back in the 1877 FA Cup Final. He was the first England player born in Scotland (Bothwell, Lanarkshire).

ALFRED
BAKER

b 27 Apr 1898   d 1 Apr 1955   RIGHT HALF
Caps: 1   Goals: 0
Only cap: 28 Nov 1927 v Wales 1–2   aged 29yr 215d
England career: P1 W0 D0 L1 – 0%
Club: Arsenal

Arsenal's jack of all trades (often a right back, once even a goalkeeper), Alf Baker was part of a hotchpotch defence against Wales: two others (TREMELLING, R OSBORNE) were also winning their only caps.

JOSEPH
HENRY
BAKER

b 17 Jul 1940   CENTRE FORWARD
Caps: 8   Goals: 3
First cap: 18 Nov 1959 v N Ireland 2–1   aged 19yr 123d
                                              (1 goal)
Last cap: 5 Jan 1966 v Poland 1–1   aged 25yr 172d
England career: 6yr 48d – P8 W3 D3 L2 – 56.25%
Clubs: Hibernian (5), Arsenal (3)
2 Goals in a game: 0   Substituted: 1

The first player to be capped by England while playing for a club from outside the Football League, Joe Baker had to wait more than five years for his seventh cap. He was substituted by N HUNTER after having scored against Spain in 1965.

ALAN
JAMES
BALL

b 12 May 1945   MIDFIELDER
Caps: 72   Goals: 8   Captain: 6
First cap: 9 May 1965 v Yugoslavia 1–1 aged 19yr 362d
Last cap: 24 May 1975 v Scotland 5–1   aged 30yr 12d
England career: 10yr 15d – P72 W46 D18 L18 – 76.38%
Clubs: Blackpool (14), Everton (39), Arsenal (33)
Substitute: 3   Substituted: 1
2 Goals in a game: 1   Goals while captain: 0
Penalties: 2   Missed: 1

Probably England's decisive player in the World Cup Final, Alan Ball was suddenly made captain by REVIE in his last six internationals, then just as abruptly dropped. Against Poland in 1973, he became the second player to be sent off (see MULLERY) while playing for the full England team; and, following his dismissal in the Under-23 match in Vienna in 1965, the only player to be sent off twice in England colours. He scored from the penalty spot against Wales in 1967 after missing against Finland the previous year.

In 1972 Farror & Lamming listed his birthday as 5 May; no doubt a simple misprint.

JOHN BALL

b 29 Sep 1899/1900   d unknown   INSIDE LEFT/GOALKEEPER
Caps: 1   Goals: 0   Goals conceded: 1
Only cap: 22 Oct 1927 v Ireland 0–2   aged 27/28yr 23d
England career: P1 W0 D0 L1 – 0%
Club: Bury

Jack Ball went in goal at half-time after HUF-TON's wrist injury, let in only Jackie Mahood's goal, and was never chosen again. He was the last to play outfield and in goal for England.

WILLIAM BALMER

b 1877   d unknown   RIGHT BACK
Caps: 1   Goals: 0
Only cap: 25 Feb 1905 v Ireland 1–1   aged 27/28
England career: P1 W0 D1 L0 – 50%
Club: Everton

One of Everton's leading players at the time, he came from a well-known footballing family (one of 'two great brothers'), which makes it strange that there should be any argument about his christian name. Books about Everton (by John Roberts and Stephen Kelly) call him Walter, whereas anything dealing with England players tends to say Billy (Jon Silk, Nick Gibbs), although this may just be following Douglas Lamming's lead – in his 1972 book, he calls him William, and doesn't change his mind in the 1990 revision. Billy seems more likely, especially as it's backed up by the Sheffield *Daily Telegraph* of 20 April 1907.

JOHN BAMBER

b 11 Apr 1895   d 1971   RIGHT HALF
Caps: 1   Goals: 0
Only cap: 14 Mar 1921 v Wales 0–0   aged 25yr 337d
England career: P1 W0 D1 L0 – 50%
Club: Liverpool

One of seven players making their debut at Ninian Park (see BROMILOW), Jack Bamber had a good game against Everton's Stan Davies and would probably have been capped again but for injury.

ARTHUR LEOPOLD BAMBRIDGE

b 16 Jun 1861   d 27 Nov 1923   LEFT BACK/FORWARD
Caps: 3   Goals: 1
First cap: 26 Feb 1881 v Wales 0–1   aged 19yr 265d

Last cap: 23 Feb 1884 v Ireland 8–1   aged 22yr 262d
(1 goal)
England career: 2yr 362d – P3 W2 D0 L1 – 66.66%
Club: Swifts (& Corinthians)

Arthur and EC BAMBRIDGE were the first brothers to score in the same match for England. Another brother, EH BAMBRIDGE, was also an international.

EDWARD CHARLES BAMBRIDGE

b 30 Jul 1858   d 8 Nov 1935   OUTSIDE/INSIDE LEFT
Caps: 18   Goals: 11   Captain: 2
First cap: 5 Apr 1879 v Scotland 5–4   aged 20yr 249d
(2 goals)
Last cap: 19 Mar 1887 v Scotland 2–3   aged 28yr 232d
England career: 7yr 348d – P18 W9 D3 L6 – 58.33%
Clubs: Swifts (13), Swifts & Corinthians (5)
3 Goals in a game: 0   2 Goals in a game: 3
Goals while captain: 1

A fast and famous winger, the first player to score 10 goals for England, Charlie Bam scored in each of eight successive seasons (1878–79 to 1885–86), unsurpassed until R CHARLTON in 1965–66. His finest hour was his first international, when England were 4–1 down at half-time. His run from halfway, rounding the keeper to pull one back, changed everything; his second goal, in the last few minutes, was the winner.

ERNEST HENRY BAMBRIDGE

b 16 May 1848   d 16 Oct 1917   FORWARD
Caps: 1   Goals: 0
Only cap: 4 Mar 1876 v Scotland 0–3   aged 27yr 292d
England career: P1 W0 D0 L1 – 0%
Club: Swifts & Corinthians

Apparently the least talented of the three brothers. The first to be capped.

GORDON BANKS

b 30 Dec 1937   GOALKEEPER
Caps: 73   Goals conceded: 57   Clean sheets: 35
First cap: 6 Apr 1963 v Scotland 1–2   aged 25yr 97d
Last cap: 27 May 1972 v Scotland 1–0   aged 34yr 148d
England career: 9yr 51d – P73 W49 D15 L9 – 77.40%
Clubs: Leicester City (37), Stoke City (36)
Penalties: 5   Saved: 1

Only SHILTON, his understudy at Leicester, challenged Fernandel's goalkeeping records and his claim to have been England's best ever. Banks was the first to play more than 33 times and the first to keep more than 10 clean sheets. He still holds the England record of 7 clean sheets in a row, finally ended only by Eusebio's late penalty in the World Cup semi-final, which also cut short the England record of 707 minutes without conceding a goal, to which SPRINGETT and BONETTI contributed. He played in 23 consecutive internationals without defeat (1964–67).

He was beaten from the penalty spot by Eusebio and (on his debut) Jim Baxter, who both sent him the wrong way; got both hands to Netzer's kick that went in off a post; and saved from Carlos Alberto as England nearly held out in Rio in 1969. Oh, and he fumbled Peter Ducke's long shot for East Germany in 1963, the 500th goal conceded by England. A rare mistake. A great keeper. The save from Pele a kind of tribute to both.

HERBERT
ERNEST
BANKS

b 1874   d 1947   **INSIDE LEFT**
Caps: 1   **Goals:** 0
Only cap: 9 Mar 1901 v Ireland 3–0   aged 26/27
England career: P1 W1 D0 L0 – 100%
Club: Millwall Athletic

Twelve players won their first caps at The Dell; eight of them didn't win a second, including big Herbert.

THOMAS
BANKS

b 10 Nov 1929   **LEFT BACK**
Caps: 6   **Goals:** 0
First cap: 18 May 1958 v USSR 1–1   aged 28yr 189d
Last cap: 4 Oct 1958 v N Ireland 3–3   aged 28yr 328d
England career: 0yr 139d – P6 W0 D5 L1 – 41.66%
Club: Bolton Wanderers

Tough (very tough) Tommy Banks was the only player to appear in six England matches without once being on the winning side.

WILLIAM
BANNISTER

b 1879   d 26 Mar 1942   **CENTRE HALF**
Caps: 2   **Goals:** 0
First cap: 18 Mar 1901 v Wales 6–0   aged 21/22
Last cap: 22 Mar 1902 v Ireland 1–0   aged 22/23
England career: 1yr 4d – P2 W2 D0 L0 –100 %
Clubs: Burnley (1), Bolton Wanderers (1)

Billy Bannister, 'a rattling man', won his first cap when the original choice FRANK FORMAN dropped out through injury.

ROBERT
BARCLAY

b 27 Oct 1906/7   d 13 Jul 1969   **INSIDE RIGHT**
Caps: 3   **Goals:** 2
First cap: 9 Apr 1932 v Scotland 3–0 aged 24/25yr 165d
                                     (1 goal)
Last cap: 4 Apr 1936 v Scotland 1–1 aged 28/28yr 160d
England career: 3yr 360d – P3 W2 D1 L0 – 83.33%
Club: Sheffield United

Bobby Barclay scored in each of his first two internationals (a virtual own goal by Allan Craig and the only goal of the match against Ireland). Had to wait more than three years for his last cap.

MARK
FRANCIS
BARHAM

b 12 Jul 1962   **OUTSIDE RIGHT**
Caps: 2   **Goals:** 0
First cap: 12 Jun 1983 v Australia 0–0   aged 20yr 335d
Last cap: 15 Jun 1983 v Australia 1–0   aged 20yr 338d
England career: 0yr 3d – P2 W1 D1 L0 – 75%
Club: Norwich City

A 'B' team went to Australia, had three woeful results, and came back with full caps, Mark Barham among them.

SAMUEL
BARKAS

b 29 Dec 1909   d 10 Dec 1989
                      INSIDE RIGHT/LEFT BACK
Caps: 5   **Goals:** 0
First cap: 9 May 1936 v Belgium 2–3   aged 26yr 132d
Last cap: 1 Dec 1937 v Czechoslovakia 5–4
                                 aged 27yr 337d
England career: 1yr 206d – P5 W3 D0 L2 – 60%
Club: Manchester City

Sam Barkas was good enough at left back to be capped while HAPGOOD was at his peak, though he actually made his debut at inside right on England's clumsy summer tour. He was on the losing side in his first two internationals and a winning captain in his last three.

JOHN
WILLIAM
BARKER

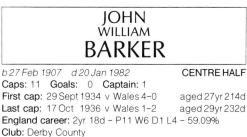

b 27 Feb 1907   d 20 Jan 1982   **CENTRE HALF**
Caps: 11   **Goals:** 0   **Captain:** 1
First cap: 29 Sept 1934 v Wales 4–0   aged 27yr 214d
Last cap: 17 Oct 1936 v Wales 1–2   aged 29yr 232d
England career: 2yr 18d – P11 W6 D1 L4 – 59.09%
Club: Derby County

Dominant, very highly rated, Jack Barker was captain in his last international.

ROBERT C
BARKER

b 19 Jun 1847   d 11 Nov 1915   KEEPER/FORWARD
Caps: 1   Goals: 0   Goals conceded: 0   Clean Sheets: 1
Only cap: 30 Nov 1872 v Scotland 0–0   aged 25yr 165d
England career: P1 W0 D1 L0 – 50%
Club: Hertfordshire Rangers (& Wanderers)

England's first ever goalkeeper. Most yearbooks list MAYNARD, but contemporary reports are quite clear about it: Barker started in goal then changed places with Maynard during the second half. Odd, because they were both forwards. Barker was probably put in goal because he was apparently the biggest and slowest in the team – he'd been a rugby player at school.

RICHARD RAINE
BARKER

b 29 May 1869   d 1 Oct 1940   HALF BACK
Caps: 1   Goals: 0
Only cap: 18 Mar 1895 v Wales 1–1   aged 25yr 293d
England career: P1 W0 D1 L0 – 50%
Club: Casuals (& Corinthians)

Barker ('much too slow for an international'), STANBROUGH and G DEWHURST made their debuts – and sank without trace.

RAYMOND
JOHN
BARLOW

b 17 Aug 1926   LEFT HALF
Caps: 1   Goals: 0
Only cap: 2 Oct 1954 v N Ireland 2–0   aged 28yr 46d
England career: P1 W1 D0 L0 – 100%
Club: West Bromwich Albion

A class act without a stage. Ray Barlow was kept out of the England team by the favoured double bill of DICKINSON and EDWARDS.

JOHN
CHARLES BRYAN
BARNES

b 7 Nov 1963   OUTSIDE LEFT
Caps: 65   Goals: 10
First cap: 28 May 1983 v N Ireland 0–0   aged 19yr 222d
(sub 66min)

Half-time approaches at the Maracana as John Barnes (11) turns after scoring his very Brazilian goal in 1984
(Bob Thomas)

Last cap: 25 May 1991 v Argentina 2–2   aged 27yr 219d
(sub'd 63min)
England career: 7yr 362d – P65 W29 D22 L14 – 61.54%
Clubs: Watford (31), Liverpool (34)
Substitute: 13   **Substituted:** 12   **2 Goals in a game:** 2

Figures seem to support the John Barnes Never Does It For England school – not enough wins, not too many goals scored (by him or the team), anonymous in the World Cup, invisible in the European Championships. But 4–4–2 had a lot to answer for, forcing one of the most talented players England have ever had had into a tiring, cramping, semi-defensive role, making him neither fish nor fowl. He's the most skilful of fish for Liverpool, where he doesn't have to constantly live up to that outrageous goal in the Maracana.

PETER
SIMON
BARNES

b 10 Jun 1957   OUTSIDE LEFT
Caps: 22   **Goals:** 4
First cap: 16 Nov 1977 v Italy 2–0   aged 20yr 159d
Last cap: 25 May 1982 v Holland 2–0   aged 24yr 349d
(sub 82min)
England career: 4yr 190d – P22 W12 D3 L7 – 61.36%
Clubs: Manchester City (20), Leeds United (2)
Substitute: 4   **Substituted:** 3   **2 Goals in a game:** 0

Ron Greenwood stuck by Peter Barnes almost to the end. A very direct (as in headlong) winger who once promised a lot for England.

HORACE
HUTTON
BARNET

b 6 Mar 1856   d 29 Mar 1941   FORWARD
Caps: 1   **Goals:** 0
Only cap: 18 Feb 1882 v Ireland 13–0   aged 25yr 349d
England career: P1 W1 D0 L0 – 100%
Club: Royal Engineers (& Corinthians)

Six forwards played against the woeful Irish first-timers; only one didn't score – or play for England again.

MALCOLM
WILLIAMSON
BARRASS

b 13 Dec 1924   CENTRE HALF
Caps: 3   **Goals:** 0
First cap: 20 Oct 1951 v Wales 1–1   aged 26yr 311d
Last cap: 18 Apr 1953 v Scotland 2–2   aged 28yr 126d
England career: 1yr 180d – P3 W1 D2 L0 – 66.66%
Club: Bolton Wanderers

Malcolm Barrass kept Trevor Ford goalless in his first international, but couldn't stop Laurie Reilly scoring twice in his last.

ALBERT
FRANK
BARRETT

b 11 Nov 1903   d ?   LEFT HALF
Caps: 1   **Goals:** 0
Only cap: 19 Oct 1929 v Ireland 3–0   aged 25yr 342d
England career: P1 W1 D0 L0 – 100%
Club: Fulham

Not to be confused with JW Barrett, who played against the same country almost exactly a year earlier, this was the next Fulham player after OLIVER to be capped by England; they were both in the Third Division at the time.

EARL
BARRETT

b 28 Apr 1967   CENTRAL DEFENDER
Caps: 1   **Goals:** 0
Only cap: 3 Jun 1991 v N Zealand 1–0   aged 24yr 36d
England career: P1 W1 D0 L0 – 100%
Club: Oldham Athletic

Very quick, looked the part especially in Oldham's high-profile 1989–90 season.

JAMES
WILLIAM
BARRETT

b 19 Jan 1907   d 25/26 Nov 1970   CENTRE HALF
Caps: 1   **Goals:** 0
Only cap: 22 Oct 1928 v Ireland 2–1   aged 21yr 277d
England career: P1 W1 D0 L0 – 100%
Club: West Ham United

An old knee injury flared up and left Jimmy Barrett with the shortest England career of all (matched only by PD WARD): just the first eight minutes at Goodison Park. He was young enough to come back, but perhaps his weight (he was between 14 and 15 stone) began to tell against him.

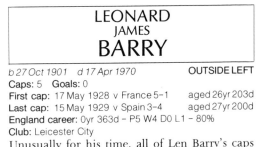

LEONARD
JAMES
BARRY

b 27 Oct 1901   d 17 Apr 1970   OUTSIDE LEFT
Caps: 5   **Goals:** 0
First cap: 17 May 1928 v France 5–1   aged 26yr 203d
Last cap: 15 May 1929 v Spain 3–4   aged 27yr 200d
England career: 0yr 363d – P5 W4 D0 L1 – 80%
Club: Leicester City

Unusually for his time, all of Len Barry's caps were won against continental opposition.

FRANK
BARSON

b 10 Apr 1891   d 13 Sep 1968 **CENTRE HALF**
Caps: 1   Goals: 0
Only cap: 15 Mar 1920 v Wales 1–2   aged 28yr 339d
England career: P1 W0 D0 L1 – 0%
Club: Aston Villa

Frank Barson was often in trouble with referees and other figures of authority. England's first defeat by Wales for 38 years may have been a good excuse to drop him.

JOHN
BARTON

b 5 Oct 1866   d 22 Apr 1910 **RIGHT HALF**
Caps: 1   Goals: 1?
Only cap: 15 Mar 1890 v Ireland 9–1   aged 23yr 164d
                                            (1? goal)
England career: P1 W1 D0 L0 – 100%
Club: Blackburn Rovers

Some reports credit Jack Barton with England's ninth goal, two minutes from time. Others don't. And anyway the Irish players claimed the ball had gone over the bar. It was that kind of match.

PERCIVAL
HARRY
BARTON

b 19 Aug 1895   d Oct 1961 **LEFT HALF**
Caps: 7   Goals: 0
First cap: 21 May 1921 v Belgium 2–0   aged 25yr 275d
Last cap: 22 Oct 1924 v Ireland 3–1   aged 29yr 64d
England career: 3yr 154d – P7 W3 D3 L1 – 64.29%
Club: Birmingham FC

Good in the tackle, rather anonymous in midfield, Percy Barton won his share of caps in an unsettled age: he had eight different half-back partners.

WILLIAM
ISAIAH
BASSETT

b 27 Jan 1869   d 8 Apr 1937 **OUTSIDE RIGHT**
Caps: 16   Goals: 7
First cap: 7 Apr 1888 v Ireland 5–1   aged 19yr 70d
Last cap: 4 Apr 1896 v Scotland 1–2   aged 27yr 67d
                                            (1 goal)
England career: 7yr 362d – P16 W12 D2 L2 – 81.25%
Club: West Bromwich Albion   2 Goals in a game: 0

Very small but strongly built, quick and elusive, he scored his share of goals from the wing and made many others, including three in ten minutes to turn a match Scotland were leading 2–1 in 1893; one of the most important players in England's most successful era.

SEGAL RICHARD
BASTARD

b 25 Jan 1854   d 20 Mar 1921 **OUTSIDE RIGHT**
Caps: 1   Goals: 0
Only cap: 13 Mar 1880 v Scotland 4–5   aged 26yr 48d
England career: P1 W0 D0 L1 – 0%
Club: Upton Park

In 1879 he'd refereed the first ever England–Wales match. In 1880 he umpired the second England–Wales match. He was the fourth England player (after ALCOCK, MORTEN AND GHH HERON) to officiate in England matches. He had a lovely name for a referee – though note that the 1972 Farror-Lamming book spelled it Segar . . .

CLIFFORD
SYDNEY
BASTIN

b 14 Mar 1912 **OUTSIDE/INSIDE LEFT**
Caps: 21   Goals: 12
First cap: 18 Nov 1931 v Wales 3–1   aged 19yr 249d
Last cap: 26 May 1938 v France 4–2   aged 26yr 73d
                                            (1 pen)
England career: 6yr 184d – P21 W10 D2 L9 – 52.38%
Club: Arsenal
Hat-tricks: 0   2 Goals in a game : 2
Penalties: 2   Missed: 0

Before the tournament, Hugo Meisl, Austria's famous manager, said his team wouldn't win the 1934 World Cup, but if he were allowed to include the one foreign player he had in mind . . .

On and off, Cliff Bastin *was* the left side of England's attack throughout the thirties, sharing the bad days as well as the good (the myth of English superiority was constantly punctured in matches abroad), his standards slipping only when deafness began to creep in. He missed a hat-trick against Switzerland in 1933 only when a second-half goal was disallowed.

DAVID
BATTY

b 2 Dec 1968 **MIDFIELDER**
Caps: 5   Goals: 0
First cap: 21 May 1991 v USSR 3–1   aged 22yr 170d
                                            (sub 70min)
Last cap: 12 Jun 1991 v Malaysia 4–2   aged 22yr 192d
England career: 0yr 22d – P5 W4 D1 L0 – 90%
Club: Leeds United
Substitute: 1   Substituted: 1

No shortage of red meat in Leeds. A limb-nibbler in the Norman Hunter mould.

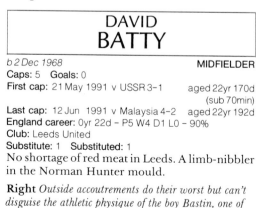

Right *Outside accoutrements do their worst but can't disguise the athletic physique of the boy Bastin, one of the great wingers* (Lamming)

RICHARD
BAUGH

b 14 Feb 1864   d 14 Aug 1929   **RIGHT BACK**
Caps: 2   Goals: 0
First cap: 13 Mar 1886 v Ireland 6–1   aged 22yr 27d
Last cap: 15 Mar 1890 v Ireland 9–0   aged 26yr 29d
England career: 4yr 2d – P2 W2 D0 L0 – 100%
Clubs: Stafford Road (1), Wolves (1)
On the same day that an amateur England team beat Wales 3–1, Dick Baugh (a late replacement for the captain Bob HOWARTH) won his last cap as part of an all-professional side in Belfast.

ALBERT EDWARD
JAMES
MATTHIAS
BAYLISS

b Aug 1863   d 19 Aug 1933   **RIGHT HALF**
Caps: 1   Goals: 0
Only cap: 7 Mar 1891 v Ireland 6–1   aged 27yr 188–218d
England career: P1 W1 D0 L0 – 100%
Club: West Bromwich Albion
Won his cap at half back, but was usually a forward. He was known as Jem, which has been explained as the sum of three of his initials; in fact, Jem was a common enough diminutive of James.

RONALD LESLIE
BAYNHAM

b 10 Jun 1929   **GOALKEEPER**
Caps: 3   Goals conceded: 2   Clean sheets: 1
First cap: 2 Oct   1955 v Denmark 5–1   aged 26yr 114d
Last cap: 30 Nov 1955 v Spain 4–1   aged 26yr 173d
England career: 0yr 59d – P3 W3 D0 L0 – 100%
Club: Luton Town
A good goalkeeper in an age of very good ones, Ron Baynham was capped after Bert WILLIAMS was dropped, did nothing very wrong in his three games, then was replaced by a Third Division player, Reg MATTHEWS.

PETER
ANDREW
BEARDSLEY

b 18 Jan 1961   **FORWARD**
Caps: 49   Goals: 7   Captain: 1
First cap: 29 Jan 1986 v Egypt 4–0   aged 25yr   11d
(sub 50min)
Last cap: 21 May 1991 v USSR 3–1   aged 30yr 123d
(sub 70min)
England career: 5yr 112d – P49 W25 D17 L7 – 68.37%
Clubs: Newcastle United (15), Liverpool (34)
Substitute: 11   Substituted: 16   2 Goals in a game: 1
Goals as substitute: 1   Goals while captain: 0

Peter Beardsley's never scored enough goals for England, but he's spoonfed LINEKER with a few (v Brazil, Colombia, Switzerland etc). A tendency to fade out of a game, but when he's in it he can still win it.

DAVID
JOHN
BEASANT

b 20 Mar 1959   GOALKEEPER
Caps: 2   Goals conceded: 0
First cap: 15 Nov 1989 v Italy 0–0   aged 30yr 240d
                                        (sub HT)
Last cap: 13 Dec 1989 v Yugoslavia 2–1 aged 30yr 268d
                                        (sub HT)
England career: 0yr 28d – P2 W1 D1 L0 – 75%
Club: Chelsea
Substitute: 2

Several goalkeepers didn't concede a goal while playing for England, but only two, HOWARD BAKER and Beasant, played as many as two games (in big Dave's case, half that). He saved a penalty in the 1988 FA Cup Final, and a very bold (last-minute?) substitution might have seen him facing a few in the World Cup semi . . .

ALBERT
BEASLEY

b 16 Jul 1913   d Feb 1986   OUTSIDE LEFT
Caps: 1   Goals: 1
Only cap: 15 Apr 1939 v Scotland 2–1   aged 25yr 293d
England career: P1 W1 D0 L0 – 100%
Club: Huddersfield

After the other new cap, Jimmy Dougall, had given Scotland the lead at Hampden, 'Pat' Beasley equalised.

WILLIAM
EDWIN
BEATS

b 13 Nov 1871   d 13 Apr 1939   CENTRE FORWARD
Caps: 2   Goals: 0
First cap: 18 Mar 1901 v Wales 6–0   aged 29yr 125d
Last cap: 3 May 1902 v Scotland 2–2   aged 30yr 171d
England career: 1yr 46d – P2 W1 D1 L0 – 75%
Club: Wolves

Billy Beats was known as an unselfish leader of the line, and in his first international his inside-forwards scored five between them (BLOOMER 4, RE FOSTER).

THOMAS
KEVIN
BEATTIE

b 18 Dec 1953   CENTRE HALF/LEFT BACK

Caps: 9   Goals: 1
First cap: 16 Apr 1975 v Cyprus 5–0   aged 21yr 119d
Last cap: 12 Oct 1977 v Luxembourg 2–0 aged 23yr 298d
                                      (sub 68min)
England career: 2yr 179d – P9 W6 D1 L2 – 72.22%
Club: Ipswich Town
Substitute: 2   Substituted: 1

Injury-prone, but once many people's idea of The New Duncan Edwards . . .

FRANCIS
BECTON

b 1873   d 6 Nov 1909   INSIDE LEFT
Caps: 2   Goals: 2
First cap: 9 Mar 1895 v Ireland 9–0   aged 21/22
                                        (2 goals)
Last cap: 29 Mar 1897 v Wales 4–0   aged 23/24
England career: 2yr 20d – P2 W2 D0 L0 – 100%
Clubs: Preston NE (1), Liverpool (1)
2 Goals in a game: 1

Frank Becton made his international debut in the same match as BLOOMER, and matched the great goalscorer goal for goal.

HENRY
BEDFORD

b 15 Oct 1899   d 24 Jun 1976   CENTRE FORWARD
Caps: 2   Goals: 1
First cap: 21 May 1923 v Sweden 4–2   aged 23yr 218d
Last cap: 22 Oct 1924 v Ireland 3–1   aged 25yr 7d
                                        (1 goal)
England career: 1yr 154d – P2 W2 D0 L0 – 100%
Club: Blackpool

After Harry Bedford had put England 2–0 ahead, Billy Gillespie replied for Ireland, the fifth match in which he'd scored against England. While Bedford was never picked again, Gillespie scored in a record sixth match in 1926.

COLIN
BELL

b 26 Feb 1946   MIDFIELDER
Caps: 48   Goals: 9   Captain: 1
First cap: 22 May 1968 v Sweden 3–1   aged 22yr 86d
Last cap: 30 Oct 1975 v Czechoslovakia 1–2
                                        aged 29yr 247d
England career: 7yr 161d – P48 W26 D12 L10 – 66.66%
Club: Manchester City
Substitute: 3   Substituted: 1
2 Goals in a game: 1   Goals while captain: 0

Hard-running midfielder ('Nijinsky') who was at last beginning to do well for England before injury. Scored twice in REVIE's first match in charge.

WALTER
BENNETT

b 1874   d 6 Apr 1908   OUTSIDE RIGHT
Caps: 2   **Goals:** 0
First cap: 18 Mar 1901 v Wales 6-0   aged 26/27
Last cap: 30 Mar 1901 v Scotland 2-2   aged 26/27
England career: 0yr 12d – P2 W1 D1 L0 – 75%
Club: Sheffield United

Thumping winger who didn't score the expected goals for England when faced by two high-class left backs: Wales' captain Charlie Morris and the fearsome Jock Drummond.

ROBERT
WILLIAM
BENSON

b 9 Feb 1883   d 19 Feb 1916   LEFT BACK
Caps: 1   **Goals:** 0
Only cap: 15 Feb 1913 v Ireland 1-2   aged 30yr 6d
England career: P1 W0 D0 L1 – 0%
Club: Sheffield United

A player of average height who weighed 14 stone, Bobby Benson died while playing in a wartime match at Highbury.

ROY
THOMAS FRANK
BENTLEY

b 17 May 1924
               CENTRE FORWARD/INSIDE LEFT/RIGHT
Caps: 12   **Goals:** 9
First cap: 13 May 1949 v Sweden 1-3   aged 24yr 361d
Last cap: 22 May 1955 v Portugal 1-3   aged 31yr 5d
                                             (1 goal)
England career: 6yr 9d – P12 W8 D1 L3 – 70.83%
Club: Chelsea
3 Goals in a game: 1   **2 Goals in a game:** 0

They didn't quite know what to do with Roy Bentley; three different positions, caps scattered over six years. Nevertheless he had his moments: a hat-trick against Wales in 1954 made him the first England player to score all three in a match.

JOSEPH
BERESFORD

b 26 Feb 1906   d 1978   INSIDE RIGHT
Caps: 1   **Goals:** 0
Only cap: 16 May 1934 v Czechoslovakia 1-2
                                             aged 28yr 79d
England career: P1 W0 D0 L1 – 0%
Club: Aston Villa

Czechoslovakia reached the World Cup Final a few weeks later. Planicka, Nejedly and Puc were giants of their day. Joe Beresford was 5 foot 5.

ARTHUR
BERRY

b 3 Jan 1888   d 15 Mar 1953   OUTSIDE RIGHT
Caps: 1   **Goals:** 0
Only cap: 13 Feb 1909 v Ireland 4-0 aged 21yr 41d
England career: P1 W1 D0 L0 – 100%
Club: Oxford University

Part of the United Kingdom team that won the 1912 Olympic gold medal.

JOHN
JAMES
BERRY

b 1 June 1926   OUTSIDE LEFT/RIGHT
Caps: 4   **Goals:** 0
First cap: 17 May 1953 v Argentina 0-0   aged 26yr 350d
Last cap: 16 May 1956 v Sweden 0-0   aged 29yr 350d
England career: 2yr 365d – P4 W1 D2 L1 – 50%
Club: Manchester United

A classic small tricky winger, Johnny Berry played well on England's South American tour in 1953 and survived the Munich air crash, though it ended his career.

JOHN
GILBERT
BESTALL

b 24 Jun 1900   d 11 Apr 1985   INSIDE RIGHT
Caps: 1   **Goals:** 0
Only cap: 6 Feb 1935 v Ireland 2-1 aged 34yr 227d
England career: P1 W1 D0 L0 – 100%
Club: Grimsby Town

Only HUDSPETH, COMPTON and perhaps MORTEN were older than Jackie Bestall when making their England debuts. Only WALDEN and possibly JF CRAWFORD were smaller.

HARRY
BETMEAD

b 11 Apr 1912   d 26 Aug 1984   CENTRE HALF
Caps: 1   **Goals:** 0
Only cap: 20 May 1937 v Finland 8-0 aged 25yr 39d
England career: P1 W1 D0 L0 – 100%
Club: Grimsby Town

Had an easy time in Helsinki, protected by the likes of WOODLEY, MALE, HAPGOOD and COPPING.

MORTON
PETO
BETTS

b 30 Aug 1847   d 19 Apr 1914   GOALKEEPER
Caps: 1   **Goals conceded:** 3

Only cap: 3 Mar 1877 v Scotland 1–3 aged 29yr 185d
England career: P1 W0 D0 L1 – 0%
Club: Old Harrovians (& Wanderers)
Played in goal in his only international, was often a full back, and scored the only goal in the first FA Cup Final while playing up front.

WILLIAM
BETTS

b 1864   d 8 Aug 1941   LEFT HALF
Caps: 1   Goals: 0
Only cap: 23 Feb 1889 v Wales 4–1 aged 24/25
England career: P1 W1 D0 L0 – 100%
Club: Sheffield Wednesday
Tough little Billy was often centre half in club football, but was capped on the left when the original choice WEIR dropped out.

JOSEPH
BEVERLEY

b 12 Nov 1856   d 21 May 1897   FULL BACK
Caps: 3   Goals: 0
First cap: 23 Feb 1884 v Ireland 8–1   aged 27yr 103d
Last cap: 17 Mar 1884 v Wales 4–0   aged 27yr 126d
England career: 0yr 23d – P3 W2 D0 L1 – 66.66%
Club: Blackburn Rovers
Left-back in his England matches, Joe Beverley was on the right in the 1884 FA Cup Final.

RALPH
JAMES EVANS
BIRKETT

b 9 Jan 1913/14   OUTSIDE RIGHT
Caps: 1   Goals: 1
Only cap: 19 Oct 1935 v Ireland 3–1 aged 21/22yr 283d
                                          (1 goal)
England career: P1 W1 D0 L0 – 100%
Club: Middlesbrough
Most modern yearbooks do Ralph Birkett no favours, crediting TILSON with two goals in Belfast. But contemporary match reports vary; he and not Fred T may have equalised after 18 minutes of the second half. He was chosen for the next match, against Germany at White Hart Lane, only to be injured and replaced by one S MATTHEWS.

REGINALD HALSEY
BIRKETT

b 28 Mar 1849   d 30 Jun 1898   GOALKEEPER
Caps: 1   Goals conceded: 4
Only cap: 5 Apr 1879 v Scotland 5–4 aged 30yr 8d
England career: P1 W1 D0 L0 – 100%
Club: Clapham Rovers
The first football international to play rugby

union for England. His son and brother were also rugby union internationals.

FRANCIS HORNBY
BIRLEY

b 14 Mar 1850   d 1 Aug 1910   HALF BACK
Caps: 2   Goals: 0
First cap: 7 Mar 1874 v Scotland 1–2   aged 23yr 358d
Last cap: 6 Mar 1875 v Scotland 2–2   aged 24yr 357d
England career: 0yr 364d – P2 W0 D1 L1 – 25%
Clubs: Oxford University (1), Wanderers (1)
May have been a member of the Wanderers as well as his university club in 1874.

GARRY
BIRTLES

b 27 Jul 1956   FORWARD
Caps: 3   Goals: 0
First cap: 13 May 1980 v Argentina 3–1   aged 23yr 304d
                                          (sub 76min)
Last cap: 15 Oct 1980 v Romania 1–2   aged 24yr 80d
                                          (sub'd 65min)
England career: 0yr 155d – P3 W1 D0 L2 – 33.33%
Club: Nottingham Forest
Substitute: 1   Substituted: 2
Had done well enough in that season's European Cup for Greenwood to gamble on him against Italy in the European Championship finals in the absence of clubmate Trevor FRANCIS. But it was asking too much too soon, and anyway there was no comparison.

SIDNEY
McDONALD
BISHOP

b 10 Feb 1900   d 4 May 1949   LEFT HALF
Caps: 4   Goals: 1
First cap: 2 Apr 1927 v Scotland 2–1   aged 27yr 53d
Last cap: 26 May 1927 v France 6–0   aged 27yr 107d
England career: 0yr 54d – P4 W4 D0 L0 – 100%
Club: Leicester City
Sid Bishop's successful little career, founded on a comfortable continental tour, would have lasted longer but for injury; he had to cry off after being recalled as captain against Scotland in 1928 and Ireland the following season. His one international goal was the fifth against Luxembourg, after England had been 2–0 down.

FREDERICK
BLACKBURN

b Sep 1879   d unknown   OUTSIDE LEFT
Caps: 3   Goals: 1
First cap: 30 Mar 1901 v Scotland 2–2
                        aged 21yr 181–210d (1 goal)

Last cap: 9 Apr 1904 v Scotland 1–0
aged 24yr 191–220d
England career: 3yr 10d – P3 W2 D1 L0 – 83.33%
Club: Blackburn Rovers
Fred Blackburn gave England the lead after 35 minutes, before the Scots hit back to lead 2–1.

GEORGE FREDERICK
BLACKBURN

b 8/18 Mar 1899   d 3 Jul 1957   LEFT HALF
Caps: 1   **Goals:** 0
Only cap: 17 May 1924 v France 3–1 aged 25yr 60/70d
England career: P1 W1 D0 L0 – 100%
Club: Aston Villa
Something of a scratch team took on the French: captain George WILSON aside, they had only 14 previous caps between them.

ERNEST
BLENKINSOP

b 20 Apr 1900/02   d 24 Apr 1969   LEFT BACK
Caps: 26   **Goals:** 0   **Captain:** 4
First cap: 17 May 1928 v France 5–1
aged 26/28yr   27d
Last cap: 1 Apr 1933 v Scotland 1–2
aged 30/32yr 346d
England career: 4yr 319d – P26 W18 D3 L5 – 75%
Club: Sheffield Wednesday
Remarkably in such a chop-and-change era, Ernie Blenkinsop's caps were all won consecutively, taking the record from WEDLOCK and keeping it until 1950 (see FRANKLIN and WA WRIGHT). Thinker as well as tackler, he was captain in his last international.

HERBERT
BLISS

b 29 Mar 1890   d 14 Jun 1968   INSIDE LEFT
Caps: 1   **Goals:** 0
Only cap: 9 Apr 1921 v Scotland 0–3 aged 31yr 11d
England career: P1 W1 D0 L0 – 0%
Club: Tottenham Hotspur
Surprisingly, at a time of wholesale clearances, the careers of only two England players were ended by the result at Hampden, both debutants: H GOUGH and Bert Bliss.

LUTHER
LOIDE
BLISSETT

b 1 Feb 1958   FORWARD
Caps: 14   **Goals:** 3
First cap: 13 Oct 1982 v W Germany 1–2 aged 24yr 254d
(sub 80min)
Last cap: 2 Jun 1984 v USSR 0–2   aged 26yr 122d
England career: 1yr 243d – P14 W5 D5 L4 – 53.57%

Clubs: Watford (9), Milan (5)
Substitute: 6   **Substituted:** 3
3 Goals in a game: 1
The year at Milan exposed Luther Blissett's shortage of real international class, but no-one tried harder on the pitch. For what it's worth, he was the first black player to score for England, and the only one to score a hat-trick, against Luxembourg in 1982.

JEFFREY
PAUL
BLOCKLEY

b 12 Sep 1949   CENTRE HALF
Caps: 1   **Goals:** 0
Only cap: 11 Oct 1972 v Yugoslavia 1–1   aged 23yr 29d
England career: P1 W0 D1 L0 – 50%
Club: Arsenal
Four other players made their debut at Wembley: CHANNON, LAMPARD, MD MILLS – and the one big Jeff was marking, Franjo Vladic, who scored the equaliser.

STEPHEN
BLOOMER

b 20 Jan 1874   d 16 Apr 1938   INSIDE RIGHT
Caps: 23   **Goals:** 28   **Captain:** 1
First cap: 9 Mar 1895 v Ireland 9–0   aged 21yr 48d
(2 goals)
Last cap: 6 Apr 1907 v Scotland 1–1   aged 33yr 76d
(1 goal)

England career: 12yr 28d – P23 W15 D6 L2 – 78.26%
Clubs: Derby County (21), Middlesbrough (2)
5 Goals in a game: 1   **4 Goals in a game:** 1
2 Goals in a game: 5   **Goals while captain:** 0
The great out-and-out goalscorers start here. Shortish, white as salt, a bad-tempered perfectionist who didn't suffer fools, England's best player before the First World War, Steve Bloomer set all manner of records for goals, goalscoring spans, and appearances.

He was the first of only two players (see R CHARLTON) to hold the England record for most goals as well as most caps. His international career was the longest before CROMPTON. His goalscoring span was the longest until S MATTHEWS and is still there in second place.

He overtook GO Smith's record of 20 caps in 1905. Most sources agree that he equalled VAUGHTON's record of five goals in one game (v Wales 1896)), and some say he did it twice – one or two credit him with five against Wales in 1901, which might have been six, if he'd been allowed to take the penalty that NEEDHAM missed.

He overhauled Lindley's record of 14 goals in total and set a mark that only WOODWARD edged past (dubiously) before 1958. He was England's annual leading scorer a record six times. He scored a total of 12 goals against Wales, the record by an England player against any one country. He scored in seven different matches against Scotland, eight goals in all, a record by a player from any country, which also equalled J Smith's record total in England–Scotland matches. He added eight against Ireland (second only to GREAVES' 10), which made him the only player to score at least eight against every other Home country.

He scored in his first 10 matches for England (a record that still stands), which helped him average 1.22 goals per game over 12 years as an international, on top of 352 in League matches. More defensive times would have reduced that ratio, but not the knack, the unexpected shooting. A phenomenon in front of goal.

FRANK
BLUNSTONE

b 17 Oct 1934   **OUTSIDE LEFT**
Caps: 5   **Goals:** 0
First cap: 10 Nov 1954 v Wales 3–2   aged 20yr 24d
Last cap: 28 Nov 1956 v Yugoslavia 3–0   aged 22yr 42d
England career: 2yr 18d – P5 W3 D0 L2 – 60%
Club: Chelsea

FINNEY's stand-in until the match against the Slavs, when the great man was at centre-forward with Sir Stan on the other wing.

RICHARD
BOND

b 14 Dec 1883   d 25 Apr 1955   **OUTSIDE RIGHT**
Caps: 8   **Goals:** 2
First cap: 25 Feb 1905 v Ireland 1–1   aged 21yr 73d
Last cap: 2 Apr 1910 v Scotland 0–2   aged 26yr 109d
England career: 5yr 36d – P8 W4 D2 L2 – 62.50%
Clubs: Preston NE (5), Bradford City (3)
2 Goals in a game: 1

Dicky Bond's second goal in the 5–0 win over Ireland in 1906 was scored in the last minute. He had to wait four seasons between his fifth and sixth caps.

PETER
PHILLIP
BONETTI

b 27 Sep 1941   **GOALKEEPER**
Caps: 7   **Goals conceded:** 4   **Clean sheets:** 5
First cap: 3 Jul 1966 v Denmark 2–0   aged 24yr 279d
Last cap: 14 Jul 1970 v W Germany 2–3   aged 28yr 290d
England career: 4yr 11d – P7 W6 D0 L1 – 85.71%
Club: Chelsea

Best remembered for a nervy last international, Peter the Cat had in fact been a high-class deputy for BANKS. Six wins out of six (including some match-winning saves against Portugal at Wembley), five clean sheets and only one goal conceded. Or put another way, 'the three best goalkeepers in the world are Lev Yashin, Gordon Banks and Peter Bonetti.' In Pele's opinion, anyway.

ALEXANDER GEORGE
BONSOR

b ?   d 17 Aug 1907   **FORWARD/GOALKEEPER**
Caps: 2   **Goals:** 1   **Goals conceded:** 0
First cap: 8 Mar 1873 v Scotland 4–2   (1 goal)
Last cap: 6 Mar 1875 v Scotland 2–2
England career: 1yr 363d – P2 W1 D1 L0 – 75%
Club: Wanderers (& Old Etonians)

A goal after 10 minutes of his first international made him briefly England's joint top scorer of all time! He played in goal for the first quarter of an hour when WH Carr was late for the 1875 match.

FRANK
BOOTH

b 1882   d 22 June 1919   **OUTSIDE LEFT**
Caps: 1   **Goals:** 0
Only cap: 25 Feb 1905 v Ireland 1–1   aged 22/23
England career: P1 W0 D1 L0 – 50%
Club: Manchester City

Six new caps, an own goal, a draw against a weak team. There was a new outside left – and a win – in each of the subsequent matches that season.

THOMAS
EDWARD
BOOTH

b 25 Apr 1874   d 7 Sep 1939   **CENTRE HALF**
Caps: 2   **Goals:** 0
First cap: 28 Mar 1898 v Wales 3–0   aged 23yr 337d
Last cap: 4 Apr 1903 v Scotland 1–2   aged 28yr 344d
England career: 5yr 7 – P2 W1 D0 L1 – 50%
Clubs: Blackburn Rovers (1), Everton (1)

England had little luck against the Scots at Bramall Lane: CROMPTON had a goal disallowed, Harry DAVIS a bruised breastbone. Bobby Hamilton, who did the bruising, was kept out by Tom Booth, but the inside-forwards Finlay Speedie and Bobby Walker scored twice in two minutes.

JOHN
WILLIAM ANSLOW
BOWERS

b 22 Feb 1908   d 4 Jul 1970   CENTRE FORWARD
Caps: 3   Goals: 2
First cap: 14 Oct 1933 v Ireland 3–0   aged 25yr 234d
                                                        (1 goal)
Last cap: 14 Apr 1934 v Scotland 3–0   aged 26yr 51d
                                                        (1 goal)
England career: 0yr 182d – P3 W2 D0 L1 – 66.66%
Club: Derby County
Long-legged Jack played throughout the Home Championship and scored two minutes from the end of his last international.

STANLEY
BOWLES

b 24 Dec 1948   FORWARD
Caps: 5   Goals: 1
First cap: 3 Apr 1974 v Portugal 0–0   aged 25yr 100d
Last cap: 9 Feb 1977 v Holland 0–2   aged 28yr 47d
England career: 2yr 310d – P5 W2 D1 L2 – 50%
Club: Queen's Park Rangers
Substituted: 1
Peter Taylor, famous judge of a player, gave Stan Bowles the chance of playing for Nottingham Forest in a European Cup Final, which he seems to have turned down; he had a high-profile gambling bug too. But once out on the pitch, there was touch, timing, personality, a nose for goal – you knew why you watched football when you watched Stan Bowles. Flaws and all, you'd have liked to watch him in a good England team.

EDWIN
RAYMOND
BOWDEN

b 13 Sep 1909   INSIDE RIGHT
Caps: 6   Goals: 1
First cap: 29 Sep 1934 v Wales 4–0   aged 25yr 16d
Last cap: 2 Dec 1936 v Hungary 6–2   aged 27yr 80d
England career: 2yr 64d – P6 W4 D0 L2 – 66.66%
Club: Arsenal
Ray Bowden played in two memorable internationals on his home club ground: against Italy in 1934, when he was one of a record seven players from the same club in an England team; and his last, when he helped clubmate Ted DRAKE to a hat-trick.

ALFRED GEORGE
BOWER

b 10 Nov 1895   d 30 Jun 1970   RIGHT/LEFT BACK
Caps: 5   Goals: 0   Captain: 3
First cap: 20 Oct 1923 v Ireland 1–2
                                            aged 27yr 344d

Last cap: 12 Feb 1927 v Wales 3–3   aged 32yr 94d
England career: 3yr 115d – P5 W2 D2 L1 – 60%
Club: Corinthians (& Casuals & Old Carthusians)
Not an especially good international player – he had terrible trouble with Billy Gillespie, for instance, in 1923 – 'Baishe' Bower was the last amateur to captain England.

SIDNEY
BOWSER

b 6 Apr 1891   d 25 Feb 1961   CENTRE HALF
Caps: 1   Goals: 0
Only cap: 25 Oct 1919 v Ireland 1–1   aged 28yr 202d
England career: P1 W0 D1 L0 – 50%
Club: West Bromwich Albion
A game of firsts. The first after the First World War, first caps for 15 of the 22. First and last for five.

PHILIP
JOHN
BOYER

b 25 Jan 1949   STRIKER
Caps: 1   Goals: 0
Only cap: 24 Mar 1976 v Wales 2–1   aged 27yr 58d
England career: P1 W1 D0 L0 – 100%
Club: Norwich City
Don REVIE picked a very experimental team for the centenary match at Wrexham, including eight new caps. Phil Boyer was still a surprise.

WALTER
EDWARD
BOYES

b 5 Jan 1913   d 16 Sep 1960   OUTSIDE LEFT
Caps: 3   Goals: 0
First cap: 18 May 1935 v Holland 1–0   aged 22yr 133d
Last cap: 26 Oct 1938 v Rest of Europe 3–0
                                            aged 25yr 294d
England career: 3yr 161d – P3 W2 D0 L1 – 66.66%
Clubs: West Bromwich Albion (1), Everton (2)
Little Wally Boyes had to wait three years for BASTIN's international career to end before he could win a second cap.

THOMAS
WILKINSON
BOYLE

b 29 Jan 1888/9   d 5 Jan 1940   CENTRE HALF
Caps: 1   Goals: 0
Only cap: 15 Feb 1913 v Ireland 1–2   aged 24/25yr 17d
England career: P1 W0 D0 L1 – 0%
Club: Burnley
A small centre-half in the WEDLOCK mould, Tommy Boyle couldn't stop centre-forward Billy

Gillespie scoring twice on his debut as Ireland beat England for the first time.

PETER

BRABROOK

b 8 Nov 1937   **OUTSIDE RIGHT**
Caps: 3   Goals: 0
First cap: 17 Jun 1958 v USSR 0–1   aged 20yr 221d
Last cap: 15 May 1960 v Spain 0–3   aged 22yr 188d
England career: 1yr 332d – P3 W0 D1 L2 – 16.66%
Club: Chelsea

England had no luck in the 1958 World Cup. Kevan might have had a penalty against Brazil; ROBSON had two goals disallowed; then Brabrook, on his debut, had a goal ruled out as well as hitting a post twice (the same one, as it happened) in the play-off. The only time the USSR hit a post, the ball went in.

PAUL
WILLIAM
BRACEWELL

b 19 Jul 1962   **MIDFIELDER**
Caps: 3   Goals: 0
First cap: 12 Jun 1985 v W Germany 3–0 aged 22yr 328d
                                     (sub 71m)
Last cap: 14 Nov 1985 v N Ireland 0–0   aged 23yr 118d
England career: 0yr 155d – P3 W2 D1 L0 – 83.33%
Club: Everton
Substitute: 1

Good, dependable part of the Everton team that won the League and Cup-Winners' Cup. Injuries stopped him proving whether he was really international class.

GEOFFREY
REGINALD WILLIAM
BRADFORD

b 18 Jul 1927   **INSIDE LEFT**
Caps: 1   Goals: 1
Only cap: 2 Oct 1955 v Denmark 5–1   aged 28yr 76d
                                        (1 goal)
England career: P1 W1 D0 L0 – 100%
Club: Bristol Rovers

Geoff Bradford scored England's fifth, eight minutes from the end. Rovers were then in the Second Division.

JOSEPH
BRADFORD

b 22 Jan 1901   d 6 Sep 1980
            CENTRE FORWARD/INSIDE LEFT
Caps: 12   Goals: 7
First cap: 20 Oct 1923 v Ireland 1–2   aged 22yr 241d
                                        (1 goal)

Last cap: 22 Nov 1930 v Wales 4–0   aged 29yr 269d
                                        (1 goal)
England career: 7yr 28d – P12 W7 D2 L3 – 66.66%
Club: Birmingham FC
3 Goals in a game: 0   2 Goals in a game: 2

It took a while for the selectors to settle on Joe Bradford. After scoring twice against Belgium in 1924, he was left out until the disastrous Wembley Wizards match of 1928 – then, oddly, he was more or less a fixture.

WARREN
BRADLEY

b 20 June 1933   **OUTSIDE RIGHT**
Caps: 3   Goals: 2
First cap: 6 May 1959 v Italy 2–2   aged 25yr 320d
                                        (1 goal)
Last cap: 28 May 1959 v USA 8–1   aged 25yr 342d
                                        (1 goal)
England career: 0yr 22d – P3 W1 D1 L1 – 50%
Club: Manchester United
Substitute: 1

Tiny winger who equalised when the USA were threatening a repeat of 1950.

FRANCIS
BRADSHAW

b 31 May 1884/85   d unknown   **CENTRE FORWARD**
Caps: 1   Goals: 3
Only cap: 8 Jun 1908 v Austria 11–1 aged 23/24 (3 goals)
England career: P1 W1 D0 L0 – 100%
Club: Sheffield Wednesday

Frank Bradshaw was the last of five players (see A ALLEN, YATES, GILLIAT, J VEITCH) to score a hat-trick while winning just a single cap, the only one to do so against European opposition. It's possible that all his goals were scored in one half (which is one way of saying full reports of the match are hard to come by).

THOMAS
HENRY
BRADSHAW

b 24 Aug 1873   d 25 Dec 1899   **OUTSIDE LEFT**
Caps: 1   Goals: 0
Only cap: 20 Feb 1897 v Ireland 6–0 aged 23yr 180d
England career: P1 W1 D0 L0 – 100%
Club: Liverpool

Harry Bradshaw, a very quick winger, died young, on the last Christmas Day of the century.

WILLIAM
BRADSHAW

b 1884/85   d unknown   **LEFT HALF**
Caps: 4   Goals: 0

First cap: 12 Feb 1910 v Ireland 1–1   aged c.25
Last cap: 17 Mar 1913 v Wales 4–3   aged c.28
England career: 3yr 33d – P4 W3 D1 L0 – 87.50%
Club: Blackburn Rovers

Nine other players made their international debuts in the same match in 1910: DUCAT, AE HALL, H MORLEY, Bill Bradshaw's club colleague A COWELL, and five of the Irish team.

GEORGE
BRANN

b 23 Apr 1865   d 14 Jun 1954
           OUTSIDE LEFT/INSIDE FORWARD
Caps: 3   **Goals:** 1
First cap: 27 Mar 1886 v Scotland 1–1   aged 20yr 338d
Last cap: 7 Mar 1891 v Wales 4–1   aged 25yr 318d
England career: 4yr 345d – P3 W2 D1 L0 – 83.33%
Club: Swifts (& Corinthians)

Typical of the time, an all-round sportsman who could play anywhere in the forward line. Still being written about 20 years after his appearances for England.

WILLIAM
FREDERICK
BRAWN

b 1 Aug 1878   d 18 Aug 1932   OUTSIDE RIGHT
Caps: 2   **Goals:** 0
First cap: 29 Feb 1904 v Wales 2–2   aged 25yr 212d
Last cap: 12 Mar 1904 v Ireland 3–1   aged 25yr 224d
England career: 0yr 12d – P2 W1 D1 L0 – 75%
Club: Aston Villa

Six other players made their debuts alongside brawny Billy: AS BROWN, Herbert BURGESS, COMMON, GH DAVIS, EA LEE and RUDDLESDIN.

JOHN
BRAY

b 22 Apr 1909   d 20 Nov 1982   LEFT HALF
Caps: 6   **Goals:** 0
First cap: 29 Sep 1934 v Wales 4–0   aged 25yr 160d
Last cap: 17 Apr 1937 v Scotland 1–3   aged 27yr 360d
England career: 2yr 200d – P6 W3 D1 L2 – 58.33%
Club: Manchester City

A respected wing-half who prompted City to a League title and an FA Cup win, Jackie Bray had an international career that fell away after a good start, with no wins in the last three matches.

EDWARD
BRAYSHAW

b 1863   d 20 Nov 1908   CENTRE HALF
Caps: 1   **Goals:** 0
Only cap: 5 Feb 1887 v Ireland 7–0 aged 23/24
England career: P1 W1 D0 L0 – 100%

Club: Sheffield Wednesday

Teddy Brayshaw had few problems against a team with eight new caps, half of whom didn't play for Ireland again.

BARRY
JOHN
BRIDGES

b 29 Apr 1941   CENTRE FORWARD
Caps: 4   **Goals:** 1
First cap: 10 Apr 1965 v Scotland 2–2   aged 23yr 346d
Last cap: 20 Oct 1965 v Austria 2–3   aged 24yr 174d
England career: 0yr 193d – P4 W1 D2 L1 – 50%
Club: Chelsea

Quick straightforward striker whose header earned England a draw in Belgrade.

GEORGE
ARTHUR
BRIDGETT

b 1882/84   d 1954   OUTSIDE LEFT
Caps: 11   **Goals:** 3
First cap: 1 Apr   1905 v Scotland 1–0   aged 20–23
Last cap: 1 Jun   1909 v Austria 8–1   aged 24–27
England career: 4yr 30d – P11 W10 D1 L0 – 95.45%
Club: Sunderland

A good crosser of the ball, maker rather than scorer of goals, Arthur Bridgett had to wait three years for a second cap, but then went on to equal RUTHERFORD's total of 11 matches without defeat – and with a higher win ratio, statistically the best record of any England player.

THOMAS
BRINDLE

b 1861?   d 15 Apr 1905   RIGHT/LEFT BACK
Caps: 2   **Goals:** 1
First cap: 13 Mar 1880 v Scotland 4–5   aged 18/19?
Last cap: 15 Mar 1880 v Wales 3–1   aged 18/19?
                                (1 goal)
England career: 0yr 2d – P2 W1 D0 L1 – 50%
Club: Darwen

The first defender to score for England, very surprising in an age when backs almost invariably stayed back.

JOHN
THOMAS
BRITTLETON

b 23 Apr 1882   d 22 Feb 1955   RIGHT HALF
Caps: 5   **Goals:** 0
First cap: 10 Feb 1912 v Ireland 6–1   aged 29yr 293d
Last cap: 16 Mar 1914 v Wales 2–0   aged 31yr 327d
England career: 2yr 34d – P5 W4 D1 L0 – 90%
Club: Sheffield Wednesday

The 1972 Farror–Lamming book lists his first name as James – but Jim Creasy's research has produced the John which is surely correct given that Charlie BUCHAN, a contemporary, called him Jack. Though oddly enough, most sources say he was known as Tom.

CLIFFORD
SAMUEL
BRITTON

b 27/29 Aug 1909   d 1 Dec 1975   **INSIDE RIGHT**
Caps: 9   Goals: 1
First cap: 19 Sep 1934 v Wales 4-0 aged 25yr 31/33d
Last cap: 17 May 1937 v Sweden 4-0
                                             aged 27yr 261/263d
England career: 2yr 230d – P9 W7 D0 L2 – 77.77%
Club: Everton
The half-back line of Britton, CULLIS and MERCER was famous in the War, but Cliff Britton was replaced, a little surprisingly, by Ken WILLINGHAM in the two years leading up to it.

PETER
FRANK
BROADBENT

b 15 May 1933   **INSIDE RIGHT**
Caps: 7   Goals: 2
First cap: 17 Jun 1958 v USSR 0-1   aged 25yr 33d
Last cap: 9 Apr 1960 v Scotland 1-1   aged 26yr 330d
England career: 1yr 297d – P7 W1 D4 L2 – 42.86%
Club: Wolves
The nearest thing to a free spirit allowed in a Stan CULLIS team, Peter Broadbent scored two equalisers in the 2–2 draw with Wales in 1958.

IVAN
ARTHUR
BROADIS

b 18 Dec 1922   **INSIDE RIGHT/LEFT**
Caps: 14   Goals: 8
First cap: 28 Nov 1951 v Austria 2-2   aged 28yr 345d
Last cap: 26 Jun 1954 v Uruguay 2-4   aged 31yr 190d
England career: 2yr 210d – P14 W5 D5 L4 – 53.57%
Clubs: Manchester City (8), Newcastle United (6)
2 Goals in a game: 2
Scored his share of goals for some rather unsuccessful England teams.

JOHN
BROCKBANK

b 22 Aug 1848   d 29 Jan 1904   **FORWARD**
Caps: 1   Goals: 0
Only cap: 30 Nov 1872 v Scotland 0-0   aged 24yr 100d
England career: P1 W0 D1 L0 – 50%
Club: Cambridge University

One of four Oxbridge players in the first ever England team, and (with GREENHALGH) the oldest.

JOHN
BRANT
BRODIE

b 1862   d 16 Feb 1925   **CENTRE FORWARD**
Caps: 3   Goals: 1   Captain: 1
First cap: 2 Mar   1889 v Ireland 6-1   aged 26/27
                                                  (1 goal)
Last cap: 7 Mar   1891 v Ireland 6-1   aged 28/29
England career: 1yr 05d – P3 W2 D0 L1 – 66.66%
Club: Wolves
Captained England on his debut, the last to do so before KNIGHT in 1919. It's possible that he scored in the match v Scotland in 1889; see WEIR.

THOMAS
GEORGE
BROMILOW

b 7 Oct 1894   d 4 Mar 1959   **LEFT HALF**
Caps: 5   Goals: 0
First cap: 14 Mar   1921 v Wales 0-0   aged 26yr 158d
Last cap: 24 Oct   1925 v Ireland 0-0   aged 31yr 17d
England career: 4yr 224d – P5 W2 D2 L1 – 60%
Club: Liverpool
Seven players won their first caps against Wales; skilful Tom (or Tommy) Bromilow was one of six who'd played for the North team that beat an England XI 6-1.

WILLIAM E
BROMLEY-
DAVENPORT

b 21 Jan 1862   d 6 Feb 1949   **CENTRE FORWARD**
Caps: 2   Goals: 2
First cap: 15 Mar   1884 v Scotland 0-1   aged 22yr 54d
Last cap: 17 Mar   1884 v Wales 4-0   aged 22yr 56d
                                                  (2 goals)
England career: 0yr 02d – P2 W1 D0 L1 – 50%
Club: Oxford University (& Old Etonians & Corinthians)
2 Goals in a game: 1
By the time he died, he'd reached a higher military rank than any other England player, and was weighed down by titles: General Sir William Bromley-Davenport DSO KCB MP, Lord Lieutenant of Cheshire. A COMMON he wasn't.

ERIC
FRED
BROOK

b 27 Nov 1907   d 29 Mar 1965   **OUTSIDE LEFT**
Caps: 18   Goals: 10

First cap: 19 Oct 1929 v Ireland 3–0   aged 21yr 326d
Last cap: 17 Nov 1937 v Wales 2–1   aged 29yr 355d
England career: 8yr 29d – P18 W12 D1 L5 – 69.44%
Club: Manchester City
Hat-tricks: 0   2 Goals in a game: 1
Penalties: 1   Missed: 1

Hard-shooting, broken-nosed Eric had to wait over three years for his second cap, but was then more or less a fixture. Carlo Ceresoli of Italy saved his penalty in 1934, making him the only player to miss one in the first minute of an England match; he then scored twice in the next 10 minutes, the second of only two players (see WH WALKER) to miss out on a hat-trick by missing a penalty.

TREVOR
DAVID
BROOKING

b 2 Oct 1948   MIDFIELDER
Caps: 47   Goals: 5
First cap: 3 Apr 1974 v Portugal 0–0   aged 25yr 183d
Last cap: 5 Jul 1982 v Spain 0–0   aged 33yr 276d
England career: 8yr 93d – P47 W25 D14 L8 – 68.09%
Club: West Ham United
Substitute: 6   Substituted: 9
2 Goals in a game: 1

It took his old club manager Greenwood to bring out the best of Trevor Brooking for England, after which he influenced and decorated any number of matches, above all the vital World Cup qualifier in Budapest, his second goal lodging against the stanchion; a memorable image.

JOHN
BROOKS

b 23 Dec 1931   INSIDE RIGHT
Caps: 3   Goals: 2
First cap: 14 Nov 1956 v Wales 3–1   aged 24yr 326d
                               (1 goal)
Last cap: 5 Dec 1956 v Denmark 5–2   aged 24yr 347d
England career: 0yr 21d – P3 W3 D0 L0 – 100%
Club: Tottenham Hotspur

England used a variety of players at inside right during the HAYNES era, strikers (ATYEO, KEVAN, GREAVES) as well as schemers (T THOMPSON, RW ROBSON, BROADBENT) – and Johnny Brooks, who did a little bit of both in his three internationals.

FRANK
HENRY
BROOME

b 11 Jun 1915   CENTRE FORWARD/OUTSIDE RIGHT/
                        INSIDE RIGHT/OUTSIDE LEFT

Caps: 7   Goals: 3

First cap: 14 May 1938 v Germany 6–3   aged 22yr 337d
                                 (1 goal)
Last cap: 24 May 1939 v Romania 2–0   aged 24yr 347d
England career: 1yr 10d – P7 W4 D1 L2 – 64.29%
Club: Aston Villa
2 Goals in a game: 0

Famously fast, Frank played for England in four forward positions, scoring from three of them.

ANTHONY
BROWN

b 3 Oct 1945   STRIKER
Caps: 1   Goals: 0
Only cap: 19 May 1971 v Wales 0–0   aged 25yr 228d
                               (sub'd 74min)
England career: P1 W0 D1 L0 – 50%
Club: West Bromwich Albion

Tony Brown had scored plenty for West Brom (he was the First Division's leading scorer that season), but Sir Alf only needed a quick look at international level. Of the players who appeared for less than 90 minutes in an England match, he was the first to be substituted without being injured.

ARTHUR
BROWN

b 1859   d 1 Jul 1909   INSIDE RIGHT
Caps: 3   Goals: 4
First cap: 18 Feb 1882 v Ireland 13–0   aged 22/23
                               (4 goals)
Last cap: 13 Mar 1882 v Wales 3–5   aged 22/23
England career: 0yr 23d – P3 W1 D0 L2 – 33.33%
Club: Aston Villa

Powerful and a natural goalscorer, but the first Irishmen were no kind of decent yardstick; even VAUGHTON found them easy targets.

ARTHUR
SAMUEL
BROWN

b 6 Apr 1885   d 27 Jun 1944   CENTRE FORWARD
Caps: 2   Goals: 1
First cap: 29 Feb 1904 v Wales 2–2   aged 18yr 328d
Last cap: 17 Feb 1906 v Ireland 5–0   aged 20yr 316d
                               (1 goal)
England career: 1yr 353d – P2 W1 D1 L0 – 75%
Club: Sheffield United

Arthur ('Boy') Brown was once thought to have been the youngest England player before D EDWARDS. See PRINSEP, ROSTRON, C MITCHELL and J BROWN.

GEORGE
BROWN

b 22 Jun 1903   d 10 Jun 1948
           INSIDE RIGHT/CENTRE FORWARD

Caps: 9   Goals: 5
First cap: 20 Oct 1926 v Ireland 3–3   aged 23yr 120d
                                                                (1 goal)
Last cap: 16 Nov 1932 v Wales 0–0   aged 29yr 147d
England career: 6yr 27d – P9 W4 D3 L2 – 61.11%
Clubs: Huddersfield Town (8), Aston Villa (1)
2 Goals in a game: 2

After a successful start to his international career, including five goals in his first six games, George Brown was recalled after more than three years for his last cap, out of position at centre forward.

There's confusion as to whether he or RIGBY scored twice against France in 1927. In his corner: *The Sporting Life*, *L'Equipe 1984–85*, *Rothmans*. In Rigby's: *The Guardian*, *L'Echo des Sports*, Gamage's and Granidge's annuals.

JAMES
BROWN

b 31 Jul 1862   d 4 Jul 1922   CENTRE FORWARD
Caps: 5   Goals: 3
First cap: 26 Feb 1881 v Wales 0–1   aged 18yr 210d
Last cap: 21 May 1885 v Scotland 1–1   aged 22yr 233d
England career: 4yr 23d – P5 W2 D2 L1 – 60%
Club: Blackburn Rovers
Hat-tricks: 0   2 Goals in a game: 1

An unusually skilful goalscorer, Jimmy Brown was one of the youngest of all England players, and (v Ireland 1882) the only teenager to score twice in a match for England.

JOHN
HENRY
BROWN

b 19 Mar 1899   d 10 Apr 1962   GOALKEEPER
Caps: 6   Goals conceded: 7   Clean sheets: 2
First cap: 12 Feb 1927 v Wales 3–3   aged 27yr 330d
Last cap: 19 Oct 1929 v Ireland 3–0   aged 30yr 214d
England career: 2yr 249d – P6 W5 D1 L0 – 91.66%
Club: Sheffield Wednesday
Penalties: 1   Saved: 0

Big heavy Jack Brown was beaten by Len Davies' penalty in his first international; after that, he played in five winning teams and didn't give much away, helped by the 1927 summer tour against weak continental teams. He kept clean sheets in his last two matches.

KENNETH
BROWN

b 16 Feb 1934   CENTRE HALF
Caps: 1   Goals: 0
Only cap: 18 Nov 1959 v N Ireland 2–1   aged 25y 275d
England career: P1 W1 D0 L0 – 100%
Club: West Ham United

England had trouble finding a central stopper to replace Billy WRIGHT. Ken Brown (later the genial and successful manager of Norwich) was given a brief chance.

WILLIAM
BROWN

b 22 Aug 1900   d Jan 1985   INSIDE RIGHT
Caps: 1   Goals: 1
Only cap: 1 Nov 1923 v Belgium 2–2 aged 23yr 71d (1 goal)
England career: P1 W0 D1 L0 – 50%
Club: West Ham United

Bill Brown scored England's first equaliser as Belgium became the first foreign team to avoid defeat against England.

JOHN
BRUTON

b 21 Nov 1903   d 13 Mar 1986   OUTSIDE RIGHT
Caps: 3   Goals: 0
First cap: 17 May 1928 v France 5–1   aged 24yr 178d
Last cap: 13 Apr 1929 v Scotland 0–1   aged 25yr 143d
England career: 0yr 331d – P3 W2 D0 L1 – 66.66%
Club: Burnley

One of six players who won their first England caps in Paris, speedy Jack Bruton was one of five who won their last at Hampden.

WILLIAM
INGRAM
BRYANT

b 1 Mar 1899   d 21 Jan 1986   CENTRE HALF
Caps: 1   Goals: 0
Only cap: 21 May 1925 v France 3–2   aged 26yr 81d
England career: P1 W1 D0 L0 – 100%
Club: Clapton

Billy Bryant played for the same amateur club as GIBBINS and EARLE.

CHARLES
MURRAY
BUCHAN

b 22 Sep 1891   d 25 Jun 1960
                INSIDE RIGHT/CENTRE FORWARD
Caps: 6   Goals: 4   Captain: 2
First cap: 15 Feb 1913 v Ireland 1–2   aged 21yr 146d
                                                                (1 goal)
Last cap: 12 Apr 1924 v Scotland 1–1   aged 32yr 202d
England career: 11yr 57d – P6 W2 D2 L2 – 50%
Club: Sunderland
2 Goals in a game: 0   Goals while captain: 1

England's first defeat against Ireland followed by a World War meant Charlie Buchan had to wait 7 years 28 days for a second cap, but England should nevertheless have built a team round him throughout the early twenties. Long-legged and

Both substitutes have something to celebrate at Hampden Park: Gascoigne a birthday, Bull a goal on his debut
(Allsport)

odd-looking, good on the ball ('like a kitten with a strange plaything'), exceptional in the air, it used to be said he was too clever for his own team mates. For the selectors, certainly.

WALTER
SCOTT
BUCHANAN

b 1 Jun 1855?   *d 11 Nov 1926?*   FORWARD
Caps: 1   **Goals:** 0
Only cap: 4 Mar 1876 v Scotland 0–3   aged 20yr 276d
England career: P1 W0 D0 L1 – 0%
Club: Clapham Rovers

No-one seems 100 per cent sure that this *was* Walter Buchanan. The late Morley Farror's records (original source unknown) say he probably was, and Douglas Lamming's latest book takes this up ('is almost certainly'). If he was, his dates of birth and death are correct.

FRANKLIN
CHARLES
BUCKLEY

b 9 Nov 1882/83   *d 22 Dec 1964*   CENTRE HALF
Caps: 1   **Goals:** 0
Only cap: 14 Feb 1914 v Ireland 0–3   aged 30/31yr 97d
England career: P1 W0 D0 L1 – 0%
Club: Derby County

Like Stan CULLIS, another England player who became a successful Wolves manager, Frank Buckley was an international centre half whose year of birth is in doubt. After service in World War I, he was forever known as Major Frank.

STEPHEN
GEORGE
BULL

b 28 Mar 1965   STRIKER
Caps: 13   **Goals:** 4
First cap: 27 May 1989 v Scotland 2–0   aged 24yr 60d
(sub 31 min, 1 goal)
Last cap: 17 Oct 1990 v Poland 2–0   aged 25yr 203d
(sub'd 57 min)

England career: 1yr 143d – P13 W8 D4 L1 – 76.92%
Club: Wolves
Substitute: 8 **Substituted:** 3
2 Goals in a game: 1

Not to everyone's taste, straightforward Steve nevertheless went through every level of china shop to get goals even in internationals. The first Third Division player to play for England since PJ TAYLOR (having just shot Wolves to promotion), he scored a goal on his debut before becoming one of only two (see CURRIE) to score in two matches as substitute, the second a last-minute equaliser in Tunis after he'd been on the pitch only 10 minutes.

FREDERICK
EDWIN
BULLOCK

b 1886 d 15 Nov 1922 　　　　　**LEFT BACK**
Caps: 1 **Goals:** 0
Only cap: 23 Oct 1920 v Ireland 2–0 　　aged 33/34
England career: P1 W1 D0 L0 – 100%
Club: Huddersfield Town

Fred Bullock died only two years after playing in an international and an FA Cup Final.

NORMAN
BULLOCK

b 8 Sep 1900 d 22 Oct 1970 　**CENTRE FORWARD**
Caps: 3 **Goals:** 2
First cap: 19 Mar 1923 v Belgium 6–1 　aged 22yr 192d
　　　　　　　　　　　　　　　　　　(1 goal)
Last cap: 20 Oct 1926 v Ireland 3–3 　aged 26yr 42d
　　　　　　　　　　　　　　　　　　(1 goal)
England career: 3yr 150d – P3 W1 D1 L1 – 50%
Club: Bury

His style of play didn't match his surname. A 'studious type of leader, not a battering ram but beating defenders by positional play', he did nothing very wrong in his appearances for England.

HARRY
BURGESS

b 20 Aug 1904 d unknown 　　**INSIDE LEFT**
Caps: 4 **Goals:** 2
First cap: 20 Oct 1930 v Ireland 5–1 　aged 26yr 61d
Last cap: 16 May 1931 v Belgium 4–1 　aged 26yr 269d
　　　　　　　　　　　　　　　　　　(2 goals)
England career: 0yr 208d – P4 W2 D0 L2 – 50%
Club: Sheffield Wednesday

Harry (pictured right) might have become the last player to score a hat-trick in his last match for England (see FR OSBORNE) if he'd taken the penalty converted by Houghton.

HERBERT
BURGESS

b 1883   d 1954   **LEFT BACK**
Caps: 4   **Goals:** 0
First cap: 29 Dec 1904 v Wales 2–2   aged 20/21
Last cap: 7 Apr 1906 v Scotland 1–2   aged 22/23
England career: 2yr 38d – P4 W2 D1 L1 – 62.50%
Club: Manchester City
Seems to have been England's shortest ever full-back at 5ft 4in.

CUTHBERT JAMES
BURNUP

b 21 Nov 1875   d 5 Apr 1960   **OUTSIDE LEFT**
Caps: 1   **Goals:** 0
Only cap: 4 Apr 1896 v Scotland 1–2   aged 20yr 135d
England career: P1 W0 D0 L1 – 0%
Club: Cambridge University (& Old Malvernians
        & Corinthians)

England had gone 20 games without losing (9–1 v Wales in the 20th) before NEEDHAM and BLOOMER, vital players both, dropped out injured prior to the match at Celtic Park. There was universal surprise and condemnation when CJ was chosen; evidence of southern bias, it was said: 'a smart little fellow, but not up to international standard.' Seems he lived down to it all ('the amateur was painfully weak, almost everything he did ending in utter failure') as Scotland ended the record run of six years without defeat. In 1900, playing cricket for the MCC, he bowled a ball that was hit for 10 runs by Derbyshire's Samuel Hill-Wood, a record in first-class cricket.

HORACE
BURROWS

b 11 Mar 1910   d 22 Mar 1969   **LEFT HALF**
Caps: 3   **Goals:** 0
First cap: 10 May 1934 v Hungary 1–2   aged 24yr 60d
Last cap: 18 May 1935 v Holland 1–0   aged 25yr 68d
England career: 1yr 08d – P3 W1 D0 L2 – 33.33%
Club: Sheffield Wednesday
Won all three caps on end-of-season tours abroad, the first two against teams of real quality, Hungary and Czechoslovakia, who both won 2–1.

FRANK ERNEST
BURTON

b 18 Mar 1865   d 10 Feb 1948   **FORWARD**
Caps: 1   **Goals:** 0
Only cap: 2 Mar 1889 v Ireland 6–1   aged 23yr 349d
England career: P1 W1 D0 L0 – 100%
Club: Nottingham Forest
Played exactly the way he was christened. Yes, honestly.

LINDSAY
BURY

b 9 July 1857   d 30 Oct 1935   **FULL BACK**
Caps: 2   **Goals:** 0
First cap: 3 Mar 1877 v Scotland 1–3   aged 19yr 237d
Last cap: 18 Jan 1879 v Wales 2–1   aged 21yr 193d
England career: 1yr 321d – P2 W1 D0 L1 – 50%
Clubs: Cambridge University & Old Etonians (1), Old
        Etonians alone (1)
Undergraduate all-rounder who was faced with an overwhelming forward line in his first international and coped well enough.

TERENCE
IAN
BUTCHER

b 28 Dec 1958   **CENTRAL DEFENDER**
Caps: 77   **Goals:** 3   **Captain:** 7
First cap: 31 May 1980 v Australia 2–1   aged 21yr 154d
Last cap: 4 Jul 1990 v W Germany 1–1 aged 31yr 188d
                                    (sub'd 70min)
England career: 10yr 34d – P77 W45 D22 L10 – 72.72%
Clubs: Ipswich Town (46), Glasgow Rangers (31)
Substituted: 3   **2 Goals in a game:** 0
Very tall (6ft 4in) and heavy (14st-plus) and not quick with it, Terry Butcher had his share of critics throughout, but England didn't lose too often when he was in the team. Without him . . . well, the 1988 European Championship finals are a case in point. He may have needed Des WALKER alongside him towards the end, but he'd paid his dues for that.

JOHN
DENNIS
BUTLER

b 14 Aug 1894   d 5 Jan 1961   **CENTRE HALF**
Caps: 1   **Goals:** 0
Only cap: 8 Dec 1924 v Belgium 4–0   aged 30yr 116d
England career: P1 W1 D0 L0 – 100%
Club: Arsenal
According to Bernard Joy, journalist and fellow Arsenal centre half, Jack Butler had trouble adapting to the more defensive duties required of a number 5 after the change in the offside law in 1925. Hardly surprising, then, that he didn't play for England after that date. Still, he had his revenge. Having won his only cap against Belgium, he coached the same country to their only win over England, in 1936.

WILLIAM
BUTLER

b 27 Mar 1900   d 11 Jul 1966   **OUTSIDE RIGHT**

Caps: 1   Goals: 0
Only cap: 12 Apr 1924 v Scotland 1–1   aged 24yr 16d
England career: P1 W0 D1 L0 – 50%
Club: Bolton Wanderers

Four players won their only cap at Wembley in 1924: Willie Cowan, Neil Harris and Jock Smith of Scotland, and Bill Butler. He died on the day England played Uruguay at the same stadium in the opening match of the 1966 World Cup finals.

GERALD
BYRNE

b 29 Aug 1938   **LEFT BACK**
Caps: 2   Goals: 0
First cap: 6 Apr 1963 v Scotland 1–2   aged 24yr 220d
Last cap: 29 Jun 1966 v Norway 6–1   aged 27yr 304d
England career: 3yr 84d – P2 W1 D0 L1 – 50%
Club: Liverpool

Ray Wilson's cover in the 1966 World Cup squad, Gerry Byrne had played through the previous year's FA Cup Final with a broken collarbone.

JOHN J
BYRNE

b 13 May 1939   **INSIDE RIGHT/CENTRE FORWARD**
Caps: 11   Goals: 8
First cap: 22 Nov 1961 v N Ireland 1–1   aged 22yr 193d
Last cap: 10 Apr 1965 v Scotland 2–2   aged 25yr 332d
England career: 3yr 139d – P11 W5 D3 L3 – 59.09%
Clubs: Crystal Palace (1), West Ham United (10)
3 Goals in a game: 1   **2 Goals in a game:** 2

Johnny Byrne talked non-stop like a budgie and scored goals like the very talented centre-forward he was; similar to Hidegkuti, but cheekier. He had a weight problem and was badly injured in his last international; otherwise – who knows? – there might have been four Hammers in the World Cup Final.

ROGER
WILLIAM
BYRNE

b 8 Feb 1929   *d 6 Feb 1958*   **LEFT BACK**
Caps: 33   Goals: 0
First cap: 3 Apr 1954 v Scotland 4–2   aged 25yr 54d
Last cap: 27 Nov 1957 v France 4–0   aged 28yr 292d
England career: 3yr 238d – P33 W20 D6 L7 – 69.69%
Club: Manchester United
Penalties: 2   **Missed:** 2

One of four players to miss two penalties while playing for England, Roger Byrne was the only one never to score an international goal any other way. Erratic at first, one of the best by the time he died at Munich, all his caps were won successively.

IAN
ROBERT
CALLAGHAN

b 10 Apr 1942   **OUTSIDE RIGHT/MIDFIELDER**
Caps: 4   Goals: 0
First cap: 26 Jun 1966 v Finland 3–0   aged 24yr 77d
Last cap: 12 Oct 1977 v Luxembourg 2–0
     aged 35yr 185d
England career: 11yr 98d – P4 W3 D1 L0 – 87.50%
Club: Liverpool
Substituted: 1

In his first match in charge, Ron Greenwood picked a Liverpool *bloc*, including Ian Callaghan, a good winger turned very good midfielder, who hadn't played international football since 1966; a record gap between England caps of 11 years 49 days. The experiment lasted two matches.

JOHN
CALVEY

b 23 June 1875   *d Jan 1937*   **CENTRE FORWARD**
Caps: 1   Goals: 0
Only cap: 22 Mar 1902 v Ireland 1–0   aged 26yr 272d
England career: P1 W1 D0 L0 – 100%
Club: Nottingham Forest

Didn't play well in Belfast but was picked out of position ('Calvey is not a centre forward'). Farror/Lamming originally listed his date of birth as 23 Aug 1876.

AUSTEN
FENWICK
CAMPBELL

b 5 May 1901   *d 8 Sep 1981*   **LEFT HALF**
Caps: 8   Goals: 0
First cap: 22 Oct 1928 v Ireland 2–1   aged 27yr 170d
Last cap: 9 Dec 1931 v Spain 7–1   aged 30yr 217d
England career: 3yr 47d – P8 W7 D0 L1 – 87.50%
Clubs: Blackburn Rovers (2), Huddersfield Town (6)

If figures ever mean anything, Austen Campbell would have had the most successful international career of any England player but for Spain's late rally in 1929. His first name is often seen spelt Austin, apparently an error.

GEORGE
HENRY
CAMSELL

b 27 Nov 1902   *d 7 Mar 1966*   **CENTRE FORWARD**
Caps: 9   Goals: 18
First cap: 9 May 1929 v France 4–1   aged 26yr 163d
     (2 goals)
Last cap: 9 May 1936 v Belgium 2–3   aged 33yr 164d
     (1 goal)
England career: 7yr – P9 W6 D1 L2 – 72.22%

Club: Middlesbrough
4 Goals in a game: 1   3 Goals in a game: 1
2 Goals in a game: 4

George Camsell's record of 59 League goals in 1926–27 was overhauled by DEAN the very next season, but his strike rate in internationals was superior – to anyone's. Of the players who scored in their every England game, no-one else played in as many as his nine (TILSON the nearest with four), and his average of exactly two a game is the highest among scorers of ten goals or more. He scored at least twice in each of his first six matches, still the England record. He scored five successive England goals in 1929 (surpassed only by MACDONALD), including the first four against Belgium, after which he was rested while Spain became the first foreign team to beat England.

Against Ireland in 1929, he was fouled for the penalty, converted by HINE, that gave England the lead, then scored the other two himself. Even in his thirties he went on scoring, including one in each of his last two internationals, the only times he was on the losing side.

JOHN CARR

b 1876   d 17 Mar 1948   **LEFT BACK**

Caps: 2   **Goals:** 0
First cap: 25 Feb 1905 v Ireland 1–1   aged 28/29
Last cap: 16 Feb 1907 v Ireland 1–0   aged 30/31
England career: 1yr 356d – P2 W1 D1 L0 – 75%
Club: Newcastle United

The scorelines don't lie: England scrambled through these matches. Hardly surprising with six new caps in the first (including Jack Carr) and five in the second.

JOHN CARR

b 26 Nov 1892   d 10 May 1942 **INSIDE/OUTSIDE RIGHT**

Caps: 2   **Goals:** 0
First cap: 25 Oct 1919 v Ireland 1–1   aged 26yr 333d
Last cap: 5 Mar 1923 v Wales 2–2   aged 30yr 99d
England career: 3yr 131d – P2 W0 D2 L0 – 50%
Club: Middlesbrough

Jackie Carr no longer had the pace to beat the bald, experienced Moses Russell at Ninian Park, and England needed luck to draw the match, though the Welsh equalised only four minutes from time.

WILLIAM HENRY CARR

b 1848   d 22 Feb 1924   **GOALKEEPER**

Caps: 1   **Goals conceded:** 2
Only cap: 6 Mar 1875 v Scotland 2–2 aged 26/27 (c.75min)
England career: P1 W0 D1 L0 – 50%
Club: Owlerton (Sheffield)

Arrived late for his only international, leaving England to play the first quarter of an hour with 10 men. He was the first to play less than 90 minutes in international football.

HORATIO STRATTON CARTER

b 21 Dec 1913   **INSIDE RIGHT**

Caps: 13   **Goals:** 7
First cap: 14 Apr 1934 v Scotland 3–0   aged 20yr 114d
Last cap: 18 May 1947 v Switzerl'd 0–1   aged 33yr 148d
England career: 13yr 34d – 13P W9 D1 L3 – 73.08%
Clubs: Sunderland (6), Derby County (7)
Hat-tricks: 0   2 Goals in a game: 1

Perhaps England's best inside-forward, one of the great playmaker–goalscorers, confident, tetchy, dominating, Raich Carter had one of the longest of all England careers – and sadly one of the longest gaps between caps (9yr 347d). World War II didn't help, but his total of caps was nevertheless ridiculously small. He scored in the first minute of England's first match after the war, against Ireland.

Horatio Stratton Carter, footballing aristocrat
(Lamming)

JOSEPH
HENRY
CARTER

b 16 Apr 1901   d 21 Jan 1977   **INSIDE RIGHT/LEFT**
Caps: 3   Goals: 4
First cap: 24 May 1926 v Belgium 5-3   aged 25yr 38d
(1 goal)
Last cap: 15 May 1929 v Spain 3-4   aged 28yr 29d
(2 goals)
England career: 2yr 356d – P3 W2 D0 L1 – 66.66%
Club: West Bromwich Albion
2 goals in a game: 1
Joe Carter scored in all three games, all against continental opposition. In Brussels in 1929, after CAMSELL had scored the first four, he added the 500th goal scored by England.

ARTHUR
EDWARD
CATLIN

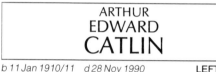

b 11 Jan 1910/11   d 28 Nov 1990   **LEFT BACK**
Caps: 5   Goals: 0
First cap: 17 Oct 1936 v Wales 1-2 aged 25/26 yr 280d
Last cap: 17 May 1937 v Sweden 4-0
aged 26/27 yr 120d
England career: 0yr 182d – P5 W4 D1 L0 – 90%
Club: Sheffield Wednesday
With his broken nose and savage haircut, Ted Catlin looked a fearsome proposition. Certainly he was good enough to keep HAPGOOD out of international football for a while. Strangely, Charlie BUCHAN referred to him as Bert, HAPGOOD himself as Ernie! He was Edward, known as Ted. Definitely.

ARTHUR
CHADWICK

b 1875   d 21 Mar 1936   **CENTRE HALF**
Caps: 2   Goals: 0
First cap: 26 Mar 1900 v Wales 1-1   aged 24/25
Last cap: 7 Apr 1900 v Scotland 1-4   aged 24/25
England career: 0yr 12d – P2 W0 D1 L1 – 25%
Club: Southampton
Died watching Exeter City playing at home. E CHADWICK was his cousin.

EDGAR
WALLACE
CHADWICK

b 14 Jun 1869   d 14 Feb 1942   **INSIDE LEFT**
Caps: 7   Goals: 3
First cap: 7 Mar 1891 v Wales 4-1   aged 21yr 266d
(1 goal)
Last cap: 3 Apr 1897 v Scotland 1-2   aged 27yr 293d
England career: 6yr 27d – P7 W5 D1 L1 – 78.57%

Club: Everton
2 Goals in a game: 0
A fast dribbler, often used on the wing, he enjoyed some good moments, including the winner against Scotland in 1891.

MARK
VALENTINE
CHAMBERLAIN

b 19 Nov 1961   **OUTSIDE RIGHT**
Caps: 8   Goals: 1
First cap: 15 Dec 1982 v Luxembourg 9-0
aged 21y 26d (sub 65min, 1 goal)
Last cap: 17 Oct 1984 v Finland 5-0
aged 22y 332d (sub 80min)
England career: 1yr 306d – P8 W3 D2 L3 – 50%
Club: Stoke City
Substitute: 3   Substituted: 2
Skilful winger, sensational start: cap after only a few months in First Division, goal after just a few minutes of international debut. Then quickly downhill.

HENRY
CHAMBERS

b 17 Nov 1896   d 29 Jun 1949
INSIDE LEFT/CENTRE FORWARD
Caps: 8   Goals: 5
First cap: 14 Mar 1921 v Wales 0-0   aged 24yr 117d
Last cap: 20 Oct 1923 v Ireland 1-2   aged 26yr 337d
England career: 2yr 220d – P8 W3 D3 L2 – 56.25%
Club: Liverpool
3 Goals in a game: 0   2 Goals in a game: 1
Big, aggressive Harry Chambers was selected against Scotland in 1924 but had to cry off and was replaced by BUCHAN. He scored the only two goals of the game against Ireland in 1922.

MICHAEL
ROGER
CHANNON

b 28 Nov 1948   **FORWARD**
Caps: 46   Goals: 21   Captain: 2
First cap: 11 Oct 1972 v Yugoslavia 1-1 aged 23yr 317d
Last cap: 7 Sep 1977 v Switzerland 0-0 aged 28yr 283d
(sub'd HT)
England career: 4yr 331d – P46 W22 D15 L9 – 64.13%
Clubs: Southampton (45), Manchester City (1)
Substitute: 2   Substituted: 5   2 Goals in a game: 4
Goals while captain: 3   Penalties: 3   Missed: 0
Teamed at times with some sub-standard players, not quite a great one himself, Mick Channon nevertheless scored in five successive seasons. He was less successful against the very best teams. As an unintentionally hilarious TV pundit, he coined that vivid verb 'to done great'.

FREDERICK
PATEY
CHAPPELL

b 1850   d 25 Sep 1907   **FORWARD**
Caps: 1   **Goals:** 0
Only cap: 30 Nov 1872 v Scotland 0–0   *aged 21/22*
England career: P1 W0 D1 L0 – 50%
Club: Oxford University

Changed his name to Frederick Brunning Maddison in 1873, and appears as such in most yearbooks.

GARY
CHARLES

b 13 April 1970   **RIGHT BACK**
Caps: 2   **Goals:** 0
First cap: 8 Jun 1991 v N Zealand 2–0   *aged 21yr 56d*
Last cap: 12 Jun 1991 v Malaysia 4–2   *aged 21yr 60d*
England career: 0yr 4d – P2 W2 D0 L0 – 100%
Club: Nottingham Forest

Quick, good on the ball; with SALAKO, one of the finds of the 1991 summer tour.

JOHN
CHARLTON

b 8 May 1935   **CENTRE HALF**
Caps: 35   **Goals:** 6
First cap: 10 Apr 1965 v Scotland 2–2   *aged 29yr 337d*
Last cap: 11 Jun 1970 v Czechoslovakia 1–0
                                          aged 35y 34d
England career: 5yr 62d – P35 W25 D8 L2 – 82.86%
Club: Leeds United
2 goals in a game: 0

Jack the Giraffe was immovable in England's central defence and carried his remarkable scoring record onto the international stage, with at least two more for England than any other out-and-out defender, including goals in consecutive games on two separate occasions. He and R CHARLTON were the last brothers to play for England. In later years he was a pain in England's side as manager of Eire.

ROBERT
CHARLTON

b 11 Oct 1937
        OUTSIDE LEFT/CENTRE FORWARD/MIDFIELD
Caps: 106   **Goals:** 49   **Captain:** 3
First cap: 19 Apr 1958 v Scotland 4–0   *aged 20yr 189d*
                                                    (1 goal)
Last cap: 14 Jun 1970 v W Germany 2–3 aged 32yr 245d
                                             (sub'd 69min)
England career: 12yr 56d – P106 W60 D24 L22 – 67.92%
Club: Manchester United

Substitute: 1   **Substituted:** 5
3 Goals in a game: 4   **2 Goals in a game:** 8
Goals while captain: 1   **Goals as sub:** 1
Penalties: 4   **Missed:** 1

We all know the story: the Italian gateman/Hungarian peasant/Colombian baggage-handler who knows only four words of English: Bobbee Chalton very good.

Why so beloved? For being the perfect gent, we're told – but the likes of Finney, Hurst, Peters, Mooro and Greavsie weren't exactly Attila and Genghis either. The skills and flair, then? There were others with more – and he wasn't an unqualified success as midfield general. What, then? The shooting, that's what then.

Nobody shot like Bobby Charlton. Either foot, any range. Nobody shot so many goals for England, five clear of GREAVES in second place. Nobody else scored in 13 successive seasons (and never mind the funny one in 1966–67) or in 27 England matches. So nobody begrudges the virtual sainthood that's been conferred on him.

His total of caps overhauled Billy WRIGHT's as a European record. His four hat-tricks equalled WOODWARD's England record (later surpassed by GREAVES). He was the second of only two players (see BLOOMER) to hold the England record for goals as well as appearances. He played at least 10 times against each of the other Home countries. He and GREAVES scored together in seven different matches, equalling another England record. His scoring (12yr 25d) and appearance spans for England are two of the longest. Made captain in his 100th international, he scored England's third goal after a mistake by Pat Jennings. He and J CHARLTON were the last brothers to play for England.

There's more, but that'll do. Bobbee Chalton pretty good all right.

RAYMOND
OGDEN
CHARNLEY

b 29 May 1935   **CENTRE FORWARD**
Caps: 1   **Goals:** 0
Only cap: 3 Oct 1962 v France 1–1   *aged 27yr 127d*
England career: P1 W0 D1 L0 – 50%
Club: Blackpool

Ray Charnley wasn't the greatest striker in the world, but he might have been given a better chance to disprove it. In the first match after the World Cup, Winterbottom put out an attack in which only GREAVES had been capped at all (see CROWE, HELLAWELL, HINTON).

CHARLES CHRISTOPHER
CHARSLEY

b 7 Nov 1864 d 10 Jan 1945 GOALKEEPER
Caps: 1 Goals conceded: 1
Only cap: 25 Feb 1893 v Ireland 6–1 aged 28yr 110d
England career: P1 W1 D0 L0 – 100%
Club: Small Heath (later Birmingham City)
An unreliable source says he was known as Chris.
Shame – Charles Charsley has a certain ring.

SAMUEL
CHEDGZOY

b 27 Jan 1889/90 d 15 Jan 1967 OUTSIDE RIGHT
Caps: 8 Goals: 0
First cap: 15 Mar 1920 v Wales 1–2 aged 30/31yr 48d
Last cap: 22 Oct 1924 v Ireland 3–1 aged 34/35yr 269d
England career: 4yr 221d – P8 W2 D3 L3 – 43.75%
Club: Everton
A good crosser of the ball who fed the very young
Dixie DEAN at club level, Sam Chedgzoy played
in some very ordinary England teams.

CHARLES JOHN
CHENERY

b 1 Jan 1850 d unknown FORWARD
Caps: 3 Goals: 1
First cap: 30 Nov 1872 v Scotland 0–0 aged 22yr 333d
Last cap: 7 Mar 1874 v Scotland 1–2 aged 24yr 66d
England career: 1yr 97d – P3 W1 D1 L1 – 50%
Club: Crystal Palace
The only player to take part in England's first
three matches. His club was the original Palace,
not the club in existence now.

TREVOR
JOHN
CHERRY

b 23 Feb 1948 RIGHT/LEFT BACK/MIDFIELD
Caps: 27 Goals: 0 Captain: 1
First cap: 24 Mar 1976 v Wales 1–2 aged 28yr 30d
Last cap: 18 Jun 1980 v Spain 2–1 aged 32yr 116d
(sub'd 83min)
England career: 4yr 86d – P27 W13 D9 L5 – 64.81%
Club: Leeds United
Substitute: 4 Substituted: 2
The only time two players were sent off in an Eng-
land match, against Argentina in 1977, Daniel
Bertoni was guilty, Trevor Cherry (who lost some
teeth) wasn't.

ALLENBY C
CHILTON

b 16 Sep 1918 CENTRE HALF
Caps: 2 Goals: 0

First cap: 7 Oct 1950 v N Ireland 4–1 aged 32yr 21d
Last cap: 3 Oct 1951 v France 2–2 aged 33yr 17d
England career: 0yr 361d – P2 W1 D1 L0 – 75%
Club: Manchester United
Good in the air but famously slow, especially by
the time he was capped.

HENRY
CHIPPENDALE

b 2 Oct 1870 d 29 Sep 1952 OUTSIDE RIGHT
Caps: 1 Goals: 0
Only cap: 3 Mar 1894 v Ireland 2–2 aged 23yr 152d
England career: P1 W1 D0 L0 – 100%
Club: Blackburn Rovers
This was the first match Ireland didn't lose to
England. None of the English had won as many
as seven caps, and six didn't win any more after
this, including hefty Harry Chippendale.

MARTIN
HARCOURT
CHIVERS

b 27 Apr 1945 STRIKER
Caps: 24 Goals: 13
First cap: 3 Feb 1971 v Malta 1–0 aged 25yr 282d
Last cap: 17 Oct 1973 v Poland 1–1 aged 28yr 173d
(sub'd 88min)
England career: 2yr 256d – P24 W15 D5 L4 – 72.92%
Club: Tottenham Hotspur
Substitute: 2 Substituted: 1
2 Goals in a game: 3
Everybody's favourite enigma. Very big and
strong – but light-footed and skilful. A world-
class finisher – but no hat-tricks in the League.
Still, big Martin was no worse than most in a team
that won matches when they didn't matter
(Greece, Malta, Austria 7÷0) and didn't when
they did (West Germany 1972 and Poland 1973).
For a while, at least he gave England a boost:
leading scorer three years in a row, regarded as
the best centre-forward in Europe (by Europeans, too). Oh, and he nearly got that elusive hat-
trick: two fine goals in the first half against Scotland, another disallowed in the second.

EDWARD
CHRISTIAN

b 14 Sep 1858 d 3 Apr 1934 FULL BACK
Caps: 1 Goals: 0
Only cap: 5 Apr 1879 v Scotland 5–4 aged 20yr 233d
England career: P1 W1 D0 L0 – 100%
Club: Old Etonians (& surely Cambridge University)
England were 4–1 down by half-time, won dra-
matically and freakishly, then dropped seven
players for good.

EDWIN HAROLD CLAMP

b 14 Sep 1934   RIGHT HALF

Caps: 4   **Goals:** 0
First cap: 18 May 1958 v USSR 1–1   aged 23yr 246d
Last cap: 15 Jun 1958 v Austria 2–2   aged 23yr 274d
England career: 0yr 28d – P4 W0 D4 L0 – 50%
Club: Wolves

Tallish and tenacious, Eddie Clamp made up an all-Wolves halfback line in the World Cup finals with SLATER and WA WRIGHT, and had a unique England career: four games, four draws.

DANIEL CLAPTON

b 22 Jul 1934 d Jun 1986   OUTSIDE RIGHT

Caps: 1   **Goals:** 0
Only cap: 26 Nov 1958 v Wales 2–2 aged 24yr 127d
England career: P1 W0 D1 L0 – 50%
Club: Arsenal

Danny Clapton was the first winger to be capped after FINNEY's departure.

THOMAS CLARE

b 1865   d 27 Dec 1929   RIGHT BACK
Caps: 4   **Goals:** 0
First cap: 2 Mar 1889 v Ireland 6–1   aged 23/24
Last cap: 7 Apr 1894 v Scotland 2–2   aged 28/29
England career: 5yr 36d – P4 W3 D1 L0 – 87.50%
Club: Stoke FC

Big Tommy, the club's first professional, made up an all-Stoke back three for England with W ROWLEY and UNDERWOOD.

The big man only knocks twice. Martin Chivers – challenged here by Pat Rice, watched by Channon and Bell – scored both of England's goals 'away' to Northern Ireland at Goodison Park in 1973 (Colorsport)

Sniffer Clarke sends Ivo Viktor (and the photographer) the wrong way to score the only goal on his debut
(Popperfoto)

ALLAN
JOHN
CLARKE

b 31 Jul 1946   STRIKER
Caps: 19   Goals: 10
First cap: 11 Jun 1970 v Czechoslovakia 1–0
aged 23yr 315d (1 pen)
Last cap: 19 Nov 1975 v Portugal 1–1   aged 29yr 111d
(sub 74min)
England career: 5yr 161d – P19 W10 D5 L4 – 65.79%
Club: Leeds United
Substitute: 3   Substituted: 3
2 Goals in a game: 2   Penalties: 4   Missed: 1

A lean, sharp, arrogant striker, part of Ramsey's brave new team after the 1970 World Cup, Allan Clarke's first 10 games were all unbeaten; then it went wrong, with no wins in the last five. Typically confident, he offered to be the penalty-taker in his first international. His last goal for England was also a penalty, the frustrating equaliser against Poland in 1973. He also scored from the spot against Malta in 1971, then missed another in the same game, the second of only two players (see R CHARLTON) to miss one and score one for England.

HENRY
ALFRED
CLARKE

b 23 Feb 1923   CENTRE HALF
Caps: 1   Goals: 0
Only cap: 3 April 1954 v Scotland 4–2 aged 31yr 39d
England career: P1 W1 D0 L0 – 100%
Club: Tottenham Hotspur

Tall, good in the air, but Harry Clarke was past his best by the time he became the first stopper to be tried out after the Hungarian visit to Wembley.

THOMAS
CLAY

b 19 Nov 1892   d 21 Feb 1949   RIGHT BACK
Caps: 4   Goals: 0
First cap: 15 Mar 1920 v Wales 1–2   aged 27yr 117d
Last cap: 8 Apr 1922 v Scotland 0–1   aged 29yr 140d
England career: 2yr 24d – P4 W1 D1 L2 – 37.50%
Club: Tottenham Hotspur

Six members of Spurs' FA winning team of 1921 played for England: B SMITH, GRIMSDELL, SEED, BLISS, DIMMOCK and Tommy Clay.

RONALD
CLAYTON

b 5 Aug 1934   RIGHT HALF
Caps: 35   Goals: 0   Captain: 5

First cap: 2 Nov 1955 v N Ireland 3-0   aged 21yr 89d
Last cap: 11 May 1960 v Yugoslavia 3-3 aged 25yr 280d
England career: 4yr 191d – P35 W19 D9 L7 – 67.14%
Club: Blackburn Rovers

The Slavs did for Ronnie Clayton. A fixture in a settled team, though never a favourite of the fans, he had a surprisingly bad match ('his performance was just too bad to be true') in a 5-0 defeat in Belgrade which put him out of the 1958 World Cup, then was captain in his last five internationals until a poor team performance at Wembley saw him abruptly dropped in favour of Bobby ROBSON.

JOHN
CHARLES
CLEGG

b 15 Jun 1850   d 26 Jun 1937   FORWARD
Caps: 1   Goals: 0
Only cap: 30 Nov 1872 v Scotland 0-0 aged 22yr 168d
England career: P1 W0 D1 L0 – 50%
Club: Sheffield Wednesday

Sir Charles Clegg was later one of the most influential men in football, as FA President from 1923 till his death. He played in the very first international, WE CLEGG in the second, the first brothers to play for England.

When he died, he was the longest-lived England player before WELCH.

WILLIAM
EDWIN
CLEGG

b 21 Apr 1852   d 22 Aug 1932   FORWARD
Caps: 2   Goals: 0
First cap: 8 Mar 1873 v Scotland 4-2   aged 20yr 321d
Last cap: 18 Jan 1879 v Wales 2-1   aged 26yr 272d
England career: 5yr 308d – P2 W2 D0 L0 – 100%
Clubs: Sheffield Wednesday (1), Sheffield Albion (1)

William Clegg was the first player to have to wait more than five years between England appearances (the first, in fact, to have a five-year England career!). He and his brother JC CLEGG were the first brothers to play for England – and the only pair to be knighted for services to football.

He was a barrister, and the story goes that he was taking part in the trial of the famous thief Charlie Peace and arrived 20 minutes late for his second international. Nice tale, but first, it seems odd that no reserve had been chosen; second, his train was supposedly delayed on the way from Sheffield, which suggests confusion with the WH CARR story; and third, match reports in *The Times*, *The Sportsman* and *Athletic News* make no mention of it. It may nevertheless be true!

RAYMOND
NEAL
CLEMENCE

b 5 Aug 1948   GOALKEEPER
Caps: 61   Captain: 1
Goals conceded: 54   Clean sheets: 27
First cap: 15 Nov 1972 v Wales 1-0   aged 24yr 102d
Last cap: 16 Nov 1983 v Luxembourg 4-0
                                      aged 35yr 103d
England career: 11yr 01d – P61 W33 D14 L14 – 65.57%
Clubs: Liverpool (56), Tottenham Hotspur (5)
Substitute: 1   Penalties: 8   Saved: 1

A natural athlete but another unreliably brilliant Liverpool keeper, (Lawrence, Grobbelaar) Ray Clemence may finally be remembered as the man who deprived SHILTON of another few dozen caps, which is unfair but perhaps not completely so. He had his moments, as when he made save after save to earn a goalless draw in Rio in 1977 – but they weren't always good ones: the Dalglish shot that went through his legs, the Bonhof free-kick. He was the first goalkeeper to captain England (v Brazil 1981) since SWIFT – and saved Dani's second, retaken penalty against Spain in 1980.

DAVID T
CLEMENT

b 2 Feb 1948   d (suicide) 31 Mar 1982   RIGHT BACK
Caps: 5   Goals: 0
First cap: 24 Mar 1976 v Wales 2-1   aged 28yr 51d
                                        (sub HT)
Last cap: 9 Feb 1977 v Holland 0-2   aged 29yr 7d
England career: 0yr 322d – P5 W3 D0 L2 – 75%
Club: Queen's Park Rangers
Substitute: 1   Substituted: 1

Dave Clement followed his club partner GILLARD into the England team, and found it just as hard, finishing with two 2-0 defeats, against Italy and Cruyff & Co.

BRIAN
HOWARD
CLOUGH

b 21 Mar 1935   CENTRE FORWARD
Caps: 2   Goals: 0
First cap: 17 Oct 1959 v Wales 1-1   aged 24yr 210d
Last cap: 28 Oct 1959 v Sweden 2-3   aged 24yr 221d
England career: 0yr 11d – P2 W0 D1 L1 – 25%
Club: Middlesbrough

There'd been a Call for Clough before the World Cup in Sweden; Winterbottom took the hulking KEVAN instead. More than a year later, he put BC in a team that included four other new caps, three strikers and no playmaker; a shambles, repeated man-for-man against the excellent

Clough senior made one of England's goals against Sweden but missed this chance and didn't get another, as player or manager (Hulton)

Swedes. So he wasn't given a chance for England, as player or manager. An unforgettable figure, still just about compulsive viewing, his record as a manager would speak for itself if it ever got a word in.

NIGEL
HOWARD
CLOUGH

b 19 Mar 1966 **CENTRE FORWARD**
Caps: 4   Goals: 0
First cap: 23 May 1989 v Chile 0–0   aged 23yr 65d
Last cap: 12 Jun 1991 v Malaysia 4–2   aged 25yr 85d
England career: 2yr 20d – P4 W2 D2 L0 – 75%
Club: Nottingham Forest
Substitute: 1
Completed the second father-and-son act to play for England (see EASTHAM). Speed of thought makes up for lack of speed.

RALPH
COATES

b 26 Apr 1946   **OUTSIDE RIGHT/MIDFIELDER**
Caps: 4   Goals: 0
First cap: 21 Apr 1970 v N Ireland 3–1   aged 23yr 360d
Last cap: 19 May 1971 v Wales 0–0   aged 25yr 23d
England career: 1yr 28d – P4 W3 D1 L0 – 87.50%
Clubs: Burnley (2), Tottenham Hotspur (2)

Substitute: 1   Substituted: 1
Everyone wanted Ralphie to do well. Dynamic and sometimes unstoppable on the ball, he gave value for money just by trying to. Never quite a winger, or a playmaker, or a success with Spurs and England, there were nevertheless times when the constant comparison with Bobby CHARLTON had nothing to do with hairstyle.

WILLIAM
NEVILL
COBBOLD

b 4 Feb 1863   *d 8 Apr 1922*
 INSIDE/OUTSIDE FORWARD
Caps: 9   Goals: 6
First cap: 24 Feb 1883 v Ireland 7–0   aged 20yr 20d
   (2 goals)
Last cap: 19 Mar 1887 v Scotland 2–3   aged 24yr 43d
England career: 4yr 23d – P9 W5 D2 L2 – 66.66%
Club: Cambridge University & Old Carthusians (6);
   Old Carthusians alone (3); Corinthians (1885–88)
Hat tricks: 0   2 Goals in a game: 1
His second goal against Ireland in 1883 was the 50th scored by England. He was nicknamed 'Nuts', because (according to CB FRY) he was 'all kernel and extremely hard to crack'. Let's hope so.

JOHN
GILBERT
COCK

b 14 Nov 1893   d 19 Apr 1966   **CENTRE FORWARD**
Caps: 2   Goals: 2
First cap: 25 Oct 1919 v Ireland 1–1   aged 25yr 345d
                                                    (1 goal)
Last cap: 10 Apr 1920 v Scotland 5–4   aged 26yr 148d
                                                    (1 goal)
England career: 0yr 168d – P2 W1 D1 L0 – 75%
Clubs: Huddersfield Town (1), Chelsea (1)

Apparently the first Cornishman to be capped, Jack Cock made a dramatic start to his international career, scoring after 30 seconds or so of England's first match after the First World War with a shot that goalkeeper Walter O'Hagan touched onto the bar and in; possibly the fastest debut goal in all international football (see NICHOLSON).

HENRY
COCKBURN

b 14 Sep 1923   **LEFT HALF**
Caps: 13   Goals: 0
First cap: 28 Sep 1946 v N Ireland 7–2   aged 23yr 14d
Last cap: 3 Oct 1951 v France 2–2   aged 28yr 19d
England career: 5yr 05d – P13 W9 D2 L2 – 76.92%
Club: Manchester United

Short, but good in the air, above all quick and dogged on the ground, a counterpoint to all the skill in England's first, successful, post-war team. He wasn't known as Harry.

GEORGE
REGINALD
COHEN

b 22 Oct 1939   **RIGHT BACK**
Caps: 37   Goals: 0
First cap: 6 May 1964 v Uruguay 2–1   aged 24yr 197d
Last cap: 22 Nov 1967 v N Ireland 2–0   aged 28yr 31d
England career: 3yr 200d – P37 W26 D8 L3 – 81.08%
Club: Fulham

Teammates chuckled (gently) at George Cohen's crosses on the overlap, but his tackling and speed of recovery made him very, very hard on wingers. Fit and strong, it was ironic that injury should make him the first of the World Cup Final team to retire from international football, and that illness should affect him afterwards.

HORACE
COLCLOUGH

b 1891   d 1941   **LEFT BACK**
Caps: 1   Goals: 0

Only cap: 16 Mar 1914 v Wales 2–0   aged 22/23
England career: P1 W1 D0 L0 – 100%
Club: Crystal Palace

Typically stiff tackler who did well to win a cap during CROMPTON's reign. The revised Lamming book calls him Henry, which may well be right. 'Horace' comes from a personal phone call to a Palace statistician. Sadly it was several years ago and his name has escaped.

ERNEST HERBERT
COLEMAN

b 19 Oct 1889   d 15 Jun 1958   **GOALKEEPER**
Caps: 1   Goals conceded: 0
Only cap: 14 March 1921 v Wales 0–0   aged 31yr 146d
England career: P1 W0 D1 L0 – 50%
Club: Dulwich Hamlet

England picked a new goalkeeper in each of the first six matches after sam HARDY's reign. Coleman, an amateur, was the second. He did nothing very wrong in the mud at Ninian Park.

JOHN GEORGE
('TIM')
COLEMAN

b 26 Oct 1881   d 20 Nov 1940   **INSIDE RIGHT**
Caps: 1   Goals: 0
Only cap: 16 Feb 1907 v Ireland 1–0   aged 25yr 113d
England career: P1 W1 D0 L0 – 100%
Club: Woolwich Arsenal

Five players won their first England caps at Goodison; all except perhaps 'Tim' Coleman were out of the very top drawer.

ALFRED
COMMON

b 25 May 1880   d 3 Apr 1946
                                   INSIDE/CENTRE FORWARD
Caps: 3   Goals: 3
First cap: 29 Feb 1904 v Wales 2–2   aged 23yr 280d
                                                    (1 goal)
Last cap: 19 Mar 1906 v Wales 1–0   aged 25yr 299d
England career: 2yr 19d – P3 W2 D1 L0 – 83.33%
Clubs: Sheffield United (2), Middlesbrough (1)
2 Goals in a game: 1

Not tall, very heavy, an out-and-out goalscorer, well known as the first player to attract a £1000 transfer fee (in 1905), Alf Common was also, a year earlier, the first to cost £500.

Note that some yearbooks (with *Rothmans* to the fore) credit G DAVIS with one of his two goals against Ireland in 1904. Match reports in *The Sporting Life*, *Athletic News*, and *Belfast Telegraph* all say Alf scored them both.

Portrait of a Common man. The first to fetch £1000
(Bob Thomas)

LESLIE
HARRY
COMPTON

b 12 Sep 1912   d 27 Dec 1984   CENTRE HALF
Caps: 2   Goals: 0
First cap: 15 Nov 1950 v Wales 4–2   aged 38yr 64d
Last cap: 22 Nov 1950 v Yugoslavia 2–2   aged 38yr 71d
(1 own goal)
England career: 0yr 7d – P2 W1 D1 L0 – 75%
Club: Arsenal

Brother of the Test cricketer, big Leslie (or MORTEN) was the oldest player to make his debut for England, perhaps for any country – and the first of two (see PEJIC) to put through his own goal in his last international, which was played on his home club ground.

JAMES
CONLIN

b 6 Jul 1881   d 23 Jun 1917   OUTSIDE LEFT
Caps: 1   Goals: 0
Only cap: 7 Apr 1906 v Scotland 1–2   aged 24yr 302d
England career: P1 W0 D0 L1 – 0%
Club: Bradford City

The epitome of the buzzing little winger at 5ft 5in and 9st 11b (the writer and amateur international Ivan Sharpe said 5ft 4in and 9st 61b), Jimmy Conlin was killed in the First World War.

JOHN
MICHAEL
CONNELLY

b 18 Jul 1938   OUTSIDE RIGHT/LEFT
Caps: 20   Goals: 7
First cap: 17 Oct 1959 v Wales 1–1   aged 21yr 91d
Last cap: 11 Jul 1966 v Uruguay 0–0   aged 27yr 358d
England career: 6yr 267d – P20 W11 D6 L3 – 70%
Clubs: Burnley (10), Manchester United (10)
2 Goals in a game: 0

John Connelly was given a fair run (and had his moments) in the England team before being one of the three wingers (PAINE and, temporarily, CALLAGHAN) dropped after a single match in the 1966 World Cup.

THOMAS
EDWIN REED
COOK

b 4 Jan/5 Feb 1901   d 15 Jan 1950   CENTRE FORWARD
Caps: 1   Goals: 0
Only cap: 28 Feb 1925 v Wales 2–1   aged 24yr 23/56d
England career: P1 W1 D0 L0 – 100%
Club: Brighton and Hove Albion

Tommy Cook made his international debut in the same match as Len GRAHAM, the last time two Third Division players appeared in the same match for England (see TITMUSS and WE RAWLINGS).

NORMAN CHARLES
COOPER

b 12 Jul 1870   d 30 Jul 1920   HALF BACK
Caps: 1   Goals: 0
Only cap: 25 Feb 1893 v Ireland 6–1   aged 22yr 228d
England career: P1 W1 D0 L0 – 100%
Club: Cambridge Univ (& Old Brightonians & Corinthians)

One of six new England caps at Perry Barr.

TERENCE
COOPER

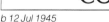

b 12 Jul 1945   LEFT BACK
Caps: 20   Goals: 0
First cap: 12 Mar 1969 v France 5–0   aged 23yr 243d
Last cap: 20 Nov 1974 v Portugal   aged 29yr 131d
(sub'd 23min)
England career: 5yr 253d – P20 W12 D6 L2 – 75%
Club: Leeds United
Substituted: 1

Terry Cooper looked good on television making those runs up the flank in the first Mexico World Cup, which left him exhausted when Jurgen Grabowski came on to turn the quarter-final round. His old club manager brought him back for a last (brief) cap after a three-year gap.

Paul Gascoigne goes past Michel de Wolf on the kind of run that made him a star of the 1990 World Cup. The last in this match against Belgium led to him being fouled; from his free-kick, David Platt volleyed England's last-minute winner
(Bob Thomas)

Above *Wembley, 30 July 1966. Ray Wilson struggles to uphold Bobby Moore, who has no such problems with the World Cup, flanked by (right to left) the tired but happy Bobby Charlton and George Cohen, the goalscorers Hurst and Peters, the hidden Hunt, Ballie, Banksie, big Jack and a sabre-toothed Stiles. England the world champions* (Popperfoto)

Above *Franz Beckenbauer, who played against England a record seven times, shakes hands with Bobby Moore (who played the same number of matches against West Germany) before the 0–0 draw in West Berlin that knocked England out of the 1972 European Championships* (Allsport)

Left *England hosted the 1966 World Cup, the team won it, the manager was knighted. Everyone was happy. Including Sir Alfred. Honest* (Allsport)

Left *John Barnes with a brilliant run, and Mark Hateley with a header, have just scored their first goals for England, who have beaten Brazil in the Maracana for the first time. 10 June 1984* (Allsport)

Below *Only a week after Heysel, England wear black armbands for their game with Italy in Mexico City. Left to right: Francis, Shilton, Wright, Hateley, Waddle, Butcher, Sansom, Wilkins, Robson, Steven, MG Stevens. Barely 8000 spectators watched a (very) friendly match* (Allsport)

Gary Lineker watches as Danny Wallace volleys a goal in his only international, against Egypt in 1986 (Bob Thomas)

Above *The 1986 World Cup is over for Ray Wilkins (sent off) and Bryan Robson (injured again) at half-time against Morocco, but just about to start for England who drew this match but won the next two 3–0 to reach the quarter-finals* (Allsport)

Below *England look good before the 1986 World Cup quarter-final against Argentina. Left to right: Shilton, Hoddle, MG Stevens, Fenwick, Lineker, Butcher, Hodge, Sansom, Steven, Reid, Beardsley. But the Hand of God is about to intervene* (Allsport)

Above *Tony Adams heads the equaliser against Holland at Wembley in 1988 to become the only player to score for each side in an England match* (Allsport)

Above *Alex McLeish is too late to stop substitute Steve Bull scoring on his England debut, at Hampden in 1989*
(Colorsport)

Marco van Basten is about to score his first goal in the 1988 European Championships. Two more in the second half made him the first player to score a hat-trick against England for nearly 30 years (Colorsport)

The first for Graham Taylor. From left: Gascoigne, Lineker (the scorer and new captain) and Platt (7) celebrate the only goal of the game against Hungary at Wembley (Allsport)

Left *The match against the Republic of Ireland wasn't the best of Italia '90, but Lineker gave it a good start, swerving past Bonner and outpacing Mick McCarthy and Chris Morris to put England ahead after just nine minutes* (Allsport)

Below *David Platt heads England in front in the quarter-final against the Cameroon* (Allsport)

Bottom *The bench rises to greet England's extra-time win. From left: Webb, Barnes, MG Stevens, Dorigo, Butcher, Bull, Beasant, McMahon* (Allsport)

Left *The England team that started the vivid semi-final against West Germany. Left to right: Butcher, Wright, Shilton, Pearce, Platt, Lineker, Walker, Waddle, Gascoigne, Beardsley, Parker* (Allsport)

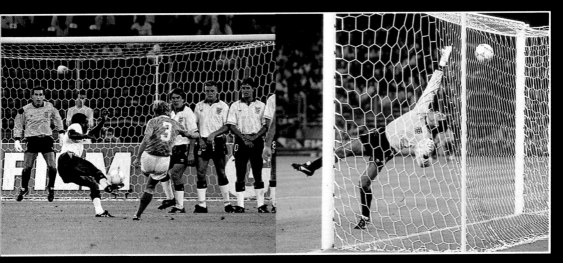

Above *For the second semi-final in a row, Andreas Brehme puts West Germany 1–0 ahead from a free-kick, his left-footed shot hitting an unlucky Paul Parker . . . and ballooning over a desperate Shilton* (Bob Thomas)

Right *Gary Lineker leaves two defenders and the goalkeeper standing as his left-footed drive brings the scores level with only ten minutes left* (Allsport)

England are unlucky to the end. Again a dead-ball kick hits someone's leg – but this time the ball stays out. Bodo Illgner goes the wrong way but stops Stuart Pearce's shot, and England are on the way to losing the penalty shoot-out (Bob Thomas)

Three men who scored go to console one who didn't: Lothar Matthaus, Peter Beardsley and David Platt scored from the spot, but Chris Waddle missed England's fifth and the Germans went on to the final (Allsport)

THOMAS COOPER

b 1904? d 25 Jun 1940 **RIGHT BACK**
Caps: 15 **Goals:** 0 **Captain:** 4
First cap: 22 Oct 1927 v Ireland 0–2 aged 22/23?
Last cap: 29 Sep 1934 v Wales 4–0 aged 29/30?
England career: 6yr 341d – P15 W8 D0 L7 – 53.33%
Club: Derby County

A hard man with a brutal haircut, a strong tackler but no great passer, Tommy Cooper was captain in the last four matches of an international career whose win–loss record says everything about England's standing at the time.

STEPHEN JAMES COPPELL

b 9 Jul 1955 **OUTSIDE RIGHT**
Caps: 42 **Goals:** 7
First cap: 16 Nov 1977 v Italy 2–0 aged 22yr 130d
Last cap: 30 Mar 1983 v Greece 0–0 aged 27yr 264d
England career: 5yr 134d – P42 W26 D8 L8 – 71.43%
Club: Manchester United
Substitute: 3 **Substituted:** 4 **2 Goals in a game:** 0

Best remembered for his all-round (i.e. defensive) abilities, Steve Coppell was a classy, attacking winger asked (too often?) to be a nursemaid for his right back. A bad foul eventually ended his international, and first-class, career. All his goals for England were scored from very close range.

WILFRED COPPING

b 17 Aug 1909 d 1980 **LEFT HALF**
Caps: 20 **Goals:** 0
First cap: 13 May 1933 v Italy 1–1 aged 23yr 269d
Last cap: 24 May 1939 v Romania 2–0 aged 29yr 280d
England career: 6yr 11d – P20 W14 D1 L5 – 72.50%
Clubs: Leeds United (8), Arsenal (12)

When they talk about Wilf Copping, they talk parts of the body. The original blue-jawed hard man, he rubbed shoulders with the best inside forwards in Britain and Europe throughout the thirties; it took a war to end his international career. The story goes that when he broke his nose in a League match, he reset it himself and played on. His shoulder-charging helped spark off the Battle of Highbury with Italy in 1934.

BERTIE OSWALD CORBETT

b 15 May 1875 d 30 Nov 1967 **OUTSIDE LEFT**
Caps: 1 **Goals:** 0

Only cap: 18 Mar 1901 v Wales 6–0 aged 25yr 309d
England career: P1 W1 D0 L0 – 100%
Club: Corinthians

He and his brother R CORBETT both won only one cap (both against Wales), both became schoolteachers, and both lived to be over 87. BO was only capped because the original choice, the classy STEVE SMITH of Aston Villa, withdrew.

REGINALD CORBETT

b 1879 d 2 Sep 1967 **OUTSIDE LEFT**
Caps: 1 **Goals:** 0
Only cap: 2 Mar 1903 v Wales 2–1 aged 23/24
England career: P1 W1 D0 L0 – 100%
Club: Old Malverians (& Corinthians)

Brother of BO CORBETT, Rex struggled on the wing against the experienced Horace Blew.

WALTER SAMUEL CORBETT

b 26 Nov 1880 d 1955 **LEFT BACK**
Caps: 3 **Goals:** 0
First cap: 6 Jun 1908 v Austria 6–1 aged 27yr 193d
Last cap: 13 Jun 1908 v Bohemia 4–0 aged 27yr 200d
England career: 0yr 7d – P3 W3 D0 L0 – 100%
Club: Birmingham FC

Leaving F BRADSHAW's single cap aside, Walter Corbett was the first England footballer to play only against foreign opposition.

JOSEPH THOMAS CORRIGAN

b 18 Nov 1948 **GOALKEEPER**
Caps: 9 **Goals conceded:** 5 **Clean sheets:** 4
First cap: 28 May 1976 v Italy 3–2 aged 27yr 191d
(sub HT)
Last cap: 2 Jun 1982 v Iceland 1–1 aged 33yr 196d
England career: 6yr 5d – P9 W3 D5 L1 – 61.11%
Club: Manchester City
Substitute: 1
Penalties: 2 **Saved:** 0

Has any country had a better trio of keepers in a World Cup than SHILTON, CLEMENCE and big Joe in 1982? The only time he was on the losing side was against Scotland in 1981.

ANTHONY RICHARD COTTEE

b 11 Jul 1965 **STRIKER**
Caps: 7 **Goals:** 0
First cap: 10 Sep 1986 v Sweden 0–1 aged 21yr 61d
(sub 58min)

Last cap: 27 May 1989 v Scotland 2–0   aged 23yr 320d
(sub'd 75min)
England career: 2yr 259d – P7 W3 D3 L1 – 64.29%
Clubs: West Ham United (3), Everton (4)
Substitute: 6   **Substituted:** 1

If Bobby ROBSON wanted Tony Cottee to score for England, he might have given him more time than this: 42min, 8min, 8min, 21min, 11min. He only started (but didn't finish) one match.

GEORGE
HUTH
COTTERILL

b 4 Apr 1868   d 1 Oct 1950   CENTRE FORWARD
Caps: 4   **Goals:** 2   **Captain:** 2
First cap: 7 Mar 1891 v Ireland 6–1   aged 22yr 337d
(1 goal)
Last cap: 1 Apr 1893 v Scotland 5–2   aged 24yr 362d
(1 goal)
England career: 2yr 25d – P4 W4 D4 L0 – 100%
Clubs: Cambridge University & Old Brightonians (1);
Old Brightonians alone (3); Corinthians throughout
Goals while captain: 1

One of the heftiest players (and moustaches, see below) of the Victorian era, and one of the most successful international careers, short but sweet. A goal in his first and last matches, goalscoring captain in the latter (no April Fool here) and four wins out of four. Called up for his last cap 'at an hour's notice' to replace John GOODALL.

JOSEPH RICHARD
COTTLE

b 1886   d 3 Feb 1958   LEFT BACK
Caps: 1   **Goals:** 0
Only cap: 13 Feb 1909 v Ireland 4–0   aged 22/23
England career: P1 W1 D0 L0 –100%
Club: Bristol City

Played in his only international alongside clubmate Billy WEDLOCK.

SAMUEL
COWAN

b 10 May 1901   d 4 Oct 1964   CENTRE/LEFT HALF
Caps: 3   **Goals:** 0
First cap: 24 May 1926 v Belgium 5–3   aged 25yr 14d
Last cap: 16 May 1931 v Belgium 4–1   aged 30yr 06d
England career: 4yr 357d – P3 W2 D1 L0 – 83.33%
Club: Manchester City

Much respected, simply a very good all-round player, Sam Cowan was largely kept out of the England team by JH HILL. His three scattered caps were all won against continental opposition.

GORDON
SIDNEY
COWANS

b 27 Oct 1958   MIDFIELDER
Caps: 10   **Goals:** 2
First cap: 23 Feb 1983 v Wales 2–1   aged 24yr 119d
Last cap: 14 Nov 1990 v Eire 1–1   aged 32yr 18d
England career: 7yr 264d – P10 W6 D4 L0 – 80%
Clubs: Aston Villa (8), Bari (2)
Substituted: 1   **2 Goals in a game:** 0

But for injuries, Gordon (Sid) Cowans might have patrolled the left side of England's midfield throughout the eighties. After more than four years, his old club manager controversially recalled him in place of GASCOIGNE in Dublin, where he looked out of place among the kicking and rushing.

One of only six England players (see HOLT, RUTHERFORD, BRIDGETT, HOLLEY, ROCASTLE) to have a 10-match unbeaten international career.

ARTHUR
COWELL

b 20 May 1886   d 12 Feb 1959   LEFT BACK
Caps: 1   **Goals:** 0
Only cap: 12 Feb 1910 v Ireland 1–1   aged 23yr 268d
England career: P1 W1 D0 L0 – 100%
Club: Blackburn Rovers

Three of the five England debutants in Belfast won only this one cap. The highly-rated Cowell was HOULKER's cousin.

JOHN
COX

b 21 Nov 1876   d unknown　　　**OUTSIDE LEFT**
Caps: 3   Goals: 0
First cap: 9 Mar   1901 v Ireland 3–0　　aged 24yr 108d
Last cap: 4 Apr   1903 v Scotland 1–2　　aged 26yr 134d
England career: 2yr 26d – P3 W1 D1 L1 – 50%
Club: Liverpool

Despite the result, Jack Cox had a good game in his last international. *The Athletic News* criticised him for 'hugging' the ball too much, but acknowledged that his dribbling and crossing had helped prevent a heavier defeat.

JOHN
DAVIES
COX

b 1870   d Jun 1957　　　**RIGHT HALF**
Caps: 1   Goals: 0
Only cap: 5 Mar 1892 v Ireland 2–0　　aged 21/22
England career: P1 W1 D0 L0 – 100%
Club: Derby County

England apparently 'played most of the game weak and foul' in Belfast, with Jack Cox described as 'the worst of the lot'. His foul on John Peden reduced Ireland to 10 men for most of the match. To be fair, a couple of reports pointed the finger at HOLT, but JD's guilty by a majority of 5–2 with two abstentions.

JOHN
FORSYTH
CRAWFORD

b 26 Sep 1896   d 27 Sep 1975　　**OUTSIDE LEFT**
Caps: 1   Goals: 0
Only cap: 28 Mar 1931 v Scotland 0–2　　aged 34yr 183d
England career: P1 W0 D0 L1 – 0%
Club: Chelsea

If Scotland had a miniature left winger (Alan Morton) at Hampden in 1931, England had a real tich. Jack Crawford may have stood only 5ft 2in and weighed only 8st 6lb. If the figures are correct, he was the smallest man ever to play for England (see WALDEN). If his date of birth is correct, he was one of the oldest to win a first cap.

RAYMOND
CRAWFORD

b 13 Jul 1936　　　**CENTRE FORWARD**
Caps: 2   Goals: 1
First cap: 22 Nov 1961 v N Ireland 1–1　　aged 25yr 132d
Last cap: 4 Apr   1962 v Austria 3–1　　aged 25yr 265d
　　　　　　　　　　　　　　　　　　(1 goal)
England career: 0yr 133d – P2 W1 D1 L0 – 75%
Club: Ipswich Town

Rugged Ray played in, and scored for, two surprise teams – Ipswich when they won the League title under RAMSEY, Colchester when they beat Leeds – and hit the bar on his England debut.

THOMAS
HENRY
CRAWSHAW

b 27 Dec 1872   d 25 Nov 1960　　**CENTRE HALF**
Caps: 10   Goals: 1
First cap: 9 Mar 1895 v Ireland 9–0　　aged 22yr 72d
Last cap: 12 Mar 1904 v Ireland 3–1　　aged 31yr 75d
England career: 9yr 3d – P10 W7 D1 L2 – 75%
Club: Sheffield Wednesday

Typical of the small and energetic centre-halves of the time, Tommy Crawshaw had a long international career but was often recalled very briefly: as late replacement for HOLT in 1896, then only one cap between 1897 and 1904.

WILLIAM
JOHN
CRAYSTON

b 9 Oct 1910　　　**RIGHT HALF**
Caps: 8   Goals: 1
First cap: 4 Dec   1935 v Germany 3–0　　aged 25yr 56d
Last cap: 1 Dec   1937 v Czechoslovakia 5–4
　　　　　　　　　　　　　　　aged 27y 53d (1 goal)
England career: 1yr 362d – P8 W4 D1 L3 – 56.25%
Club: Arsenal

Before being rescued by a Stanley MATTHEWS hat-trick, England were deep in the wars against Czechoslovakia. Tall Jack Crayston scored after 10 minutes, short Jack MORTON after 18; both were injured and hobbled on the wing, neither played for England again.

FREDERICK
NORMAN
SMITH
CREEK

b 12 Jan 1898   d 26 Jul 1980　　**CENTRE FORWARD**
Caps: 1   Goals: 1   Captain: 1
Only cap: 10 May 1923 v France 4–1　　aged 25yr 120d
England career: P1 W1 D0 L0 – 100%
Club: Corinthians (& Darlington)

Better known, perhaps, as a journalist who wrote a history of the Corinthians, he put England 3–0 ahead in Paris.

WARNEFORD
CRESSWELL

b 5 Nov 1894/97   d 20 Oct 1973　　**RIGHT BACK**
Caps: 7   Goals: 0

Right *Smouldering Sam Crooks, Thirties hot shot*
(Lamming)

First cap: 14 Mar 1921 v Wales 0–0 aged 23/26yr 129d
Last cap: 19 Oct 1929 v Ireland 3–0 aged 31/34yr 348d
England career: 8yr 219d – P7 W3 D3 L1 – 64.29%
Clubs: South Shields (1), Sunderland (5), Everton (1)

In Charlie BUCHAN's opinion, a change from right flank to left turned Warney Cresswell from an average, non-tackling full back into 'the complete defender, worthy to rank with the Howard SPENCERs, the Bob CROMPTONs and the Jesse PENNINGTONs.' Yet, oddly enough, he's listed at number 2 in all his internationals. Even more strangely, he never played in two consecutive England matches; he was recalled after almost exactly three years for his last cap.

Note that the 1972 Farror–Lamming book and Jim Creasy give 1894 as his year of birth, whereas the 1990 Lamming revision shows 1897.

ROBERT
CROMPTON

b 26 Sep 1879   d 16 Mar 1941   **RIGHT BACK**
Caps: 41   **Goals:** 0   **Captain:** 23
First cap: 3 Mar 1902 v Wales 0–0   aged 22yr 158d
Last cap: 4 Apr 1914 v Scotland 1–3   aged 34yr 190d
England career: 12yr 32d – P41 W27 D8 L6 – 75.61%
Club: Blackburn Rovers

Burly Bob broke all the major England records for caps, captaincy, and length of international career.

He took two of them from BLOOMER. His career was only four days longer – but he modernised the record for the highest number of appearances with his world record 41, only overhauled as the England best by WA WRIGHT in 1952. His 23 games as captain alone equalled Bloomer's *total* number of caps (no-one captained England more often until Wright, again, in 1951). His total would have been higher but for the war and the selectors' insistence on an amateur captain (WOODWARD) for the contintental tours of 1908 and 1909. His 19th consecutive cap (1909) broke GO SMITH's record of 15 and was itself overtaken by WEDLOCK.

In the first minute of the match against Scotland in 1907, he became the first England captain to score an own goal. He missed a game here and there, but played in 11 successive England wins, one short of WARREN's record. Captain in his last 14 internationals, he was a high-class defender in an antique sort of way, the shoulder charge a staple weapon. As Charlie BUCHAN said, 'it would not be allowed today'.

SAMUEL
DICKINSON
CROOKS

b 16 Jan 1908/9   d 5 Feb 1981   **OUTSIDE RIGHT**
Caps: 26   **Goals:** 7
First cap: 5 Apr 1930 v Scotland 5–2 aged 21/22yr 79d
Last cap: 2 Dec 1936 v Hungary 6–2 aged 27/28yr 320d
England career: 6yr 241d – P26 W15 D4 L7 – 65.38%
Club: Derby County
Hat tricks: 0   **2 Goals in a game:** 1

A goalscoring winger, Sammy Crooks seemed to lose the knack towards the end of his international career, with no goals in his last 11 games. Before that, he was an important cog in various England attacks, scoring twice in the 7–1 win over Spain in 1931, making the first four goals against Scotland in 1930.

CHRISTOPHER
CROWE

b 11 Jun 1939   **INSIDE RIGHT**
Caps: 1   **Goals:** 0
Only cap: 3 Oct 1962 v France 1–1   aged 23yr 114d
England career: P1 W0 D1 L0 – 50%
Club: Wolves

England didn't take the early European Nations Cups too seriously, picking four new forwards (CHARNLEY, HELLAWELL, HINTON and

Chris Crowe) for the first match after the World Cup, needing a FLOWERS penalty to draw with a French team led by the great Raymond Kopa.

FRANCIS
CUGGY

b 16 Jun 1889   d 27 Mar 1965   **RIGHT HALF**
Caps: 2   **Goals:** 0
First cap: 15 Feb 1913 v Ireland 1–2   aged 23yr 244d
Last cap: 14 Feb 1914 v Ireland 0–3   aged 24yr 243d
England career: 0yr 364d – P2 W0 D0 L2 – 0%
Club: Sunderland

Frank Cuggy, who made his international debut alongside clubmates BUCHAN (who called him 'the nearest thing to perpetual motion I ever saw') and MORDUE, had no luck with the Irish; in his first match they beat England for the first time, in the second, they scored their only three-goal win over England.

STANLEY
CULLIS

b 25 Oct 1915/16   **CENTRE HALF**
Caps: 12   **Goals:** 0   **Captain:** 1
First cap: 23 Oct 1937 v Ireland 5–1
                                 aged 20/21yr 363d
Last cap: 24 May 1939 v Romania 22–0
                                 aged 22/23yr 211d
England career: 1yr 213d – P12 W9 D1 L2 – 79.16%
Club: Wolves

More than just a stopper (though he could stop with the best of them), later Wolves' dogmatic, domestically successful manager, Stan Cullis was England's last captain before the Second World War – and one of the youngest, though there's a doubt about the exact year he was born.

ARTHUR
CUNLIFFE

b 5 Feb 1909   d 28 Aug 1986   **OUTSIDE LEFT**
Caps: 2   **Goals:** 0
First cap: 17 Oct 1932 v Ireland 1–0   aged 23yr 255d
Last cap: 16 Nov 1932 v Wales 0–0   aged 23yr 285d
England career: 0yr 30d – P2 W1 D1 L0 – 75%
Club: Blackburn Rovers

Two drab performances led to the dropping of the entire left wing after the Wales match.

DANIEL
CUNLIFFE

b 1875   d 28 Dec 1937   **INSIDE RIGHT**
Caps: 1   **Goals:** 0
Only cap: 17 Mar 1900 v Ireland 2–0   aged 24/25
England career: P1 W1 D1 L0 – 100%
Club: Portsmouth

The England attack made hard work of it at Lansdowne Road, but they were barely on first-name terms: GO SMITH was winning his 17th cap, the others their first.

JAMES
NATHANIEL
CUNLIFFE

b 5 Jul 1912   d 21 Nov 1986   **INSIDE LEFT**
Caps: 1   **Goals:** 0
Only cap: 9 May 1936 v Belgium 2–3   aged 23yr 309d
England career: P1 W0 D0 L1 – 0%
Club: Everton

Six players won their last caps at the Heysel including Arthur CUNLIFFE's skilful cousin, who seems to have been known as Nat as well as Jimmy.

LAWRENCE
PAUL
CUNNINGHAM

b 8 Mar 1956   d 15 Jul 1989   **OUTSIDE RIGHT**
Caps: 6   **Goals:** 0
First cap: 23 May 1979 v Wales 0–0   aged 23yr 76d
Last cap: 15 Oct 1980 v Romania 1–2   aged 24yr 221d
                                          (sub 65min)
England career: 1yr 145d – P6 W2 D2 L2 – 50%
Clubs: West Bromwich Albion (3), Real Madrid (3)
Substitute: 3

For a number of reasons, you wanted Laurie Cunningham and his skills to succeed. For one reason or another (injuries were one) it didn't happen for England. Then the early death in a road accident. Sadness and a sense of waste.

EDMUND SAMUEL
CURREY

b 28 Jan 1868   d 12 Mar 1920   **INSIDE FORWARD**
Caps: 2   **Goals:** 2
First cap: 15 Mar 1890 v Wales 3–1   aged 22yr 46d
                                          (2 goals)
Last cap: 5 Apr 1890 v Scotland 1–1   aged 22yr 67d
England career: 0yr 21d – P2 W1 D1 L0 – 75%
Club: Oxford University (& Old Carthusians & Corinthians)
2 Goals in a game: 1

Big, quick young student who was 'promoted' from the team to play Ireland as late replacement for COTTERILL at Wrexham, he scored twice and may have made the other (as well as missing a hat-trick only by hitting a post) on his debut but was found out (and 'fagged out', said *The Athletic News*) by the hardened Scots. The original Farror–Lamming Who's Who called him Edward.

ANTHONY
WILLIAM
CURRIE

b 1 Jan 1950   **MIDFIELDER**
Caps: 17   Goals: 3
First cap: 23 May 1972 v N Ireland 0–1   aged 22yr 143d
                                                (sub'd 59min)
Last cap: 10 Jun 1979 v Sweden 0–0   aged 29yr 160d
England career: 7yr 18d – P17 W10 D4 L3 – 70.59%
Clubs: Sheffield United (7), Leeds United (10)
Substitute: 2   Substituted: 2
2 Goals in a game: 0

Tony Currie had a poor start to his international career, taken off as the Irish beat England for the last time, and no manager seems to have known quite what to do with his brand of skill. Just two more caps from RAMSEY, an ultimatum from REVIE, in-and-out by Greenwood. Still, he had his moments: two spanking long shots in 1978, against Wales and Hungary, made him the first substitute to score in two separate matches for England.

ARTHUR
WILLIAM
CURSHAM

b 14 Mar 1853   d 24 Dec 1884   **FORWARD**
Caps: 6   Goals: 2   Captain: 2?
First cap: 4 Mar 1876 v Scotland 0–3   aged 22yr 355d
Last cap: 10 Mar 1883 v Scotland 2–3   aged 29yr 361d
England career: 7yr 6d – P6 W2 D0 L4 – 33.33%
Club: Notts County
Goals while captain: 1

Arthur Cursham, brother of HA CURSHAM, may well have been England's first captain against Wales (1879). But see WACE.

HENRY
ALFRED
CURSHAM

b 27 Nov 1859   d 6 Aug 1941   **OUTSIDE LEFT/RIGHT**
Caps: 8   Goals: 5
First cap: 15 Mar 1880 v Wales 3–2   aged 20yr 109d
Last cap: 23 Feb 1884 v Ireland 8–1   aged 24yr 88d
                                              (3 goals)
England career: 3yr 345d – P8 W5 D0 L3 – 62.50%
Club: Notts County (& Corinthians 1882–86)
3 Goals in a game: 1
2 Goals in a game: 0

While winning a record seventh successive cap, flash Harry became the first player to score a hat-trick in his last match for England; it was also the first for any country in the Home Championship. One of the fastest dribblers of his time, 'the lion of the day' against Scotland in 1883, he was AW CURSHAM's brother.

HARRY
BUTLER
DAFT

b 5 April 1866   d 12 Jan 1945   **LEFT-SIDED FORWARD**
Caps: 5   Goals: 3
First cap: 2 Mar 1889 v Ireland 6–1   aged 22yr 331d
Last cap: 5 Mar 1892 v Ireland 2–0   aged 25yr 334d
                                              (2 goals)
England career: 3yr 3d – P5 W4 D1 L0 – 90%
Clubs: Notts County & Corinthians (3);
            Notts County alone (2)
2 Goals in a game: 1

Harry Daft scored in his last two internationals – and (as an amateur among professionals) may possibly have captained England in the very last, in which *The Athletic News* credits him with only the second goal (but see DEVEY).

THOMAS
DANKS

b 30 May 1863   d 27 Apr 1908   **FORWARD**
Caps: 1   Goals: 0
Only cap: 21 Mar 1885 v Scotland 1–1   aged 21yr 295d
England career: P1 W0 D1 L0 – 50%
Club: Nottingham Forest

Tom Danks was surrounded by famous fellow forwards at the Oval, but struggled against the veteran Charlie Campbell.

JAMES
KENYON
DAVENPORT

b 23 Mar 1862   d 29 Sep 1908   **INSIDE/OUTSIDE RIGHT**
Caps: 2   Goals: 2
First cap: 14 Mar 1885 v Wales 1–1   aged 22yr 356d
Last cap: 15 Mar 1890 v Ireland 9–1   aged 27yr 358d
                                              (2 goals)
England career: 5yr 1d – P2 W1 D1 L0 – 75%
Club: Bolton Wanderers

Kenny Davenport had to wait five years for his second cap. His obituary in the *Sporting Chronicle* confirms his christian names (not Kenneth as was once thought). It's possible that he scored no goals at all against Ireland; see GEARY.

PETER
DAVENPORT

b 24 Mar 1961   **FORWARD**
Caps: 1   Goals: 0
Only cap: 26 Mar 1985 v Eire 2–1 aged 24yr 2d (sub 73min)
England career: P1 W1 D0 L0 – 100%
Club: Nottingham Forest

Bobby ROBSON gave him just 17 minutes of international football. He did at least make an impression, laying on a goal for LINEKER.

GEORGE HENRY DAVIS

b 5 Jun 1881   d 28 Apr 1969   **OUTSIDE LEFT**
Caps: 2   Goals: 0
First cap: 29 Feb 1904 v Wales 2–2   aged 22yr 269d
Last cap: 12 Mar 1904 v Ireland 3–1   aged 22yr 281d
England career: 0yr 12d – P2 W1 D1 L0 – 75%
Club: Derby County

Some modern sources credit George Davis with a goal in his last international – but see COMMON. One of seven new caps at Wrexham.

HENRY DAVIS

b 1880   d unknown   **OUTSIDE RIGHT**
Caps: 3   Goals: 1
First cap: 14 Feb 1903 v Ireland 4–0   aged 22/23
(1 goal)
Last cap: 4 Apr 1903 v Scotland 1–2   aged 22/23
England career: 0yr 49d – P3 W2 D0 L1 – 66.66%
Club: Sheffield Wednesday

At 5ft 4in, Harry Davis seems to have been the shortest man to play for England before WALDEN, but was compensatingly quick.

JOHN EDWARD DAVISON

b 2 Sep 1887   d 1971   **GOALKEEPER**
Caps: 1   Goals conceded: 0
Only cap: 13 Mar 1922 v Wales 1–0   aged 34yr 192d
England career: P1 W1 D0 L0 – 100%
Club: Sheffield Wednesday

At 5ft 7in reportedly the shortest goalkeeper ever to play for England, Teddy Davison was also the oldest England debutant (apart perhaps from MORTEN) before HUDSPETH.

JEREMIAH DAWSON

b 18 Mar 1888   d 8 Aug 1970   **GOALKEEPER**
Caps: 2   Goals conceded: 2
First cap: 22 Oct 1921 v Ireland 1–1   aged 33yr 218d
Last cap: 8 Apr 1922 v Scotland 0–1   aged 34yr 21d
England career: 0yr 168d – P2 W0 D1 L1 – 25%
Club: Burnley

Gave away the goal that cost England the match against Scotland, as his punt hit Sam WADS-WORTH and rebounded towards the empty goal; Andy N Wilson couldn't miss. Nevertheless this was a goalkeeper good enough to have another one named after him; John Dawson, who played for Scotland against England from 1936–39, was nicknamed Jerry.

SAMUEL HULME DAY

b 29 Dec 1878   d 21 Feb 1950   **INSIDE FORWARD**
Caps: 3   Goals: 2
First cap: 17 Feb 1906 v Ireland 5–0   aged 27yr 50d
(1 goal)
Last cap: 7 Apr 1906 v Scotland 1–2   aged 27yr 99d
England career: 0yr 49d – P3 W2 D0 L1 – 66.66%
Club: Old Malvernians (& Corinthians)
2 Goals in a game: 0

Like ASHCROFT, Sammy Day won all three of his caps in 1906. He scored in the first two, and heavily in amateur internationals.

WILLIAM RALPH DEAN

b 22 Jan 1907   d 1 Mar 1980   **CENTRE FORWARD**
Caps: 16   Goals: 18
First cap: 12 Feb 1927 v Wales 3–3   aged 20yr 21d
(2 goals)
Last cap: 17 Oct 1932 v Ireland 1–0   aged 25yr 268d
England career: 5yr 247d – P16 W10 D1 L5 – 65.56%
Club: Everton
3 Goals in a game: 2   2 Goals in a game: 5

Dixie owed his inflated fame to youthful pace, strength in the air, and the change in the offside rule in 1925. He scored at least twice in each of his first five internationals, the England record before CAMSELL and still the record for an uninterrupted sequence, but after that the goals dried up (stopper centre-halves appeared and he only scored once for England after 1928) and his international career was over at 25. He matched WOODWARD in scoring hat-tricks in consecutive games, against Belgium and Luxembourg in 1927 (see T TAYLOR).

BRIAN DEANE

b 7 Feb 1968   **CENTRE FORWARD**
Caps: 2   Goals: 0
First cap: 3 Jun 1991 v N Zealand 1–0   aged 23yr 116d
(sub HT)
Last cap: 8 Jun 1991 v N Zealand 2–0   aged 23yr 121d
(sub'd HT)
England career: 0yr 05d – P2 W2 D0 L0 – 100%
Club: Sheffield United

The fact that he was taken off in Wellington because England had to play against the wind in the second half says it all: 6ft 3in but rather short on the ground. A taker as well as a disher-out.

NORMAN
VICTOR
DEELEY

b 30 Nov 1933   OUTSIDE RIGHT
Caps: 2   **Goals:** 0
First cap: 13 May 1959 v Brazil 0–2   aged 25yr 164d
Last cap: 17 May 1959 v Peru 1–4   aged 25yr 168d
England career: 0yr 04d – P2 W0 D0 L2 – 0%
Club: Wolves

Little Norman Deeley was one of three wingers (see BRADLEY and AD HOLDEN) who disappeared without trace in South America.

PERCY JOHN
DE PARAVICINI

b 15 Jul 1862   d 11 Oct 1921   RIGHT BACK
Caps: 3   **Goals:** 0
First cap: 3 Feb 1883 v Wales 5–0   aged 20yr 203d
Last cap: 10 Mar 1883 v Scotland 2–3   aged 20yr 238d
England career: 0yr 35d – P3 W2 D0 L1 – 66.66%
Club: Cambridge University (& Old Etonians)

'Para', later a CVO and MVO, was mentioned in despatches from all three of the 1883 internationals. He played at left back in two FA Cup Finals.

JOHN
HENRY GEORGE
DEVEY

b 26 Dec 1866   d 11 Oct 1940   FORWARD
Caps: 2   **Goals:** 1
First cap: 5 Mar 1892 v Ireland 2–0   aged 25yr 69d
Last cap: 3 Mar 1894 v Ireland 2–2   aged 27yr 67d
                            (1 goal)
England career: 1yr 363d – P2 W1 D1 L0 – 75%
Club: Aston Villa

Grim-faced, good in the air, leader of the attack in the Villa team that won the League and Cup double in 1897, Jack Devey is credited with a goal in his first as well as his last international by *The Athletic News*, but the reporter was confused by his header that went just over the bar. The press must have been a long way from the action: another source credits the goal to HODGETTS. However, *The Times, The Guardian, The Sportsman, The Field* and the *Belfast Telegraph* all say DAFT scored both goals against Ireland.

ALAN
ERNEST
DEVONSHIRE

b 13 Apr 1956   MIDFIELDER
Caps: 8   **Goals:** 0
First cap: 20 May 1980 v Ireland 1–1   aged 24yr 38d
Last cap: 16 Nov 1983 v Luxembourg 4–0
                             aged 27yr 218d

England career: 3yr 180d – P8 W4 D3 L1 – 68.75%
Club: West Ham United
Substitute: 1   **Substituted:** 3

Injuries held Alan Devonshire back. He might perhaps have filled the hole in the left side of England's midfield with his clever running. But it's a big perhaps.

FREDERICK
DEWHURST

b 16 Dec 1863   d 21 Apr 1895   INSIDE RIGHT/LEFT
Caps: 9   **Goals:** 12
First cap: 13 Mar 1886 v Ireland 6–1   aged 22yr 87d
Last cap: 23 Feb 1889 v Wales 4–1   aged 25yr 347d
England career: 2yr 347d – P9 W8 D0 L1 – %
Clubs: Preston North End (& Corinthians)
3 Goals in a game: 1   **2 Goals in a game:** 2

Strong on the ball, a great finisher, with one of the most successful England careers: only one defeat, only one game in which he didn't score, goals in his first three and last five. He and LINDLEY scored in seven together, still the England record though equalled by GREAVES with RA SMITH and R CHARLTON.

Fred Dewhurst was the first to score 12 goals for England. Most yearbooks credit him with 11, but contemporary papers (*Sporting Life, Wrexham Advertiser, The Guardian* etc) report that he scored three, not two, against Wales in 1888. There's a small doubt about his goal against Scotland in 1887 – the *Daily Mail* match report says Cobbold deflected in his shot – but most sources agree with the *Glasgow Evening News*: it belongs to Fred.

Note that *The Athletic News* of 1 February 1892 says he was born on 14 December 1863.

GERALD
POWYS
DEWHURST

b 14 Feb 1872   d 29 Mar 1956   INSIDE FORWARD
Caps: 1   **Goals:** 0
Only cap: 18 Mar 1895 v Wales 1–1 aged 23yr 32d
England career: P1 W0 D1 L0 – 50%
Club: Liverpool Ramblers (& Corinthians)

His 'selfish' play helped Wales to escape with a draw.

JAMES
WILLIAM
DICKINSON

b 24 Apr 1925   d 9 Nov 1982   LEFT/RIGHT HALF
Caps: 48   **Goals:** 0   **Own goals:** 1
First cap: 18 May 1949 v Norway 4–1   aged 24yr 24d
Last cap: 5 Dec 1956 v Denmark 5–2   aged 31yr 225d
England career: 7yr 201d – P48 W27 D12 L9 – 68.75%
Club: Portsmouth

Jimmy Dickinson played in 25 consecutive internationals (1951–54), which just about sums him up. Mr Consistency, never putting a foot wrong, partly because he seems to have never put a foot anywhere. Hardly a mention in any match report; no goals, no decisive pieces of play.

His only international goal came in the 1954 World Cup finals. A header from Marcel Dries' free-kick in extra time, Belgium's final equaliser in a 4–4 draw.

JAMES
HENRY
DIMMOCK

b 5 Dec 1900   d 23 Dec 1972   OUTSIDE LEFT
Caps: 3   Goals: 0
First cap: 9 Apr   1921 v Scotland 0–3   aged 20yr 125d
Last cap: 24 May 1926 v Belgium 5–3   aged 25yr 170d
England career: 5yr 45d – P3 W1 D0 L2 – 33.33%
Club: Tottenham Hotspur

A great individualist, first capped a fortnight before running through to score the only goal of the FA Cup Final, tricky Jimmy Dimmock appears to have been the first player born in the 20th century to play for England. He had to wait 4 years 326 days for his third cap – and first win.

EDWIN
GEORGE
DITCHBURN

b 24 Oct 1921   GOALKEEPER
Caps: 6   Goals conceded: 9   Clean sheets: 2
First cap: 2 Dec 1948 v Switzerland 6–0 aged 27yr 39d
Last cap: 5 Dec 1956 v Denmark 5–2   aged 35yr 42d
England career: 8yr 3d – P6 W5 D0 L1 – 83.33%
Club: Tottenham Hotspur
Penalties: 1   Saved: 0

A goalkeeping pro's pro, Ted Ditchburn played for England before and after BF WILLIAMS, before during and after MERRICK; just one game in eight years during which George Atheneos of the USA beat him from the penalty spot at Yankee Stadium.

RONALD
WILLIAM
DIX

b 5 Sep 1912   INSIDE LEFT
Caps: 1   Goals: 1
Only cap: 9 Nov 1938 v Norway 4–0
                          aged 26yr 65d (1 goal)
England career: P1 W1 D0 L0 – 100%
Club: Derby County

England scored all four in the first half, Ronnie Dix getting the second after 19 minutes.

JOHN
AUGER
DIXON

b 27 May 1861   d 8 Jun 1931   LEFT-SIDED FORWARD
Caps: 1   Goals: 0
Only cap: 14 Mar 1885 v Wales 1–1   aged 23yr 291d
England career: P1 W0 D1 L0 – 50%
Club: Notts County (& Corinthians)

England had beaten Wales 4–0 the previous year. In Blackburn, they could hardly put two passes together.

KERRY M
DIXON

b 24 Jul 1961   STRIKER
Caps: 8   Goals: 4
First cap: 9 Jun   1985 v Mexico 0–1   aged 23yr 319d
                                               (sub 80min)
Last cap: 10 Sep 1986 v Sweden 0–1   aged 25yr 46d
England career: 1yr 93d – P8 W5 D1 L2 – 68.75%
Club: Chelsea
Substitute: 3   Substituted: 1
2 Goals in a game: 2

Good in the air, quick on the ground, Kerry Dixon found his right international level, scoring two goals in each of his first two complete matches against a jet-lagged West Germany and some US college boys.

LEE
MICHAEL
DIXON

b 17 Mar 1964   RIGHT BACK
Caps: 8   Goals: 1
First cap: 25 Apr 1990 v Czechoslovakia 4–2
                                               aged 26yr 39d
Last cap: 25 May 1991 v Argentina 2–2   aged 27yr 69d
England career: 1yr 30d – P8 W5 D3 L0 – 81.25%
Club: Arsenal

Graham Taylor's replacement for, but not yet obvious improvement upon, MG STEVENS.

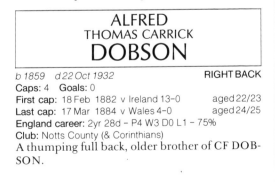

ALFRED
THOMAS CARRICK
DOBSON

b 1859   d 22 Oct 1932   RIGHT BACK
Caps: 4   Goals: 0
First cap: 18 Feb 1882 v Ireland 13–0   aged 22/23
Last cap: 17 Mar 1884 v Wales 4–0   aged 24/25
England career: 2yr 28d – P4 W3 D0 L1 – 75%
Club: Notts County (& Corinthians)

A thumping full back, older brother of CF DOBSON.

Somewhere there's a crowd of 10 000 watching Kerry Dixon score against the USA in 1985 (Allsport/Tony Duffy)

CHARLES
FREDERICK
DOBSON

b 9 Sep 1862   d 18 May 1939   **HALF BACK**
Caps: 1   **Goals:** 0
Only cap: 13 Mar 1886 v Ireland 6–1   aged 23yr 185d
England career: P1 W1 D0 L0 – 100%
Club: Notts County (& Corinthians)

Alf DOBSON's brother Charley was one of four not to win another cap.

JOHN
MARTIN
DOBSON

b 14 Feb 1948   **MIDFIELDER**
Caps: 5   **Goals:** 0
First cap: 3 Apr 1974 v Portugal 0–0   aged 26yr 48d
Last cap: 30 Oct 1974 v Czechoslovakia 3–0
                    aged 26y 258d (sub'd 62min)
England career: 0yr 210d – P5 W2 D3 L0 – 70%
Clubs: Burnley (4), Everton (1)
Substituted: 1

A skilful all-round midfielder who played under three managers in five internationals, Martin Dobson might have done a job for England, given the time that, say, BROOKING was given.

ALEXANDER
GRAHAM
DOGGART

b 2 Jun 1897   d 7 Jun 1963   **INSIDE LEFT**
Caps: 1   **Goals:** 0   **Captain:** 1
Only cap: 1 Nov 1923 v Belgium 2–2   aged 26yr 152d
England career: P1 W0 D1 L0 – 50%
Club: Corinthians

One of the last amateur captains, in the first match England failed to win against foreign opposition.

TONY
DORIGO

b 31 Dec 1965   **LEFT BACK**
Caps: 6   **Goals:** 0
First cap: 13 Dec 1989 v Yugoslavia 2–1 aged 23yr 347d
                                        (sub HT)
Last cap: 21 May 1991 v USSR 3–1   aged 25yr 141d
England career: 1yr 159d – P6 W5 D0 L1 – 83.33%
Club: Chelsea
Substitute: 4

Half-time substitute in three of his first four internationals. Looked good in the first he started, crossing for PLATT to head the equaliser against Italy in Bari.

ARTHUR
REGINALD
DORRELL

b 30 Mar 1896/98   d 13/14 Sep 1942   **OUTSIDE LEFT**
Caps: 4   **Goals:** 1
First cap: 8 Dec 1924 v Belgium 4–0
                              aged 26/28yr 253d
Last cap: 24 Oct 1925 v Ireland 0–0 aged 27/29yr 208d
England career: 0yr 320d – P4 W3 D1 L0 – 87.50%
Club: Aston Villa

Provoked an own goal then scored himself in the narrow win over France in 1925.

BRYAN
DOUGLAS

b 27 May 1934   **OUTSIDE RIGHT**
Caps: 36   **Goals:** 11
First cap: 19 Oct 1957 v Wales 4–0   aged 23yr 206d
Last cap: 5 Jun 1963 v Switzerland 8–1 aged 29yr   9d
England career: 5yr 229d – P36 W17 D11 L8 – 62.50%
Club: Blackburn Rovers
2 Goals in a game: 1

An important part of several successful England teams, the natural successor to MATTHEWS; small, skilful – though not so robust. Scored in his last three internationals.

JOHN THOMAS
DOWNS

b 13 Aug 1886   d 24 Mar 1949   **RIGHT BACK**
Caps: 1   **Goals:** 0
Only cap: 23 Oct 1920 v Ireland 2–0   aged 34yr 71d
England career: P1 W1 D0 L0 – 100%
Club: Everton

The 1972 Farror–Lamming book lists him as Richard W Downs, but that appears to have been an educated guess following the assumption that 'Dicky' was his real name instead of a (predictable?) nickname for a man called John Thomas.

Charlie BUCHAN credits 'the sturdy Barnsley miner' with being the first player to use the sliding tackle, thereby speeding up the game and bringing about more injuries.

MICHAEL
DOYLE

b 25 Nov 1946   **CENTRAL DEFENDER**
Caps: 5   **Goals:** 0
First cap: 24 Mar 1976 v Wales 2–1   aged 29yr 120d
Last cap: 9 Feb 1977 v Holland 0–2   aged 30yr 77d
England career: 0yr 322d – P5 W2 D0 L3 – 40%
Club: Manchester City
Substitute: 1

REVIE surpassed himself against the brilliant Dutch at Wembley, picking three centre halves

(BEATTIE, DV WATSON, Mick Doyle – and maybe MADELEY) against a team with no centre forward.

EDWARD
JOSEPH
DRAKE

b 16 Aug 1912 CENTRE FORWARD
Caps: 5 Goals: 6
First cap: 14 Nov 1934 v Italy 3–2 aged 22yr 90d
(1 goal)
Last cap: 26 May 1938 v France 4–2 aged 25yr 283d
(2 goals)
England career: 3yr 193d – P5 W4 D0 L1 – 80%
Club: Arsenal
3 Goals in a game: 1 2 Goals in a game: 1

Ted Drake was only third choice against Italy (TILSON and GS HUNT had to cry off before he could make his debut on his home club ground) and the selectors never tried very hard to select him, opting for GURNEY, W RICHARDSON or STEELE, or recalling CAMSELL. But when he was in, nothing could stop him going for goal; he put his head down and damned the consequences, which cost him dear against Wales in 1936 – stitches over one eye, concussion, a displaced cartilage. A fairly typical day at the office for EJ Drake, who'd played with a broken wrist, stitches in a head wound, an injured knee, a slipped disc . . . When he managed to stay out of Casualty, he generally scored goals.

ANDREW
DUCAT

b 16 Feb 1886 d 23 Jul 1942 RIGHT HALF
Caps: 6 Goals: 1
First cap: 12 Feb 1910 v Ireland 1–1 aged 23yr 361d
Last cap: 23 Oct 1920 v Ireland 2–0 aged 34yr 250d
England career: 10yr 254d – P6 W3 D1 L2 – 58.33%
Clubs: Woolwich Arsenal (3), Aston Villa (3)

Having scored the only goal of the game against Wales in his second international, Andy Ducat had to wait 9 years 347 days between his fourth and fifth, easily the England record before CALLAGHAN. He was perhaps more of a cricketer, playing for Surrey for 25 years and winning a single Test cap alongside Wally HARDINGE (who also played in just this one Test) against the all-conquering Australians of 1921.

ARTHUR
TEMPEST BLAKISTON
DUNN

b 12 Aug 1860 d 20 Feb 1902
CENTRE FORWARD/RIGHT BACK

Caps: 4 Goals: 2 Captain: 2
First cap: 24 Feb 1883 v Ireland 7–0 aged 22yr 196d
(2 goals)
Last cap: 2 Apr 1892 v Scotland 4–1 aged 31yr 234d
England career: 9yr 38d – P4 W4 D0 L0 – 100%
Clubs: Cambridge University & Old Etonians (2),
Old Etonians & Corinthians (2)
2 Goals in a game: 1

Played in the forward line in his first two internationals, then had to wait 8 years 10 days before his third cap (as full back and captain, a late replacement for Bob HOLMES), a record gap until DUCAT in 1920.

MICHAEL
DUXBURY

b 1 Sep 1959 RIGHT BACK
Caps: 10 Goals: 0
First cap: 16 Nov 1983 v Luxembourg 4–0 aged 24yr 76d
Last cap: 17 Oct 1984 v Finland 5–0 aged 25yr 46d
(sub'd HT)
England career: 0yr 336d – P10 W4 D2 L4 – 50%
Club: Manchester United
Substituted: 1

For a year, Mike Duxbury was a fixture in an England team that beat a very weak Brazil in Rio but otherwise had some very poor results, thanks partly to his mistakes: allowing centres to go over his head for Platini and Mark McGhee to head in, treading on the ball for Gotsmanov to score at Wembley.

STANLEY
GEORGE JAMES
EARLE

b 6 Sep 1897 d 26 Sep 1971 INSIDE RIGHT
Caps: 2 Goals: 0
First cap: 17 May 1924 v France 3–1 aged 26yr 254d
Last cap: 22 Oct 1927 v Ireland 0–2 aged 30yr 46d
England career: 3yr 158d – P2 W1 D0 L1 – 50%
Clubs: Clapton (1), West Ham United (1)

One of several amateurs who enjoyed end-of-season junkets to the Continent but weren't often trusted with the Home Championship.

GEORGE
EDWARD
EASTHAM

b 23 Sep 1936 INSIDE LEFT
Caps: 19 Goals: 2
First cap: 8 May 1963 v Brazil 1–1 aged 26yr 227d
Last cap: 3 Jul 1966 v Denmark 2–0 aged 29yr 284d
(1 goal)
England career: 3yr 56d – P19 W14 D2 L3 – 78.95%
Club: Arsenal
Substituted: 1

Small and thin, RAMSEY's first playmaker and a very successful one. Son of George senior.

GEORGE
RICHARD
EASTHAM

b 13 Sep 1913/14   INSIDE RIGHT
Caps: 1   Goals: 0
Only cap: 18 May 1935 v Holland 1–0   aged 20/21yr 247d
England career: P1 W1 D0 L0 – 100%
Club: Bolton Wanderers

George Eastham senior and junior were the first father and son to play for England. See CLOUGH.

WILLIAM
ECKERSLEY

b 16 July 1925/26   d 25 Oct 1982   LEFT BACK
Caps: 17   Goals: 0
First cap: 2 Jul   1950 v Spain 0–1   aged 23/24yr 352d
Last cap: 25 Nov 1953 v Hungary 3–6
                        aged 27/28yr 132d
England career: 3yr 146d – P17 W8 D5 L4 – 61.76%
Club: Blackburn Rovers

Small, a good tackler, none too adaptable. Like so much else, his 15-match partnership with RAMSEY was ended by the Hungarian takeover of Wembley.

DUNCAN
EDWARDS

b 1 Oct 1936   d 21 Feb 1958   LEFT HALF
Caps: 18   Goals: 5
First cap: 2 Apr   1955 v Scotland 7–2   aged 18yr 183d
Last cap: 27 Nov 1957 v France 4–0   aged 21yr   57d
England career: 2yr 239d – P18 W10 D5 L3 – 69.44%
Club: Manchester United
2 Goals in a game: 1

The shortest-lived England player and the youngest this century, he scored twice and hit a post against Denmark in 1956.

WILLIS
EDWARDS

b 28 Apr 1903   d 27 Sep 1988   RIGHT HALF
Caps: 16   Goals: 0   Captain: 5
First cap: 1 Mar   1926 v Wales 1–3   aged 22yr 307d
Last cap: 20 Nov 1929 v Wales 6–0   aged 26yr 206d
England career: 3yr 264d – P16 W10 D2 L4 – 68.75%
Club: Leeds United

Classic jack-of-all-trades English half back, as good as any of his day. Captain in his last five internationals as well as being the 500th player to be capped in England.

The cap fits. Willis Edwards, one of the best of the first 500 (Lamming)

WILLIAM
ELLERINGTON

b 30 Jun 1923   RIGHT BACK
Caps: 2   Goals: 0
First cap: 18 May 1949 v Norway 4–1   aged 25yr 322d
Last cap: 22 May 1949 v France 3–1   aged 25yr 326d
England career: 0yr 04d – P2 W2 D0 L0 – 100%
Club: Sunderland

Georges Moreel had only been playing international footbal for 28 seconds when he escaped his marker, big strong Billy Ellerington, to put France ahead at the Stade Colombes.

GEORGE
WASHINGTON
ELLIOTT

b 1889   d 27 Nov 1948   CENTRE FORWARD
Caps: 3   Goals: 0
First cap: 15 Feb 1913 v Ireland 1–2   aged 23/24
Last cap: 15 Mar 1920 v Wales 1–2   aged 30/31
England career: 7yr 29d – P3 W0 D0 L3 – 0%
Club: Middlesbrough

George Elliott didn't have much luck in his international career, which had 6 years 29 days taken out of it by the First World War. In his first match, Ireland beat England for the first time; in his last, Wales did the same for the first time since 1882.

WILLIAM
HENRY
ELLIOTT

b 20 Mar 1925   **OUTSIDE LEFT**
Caps: 5 **Goals:** 3
First cap: 18 May 1952 v Italy 1–1   aged 27yr 59d
Last cap: 26 Nov 1952 v Belgium 5–0   aged 27yr 251d
(2 goals)
England career: 0yr 192d – P5 W3 D2 L0 – 80%
Club: Burnley
Billy Elliott's very late goal salvaged a 2–2 draw in Belfast; another in the third minute set England on the way against Belgium.

ROBERT
ERNEST
EVANS

b 21 Nov 1885 d 28 Nov 1965   **OUTSIDE LEFT**
Caps: 4 **Goals:** 1
First cap: 11 Feb 1911 v Ireland 2–1   aged 25yr 82d
(1 goal)
Last cap: 11 Mar 1912 v Wales 2–0   aged 26yr 110d
England career: 1yr 28d – P4 W3 D1 L0 – 87.50%
Club: Sheffield United
A tall galloping winger, second of two players (see REYNOLDS) who appeared for and against England, Bobby Evans had won his 10th cap for Wales as recently as 1910. He'd scored twice for them, and played four times against England.

FREDERICK
HAROLD
EWER

b 30 Sep 1898 d 29 Jan 1971   **RIGHT/LEFT HALF**
Caps: 2 **Goals:** 0
First cap: 17 May 1924 v France 3–1   aged 25yr 230d
Last cap: 8 Dec 1924 v Belgium 4–0   aged 26yr 69d
England career: 0yr 205d – P2 W2 D0 L0 – 100%
Club: Casuals (& Corinthians)
Freddie Ewer was one of several twenties amateurs who were picked against continental opposition while the professionals played in the Home Championship.

PERCY
FAIRCLOUGH

b 1 Feb 1858 d 22 Jun 1947   **FORWARD**
Caps: 1 **Goals:** 0

Only cap: 2 Mar 1878 v Scotland 2–7   aged 20yr 29d
England career: P1 W0 D0 L1 – 0%
Club: Old Foresters (& Corinthians)
Took over from WELCH as the longest-lived England player (89yr 141d) until WACE died later in the same year.

DAVID
LIDDLE
FAIRHURST

b 20 Jul 1906/7 d 26 Oct 1972   **LEFT BACK**
Caps: 1 **Goals:** 0
Only cap: 6 Dec 1933 v France 4–1   aged 26/27yr 139d
England career: P1 W1 D0 L0 – 100%
Club: Newcastle United
A strong and dependable tackler, but probably didn't expect a second cap; Eddie HAPGOOD was around.

JOHN
FANTHAM

b 6 Feb 1939   **INSIDE RIGHT**
Caps: 1 **Goals:** 0
Only cap: 28 Sep 1961 v Luxembourg 4–1 aged 22yr 234d
England career: P1 W1 D0 L0 – 100%
Club: Sheffield Wednesday
The inside-forward trio of POINTER, VIOLLET and Johnny Fantham had only one previous cap between them; it took two late goals from Bobby CHARLTON to cover their embarrassment.

JOHN
FASHANU

b 18 Sep 1962   **CENTRE FORWARD**
Caps: 2 **Goals:** 0
First cap: 23 May 1989 v Chile 0–0   aged 26yr 247d
(sub'd 70min)
Last cap: 27 May 1989 v Scotland 2–0   aged 26yr 251d
(sub'd 31min)
England career: 0yr 4d – P2 W1 D1 L0 – 75%
Club: Wimbledon
Fash the Bash was called up as something like fourth choice to become the first Wimbledon player to win an England cap, even though he was already injured and didn't last out either match; he stayed on long enough to be booked for a foul on his debut. The smallest crowd for any international at Wembley came to hear the sound of barrels being scraped . . .

WILLIAM
FELTON

b 1 Aug 1900 d 22 Apr 1977   **LEFT BACK**
Caps: 1 **Goals:** 0
Only cap: 21 May 1925 v France 3–2   aged 24yr 293d

England career: P1 W1 D0 L0 – 100%
Club: Sheffield Wednesday

One of eight England players who didn't win another cap after 'FOX's Match', Billy Felton was Sam BARKAS's cousin.

MICHAEL
FENTON

b 30 Oct 1913   CENTRE FORWARD
Caps: 1   Goals: 0
Only cap: 9 Apr 1938 Scotland 0–1   aged 24yr 161d
England career: P1 W0 D0 L1 – 0%
Club: Middlesbrough

Both Mickey Fenton and the centre half who marked him, Tommy Smith, were winning their last caps at Wembley.

TERENCE
WILLIAM
FENWICK

b 17 Nov 1959   CENTRAL DEFENDER
Caps: 20   Goals: 0
First cap: 2 May 1984 v Wales 0–1   aged 24yr 167d
(sub 80min)
Last cap: 17 Feb 1988 v Israel 0–0   aged 28yr 92d
(sub 74min)
England career: 3yr 291d – P20 W6 D7 L7 – 47.50%
Clubs: Queen's Park Rangers (19), Tottenham Hotspur (1)
Substitute: 2

Booked against Portugal and Poland in the Mexico World Cup, Terry Fenwick was banned for one match, returned against Argentina – and was booked again. No-one was unduly surprised. Three cautions seems to be a World Cup finals record. Statistically his international career was nothing to write home about.

EDGAR
FIELD

b 29 Jul 1854   d 11 Jan 1934   FULL BACK
Caps: 2   Goals: 0
First cap: 4 Mar 1876 v Scotland 0–3   aged 21yr 219d
Last cap: 12 Mar 1881 v Scotland 1–6   aged 26yr 226d
England career: 5yr 8d – P2 W0 D0 L2 –0 %
Club: Clapham Rovers

At least two sources say he scored an own goal in his last international. If he did (most reports credit John Smith with a hat-trick), he was the first player to do so in an England match.

THOMAS
FINNEY

b 5 Apr 1922
OUTSIDE RIGHT/LEFT/CENTRE FORWARD
Caps: 76   Goals: 30

First cap: 28 Sep 1946 v N Ireland 7–2   aged 24yr 176d
(1 goal)
Last cap: 22 Oct 1958 v USSR 5–0   aged 36yr 200d
England career: 12yr 24d – P76 W51 D13 L12 – 75.66%
Club: Preston North End
4 Goals in a game: 1 (2 pen)   3 Goals in a game: 0
2 Goals in a game: 3   Penalties: 5   Missed: 2

One of the greatest players of all time – though his reputation was never so big abroad (he was anonymous in two World Cups and injured in the third) – Tom Finney had one of the longest England careers, with one of the longest scoring spans, was one of the oldest England players, and above all broke WOODWARD's 47-year-old record with his 30th goal (equalled by N LOFTHOUSE in Finney's last match). By common consent, the Finney-or-MATTHEWS argument should never have been started; the first time they played together for England, they both scored, and made eight more for MORTENSEN and LAWTON in a 10–0 win in Lisbon. He and MORTENSEN scored in six matches together.

HAROLD
JOHN
FLEMING

b 30 Apr 1887   d 23 Aug 1955   INSIDE RIGHT
Caps: 11   Goals: 9
First cap: 3 Apr 1909 v Scotland 2–0   aged 21yr 338d
Last cap: 4 Apr 1914 v Scotland 1–3   aged 26yr 339d
England career: 5yr 01d – P11 W9 D1 L1 – 86.36%
Club: Swindon Town
3 Goals in a game: 1   2 Goals in a game: 1

Very comfortable on the ball, an exceptional goalscorer, one of several England players who had statistically very successful careers just before World War I, Harold Fleming was on the losing side only in the last peacetime international. His hat-trick was scored against Ireland in a 6–1 win in 1912.

ALBERT THOMAS
FLETCHER

b 4 Jun 1867   d 1940   RIGHT HALF
Caps: 2   Goals: 0
First cap: 23 Feb 1889 v Wales 4–1   aged 21yr 264d
Last cap: 15 Mar 1890 v Wales 3–1   aged 22yr 284d
England career: 1yr 20d – P2 W2 D0 L0 – 100%
Club: Wolves

Scored direct from a free-kick in his last international, disallowed because the ball didn't touch an opponent *en route.*

Overleaf *65 000 watched Tom Finney score twice in the second half against the brilliant 'Bagica' as England beat the world champions 4–0 in Turin in 1948* (Hulton)

RONALD
FLOWERS

b 28 Jul 1934　　　　　　　　**RIGHT/LEFT HALF**
Caps: 49　Goals: 10　Captain: 3
First cap: 15 May 1955 v France 0–1　　aged 20yr 291d
Last cap: 29 Jun 1966 v Norway 6–1　　aged 31yr 336d
England career: 11yr 45d – P49 W24 D12 L13 – 61.22%
Club: Wolves
Substitute: 1
2 Goals in a game: 1
Penalties: 6　Missed: 0

No-one took more penalties for England than Ron Flowers; no-one stopped one. He scored from the spot in three consecutive matches in 1962 (v Peru, and in the World Cup finals v Hungary, Argentina). Quite tall, defensively strong, rather unexceptional, he had to wait more than three years for a second cap, then won 40 in a row, second only to Billy WRIGHT.

FRANK
FORMAN

b 23 May 1875　d 4 Dec 1961　　**HALF BACK**
Caps: 9　Goals: 1　Captain: 1
First cap:　5 Mar 1898 v Ireland 3–2　　aged 22yr 286d
Last cap:　2 Mar 1903 v Wales 2–1　　aged 27yr 283d

England career: 4yr 362d – P9 W7 D2 L0 – 88.88%
Club: Nottingham Forest
Goals while captain: 0

Brother of FR Forman, brother-in-law of LINACRE, perhaps the leading half back of his time, one match report credits him with two goals against Ireland in 1899.

FREDERICK
RALPH
FORMAN

b 8 Nov 1873　d 14 Jun 1910　　**OUTSIDE LEFT**
Caps: 3　Goals: 3
First cap: 18 Feb 1899 v Ireland 13–2　　aged 25yr 102d
　　　　　　　　　　　　　　　　　　　　　(2 goals)
Last cap:　8 Apr 1899 v Scotland 2–1　　aged 25yr 151d
England career: 0yr 49d – P3 W3 D0 L0 – 100%
Club: Nottingham Forest
2 Goals in a game: 1

Fred Forman had a single, successful, season in international football alongside his brother and club colleague FRANK FORMAN. His sister married JH LINACRE.

JAMES HENRY (JIMMY) FORREST

b 24 Jun 1864   d 30 Dec 1925

LEFT HALF/CENTRE HALF

Caps: 11   Goals: 0
First cap: 17 Mar 1884 v Wales 4–0   aged 19yr 267d
Last cap: 15 Mar 1890 v Ireland 9–1   aged 25yr 264d
England career: 5yr 363d – P11 W6 D3 L2 – 68.18%
Club: Blackburn Rovers

The template for all early half backs; small and slight but good defensively, great judge of the timing of a pass – and traditionally the first professional to play for England, though there were probably a number of 'shamateurs' before him. J HUNTER, for instance.

JOHN FORT

b 15 Apr 1888   d 23 Nov 1965

RIGHT BACK

Caps: 1   Goals: 0
Only cap: 21 May 1921 v Belgium 2–0   aged 33yr 36d
England career: P1 W1 D0 L0 – 100%
Club: Millwall

Jack Fort was the first Third Division player to play for England. Note that the 1990 Lamming book lists his club under its old name of Millwall Athletic; Rothmans say it had dropped the Athletic in 1920.

REGINALD ERSKINE FOSTER

b 16 Apr 1878   d 13 May 1914   **INSIDE FORWARD**

Caps: 5   Goals: 3   Captain: 1
First cap: 26 Mar 1900 v Wales 1–1   aged 21yr 344d
Last cap: 3 Mar 1902 v Wales 0–0   aged 23yr 321d
England career: 1yr 342d – P5 W2 D3 L0 – 70%
Clubs: Oxford University & Old Malvernians (1);
        Old Malvernians alone (4); Corinthians throughout
3 Goals in a game: 0   2 Goals in a game: 1
Goals while captain: 0

Captain in his last football international, 'Tip' Foster played Test cricket in 1903 and 1907 and was the only player to captain England at both sports. Note that he may have scored only once against Ireland in 1901. See HEDLEY.

STEPHEN B FOSTER

b 24 Sep 1957   **CENTRE HALF**

Caps: 3   Goals: 0
First cap: 23 Feb 1982 v N Ireland 4–0   aged 24yr 152d
Last cap: 25 Jun 1982 v Kuwait 1–0   aged 24yr 274d
England career: 0yr 122d – P3 W3 D0 L0 – 100%
Club: Brighton & Hove Albion

RE Foster, effortless double-century maker and strolling goalscorer. A white collar worker, alright (Lamming)

Big and ordinary, Steve Foster and his headband only played international football because Dave V WATSON grew too old, but no-one scored against England in those three matches.

WILLIAM HENRY FOULKE

b 12 Apr 1874   d 1 May 1916   **GOALKEEPER**

Caps: 1   Goals conceded: 0
Only cap: 29 Mar 1897 v Wales 4–0   aged 22yr 351d
England career: P1 W1 D0 L0 – 100%
Club: Sheffield United

The heaviest man ever to have played for England, Willie Foulke was apparently only (!) 15 stone in 1892. By the turn of the century, he was anything between 20–24 stone, depending on what you read, none of it easy to imagine. How *did* he manage to keep goal? A one-off, a fantastic footballer.

WILLIAM
ANTHONY
FOULKES

b 5 Jan 1932   **RIGHT BACK**
Caps: 1   **Goals:** 0
Only cap: 2 Oct 1954 v N Ireland 2–0 aged 22yr 270d
England career: P1 W1 D0 L0 – 100%
Club: Manchester United

Bill Foulkes scored the goal that put United into the European Cup Final, ten years after the Munich air crash he survived.

FREDERICK
SAMUEL
FOX

b 22 Nov 1898   d 1968   **GOALKEEPER**
Caps: 1   **Goals conceded:** 2
Only cap: 21 May 1925 v France 3–2 aged 26yr 180d
(76min)
England career: P1 W1 D0 L0 – 100%
Club: Milwall

Fred Fox's international career was like a clown hurting himself in a single pratfall. Laugh? He nearly bled. England led 3–0, the French pulled one back, then he was injured while being barged into the net for their second goal and had to leave the field.

He was selected against France while still with Gillingham, but was transferred to Millwall (another Third Division club) in the same month that the match was played. It's a moot point whether he should be a Gillingham or Millwall player in the record books; newspaper reports are divided, with a slight bias towards Cold Blow Lane. You pays your money . . .

GERALD
CHARLES JAMES
FRANCIS

b 6 Dec 1951   **MIDFIELDER**
Caps: 12   **Goals:** 3   **Captain:** 8
First cap: 30 Oct 1974 v Czechoslovakia 3–0
aged 22yr 328d
Last cap: 13 Jun 1976 v Finland 4–1   aged 24yr 190d
England career: 1yr 227d – P12 W6 D3 L3 – 62.50%
Club: Queen's Park Rangers
2 Goals in a game: 1
Goals while Captain: 1

How would it have turned out for the maligned REVIE if the entire, classy, engine room hadn't been shut down by injury: Gerry Francis, who was captain in his last eight matches, and Colin BELL?

TREVOR
JOHN
FRANCIS

b 19 Apr 1954   **FORWARD**
Caps: 52   **Goals:** 12
First cap: 9 Feb 1977 v Holland 0–2   aged 22yr 294d
Last cap: 23 Apr 1986 v Scotland 2–1   aged 32yr 4d
England career: 9yr 75d – P52 W25 D14 L13 – 61.54%
Clubs: Birmingham City (12), Nottm Forest (10),
Man City (10), Sampdoria (20)
Substitute: 10   **Substituted:** 8
2 Goals in a game: 2   **Penalties:** 1   **Missed:** 1

The boy wonder grew into a very fine player with an international career full of ifs and the suspicion that he might have done more. But just as he was running into exciting form at his peak, scoring twice against Northern Ireland, once (very smoothly) against Spain, and the goal that took Forest to another European Cup Final – just then, he tore an Achilles tendon. Without him, England weren't the same in the European Championship finals. His international career was mixed, but never lucky.

In the third match of a virtual B tour to Australia, he scored, missed a twice-taken penalty, and was booked. Mixed, but never lucky.

CORNELIUS
FRANKLIN

b 24 Jan 1922   **CENTRE HALF**
Caps: 27   **Goals:** 0
First cap: 28 Sep 1946 v N Ireland 7–2   aged 24yr 247d
Last cap: 15 Apr 1950 v Scotland 1–0   aged 28yr 81d
England career: 3yr 229d – P27 W20 D3 L4 – 79.63%
Club: Stoke City

When Neil Franklin went to Colombia in search of El Dorado in 1950, he left a hole in central defence that wasn't filled till Billy WRIGHT made the switch in 1954. He and Wright played in England's first 27 matches after the war, overtaking BLENKINSOP's record for consecutive appearances. There was no gold mine in Bogota and he came back to a country that needed him and could have picked him any time it chose, but didn't forgive.

BERTRAM
CLEWLEY
FREEMAN

b Oct 1885   d 11 Aug 1955   **CENTRE FORWARD**
Caps: 5   **Goals:** 3   **Captain:** 0
First cap: 15 Mar 1909 v Wales 2–0
aged 23y 135–165d (1 goal)
Last cap: 23 Mar 1912 v Scotland 1–1
aged 26y 143–173d
England career: 3yr 8d – P5 W4 D1 L0 – 90%

Clubs: Everton (2), Burnley (3)
2 Goals in a game: 0
Bert Freeman and George HOLLEY won their first caps in the same match. Holley scored first, then Freeman, and England won 2–0. Three years later against the same country, Holley again scored first, then Freeman, and England again won 2–0 with both goals (yet again) coming in the first half.

JACK
FROGGATT

b 17 Nov 1922   **OUTSIDE LEFT/CENTRE HALF**
Caps: 13   **Goals:** 2
First cap: 16 Nov 1949 v N Ireland 9–2   aged 26yr 364d
                 (1 goal)
Last cap: 8 Jun 1953 v USA 6–3   aged 30yr 203d
England career: 3yr 204d – P13 W8 D4 L1 – 76.92%
Club: Portsmouth
The only player of the modern era to appear regularly in both defence and attack for England, Jack Froggatt scored against the Irish as a winger and against the Welsh in 1952 as a centre half (revenge for the two goals Trevor Ford put over him in the same match). He and cousin R FROGGATT won their last caps in the same match.

REDFERN
FROGGATT

b 23 Aug 1923/24   **INSIDE RIGHT/LEFT**
Caps: 4   **Goals:** 2
First cap: 12 Nov 1952 v Wales 5–2   aged 28/29yr 81d
Last cap: 8 Jun 1953 v USA 6–3   aged 28/29yr 289d
                 (1 goal)
England career: 0yr 208d – P4 W3 D1 L0 – 87.50%
Club: Sheffield Wednesday
A tale of two cousins. When Redfern played in his first international, Jack was there; Jack scored. When Redfern played in his last international, Jack was there again (it was his last one too); Redfern scored.

CHARLES
BURGESS
FRY

b 25 Apr 1872   *d 7 Sep 1956*   **RIGHT BACK**
Caps: 1   **Goals:** 0
Only cap: 9 Mar 1901 v Ireland 3–0   aged 28yr 318d
England career: P1 W1 D0 L0 – 100%
Club: Southampton (& Corinthians)
It all happened for CB Fry. He was a leading Test batsman (and captain of England) in the Edwardian golden age. He played in the 1902 FA Cup Final. He equalled an unofficial world long jump record. He played rugby for the Barbarians. He won a First at Oxford. The story goes that he was offered the throne of Albania (though nobody explains why). By all accounts, he was a very moderate full-back.

His only football international was played at The Dell, his home club ground.

WILLIAM
ISAAC
FURNESS

b 8 Jun 1909   *d 29 Aug 1980*   **INSIDE LEFT**
Caps: 1   **Goals:** 0
Only cap: 13 May 1933 v Italy 1–1   aged 23yr 339d
England career: P1 W0 D1 L0 – 50%
Club: Leeds United
England drew against a strong and experienced Italian team despite fielding eight players with only two previous caps between them, including six making their debut: COPPING, GELDARD, HAPGOOD, JR RICHARDSON, WHITE and Bill Furness.

THOMAS
GALLEY

b 4 Aug 1915/17   **INSIDE RIGHT**
Caps: 2   **Goals:** 1
First cap: 14 May 1937 v Norway 6–0
             aged 19/21yr 283d (1 goal)
Last cap: 17 May 1937 v Sweden 4–0
               aged 19/21yr 286
England career: 0yr 3d – P2 W2 D0 L0 – 100%
Club: Wolves
England used seven forwards on their Scandinavian leisure trip; they all scored, including Tom Galley.

THOMAS
GARDNER

b 28 May 1910   *d May 1970*   **RIGHT HALF**
Caps: 2   **Goals:** 0
First cap: 16 May 1934 v Czechoslovakia 1–2
               aged 23yr 353d
Last cap: 18 May 1935 v Holland 1–0   aged 24yr 355d
England career: 1yr 2d – P2 W1 D0 L1 – 50%
Club: Aston Villa
Famous for WEAVER-like long throws.

BEN
WALTER
GARFIELD

b 4 Apr 1872   *d 1942*   **OUTSIDE LEFT**
Caps: 1   **Goals:** 0
Only cap: 5 Mar 1898 v Ireland 3–2   aged 25yr 335d
England career: P1 W1 D0 L0 – 100%
Club: West Bromwich Albion

Ben Garfield and the other inside-forward making his debut, Charlie RICHARDS, were essentially stop-gaps; the first attempt to replace the MILWARD-CHADWICK axis.

WILLIAM
GARRATY

b 6 Oct 1878   d 6 May 1931   **INSIDE RIGHT**
Caps: 1   **Goals:** 0
Only cap: 2 Mar 1903 v Wales 2–1   aged 24yr 147d
England career: P1 W1 D0 L0 – 100%
Club: Aston Villa

Had been selected for the previous match, against Ireland, but withdrew at the last minute. Some sources spell his surname with two Ts, but this appears to be a mistake.

THOMAS H
GARRETT

b 28 Feb 1927   **LEFT/RIGHT BACK**
Caps: 3   **Goals:** 0
First cap: 5 Apr 1952 v Scotland 2–1   aged 25yr 37d

Last cap: 10 Oct 1953 v Wales 4–1   aged 26yr 213d
England career: 1yr 188d – P3 W2 D1 L0 – 83.33%
Club: Blackpool

Did nothing very wrong as RAMSEY's full-back partner, but was really only a stand-in for ECKERSLEY.

PAUL
JOHN
GASCOIGNE

b 27 May 1967   **MIDFIELDER**
Caps: 20   **Goals:** 2
First cap: 14 Sep 1988 v Denmark 1–0   aged 21yr 110d
                                                  (sub 85min)
Last cap: 6 Feb 1991 v Cameroon 2–0 aged 23yr 255d
                                                  (sub'd 66min)
England career: 2yr 145d – P20 W12 D7 L1 – 76.50%
Club: Tottenham Hotspur
Substitute: 6   **Substituted:** 1   **2 Goals in a game:** 0

Those semi-final tears were enough to make him BBC Sports Personality of 1990 – but that was hardly his fault. Anyway, it was probably time for a little recognition; Bobby ROBSON had taken a while making up his mind about the great Gazza

Gazza azza go at Brehme and Augenthaler (5) on one of the runs that made his name (Colorsport)

– a total of 49 minutes in his first three internationals (time enough to score a classy last minute goal against Albania), a total of 93 in six of his first seven. Then, given his head against Czechoslovakia at Wembley, he made the first three goals with his right foot and scored the last himself with his left in the final minute – a conjuror's exit. Sobbing aside, he was one of the better young players in the World Cup, all close control and muscle when he ran at defenders – only to be dropped by Graham Taylor for the traditional blood 'n guts in Dublin. Controversy as well as excitement – witness the screaming free kick in the FA Cup semi, followed by the self-inflicted injury in the Final. One way or another, always has the public holding its breath. Watch this space.

ERIC
LAZENBY
GATES

b 28 Jun 1955   MIDFIELDER
Caps: 2   Goals: 0
First cap: 10 Sep 1980 v Norway 4–0   aged 25yr 75d
Last cap: 15 Oct 1980 v Romania 1–2   aged 25yr 110d
                                                   (sub'd HT)
England career: 0yr 35d – P2 W1 D0 L1 – 50%
Club: Ipswich Town
Substituted: 1

Because of his height, his buzzing style, the way he played just behind the main strikers, even his hairstyle, Eric Gates was looked upon as the new Kevin KEEGAN. It was asking too much.

LESLIE
HEWITT
GAY

b 24 Mar 1871   d 1 Nov 1949   GOALKEEPER
Caps: 3   Goals conceded: 5   Clean sheets: 0
First cap: 1 Apr 1893 v Scotland 5–2   aged 22yr 8d
Last cap: 7 Apr 1894 v Scotland 2–2   aged 23yr 14d
England career: 1yr 6d – P3 W2 D1 L0 – 83.33%
Clubs: Cambridge University & Old Brightonians (1);
     Old Brightonians alone (2); Corinthians throughout

Despite a brave and agile performance at Celtic Park, Leslie Gay's next cap was at the Sydney Cricket Ground later in the year. He was the only player to keep goal and wicket for England.

FRED
GEARY

b 23 Jan 1868   d 8 Jan 1955   CENTRE FORWARD
Caps: 2   Goals: 3?
First cap: 15 Mar 1890 v Ireland 9–1   aged 22yr 52d
                                              (3? goals)
Last cap: 4 Apr 1891 v Scotland 2–1   aged 23yr 71d

England career: 1yr 20d – P2 W2 D0 L0 – 100%
Club: Everton

Note that a (not altogether coherent) match report in *The Field* credits him with four goals against Ireland, and that a (very confused) summary in *The Athletic News* maintains that 'the clever little Everton centre was responsible for five of the goals, and beauties they were. Clugstone (sic) tried to hold one of them, but he felt it going, and he let it go – he couldn't help it.' *The Northern Whig* (Belfast) also credits him with five.

The truth is that several of England's goals were typical of the time, scored from massed scrimmages in muddy goalmouths (team efforts, in effect) – and several match reports don't even pretend to know the identity of the last player to touch the ball. *The Sporting Chronicle*, for instance, credits Fred with only two of the goals. The consensus is that he scored three. Or four. Or . . .

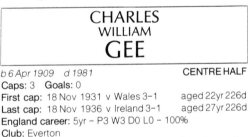

RICHARD LYON
GEAVES

b 6 May 1854   d 21 Mar 1935   OUTSIDE LEFT
Caps: 1   Goals: 0
Only cap: 6 Mar 1875 v Scotland 2–2   aged 20yr 304d
England career: P1 W0 D1 L0 – 50%
Club: Clapham Rovers

Seems to have got lost in the scrummages of a bruising match at the Oval.

CHARLES
WILLIAM
GEE

b 6 Apr 1909   d 1981   CENTRE HALF
Caps: 3   Goals: 0
First cap: 18 Nov 1931 v Wales 3–1   aged 22yr 226d
Last cap: 18 Nov 1936 v Ireland 3–1   aged 27yr 226d
England career: 5yr – P3 W3 D0 L0 – 100%
Club: Everton

Charlie Gee kept the dangerous Dai Astley quiet in his first international, had no trouble with the Spanish attack, yet had to wait very nearly five years for his last cap. England won, but Ireland's centre-forward Tommy Davis scored and that seems to have been that.

ALBERT
GELDARD

b 11 Apr 1914   d 19 Oct 1989   OUTSIDE RIGHT
Caps: 4   Goals: 0
First cap: 13 May 1933 v Italy 1–1   aged 19yr 32d
Last cap: 23 Oct 1937 v Ireland 5–1   aged 23yr 195d
England career: 4yr 163d – P4 W2 D1 L1 – 62.50%
Club: Everton

A boy wonder, thrown into the lions' den at 19. Speed and great trickery helped him survive.

Charlie George's one crowded hour (or so) against the Irish at Wembley (Hulton)

CHARLES
FREDERICK
GEORGE

b 10 Oct 1950　　　　　　　　**MIDFIELDER**
Caps: 1　**Goals:** 0
Only cap: 8 Sep 1976 v Eire 1–1
　　　　　　　　aged 25yr 334d (sub'd 65min)
England career: P1 W0 D1 L0 – 50%
Club: Derby County
Less than one full match for one of the best players in the country; playmaker, striker, professional entertainer. It looks a poor reward from REVIE (who was grudging with all the touch players: CURRIE, HUDSON, BOWLES), but then neither RAMSEY nor MERCER capped Charlie George at all . . .

WILLIAM
GEORGE

b 29 Jun 1874　d 4 Dec 1933　　**GOALKEEPER**
Caps: 3　**Goals conceded:** 2　**Clean sheets:** 2
First cap:　3 Mar 1902 v Wales 0–0　　aged 27yr 247d
Last cap:　3 May 1902 v Scotland 2–2　aged 27yr 308d
England career: 0yr 61d – P3 W1 D2 L0 – 66.66%
Club: Aston Villa
Penalties: 1　**Saved:** 1
Already a Warwickshire cricketer, big Bill George kept a clean sheet in each of his first two internationals, coming off his line to save Bob Milne's penalty in the game against Ireland.

WILLIAM
VIVIAN
TALBOT
GIBBINS

b 10 Aug 1901　d 21 Nov 1979　**CENTRE FORWARD**
Caps: 2　**Goals:** 3
First cap:　17 May 1924 v France 3–1　　aged 22yr 281d
　　　　　　　　　　　　　　　　(2 goals)
Last cap:　21 May 1925 v France 3–2　　aged 23yr 285d
　　　　　　　　　　　　　(c.35min, 1 goal)
England career: 1yr 04d – P2 W2 D0 L0 – 100%
Club: Clapton
Viv Gibbins enjoyed himself against the second-rate French (scoring the first goal each time) until an injury forced him to leave the pitch before half-time in the second match. Note that the original Farror–Lamming book lists his date of birth as 7 Jan 1903. Clapton, the amateur club, had nothing to do with Clapton (later Leyton) Orient.

JOHN
GIDMAN

b 10 Jan 1954　　　　　　　　**RIGHT BACK**
Caps: 1　**Goals:** 0

Only cap: 30 Mar 1977 v Luxembourg 5–0　aged 23yr 79d
England career: P1 W1 D0 L0 – 100%
Club: Aston Villa
Picked as an attacking full back by REVIE, who needed World Cup goals after a defeat in Rome. It worked, eventually and just about.

IAN
TERRY
GILLARD

b 9 Oct 1950　　　　　　　　**LEFT BACK**
Caps: 3　**Goals:** 0
First cap: 12 Mar 1975 v W Germany 2–0 aged 24yr 154d
Last cap: 30 Oct 1975 v Czechoslovakia 1–2
　　　　　　　　　　　　　　aged 25yr　21d
England career: 0yr 232d – P3 W1 D1 L1 – 50%
Club: Queen's Park Rangers
Miljan Miljanic, accomplished manager of Yugoslavia and Real Madrid, had his doubts about the England team in the early Revie era, mentioning the left back by name. Sure enough, the elusive little Czech Marian Masny gave big Ian big trouble in Bratislava, making both the goals that effectively knocked England out of the European Championship.

WALTER
EVELYN
GILLIAT

b 22 Jul 1869　d 2 Jan 1963　**INSIDE FORWARD**
Caps: 1　**Goals:** 3
Only cap: 25 Feb 1893 v Ireland 6–1
　　　　　　　　　　　　aged 23yr 218d (3 goals)
England career: P1 W1 D0 L0 – 100%
Club: Old Carthusians
Of the five players who scored a hat-trick in their only game for England, he was the ony one to score all three in the first half. However, see F BRADSHAW.

PAUL
GODDARD

b 12 Oct 1959　　　　　　　　**STRIKER**
Caps: 1　**Goals:** 1
Only cap: 2 June 1982 v Iceland 1–1
　　　　　　　　　aged 22yr 232d (sub 40min, 1 goal)
England career: P1 W0 D1 L0 – 50%
Club: West Ham United
The only player to score while playing a total of less than 90 minutes for England.

FREDERICK
ROY
GOODALL

b 31 Dec 1902　d 19 Jan 1982　**RIGHT BACK**

Caps: 25　Goals: 0　Captain: 11
First cap: 17 Apr 1926 v Scotland 0–1　aged 23yr 107d
Last cap: 6 Dec 1933 v France 4–1　aged 30yr 340d
England career: 7yr 233d – P25 W16 D4 L5 – 72.00%
Club: Huddersfield Town
Penalties: 1　Missed: 1

Tall and bony, the classic pre-war (pre-HAPGOOD, at least) fullback-captain, Roy Goodall was the first player to lead England out ten times after the First World War.

JOHN

GOODALL

b 19 Jun 1863　d 20 May 1942
INSIDE FORWARD/CENTRE FORWARD
Caps: 14　Goals: 11　Captain: 2
First cap: 4 Feb 1888 v Wales 5–1　aged 24yr 230d
　　　　　　　　　　　　　　　　　　　　(1 goal)
Last cap: 28 Mar 1898 v Wales 3–0　aged 34yr 282d
England career: 10yr 52d – P14 W11 D1 L2 – 82.14%
Clubs: Preston NE (4), Derby County (10)
Hat-tricks: 0　2 Goals in a game: 2
Goals while captain: 2 (in separate matches)

One of the leading players in the early years, a fine passer and goalscorer, his ball control perhaps the best in the country, he set several England records: the first to play 10 years of international football: the longest scoring span (8yr 40d) before BLOOMER; and, perhaps, still the record for scoring in most consecutive games – there's a faint possibility that he scored England's first goal against Scotland in 1889. If he did, he scored in 10 matches in a row (as opposed to the 6 he's usually credited with), which would match BLOOMER's record. It's a *very* faint possibility.

His parents were Scottish. He was born in London. His brother Archie was born in Ireland and played four times against England.

He's usually credited with 12 international goals in all, but see F DEWHURST.

HARRY CHESTER

GOODHART

b 17 Jul 1858　d 21 Apr 1895　**FORWARD**
Caps: 3　Goals: 0
First cap: 3 Feb 1883 v Wales 5–0　aged 24yr 201d
Last cap: 10 Mar 1883 v Scotland 2–3　aged 24yr 236d
England career: 0yr 35d – P3 W2 D0 L1 – 66.66%
Club: Old Etonians (& Corinthians)

Didn't score, but did his share of the providing – England scored 12 goals in his first two matches.

ALFRED GEORGE

GOODWYN

b 1849/50　d 14 Mar 1874　**HALF BACK**
Caps: 1　Goals: 0

Only cap: 8 Mar 1873 v Scotland 4–2　aged 22/24
England career: P1 W1 D0 L0 – 100%
Club: Royal Engineers

Already a lieutenant by the time he played for England.

ARTHUR COPELAND
GOODYER

b 1854　d 8 Jan 1932　**OUTSIDE RIGHT**
Caps: 1　Goals: 1
Only cap: 5 Apr 1879 v Scotland 5–4 aged 24/25 (1 goal)
England career: P1 W1 D0 L0 – 100%
Club: Nottingham Forest

Scored the third goal in the only match England have won from three down.

ROBERT
CUNLIFFE

GOSLING

b 15 Jun 1868　d 18 Apr 1922
OUTSIDE/INSIDE FORWARD
Caps: 5　Goals: 2　Captain: 1 (2?)
First cap: 5 Mar 1892 v Wales 2–0　aged 23yr 263d
Last cap: 6 Apr 1895 v Scotland 3–0　aged 26yr 295d
England career: 3yr 32d – P5 W4 D1 L0 – 90%
Club: Old Etonians (& Corinthians)
2 Goals in a game: 0　Goals while captain: 0

A tall, unselfish, rawboned forward, perfectly capable of looking after himself, Cunliffe Gosling was possibly captain against Wales in 1894, certainly captain in his last international – and, it was said, 'the richest man who ever played for England at the side of a professional'. A banker, he left £700 000 in his will.

ALBERT ARTHUR

GOSNELL

b 10 Feb 1880　d 6 Jan 1972　**OUTSIDE LEFT**
Caps: 1　Goals: 0
Only cap: 17 Feb 1906 v Ireland 5–0　aged 26yr 7d
England career: P1 W1 D0 L0 – 100%
Club: Newcastle United

England fielded another one-cap player at outside left in each of the two subsequent matches that season.

HAROLD

GOUGH

b 31 Dec 1890　d 1970　**GOALKEEPER**
Caps: 1　Goals conceded: 3
Only cap: 9 Apr 1921 v Scotland 0–3　aged 30yr 99d
England career: P1 W0 D0 L1 – 0%
Club: Sheffield United

One of a sequence of goalkeepers seemingly rewarded for waiting in line behind S HARDY, by being given a cap or two when they passed 30.

LEONARD ARTHUR
GOULDEN

b 16 Jul 1912   INSIDE LEFT/RIGHT
Caps: 14   Goals: 4
First cap: 14 May 1937 v Norway 6–0   aged 24yr 302d
(1 goal)
Last cap: 24 May 1939 v Romania 2–0   aged 26yr 312d
(1 goal)
England career: 2yr 10d – P14 W10 D1 L3 – 75%
Club: West Ham United
2 Goals in a game: 0

A skilful, sometimes brilliant, left-footed schemer, Len Goulden was on the winning side in his first six internationals.

LEONARD
GRAHAM

b 20 Aug 1901   d 21 Dec 1962   LEFT HALF
Caps: 2   Goals: 0
First cap: 28 Feb 1925 v Wales 2–1   aged 23yr 192d
Last cap: 4 Apr 1925 v Scotland 0–2   aged 23yr 227d
England career: 0yr 35d – P2 W1 D0 L1 – 50%
Club: Millwall

Len Graham and Tommy COOK, both Third Division players, made their debuts on a Vetch Field mudheap, a match won by two early goals from Frank ROBERTS.

THOMAS
GRAHAM

b 5 Mar 1907   d 29 Mar 1983   CENTRE HALF
Caps: 2   Goals: 2
First cap: 14 May 1931 v France 2–5   aged 24yr 80d
Last cap: 17 Oct 1931 v Ireland 6–2   aged 24yr 236d
England career: 0yr 156d – P2 W1 D0 L1 – 50%
Club: Nottingham Forest

Tommy Graham may have been lucky to play for England twice; the defence was overrun in Paris, centre-forward Robert Mercier scoring twice on his debut. Surprisingly enough, the only defender on either side not to win another cap was Marcel Capelle.

COLIN
GRAINGER

b 10 Jun 1933   OUTSIDE LEFT
Caps: 7   Goals: 3
First cap: 9 May 1956 v Brazil 4–2   aged 22yr 334d
(2 goals)
Last cap: 6 Apr   1957 v Scotland 2–1   aged 23yr 300d
England career: 0yr 332d – P7 W5 D2 L0 – 85.71%
Clubs: Sheffield United (6), Sunderland (1)
2 Goals in a game: 1

Scored five minutes from the start and five min-

utes from the end of his first international, and against the world champions in West Berlin. Ed HOLLIDAY was his cousin.

JAMES PETER
GREAVES

b 20 Feb 1940   GOALSCORER
Caps: 57   Goals: 44
First cap: 17 May 1959 v Peru 1–4   aged 19yr 86d
(1 goal)
Last cap: 27 May 1967 v Austria 1–0   aged 27yr 96d
England career: 8yr 10d – P57 W30 D13 L14 – 64.03%
Clubs: Chelsea (15), Tottenham Hotspur (42)
4 Goals in a game: 2   3 Goals in a game: 4
2 Goals in a game: 3

It's one of the nicer clichés: Jimmy Greaves always scored on his debut – for Chelsea, for Spurs, in his testimonial, even for England, at 19, while the sinking ship went down in Lima. He went on to break the national scoring record (which R CHARLTON would surely never have regained if Jimbo had stayed in Sir Alf's plans for even one more year); he scored 13 goals in 1960–61, still the record for a single season, including England's 1000th goal (v Wales) and seven in all in the Home Championship, a record he still shares with Hughie Gallacher. He and RA SMITH scored in seven matches together, as did he and R CHARLTON, equalling F DEW-HURST and LINDLEY's record. He alone scored six hat-tricks for England, and 10 goals v Northern Ireland.

The figures are a little deceptive in that he tended to score in batches against weak opposition; four in an 8–3 win, three in a 9–3 or a 9–0, that kind of thing (although, curiously, he didn't score at all in two 8–1 wins, over the USA and Switzerland). His victims were usually of the Luxembourg, Norway, Wales and Northern Ireland type – and he scored only once in seven matches in the World Cup finals.

None of which matters very much. The cheek and style of the finishing, the omission from the World Cup Final, the alcoholism – frailty and goals, the stuff of folk heroes. What's Lineker, after all? Just the rich man's Greavsie.

FREDERICK THOMAS
GREEN

b 21 Jun 1851   d 6 Jun 1928   FULL BACK
Caps: 1   Goals: 0
Only cap: 4 Mar 1876 v Scotland 0–3   aged 24yr 256d
England career: P1 W0 D0 L1 – 0%
Club: Wanderers (& probably Old Wykehamists)

One of six never picked again for England.

Greavsie didn't always score against the best teams – but he was invariably tightly marked, here by Zozimo as Brazil win the 1962 World Cup quarter-final 3–1 (Popperfoto)

GEORGE
HENRY
GREEN

b 2 May 1901   d 1980   **LEFT HALF**
Caps: 8   **Goals:** 0
First cap: 21 May 1925 v France 3–2   aged 24yr 19d
Last cap: 19 May 1928 v Belgium 3–1   aged 27yr 17d
England career: 2yr 363d – P8 W4 D2 L2 – 62.50%
Club: Sheffield United

A classic English half back, hard, dependable, not outrageously good on the ball, George Green won a relatively large number of caps for such an unpredictable, and for England unsuccessful, era.

ERNEST
HARWOOD
GREENHALGH

b 22 Aug 1848?   d 11 Jul 1922   **DEFENDER**
Caps: 2   **Goals:** 0
First cap: 30 Nov 1872 v Scotland 0–0   aged 24yr 100d
Last cap: 8 Mar 1873 v Scotland 4–2   aged 24yr 198d

England career: 0yr 98d – P2 W1 D1 L0 – 50%
Club: Notts County

One of only two players (see CHENERY) to play in England's first two matches. There's some doubt about his date of birth, but it seems he was born on exactly the same day – and made his debut in the same match – as BROCKBANK. They were the oldest players in the first England team.

BRIAN
GREENHOFF

b 28 Apr 1953   **MIDFIELDER**
Caps: 18   **Goals:** 0
First cap: 8 May 1976 v Wales 1–0   aged 23yr 10d
Last cap: 31 May 1980 v Australia 2–1   aged 27yr 33d
                                              (sub 88min)
England career: 4yr 23d – P18 W9 D5 L4 – 63.88%
Clubs: Manchester United (17), Leeds United (1)
Substitute: 3   **Substituted:** 3

Won the ball a little, used it a little. Not a lot at international level.

DOCTOR
HAYDOCK
GREENWOOD

b 31 Oct 1860 d 3 Nov 1951 RIGHT/LEFT BACK
Caps: 2 **Goals:** 0
First cap: 18 Feb 1882 v Ireland 13–0 aged 21yr 110d
Last cap: 11 Mar 1882 v Scotland 1–5 aged 21yr 131d
England career: 0yr 21d – P1 W1 D0 L1 – 50%
Club: Blackburn Rovers

A very good player, not to be blamed for the defeat at Hampden. And yes, Doctor's a christian name not a professional title – though the situation used to be complicated by writers calling him Dock (probably from Haydock) as well as Doc (definitely from Doctor). Phew.

JOHN
CHARLES
GREGORY

b 11 May 1954 MIDFIELDER
Caps: 6 **Goals:** 0
First cap: 12 Jun 1983 v Australia 0–0 aged 29yr 32d
Last cap: 2 May 1984 v Wales 0–1 aged 29yr 357d
England career: 0yr 325d – P6 W2 D2 L2 – 50%
Club: Queen's Park Rangers

Bobby ROBSON, still finding his feet as an England manager, could claim he was experimenting . . .

ARTHUR
GRIMSDELL

b 23 Mar 1894 d 12 Mar 1963 LEFT HALF
Caps: 6 **Goals:** 0 **Captain:** 3
First cap: 15 Mar 1920 v Wales 1–2 aged 25yr 357d
Last cap: 5 Mar 1923 v Wales 2–2 aged 28yr 347d
England career: 2yr 355d – P6 W3 D1 L2 – 58.33%
Club: Tottenham Hotspur

Enthusiastic, attacking half-back, better known for his leadership than his actual play. Captain in his last three internationals.

ARTHUR
THOMAS
GROSVENOR

b 22 Nov 1908 d 31 Oct 1972 INSIDE RIGHT
Caps: 3 **Goals:** 2
First cap: 14 Oct 1933 v Ireland 3–0 aged 24yr 326d
(1 goal)
Last cap: 6 Dec 1933 v France 4–1 aged 25yr 14d
(1 goal)
England career: 0yr 53d – P3 W2 D0 L1 – 66.66%
Club: Birmingham FC

Like Jack BOWERS, Tom Grosvenor played in three internationals in 1933–34 and scored in his first and last. Note that the original Farror–

Lamming book gives Albert as his first name. He was definitely known by his second.

WILLIAM
GUNN

b 4 Dec 1858 d 29 Jan 1921 FORWARD
Caps: 2 **Goals:** 1
First cap: 15 Mar 1884 v Scotland 0–1 aged 25yr 102d
Last cap: 17 Mar 1884 v Wales 4–0 aged 25yr 104d
(1 goal)
England career: 0yr 2d – P2 W1 D0 L1 – 50%
Club: Notts County

He and CORRIGAN, who was also 6ft 4½in, seem to have been the tallest men ever to play for England; Billy Gunn was almost certainly the tallest outfield player. He played 11 times for England at cricket and scored the first Test century ever seen at Old Trafford, in 1893.

His England career spanned just two days and two matches, the same two as BROMLEY-DAVENPORT and CP WILSON.

ROBERT
GURNEY

b 13 Oct 1906/07 CENTRE FORWARD
Caps: 1 **Goals:** 0
Only cap: 6 Apr 1935 v Scotland 0–2 aged 27/28yr 175d
England career: P1 W0 D0 L1 – 0%
Club: Sunderland

Like Walter ALSFORD in the same match, Bob Gurney was an experiment that was never very likely to work; against an experienced defence, in front of 130 000 Scots, he failed to score while Dally Duncan was heading two goals at the other end.

JOHN
HACKING

b 22 Dec 1897 d 1 Jun 1955 GOALKEEPER
Caps: 3 **Goals conceded:** 4 **Clean sheets:** 0
First cap: 22 Oct 1928 v Ireland 2–1 aged 30yr 304d
Last cap: 13 Apr 1929 v Scotland 0–1 aged 31yr 112d
England career: 0yr 173d – P3 W2 D0 L1 – 66.66%
Club: Oldham Athletic

Jack Hacking played in all three Home Championship matches in 1928–29, then paid the penalty for letting in Alex Cheyne's goal direct from a corner in the last minute.

HAROLD
HADLEY

b 1877/78 d unknown LEFT HALF
Caps: 1 **Goals:** 0
Only cap: 14 Feb 1903 v Ireland 4–0 aged 24–26

England career: P1 W1 D0 L0 – 100%
Club: West Bromwich Albion
One of three winning their only cap.

JAMES

HAGAN

b 21 Jan 1918   INSIDE RIGHT
Caps: 1   Goals: 0
Only cap: 26 Sep 1948 v Denmark 0–0   aged 30yr 249d
England career: P1 W0 D1 L0 – 50%
Club: Sheffield United

The real thing came too late for Jimmy Hagan; a single appearance, in a poor team performance in Copenhagen that also cost LAWTON his place. But he was a very fine playmaker. Sixteen wartime caps go some way to proving it.

JOHN
THOMAS WILLIAM

HAINES

b 24 Mar 1920   d 19 Mar 1987   INSIDE LEFT
Caps: 1   Goals: 2
Only cap: 2 Dec 1948 v Switzerland 6–0
                                    aged 28y 253 (2 goals)
England career: P1 W1 D0 L0 – 100%
Club: West Bromwich Albion

Jolly Jack Haines scored both his goals in the first half at Highbury, the first after only five minutes. Injury ruled out the chance of further caps.

ALBERT EDWARD
HALL

b 1882   d 17 Oct 1957   OUTSIDE LEFT
Caps: 1   Goals: 0
Only cap: 12 Feb 1910 v Ireland 1–1   aged 27/28
England career: P1 W0 D1 L0 – 50%
Club: Aston Villa

The result ended the run of 10 successive wins (still the record) so COWELL, MORLEY and the aggressive Hall won only this one cap.

GEORGE
WILLIAM

HALL

b 12 Mar 1912   d 22/23 Mar 1967   INSIDE LEFT/RIGHT
Caps: 10   Goals: 9
First cap: 6 Dec 1933 v France 4–1   aged 21yr 269d
Last cap: 18 May 1939 v Yugoslavia 1–2 aged 27yr 67d
England career: 5yr 163d – P10 W7 D1 L2 – 75%
Club: Tottenham Hotspur
5 Goals in a game: 1   2 Goals in a game: 0

Willie Hall was kept waiting till 1937 for his second cap, scoring against Ireland on his recall. Against the same country the following year, he scored three times in little more than three min-

utes (possibly the fastest hat-trick in any international) and five in the match, equalling the England record (see VAUGHTON, BLOOMER, GO SMITH, MACDONALD); he scored all five in a row, equalling a record broken only by MAC-DONALD. Oddly enough, he was in the team for his passing.

JEFFREY
JAMES

HALL

b 7 Sep 1929   d 4 Apr 1959   RIGHT BACK
Caps: 17.   Goals: 0
First cap: 2 Oct 1955 v Denmark 5–1   aged 26yr 25d
Last cap: 19 May 1957 v Eire 1–1   aged 27yr 254d
England career: 1yr 229d – P17 W12 D4 L1 – 82.35%
Club: Birmingham City

Jeff Hall had a good thing going with Roger BYRNE (17 games in a row as full-back partners, no defeats in the last 15) before polio struck. He would have had statistically the best record of any England player if Wales hadn't won 2–1 in 1955.

HAROLD
JAMES

HALSE

b Jan 1886   d Apr 1951   INSIDE RIGHT
Caps: 1   Goals: 2
Only cap: 1 June 1909 v Austria 8–1   aged 23yr 121–151d
England career: P1 W1 D0 L0 – 100%
Club: Manchester United

The Austrians were easy meat for Harold Halse, who scored England's second and seventh goals. He appeared in FA Cup Finals with three different clubs; Man Utd in 1909, Aston Villa in 1913 and Chelsea (who lost) in 1915.

HENRY EDWARD DENISON
HAMMOND

b 26 Nov 1866   d 16 Jun 1910   HALF BACK
Caps: 1   Goals: 0
Only cap: 13 Apr 1889 v Scotland 2–3   aged 22yr 138d
England career: P1 W0 D0 L1 – 0%
Club: Oxford University & Lancing Old Boys (& Corinthians)

Won his only cap in the last match before the start of England's record sequence of 6 years and 20 games without defeat.

JAMES

HAMPSON

b 23 Mar 1906   d 10 Jan 1938   CENTRE FORWARD
Caps: 3   Goals: 5
First cap: 20 Oct 1930 v Ireland 5–1   aged 24yr 211d
                                              (1 goal)
Last cap: 7 Dec 1932 v Austria 4–3   aged 26yr 259d
                                              (2 goals)

England career: 2yr 48d – P3 W3 D0 L0 – 100%
Club: Blackpool
2 Goals in a game: 2
Jimmy Hampson, he of the ferocious crewcut, had one of the most successful short careers, with three wins out of three and goals in every game. He scored twice to put England 2–0 ahead at half-time against Austria, then, like three of the other forwards (HOUGHTON, JACK and WALKER) was never picked again.

HENRY (?)
HAMPTON

b 21 Apr 1885   d 15 Mar 1963   CENTRE FORWARD
Caps: 4   Goals: 2
First cap: 17 Mar 1913 v Wales 4–3   aged 27yr 330d
                                                                       (1 goal)
Last cap: 4 Apr 1914 v Scotland 1–3   aged 28yr 348d
England career: 1yr 18d – P4 W3 D0 L1 – 75%
Club: Aston Villa
Eight years after scoring twice to win the FA Cup Final, 'Happy Harry' won another winner's medal and scored the winning goal in his first international, then the only goal (by barging keeper Jimmy Brownlie over the line) against Scotland in his second.

JOHN
HANCOCKS

b 30 Apr 1919   OUTSIDE LEFT/RIGHT
Caps: 3   Goals: 2
First cap: 2 Dec 1948 v Switzerland 6–0 aged 29yr 216d
                                                                       (2 goals)
Last cap: 22 Nov 1950 v Yugoslavia 2–2   aged 31yr 211d
England career: 1yr 355d – P3 W2 D1 L0 – 83.33%
Club: Wolves
England capped five distinguished newcomers against Switzerland: DITCHBURN, HAINES, RAMSEY, ROWLEY, and Johnny Hancocks who hit the ball very hard with size 2 boots.

EDRIS
ALBERT
HAPGOOD

b 24 Sep 1908   d 20 Apr 1973   LEFT BACK
Caps: 30   Goals: 0   Captain: 21
First cap: 13 May 1933 v Italy 1–1   aged 24yr 231d
Last cap: 18 May 1939 v Yugoslavia 1–2 aged 30yr 236d
England career: 6yr 5d – P30 W16 D3 L11 – 58.33%
Club: Arsenal
Self-confident, good in the tackle, one of the first footballing full backs, Eddie Hapgood played for (and captained) England more times than anyone else between the wars; but for the Second, he might have passed CROMPTON's totals. His first and last matches as captain were traumatic:

his nose was broken in a brutal match against Italy on his home club ground in 1934 and his ankle ligaments were torn in Belgrade. He finished both games. He was captain in his last 11 internationals.

He would have become the last to play for England in goal as well as outfield if Vic WOODLEY hadn't recovered during the 1937 tour.

HAROLD THOMAS WILLIAM
HARDINGE

b 25 Feb 1886   d 8 May 1965   INSIDE LEFT
Caps: 1   Goals: 0
Only cap: 2 Apr 1910 v Scotland 0–2   aged 24yr 36d
England career: P1 W0 D0 L1 – 0%
Club: Sheffield United
'Wally' Hardinge played international football alongside cricketers, and international cricket alongside a footballer. He himself was both.

He won only one cap at each sport: football in the same team as DUCAT and MAKEPEACE, cricket with Ducat alone (in 1921), both playing in their only Test. He might have won more caps if his debuts hadn't been against England's leading rivals each time, Scotland and Australia.

Note that Farror–Lamming originally listed Walter as his third name, which may have involved some educated guesswork (Walter= Wally). The revised Lamming book reflects Jim Creasy's findings in the newspaper library, which tie in with two major cricketing Who's Whos.

HAROLD
PAYNE
HARDMAN

b 4 Apr 1882   d 9 Jun 1965   OUTSIDE LEFT
Caps: 4   Goals: 1
First cap: 27 Mar 1905 v Wales 3–1   aged 22yr 357d
Last cap: 16 Mar 1908 v Wales 7–1   aged 25yr 346d
England career: 2yr 354d – P4 W3 D1 L0 – 87.50%
Club: Everton
A small, slim winger who didn't live up to his surname, Harold Hardman won an Olympic gold medal with the 1908 United Kingdom team and later became chairman of Manchester United.

GEORGE
FRANCIS MOUTREY
HARDWICK

b 2 Feb 1920   LEFT BACK
Caps: 13   Goals: 0   Captain: 13
First cap: 28 Sep 1946 v N Ireland 7–2   aged 26yr 239d
Last cap: 10 Apr 1948 v Scotland 2–0   aged 28yr 68d
England career: 1yr 195d – P13 W10 D2 L1 – 84.62%
Club: Middlesbrough

Penalties: 1 Missed: 1

Dapper all round (clean tackle, good distribution, Ronald Colman moustache), captain in the first 13 matches after the Second World War, George Hardwick was the last player to lead England out on his debut; of those who were captain in their every international, he played in far and away the most matches. Injured against Scotland, he didn't recover in time for the summer tour and let in SWIFT as the first goalkeeper to captain England this century. His missed penalty didn't matter much to the scoreline (England were leading 6–1 on the way to beating Holland 8–2) but did perhaps to LAWTON, who might have scored five in the match if he'd taken it.

HENRY
HARDY

b 14 Jan 1895   d 17 Feb 1969   GOALKEEPER
Caps: 1   Goals conceded: 0
Only cap: 8 Dec 1924 v Belgium 4–0   aged 29yr 328d
England career: P1 W1 D0 L0 – 100%
Club: Stockport County

Harry Hardy was the only player ever to have been capped while with Stockport. They were in the Second Division at the time.

SAMUEL
HARDY

b 25 Aug 1883   d 24 Oct 1966   GOALKEEPER
Caps: 21   Goals conceded: 25   Clean sheets: 7
First cap: 16 Feb 1907 v Ireland 1–0   aged 23yr 175d
Last cap: 10 Apr 1920 v Scotland 5–4   aged 36yr 228d
England career: 13yr 54d – P21 W12 D5 L4 – 69.04%
Clubs: Liverpool (14), Aston Villa (7)
Penalties: 3   Saved: 1

In terms of ability and statistics, Sam Hardy set all the standards for an England goalkeeper. No-one kept more clean sheets before HIBBS; he was the first to keep three in a row (1909); his career was the longest for any England player until S MATTHEWS in 1947, and for a goalkeeper until SHILTON in 1983 – and he may have been the oldest ever England player before COMPTON (see MORTEN and PENNINGTON). He would have won more caps but for World War I, which opened a gap of 5 years 204 days in his international career.

He saved the penalty which James Stark of Scotland hit straight at him in 1909.

MICHAEL G
HARFORD

b 12 Feb 1959   CENTRE FORWARD
Caps: 2   Goals: 0

First cap: 17 Feb 1988 v Israel 0–0   aged 29yr 05d
                                          (sub 68min)
Last cap: 14 Sep 1988 v Denmark 1–0   aged 29yr 215d
                                          (sub'd 69min)
England career: 0yr 210d – P2 W1 D1 L0 – 75%
Club: Luton Town

The English admiration for the blunderbuss survives in the face of all modern technology (Rossi, Rummenigge, Careca, Gerd Muller, LINEKER) especially when it's ageing and not firing as it used to (LOFTHOUSE, WITHE, Mick Harford).

FREDERICK
WILLIAM
HARGREAVES

b 16 Aug 1858   d 5 Apr 1857   HALF BACK
Caps: 3   Goals: 0
First cap: 15 Mar 1880 v Wales 3–2   aged 21yr 212d
Last cap: 23 Feb 1882 v Ireland 13–0   aged 23yr 192d
England career: 1yr 345d – P3 W2 D0 L1 – 66.66%
Club: Blackburn Rovers

Fred Hargreaves and brother Jack played once together for England, in 1881 when Wales beat England for the first time.

JOHN
HARGREAVES

b 13 Dec 1860   d 13 Jan 1903   OUTSIDE RIGHT/LEFT
Caps: 2   Goals: 0
First cap: 26 Feb 1881 v Wales 0–1   aged 20yr 75d
Last cap: 12 Mar 1881 v Scotland 1–6   aged 20yr 89d
England career: 0yr 14d – P2 W0 D0 L2 – 0%
Club: Blackburn Rovers

One of the first football Jonahs (see ROSTRON and PP HARRIS)? Jack Hargreaves played in Wales' first win over England, and England's heaviest ever defeat at home. When there was a chance of easier pickings, he had to drop out of the team that beat Ireland 7–0 in 1883. His brother Fred had a better time in internationals.

EDWARD
CASHFIELD
HARPER

b 22 Aug 1901/02   d 22 Jul 1959   CENTRE FORWARD
Caps: 1   Goals: 0
Only cap: 17 Apr 1926 v Scotland 0–1
                                  aged 23/24yr 238d
England career: P1 W0 D0 L1 – 0%
Club: Blackburn Rovers

Bill Harper the Scottish goalkeeper kept out Ted Harper the English attacker at Old Trafford. Neither played international football again.

GORDON
HARRIS

b 2 Jun 1940   OUTSIDE LEFT
Caps: 1   Goals: 0
Only cap: 5 Jan 1966 v Poland 1–1   aged 25yr 217d
England career: P1 W0 D1 L0 – 50%
Club: Burnley

Right to the last minute, Sir Alf was looking for World Cup wingers: PAINE, CONNELLY, TEMPLE, CALLAGHAN . . .

PETER
PHILIP
HARRIS

b 19 Dec 1925   OUTSIDE RIGHT
Caps: 2   Goals: 0
First cap: 21 Sep 1949 v Eire 0–2   aged 23yr 276d
Last cap: 23 May 1954 v Hungary 1–7   aged 28yr 155d
England career: 4yr 244d – P2 W0 D0 L2 – 0%
Club: Portsmouth

Peter Harris had no luck in international football. With the score still 1–0, he hit the bar against the Irish as England lost at home for the first time to a country from outside the Home Championship. Then came a five-year wait before the selectors took him to Budapest (in place of MATTHEWS) to help avenge the first home defeat by a country from outside the British Isles – and came back with England's worst defeat by anyone anywhere. No more caps after that; imagine the insurance premiums.

STANLEY
SCHUTE
HARRIS

b 19 Jul 1881   *d 4 May 1926*   INSIDE FORWARD
Caps: 6   Goals: 2   Captain: 4
First cap: 9 Apr 1904 v Scotland 1–0   aged 22yr 265d
Last cap: 7 Apr 1906 v Scotland 1–2   aged 24yr 262d
England career: 1yr 363d – P6 W4 D1 L1 – 75%
Clubs: Old Westminsters & Cambridge University (1);
     Old Westminsters alone (5); Corinthians throughout.
2 Goals in a game: 0   Goals while captain: 1

The policy of appointing an amateur forward whenever possible led to Stanley Harris captaining the team in his last three internationals. Note that the revised Lamming Who's Who spells his second name Shute and a 1907 Who's Who says it was Slater.

ALBAN HUGH
HARRISON

b 30 Nov 1869   *d 15 Aug 1943*   RIGHT BACK
Caps: 2   Goals: 0

First cap: 25 Feb 1893 v Ireland 6–1   aged 23yr 87d
Last cap: 1 Apr 1893 v Scotland 5–2   aged 23yr 122d
England career: 0yr 35d – P2 W2 D0 L0 – 100%
Club: Old Westminsters (& Corinthians)

Also picked to play Wales in 1894 but withdrew with an injured ankle.

GEORGE
HARRISON

b 18 Jul 1892   *d 12 Mar 1939*   OUTSIDE LEFT
Caps: 2   Goals: 0
First cap: 21 May 1921 v Belgium 2–0   aged 28yr 307d
Last cap: 22 Oct 1921 v Ireland 1–1   aged 29yr 96d
England career: 0yr 154d – P2 W1 D1 L0 – 75%
Club: Everton

'Jud' Harrison didn't have it easy in internationals. His opponents (Swartenbroeks and McCracken) were two of the best.

JACK
HARRY
HARROW

b 8 Oct 1888   *d 19 Jul 1958*   LEFT BACK
Caps: 2   Goals: 0
First cap: 21 Oct 1922 v Ireland 2–0   aged 34yr 13d
Last cap: 21 May 1923 v Sweden 4–2   aged 34yr 225d
England career: 0yr 212d – P2 W2 D0 L0 – 100%
Club: Chelsea

Short, tough, still quite quick, he was a little lucky that Ireland and Sweden's attacking strength was in the middle and not on the wings.

ERNEST
ARTHUR
HART

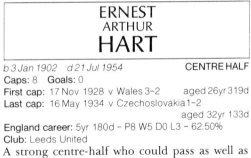

b 3 Jan 1902   *d 21 Jul 1954*   CENTRE HALF
Caps: 8   Goals: 0
First cap: 17 Nov 1928 v Wales 3–2   aged 26yr 319d
Last cap: 16 May 1934 v Czechoslovakia 1–2
                              aged 32yr 133d
England career: 5yr 180d – P8 W5 D0 L3 – 62.50%
Club: Leeds United

A strong centre-half who could pass as well as defend, Ernie Hart was awarded his caps in small clusters, including his last three in a row. His international career ended in 2–1 defeats in Budapest and Prague, where he had trouble with the more fluid Danubian forward lines.

FRANK
HARTLEY

b 20 Jul 1896   *d 20 Oct 1965*   INSIDE LEFT
Caps: 1   Goals: 0
Only cap: 10 May 1923 v France 4–1   aged 26yr 294d
England career: P1 W1 D0 L0 – 100%

Ernie Hart's best moment was against Scotland in 1934, when he kept out the great Gallacher as England won 3–0 (Lamming)

Club: Oxford City (& Tottenham Hotspur)

He was once thought to be called Fred, but there was apparently confusion with a well-known pianist of the time! The *Wisden Book of Obituaries*, Charlie BUCHAN (a contemporary) and a newspaper discovered by Jim Creasy in Colindale all confirm him as Frank.

Two other members of the forward line against France were fellow amateurs: CREEK and HEGAN.

A
HARVEY

b unknown   d unknown　　　　　　　**FULL BACK**
Caps: 1   Goals: 0
Only cap: 26 Feb 1881 v Wales 0–1
England career: P1 W0 D0 L1 – 0%
Club: Wednesbury Strollers

One of the two great unknowns (see SAVAGE). Jon Silk, quoting 'the Aston Villa records', says his christian name was Alf. Apparently an article, including his photograph, appears in an 'old publication'. Quite possibly, but rather vague. Was he the right A Harvey? Neither of the Lamming books mentions any link with Villa.

JAMES
COLIN
HARVEY

b 16 Nov 1944　　　　　　　　　　**MIDFIELDER**
Caps: 1   Goals: 0
Only cap: 3 Feb 1971 v Malta 1–0　　　aged 26yr 79d
England career: P1 W1 D0 L0 – 100%
Club: Everton

Part of the fine midfield that won the League title in 1970, Colin Harvey played in an England team with three other new caps (CHIVERS, McFARLAND and ROYLE) and a new captain (MULLERY, after MOORE was suspended following the Blackpool Affair), on a bone-hard dustbowl near Valletta. Odds heavily stacked.

HAROLD
WILLIAM
HASSALL

b 4 Mar 1929　　　　　　　　　**INSIDE LEFT**
Caps: 5   Goals: 4
First cap: 14 Apr 1951 v Scotland 2–3　　aged 22yr 41d
　　　　　　　　　　　　　　　　　　　　(1 goal)
Last cap: 11 Nov 1953 v N Ireland 3–1　aged 24yr 252d
　　　　　　　　　　　　　　　　　　　　(2 goals)
England career: 2yr 211d – P5 W3 D1 L1– 70%
Clubs: Huddersfield Town (4), Bolton Wanderers (1)

Always something of a surprise choice, Harold Hassall put England 1–0 up before the Scots made their extra man tell after MANNION's injury. Recalled after two years and four caps, he scored in the first minute and on the hour against the Irish at Goodison. His virtual own goal in the MATTHEWS Cup Final has been given to MORTENSEN as part of his hat-trick.

MARK
WAYNE
HATELEY

b 7 Nov 1961　　　　　　　　**CENTRE FORWARD**
Caps: 31   Goals: 9
First cap:　2 Jun 1984 v USSR 0–2　　　aged 22yr 208d
　　　　　　　　　　　　　　　　　　　(sub 70min)
Last cap: 18 Jun 1988 v USSR 1–3　　　aged 26yr 224d
　　　　　　　　　　　　　　　　　　　(sub 69min)
England career: 4yr 16d – P31 W11 D10 L10 – 51.61%
Clubs: Portsmouth (4), Milan (20), Monaco (7)
Substitute: 12   Substituted: 4   2 Goals in a game: 2

Things started with a bang for Mark Hateley in Milan: five goals very early in the season, problems for all defences ('Attila') with headwork reminiscent of his father; then things tailed off through injury and loss of form. Much the same with his England career: a bright beginning, several important goals on the road to Mexico – then a remarkable collapse, with no goals in his last 13 matches and no wins in the last 10, though his scoring rate would look better if he hadn't been a substitute in 10 of the last 11.

ROBERT
MURRAY
HAWKES

b 18 Oct 1880   d 12 Sep 1945 **LEFT HALF**
Caps: 5   **Goals:** 0
First cap: 16 Feb 1907 v Ireland 1–0   aged 26yr 121d
Last cap: 13 Jun 1908 v Bohemia 4–0   aged 27yr 239d
England career: 1yr 118d – P5 W5 D0 L0 – 100%
Club: Luton Town

The midfield firm of WARREN, WEDLOCK and Hawkes was much too good for the continental amateurs on England's first overseas tour. A ball-playing half back, Bob Hawkes was said to have a metal plate in his skull, hence an aversion to heading the ball. Probably gold, if his international record's anything to go by; only HINE and W WILLIAMS had longer 100% records when playing for England.

JOHN
HAWLEY EDWARDS

b 1850   d 14 Jan 1893 **FORWARD**
Caps: 1   **Goals:** 0
Only cap: 7 Mar 1874 v Scotland 1–2   aged 23/24
England career: P1 W0 D0 L1 – 0%
International career: 2yr 18d – P2 W0 D0 L2 – 0%
Club: Shropshire Wanderers (& apparently Shrewsbury FC); The Wanderers at the time of his match for Wales.

The first player to play full international football for two different countries (Wales v Scotland 1876), he was born in Shrewsbury. Modern yearbooks list him under Edwards, but *The Football Encyclopaedia 1934*, a match report in *The Sporting Life*, and Charles ALCOCK himself, call him J Hawley-Edwards.

Charles Alcock, in his Football Annuals of 1874 and 1892, refers to WYLIE having played in the 1874 international. However, elsewhere he also mentions the exact opposite – and all subsequent record books go along with that. The confusion must have arisen because the two players were clubmates and Hawley Edwards actually replaced Wylie in the team.

GEORGE
HAWORTH

b 17 Oct 1864   d unknown **HALF BACK**
Caps: 5   **Goals:** 0
First cap: 5 Feb   1887 v Ireland 7–0   aged 22yr 111d
Last cap: 5 Apr   1890 v Scotland 1–1   aged 25yr 170d
England career: 3yr 59d – P5 W3 D1 L1 – 70%
Club: Accrington FC

A fearsome proposition on a heavy pitch, he and HOWARTH made their England debuts in the same match. Whatever contemporary match reports may have said, the spelling bears no relation.

JOHN PURVIS
HAWTREY

b 19 Jul 1850   d 17 1925 **GOALKEEPER**
Caps: 2   **Goals conceded:** 7
First cap: 26 Feb 1881 v Wales 0–1   aged 30yr 222d
Last cap: 12 Mar 1881 v Scotland 1–6   aged 30yr 236d
England career: 0yr 14d – P2 W0 D0 L2 – 0%
Club: Remnants (& Old Etonians)

'Feeble and uncertain' as the invaders poured down on him in England's heaviest ever home defeat.

EDWARD BROWNLOW
HAYGARTH

b 26 Apr 1854   d 14 Apr 1915 **FULL BACK**
Caps: 1   **Goals:** 0
Only cap: 6 Mar 1875 v Scotland 2–2 aged 20yr 314d
England career: P1 W0 D1 L0 – 50%
Club: Swifts (and probably Lancing Old Boys & Wanderers)

Got through a lot of work in an Oval mudbath; couldn't stop the Scots scoring twice.

JOHN
NORMAN
HAYNES

b 17 Oct 1934 **INSIDE LEFT/RIGHT**
Caps: 56   **Goals:** 18   **Captain:** 22
First cap: 2 Oct 1954 v N Ireland 2–0   aged 19yr 350d
(1 goal)
Last cap: 10 Jun 1962 v Brazil 1–3   aged 27yr 236d
England career: 7yr 251d – P56 W30 D14 L12 – 66.07%
Club: Fulham
Substituted: 1   **Goals while captain:** 4
3 Goals in a game: 1   **2 Goals in a game:** 2

The wonder boy became the first £100-a-week man, the hub of two successful England teams – but his through-passes didn't work against World Cup defences. A combination of bad injury and good old Alf meant no more caps after 1962, though the Bring Back Johnny campaigns lasted a fair while. He was scoring regularly for England at the time of his hat-trick against the USSR in 1958, but was already playing deeper when scoring twice in the 9–3 romp against Scotland in 1961, and there were no goals in his last 15 internationals. The cares of captaincy, perhaps; he led England in his last 22 matches.

HENRY
HEALLESS

b 9/10 Feb 1893 d 11 Jan 1972 CENTRE/LEFT HALF
Caps: 2 Goals: 0
First cap: 22 Oct 1924 v Ireland 3–1
aged 31yr 255/256d
Last cap: 31 Mar 1928 v Scotland 1–5
aged 35yr 50/51d
England career: 3yr 161d – P2 W1 D0 L1 – 50%
Club: Blackburn Rovers

Harry Healless, a late replacement for the original captain Sid BISHOP, was one of five players whose England careers were ended by the Wembley Wizards. See H JONES, KELLY, WH SMITH, T WILSON.

KEVIN
JAMES
HECTOR

b 2 Nov 1944 LEFT-SIDED FORWARD
Caps: 2 Goals: 0
First cap: 17 Oct 1973 v Poland 1–1
aged 28yr 349d
(sub 88min)
Last cap: 14 Nov 1973 v Italy 0–1
aged 29yr 12d
(sub 74min)
England career: 0yr 28d – P2 W0 D1 L1 – 25%
Club: Derby County
Substitute: 2

Kevin Hector almost scored and took England to the World Cup finals in his two minutes against Poland. If that second cap was meant to be a consolation prize, it was a very small one; he played a total of 18 minutes in international football.

GEORGE
ALBERT
HEDLEY

b 20 Jul 1876 d 16 Aug 1942 CENTRE FORWARD
Caps: 1 Goals: 0 (1?)
Only cap: 9 Mar 1901 v Ireland 3–0 aged 24yr 232d
England career: P1 W1 D0 L0 – 100%
Club: Sheffield United

There's good reason for believing that George Hedley scored in his only international: at least two sources (including *Ireland's Saturday Night*) credit him with England's second, after 81 minutes. Modern yearbooks say RE FOSTER scored both the last two goals.

KENNETH EDWARD
HEGAN

b 24 Jan 1901 d ? OUTSIDE LEFT/RIGHT
Caps: 4 Goals: 4
First cap: 19 Mar 1923 v Belgium 6–1 aged 22yr 54d
(2 goals)
Last cap: 1 Nov 1923 v Belgium 2–2 aged 22yr 281d
England career: 0yr 227d – P4 W2 D1 L1 – 62.50%
Club: Corinthians (also Army football)
2 Goals in a game: 2

Lieutenant 'Jackie' Hegan scored two goals in each of his first two internationals, against Belgium and France.

MICHAEL
STEPHEN
HELLAWELL

b 30 June 1938 OUTSIDE RIGHT
Caps: 2 Goals: 0
First cap: 3 Oct 1962 v France 1–1 aged 24yr 95d
Last cap: 20 Oct 1962 v N Ireland 3–1 aged 24yr 112d
England career: 0yr 17d – P2 W1 D1 L0 – 75%
Club: Birmingham City

Mike Hellawell was very quick, could shoot, and was unlucky to be pitched into two very experimental England forward lines.

ARTHUR GEORGE
HENFREY

b 1868 d 17 Oct 1929 HALF BACK/FORWARD
Caps: 5 Goals: 2
First cap: 7 Mar 1891 v Ireland 6–1 aged 22/23
(1 goal)
Last cap: 4 Apr 1896 v Scotland 1–2 aged 27/28
England career: 5yr 28d – P5 W3 D1 L1 – 70%
Clubs: Cambridge University & Corinthians (1),
Corinthians alone (4)

A hard player 'but not good in kicking', he nevertheless almost certainly scored in his first two internationals. *The Athletic News* and *The Field* credit him with the first goal against Wales in 1891, although *The Times* (less of a sports newspaper than the others) awards it to COTTERILL. According to one report, he was still at university when he won his second cap. Like BURNUP, he ran out of steam among the professionals at Parkhead.

RONALD
PATRICK
HENRY

b 17 Aug 1934 LEFT BACK
Caps: 1 Goals: 0
Only cap: 27 Feb 1963 v France 2–5 aged 28yr 194d
England career: P1 W0 D0 L1 – 0%

Not only fools and horses. The Corinthian Henfrey, Rodney Trotter look-alike and hard-working midfielder (Lamming)

Club: Tottenham Hotspur
Elegant full-back in the Spurs Double team who ran into a nightmare in Paris where the French wingers (Maryan Wisnieski and Lucien Cossou) each scored twice.

CHARLES
FRANCIS
WILLIAM
HERON

b 1853 d 23 Oct 1914   FORWARD
Caps: 1 **Goals:** 0
Only cap: 4 Mar 1876 v Scotland 0–3   aged 22/23
England career: P1 W0 D0 L1 – 0%
Club: Wanderers
Frank Heron played alongside his older brother Hubert in his only international.

GEORGE
HUBERT
HUGH
HERON

b 30 Jan 1852 d 5 June 1914   FORWARD

Caps: 5 **Goals:** 0 **Captain:** 1
First cap: 8 Mar 1873 v Scotland 4–2   aged 21yr 37d
Last cap: 2 Mar 1878 v Scotland 2–7   aged 26yr 31d
England career: 4yr 360d – P5 W1 D1 L3 – 30%
Club: Uxbridge (& Wanderers, and probably Swifts)
A great dribbler in a dribbling age, Hubert Heron was the first player to win five England caps.

WILLIAM
HIBBERT

b 21 Sep 1884 d 16 Mar 1949   INSIDE RIGHT
Caps: 1 **Goals:** 0
Only cap: 2 Apr 1910 v Scotland 0–2   aged 25yr 193d
England career: P1 W0 D0 L1 – 0%
Club: Bury
The defeat at Hampden ended the international careers of four of the England forwards, including the entire inside-forward trio who had only one previous cap between them – PARKINSON, HARDINGE and Billy Hibbert – and outside-right Dicky BOND.

HENRY
EDWARD
HIBBS

b 27 May 1905/06 d 23 Apr 1984   GOALKEEPER
Caps: 25 **Goals conceded:** 26 **Clean sheets:** 10
First cap: 20 Nov 1929 v Wales 6–0 aged 23/24yr 177d
Last cap: 5 Feb 1936 v Wales 1–2 aged 29/30yr 253d
England career: 6yr 77d – P25 W16 D4 L5 – 72%
Club: Birmingham FC
Penalties faced: 3 **Saved:** 1 **Missed:** 2
No-one put a penalty-kick past Harry Hibbs in an international; he saved from Fred Keenor of Wales in 1930, Billy Evans of Wales shot wide in 1934, and Jackie Coulter of Ireland hit the bar in 1935. The days of English goalkeepers coming far off their line were still in the future, but he was one of the best in the world at what he did. Brave and agile, he overtook S HARDY's record number of caps for an England goalkeeper, as well as his total number of clean sheets, setting targets for SPRINGETT and G BANKS respectively.

FREDERICK
HILL

b 17 Jan 1940   INSIDE RIGHT
Caps: 2 **Goals:** 0
First cap: 20 Oct 1962 v N Ireland 3–1 aged 22yr 276d
Last cap: 21 Nov 1962 v Wales 4–0 aged 22yr 308d
England career: 0yr 32d – P2 W2 D0 L0 – 100%
Club: Bolton Wanderers
Malcolm Allison brought flash Freddie to Maine Road when he was over 30 but he was never likely to be in RAMSEY's teams.

GORDON
ALEC
HILL

b 1 Apr 1954   OUTSIDE LEFT
Caps: 6   Goals: 0
First cap: 28 May 1976 v Italy 3–2   aged 22yr 57d
Last cap: 12 Oct 1977 v Luxembourg 2–0
                           aged 23yr 194d
England career: 1yr 137d – P6 W4 D2 L0 – 83.33%
Club: Manchester United
Substitute: 3

Stocky, cocky, exasperating, sometimes a match-winner, never for England. The opposite wing to COPPELL at United, he was capped, incredibly, before him.

JOHN
HENRY
HILL

b 2 Mar 1897/99   d Apr 1972   RIGHT/CENTRE HALF
Caps: 11   Goals: 0   Own goals: 1   Captain: 8
First cap: 28 Feb 1925 v Wales 2–1   aged 25/27yr 363d
Last cap: 15 May 1929 v Spain 3–4   aged 30/32yr 74d
England career: 4yr 76d – P11 W6 D1 L4 – 59.09%
Clubs: Burnley (8), Newcastle United (3)

Very tall, hugely difficult to pass, captain in his last eight internationals, big Jack may have scored in the very last one (see J BRADFORD).

There's no doubt about his own goal. He and Fred Keenor, the two captains, scored one apiece in the second England–Wales match of 1927.

RICHARD
HENRY
HILL

b 26 Nov 1893   d Apr 1971   LEFT BACK
Caps: 1   Goals: 0
Only cap: 24 May 1926 v Belgium 5–3   aged 32yr 179d
England career: P1 W1 D0 L0 – 100%
Club: Millwall

Dick Hill was Millwall's fourth England international (after FORT, L GRAHAM and FOX) while they were in the Third Division. Yearbooks used to confuse him with JH HILL, who also played for England in the 1920s.

RICKY
ANTHONY
HILL

b 5 Mar 1959   MIDFIELDER
Caps: 3   Goals: 0
First cap: 22 Sep 1982 v Denmark 2–2   aged 23yr 201d
                           (sub 83min)
Last cap: 29 Jan 1986 v Egypt 4–0   aged 26yr 299d
                           (sub 76min)

England career: 3yr 98d – P3 W1 D1 L1 – 50%
Club: Luton Town
Substitute: 2

The first new cap picked by Bobby ROBSON, Ricky Hill was recalled after three years for his last game, playing only a couple of hours for England in total.

JOHN
HILLMAN

b 1871   d 1 Aug 1955   GOALKEEPER
Caps: 1   Goals conceded: 2
Only cap: 18 Feb 1899 v Ireland 13–2   aged 27/28
England career: P1 W1 D0 L0 – 100%
Club: Burnley
Penalties: 1   Saved: 0

Big Jack Hillman was beaten by the first penalty-kick ever conceded by England (taken by the Irish captain Joe McAllen) Earlier in the same game, CRABTREE had missed the first penalty ever taken by an England player.

ARNOLD FRANK
HILLS

b 12 Mar 1857   d 7 Mar 1927   FORWARD
Caps: 1   Goals: 0
Only cap: 5 Apr 1879 v Scotland 5–4   aged 22yr 24d
England career: P1 W1 D0 L0 – 100%
Club: Old Harrovians

The season after winning the AAA mile, he was one of eight new caps, and one of seven who didn't play for England again.

GEORGE
RICHARD
HILSDON

b 10 Aug 1885   d 10 Sep 1941   CENTRE FORWARD
Caps: 8   Goals: 14
First cap: 16 Feb 1907 v Ireland 1–0   aged 21yr 190d
Last cap: 13 Feb 1909 v Ireland 4–0   aged 23yr 187d
                           (2 goals, 1 pen)
England career: 1yr 362d – P8 W7 D1 L0 – 87.50%
Club: Chelsea
4 Goals in a game: 1   2 Goals in a game: 5

George Hilsdon had one of the very best strike records. He scored twice in each of four consecutive internationals, the England record before DEAN. In 1908 he became the first to score five England goals in succession (the last three against Hungary, the first two against Bohemia), a total exceeded only by MACDONALD. Of players who scored at least 10 goals for England, his average of 1.75 is second only to CAMSELL. His 12 goals in 1907–08 were a record for a single season, surpassed only by GREAVES in 1960–61. He was the first player to score from two penalties for England, and he did it in successive games (v Bohemia 1908, Ireland 1909). No-one scored from three penalties until RAMSEY in 1953.

Oh, and it's unlikely any other England player will score twice against Bohemia.

ERNEST
WILLIAM
HINE

b 9 Apr 1900/01   d 1974   INSIDE RIGHT/LEFT
Caps: 6   Goals: 4
First cap: 22 Oct 1928 v Ireland 2–1 aged 27/28yr 196d
Last cap: 18 Nov 1931 v Wales 3–1 aged 30/31yr 223d
(1 goal)

England career: 3yr 27d – P6 W6 D0 L0 – 100%
Club: Leicester City
2 Goals in a game: 0   **Penalties:** 1   **Missed:** 0
Ernie Hine matched W WILLIAMS' England record of Played 6, Won 6. He scored in his last two internationals as well as the first goal against Wales in 1929 from the penalty spot, after which CAMSELL scored twice.

ALAN
THOMAS
HINTON

b 6 Oct 1942   OUTSIDE LEFT
Caps: 3   Goals: 0
First cap: 3 Oct 1962 v France 1–1   aged 19yr 362d
Last cap: 18 Nov 1964 v Wales 2–1   aged 22yr 43d
England career: 2yr 46d – P3 W1 D2 L0 – 66.66%
Club: Wolves (1), Nottingham Forest (2)
Capped young, Alan Hinton was a better player ten years later for Derby. But there was talk of a lack of physical courage, hardly likely to endear him to Sir Alf.

DAVID
HIRST

b 7 Dec 1967   STRIKER
Caps: 2   Goals: 1
First cap: 1 Jun 1991 v Australia 1–0   aged 23yr 176d
(sub'd HT)
Last cap: 8 Jun 1991 v N Zealand 2–0 aged 23yr 183d
(sub HT, 1 goal)
England career: 0yr 07d – P2 W2 D0 L0 – 100%
Club: Sheffield Wednesday
Erratic but dangerous. Scored over 30 goals to help Wednesday win promotion and the League Cup in 1990–91, two more on his England B debut, and one five minutes after coming on in Wellington.

GERALD
ARCHIBALD
HITCHENS

b 8 Oct 1934   CENTRE FORWARD
Caps: 7   Goals: 5
First cap: 10 May 1961 v Mexico 8–0   aged 26yr 214d
(1 goal)
Last cap: 10 Jun 1962 v Brazil 1–3   aged 27yr 245d
(1 goal)

England career: 1yr 31d – P7 W4 D0 L3 – 57.14%
Clubs: Aston Villa (3), Internazionale (4)
2 Goals in a game: 1
Strong, uncomplicated, an out-and-out trier, Gerry Hitchens scored after only two minutes of his debut, and twice against Italy in Rome, after which Inter bought him and got a year's value for money before replacing him with the flying Jair.

HAROLD
HENRY FRANK/FREDERICK
HOBBIS

b 9 Mar 1913   d 1991   OUTSIDE LEFT
Caps: 2   Goals: 1
First cap: 6 May 1936 v Austria 1–2   aged 23yr 58d
Last cap: 9 May 1936 v Belgium 2–3   aged 23yr 61d
(1 goal)

England career: 0yr 3d – P2 W0 D0 L2 – 0%
Club: Charlton Athletic
Harold Hobbis had just helped Charlton win promotion to the first Division but couldn't stop Austria and Belgium beating England for the first time. He scored two minutes from the end of his international career.

GLENN
HODDLE

b 27 Oct 1957   MIDFIELDER
Caps: 53   Goals: 8
First cap: 22 Nov 1979 v Bulgaria 2–0   aged 22yr 26d
(1 goal)
Last cap: 18 Jun 1988 v USSR 1–3   aged 30yr 234d
England career: 8yr 208d – P53 W27 D11 L15 – 61.32%
Clubs: Tottenham Hotspur (44), Monaco (9)
Substitute: 10   **Substituted:** 7   **2 Goals in a game:** 0
The football world was probably divided straight down the middle; managers v fans, WILKINS v Hoddle. Managers picked teams, fans lost out.

Ron Greenwood had a number of good managerial reasons for not picking Glenn Hoddle ahead of, say, Terry McDERMOTT: early on he lacked stamina, he didn't follow a move through, didn't dominate an entire match . . . fair enough, but it's equally true that on his debut he made the first goal, scored a confident, exciting second, did dominate the entire match – and wasn't picked for the next three games. Equally true that he was sometimes played out of position wide on the right, presumably with instructions to stay there; that he was a player who needed a team built around him (à la Netzer) and that Greenwood – and ROBSON – rarely built it. When they did, with Bryan ROBSON and other workhorses around him, he often pulled some sweet strings: in Budapest in 1983, when he scored from a free-kick and England won 3–0; in the later matches in Mexico.

No-one, for or against, was ever absolutely certain about him. What isn't in doubt is that he was as lavishly skilled as anyone in world football (ask Ardiles), that he scored some breathtaking goals for country as well as club (and several more than Wilkins in far fewer games), that everyone was glad to have seen Glenn Hoddle play. Even his kick-about before a match was as good as Puskas', except that 'Glennda' used both feet.

He was the last player to miss a penalty (v USA in 1985) while playing for England.

STEPHEN BRIAN
HODGE

b 25 Oct 1962   MIDFIELDER
Caps: 24   Goals: 0
First cap: 26 Mar 1986 v USSR 1–0   aged 23yr 152d
Last cap: 1 May 1991 v Turkey 1–0   aged 28yr 188d
(sub HT)
England career: 5yr 36d – P24 W15 D5 L4 – 72.92%
Clubs: Aston Villa (11), Tottenham Hotspur (4), Nottingham Forest (9)
Substitute: 6   Substituted: 5

Tidied up the left flank, especially in the Mexico World Cup, but it's debatable whether he's ever really done enough going forward for England. Those 24 caps, 11 of them admittedly incomplete, look rather a lot.

DENNIS
HODGETTS

b 28 Nov 1863   d 26 Mar 1945   INSIDE/OUTSIDE LEFT
Caps: 6   Goals: 1
First cap: 4 Feb 1888 v Wales 5–1   aged 24yr 68d
Last cap: 3 Mar 1894 v Ireland 2–2   aged 30yr 95d
England career: 6yr 27d – P6 W5 D1 L0 – 91.66%
Club: Aston Villa

Powerful, chubby-cheeked, never out of place in an England team, he moved on before Villa won their Double, but won either the League or the Cup in each of the previous seasons.

ALAN
HODGKINSON

b 16 Oct 1936   GOALKEEPER

Caps: 5   Goals conceded: 5   Clean sheets: 0
First cap: 6 Apr 1957 v Scotland 2–1   aged 20yr 172d
Last cap: 23 Nov 1960 v Wales 5–1   aged 24yr 38d
England career: 3yr 231d – P5 W4 D1 L0 – 90%
Club: Sheffield United

Recalled for his last cap after more than three years, conceded exactly one goal in every game. At Hampden in 1957 he dropped the ball and Willie Fernie put it in the net; it was disallowed because Laurie Reilly had charged the new keeper while both his feet were off the ground. Welcome to international football.

GORDON
HODGSON

b 16 Apr 1904   d 14 Jun 1951   INSIDE RIGHT
Caps: 3   Goals: 1
First cap: 20 Oct 1930 v Ireland 5–1   aged 26yr 187d
Last cap: 28 Mar 1931 v Scotland 0–2   aged 26yr 346d
England career: 0yr 159d – P3 W2 D0 L1 – 66.66%
Club: Liverpool

Born in South Africa, capped by South Africa at amateur level, came over with a South African touring team. English parents.

JOSEPH
HODKINSON

b 1889   d 18 Jun 1954   OUTSIDE LEFT
Caps: 3   Goals: 0
First cap: 17 Mar 1913 v Wales 4–3   aged 23/24
Last cap: 25 Oct 1919 v Ireland 1–1   aged 29/30
England career: 6yr 222d – P3 W2 D1 L0 – 83.33%
Club: Blackburn Rovers

Like several other players at the time, Joe Hodkinson had his international career severely interrupted by the First World War (and the selectors), losing 6 years 222 days in all.

WILLIAM
HOGG

b 29 May 1879   d 30 Jan 1937   OUTSIDE RIGHT
Caps: 3   Goals: 0
First cap: 3 Mar 1902 v Wales 0–0   aged 22yr 278d
Last cap: 3 May 1902 v Scotland 2–2   aged 22yr 339d
England career: 0yr 61d – P3 W1 D2 L0 – 66.66%
Club: Sunderland

England struggled for goals in 1902, despite the presence of BLOOMER. Billy Hogg was one of those laid off for not laying on.

GEORGE HENRY
HOLDCROFT

b 23 Jan 1909   d 17 Apr 1983   GOALKEEPER

Caps: 2   Goals conceded: 3
First cap: 17 Oct 1936 v Wales 1–2   aged 27yr 268d
Last cap: 18 Nov 1936 v Ireland 3–1   aged 27yr 300d
England career: 0yr 32d – P2 W1 D0 L1 – 50%
Club: Preston North End

Wales beat England for the first time at home since 1882 when Harry Holdcroft let another new cap, Seymour Morris, equalise direct from a corner.

ALBERT
DOUGLAS
HOLDEN

b 28 Sep 1930   OUTSIDE LEFT/RIGHT
Caps: 5   Goals: 0
First cap: 11 Apr 1959 v Scotland 1–0   aged 28yr 195d
Last cap: 24 May 1959 v Mexico 1–2   aged 28yr 238d
                                              (sub'd)
England career: 0yr 43d – P5 W1 D1 L3 – 30%
Club: Bolton Wanderers
Substituted: 1

The first time England used two substitutes in a match, Doug Holden and McGUINNESS came off and didn't play international football again.

GEORGE
HENRY
HOLDEN

b 6 Oct 1859   d 1920s   OUTSIDE RIGHT
Caps: 4   Goals: 0
First cap: 12 Mar 1881 v Scotland 1–6   aged 21yr 157d
Last cap: 17 Mar 1884 v Wales 4–0   aged 24yr 162d
England career: 3yr 5d – P4 W2 D0 L2 – 50%
Club: Wednesbury Old Athletic

A respected player who survived England's worst ever home defeat.

CECIL
HENRY
HOLDEN-WHITE

b 1861   d 21 Sep 1934   LEFT HALF
Caps: 2   Goals: 0
First cap: 4 Feb 1888 v Wales 5–1   aged 26/27
Last cap: 17 Mar 1888 v Scotland 5–0   aged 26/27
England career: 0yr 42d – P2 W2 D0 L0 – 100%
Club: Swifts (& Corinthians, and perhaps Clapham Rovers)

There used to be some confusion as to whether he or FORREST played v Scotland. Alcock's and Gamage's annuals said Forrest (but were presumably listing the team as originally selected), *The Sporting Life* was vague – but most sources include HW in the line-up, and match reports in *The Sportsman* and *The Field* confirm it: he took Forrest's place in the original team.

THOMAS
HOLFORD

b 28 Jan 1878   d 6 Apr 1964   CENTRE HALF
Caps: 1   Goals: 0
Only cap: 14 Feb 1903 v Ireland 4–0   aged 25yr 17d
England career: P1 W1 D0 L0 – 100%
Club: Stoke FC

At 5ft 6in or so, Tom Holford was typical of the short – and attacking – centre halves of the time.

GEORGE H
HOLLEY

b 20/25 Nov 1885   d 27 Aug 1942   INSIDE FORWARD
Caps: 10   Goals: 8
First cap: 15 Mar 1909 v Wales 2–0
                              aged 23yr 110/115d (1 goal)
Last cap: 5 Apr 1913 v Scotland 1–0
                                   aged 27yr 131/136d
England career: 4yr 21d – P10 W9 D1 L0 – 95%
Club: Sunderland
Hat-tricks: 0   2 Goals in a game: 2

George Holley was yet another of the players whose flattering statistics were founded on easy matches against early continental opposition – but there was little doubt as to his class. Charlie BUCHAN thought him 'one of the greatest all-round forwards of my time'. He appeared on the winning side in his first seven internationals and scored twice in each of two consecutive matches, against Hungary and Austria in 1909.

EDWIN
HOLLIDAY

b 7 Jun 1939   OUTSIDE LEFT
Caps: 3   Goals: 0
First cap: 17 Oct 1959 v Wales 1–1   aged 20yr 132d
Last cap: 18 Nov 1959 v N Ireland 2–1   aged 20yr 164d
England career: 0yr 32d – P3 W1 D1 L1 – 50%
Club: Middlesbrough

Colin GRAINGER, who played for England only three years earlier, was Ed Holliday's uncle.

JOHN
WILLIAM
HOLLINS

b 16 Jul 1946   MIDFIELDER
Caps: 1   Goals: 0
Only cap: 24 May 1967 v Spain 2–0   aged 20yr 312d
England career: P1 W1 D0 L0 – 100%
Club: Chelsea

John Hollins was good enough to win more caps, and had 10 more years in which to do so. At his peak, Chelsea were successful and England weren't. Something didn't add up.

ROBERT J
HOLMES

b 23 Jun 1867   d 17 Nov 1955   **FULL BACK/HALF BACK**
Caps: 7   Goals: 0   Captain: 3
First cap: 7 Apr 1888 v Ireland 5–1   aged 20yr 319d
Last cap: 9 Mar 1895 v Ireland 9–0   aged 27yr 259d
England career: 6yr 336d – P7 W6 D1 L0 – 92.86%
Club: Preston NE

One of the hard men who made Preston Proud (see HOWARTH), Bob Holmes was captain in his last two internationals.

JOHN
HOLT

b 10 Apr 1865   d unknown   **CENTRE HALF**
Caps: 10   Goals: 0
First cap: 15 Mar 1890 v Wales 3–1   aged 24yr 339d
Last cap: 17 Mar 1900 v Ireland 2–0   aged 34yr 341d
England career: 10yr 02d – P10 W8 D2 L0 – 90%
Clubs: Everton (9), Reading (1)

A very small jack-in-the-box centre half, Johnny Holt was the first player to win ten England caps without appearing on a losing side.

EDWARD
HOPKINSON

b 29 Oct 1935   **GOALKEEPER**
Caps: 14   Goals conceded: 24   Clean sheets: 4
First cap: 19 Oct 1957 v Wales 4–0   aged 21yr 355d
Last cap: 28 Oct 1959 v Sweden 2–3   aged 23yr 364d
England career: 2yr 9d – P14 W6 D2 L6 – 50%
Club: Bolton Wanderers
Penalties: 1   Saved: 0

A good little 'un and brave with it, three of Eddie Hopkinson's first four internationals were 4–0 wins, but then he played against the likes of Yugoslavia in 1958 (0–5) and Peru in 1959 (1–4).

ANTHONY HENRY
HOSSACK

b 2 May 1867   d 24 Jan 1926   **RIGHT HALF**
Caps: 2   Goals: 0
First cap: 5 Mar 1892 v Wales 2–0   aged 24yr 306d
Last cap: 12 Mar 1894 v Wales 5–1   aged 26yr 313d
England career: 2yr 7d – P2 W2 D0 L0 – 100%
Club: Corinthians

Recovered from 'flu to win a second cap, taking his place alongside ten other Corinthians.

WILLIAM
ERIC
HOUGHTON

b 29 Jun 1910   **OUTSIDE LEFT**
Caps: 7   Goals: 5

Left *Beneath the Nigel Kennedy hair, one of the hardest shots in the game. Get in the way of Eric Houghton's left foot and you never played the violin again* (Lamming)

First cap: 20 Oct 1930 v Ireland 5–1   aged 20yr 113d
(1 goal)
Last cap: 7 Dec 1932 v Austria 4–3   aged 22yr 161d
(1 goal)
England career: 2yr 48d – P7 W6 D0 L1 – 85.71%
Club: Aston Villa
Hat-tricks: 0   2 Goals in a game: 1
Penalties: 1   Missed: 0

The international careers of Eric Houghton and Jimmy HAMPSON began and ended with them both scoring in the same matches. Houghton was well known for his fierce left-footed shooting (and an amazing stand-up, short-back-and sides haircut), but took penalties with his right for more accuracy; he equalised from the spot in Brussels as England went on to win 4–1 in 1931.

ALBERT EDWARD
('KELLY')
HOULKER

b 27 Apr 1872   d 27 May 1962   **LEFT HALF**
Caps: 5   Goals: 0
First cap: 3 May 1902 v Scotland 2–2   aged 30yr   6d
Last cap: 19 Mar 1906 v Wales 1–0   aged 33yr 326d
England career: 3yr 320d – P5 W3 D1 L1 – 70%
Clubs: Blackburn Rovers (1), Portsmouth (2),
    Southampton (2)
Exuberant clockwork half-back, cousin of COWELL.

BENJAMIN
HOWARD BAKER

b 13 Feb 1892   d 10 Sep 1987   **GOALKEEPER**
Caps: 2   Goals conceded: 0
First cap: 21 May 1921 v Belgium 2–0   aged 29yr 98d
Last cap: 24 Oct 1925 v Ireland 0–0   aged 33yr 254d
England career: 4yr 156d – P2 W1 D1 L0 – 75%
Clubs: Everton (1), Chelsea (1); Corinthians throughout
Of the goalkeepers who didn't concede a goal while playing for England, Ben Howard Baker was the only one to play as many as two complete matches (see BEASANT). Better known as a high jumper, he won his first cap at football in the same city (Antwerp) where he finished sixth in the 1920 Olympics. He also competed in the Games of 1912, won the AAA title six times between 1910 and 1921, and set a UK record of 1.95m (6ft 5in) that lasted from 1921 to 1946. When he died, he overtook WACE as the longest-lived England footballer of all time, since outlasted only by PYM.

There's doubt about whether Howard was a christian name or part of his surname. Most current yearbooks list him under Baker, but according to contemporary profiles and match reports he seems to have been double-barrelled and known as Ben.

ROBERT
HENRY
HOWARTH

b 20 Jun 1865   d 20 Aug 1938   **RIGHT BACK**
Caps: 5   Goals: 0
First cap: 5 Feb 1887 v Ireland 7–0   aged 21yr 230d
Last cap: 3 Mar 1894 v Ireland 2–2   aged 28yr 256d
England career: 7yr 26d – P5 W4 D1 L0 – 90%
Clubs: Preston NE (4), Everton (1)
A fierce tackler, a highly respected full back, Bob Howarth was chosen to captain England against Ireland in 1890 but had to drop out.

DONALD
HOWE

b 12 Oct 1935   **RIGHT BACK**
Caps: 23   Goals: 0
First cap: 19 Oct 1957 v Wales 4–0   aged 22yr 7d
Last cap: 18 Nov 1959 v N Ireland 2–1   aged 24yr 37d
England career: 2yr 30d – P23 W8 D8 L7 – 52.17%
Club: West Bromwich Albion
Given all his coaching success, it sounds too easy to call Don Howe the thinking man's full back, but that's how it was. Adaptable and constructive, he didn't miss a match throughout his England career, the second half of which coincided with a highly unsuccessful period, the 1958 World Cup and 1959 South American tour, including only 2 wins in 13 matches.

JOHN
ROBERT
HOWE

b 7 Oct 1915   d 5 Apr 1987   **LEFT BACK**
Caps: 3   Goals: 0
First cap: 16 Nov 1948 v Italy 4–0   aged 32yr 221d
Last cap: 9 Apr 1949 v Scotland 1–3   aged 33yr 184d
England career: 0yr 328d – P3 W2 D0 L1 – 66.66%
Club: Derby County
Jack Howe was apparently the first to play for England while wearing contact lenses.

LEONARD SIDGWICK
HOWELL

b 6 Aug 1848   d 7 Sep 1895   **DEFENDER**
Caps: 1   Goals: 0
Only cap: 8 Mar 1873 v Scotland 4–2   aged 24yr 214d
England career: P1 W1 D0 L0 – 100%
Club: Wanderers (& probably Old Wykehamists)
Although he was a defender and there were eight

forwards in the team, he kicked off England's first ever home match.

RABBI
HOWELL

b 12 Oct 1869   d 1937   RIGHT HALF
Caps: 2   Goals: 1
First cap: 9 Mar 1895 v Ireland 9–0   aged 25yr 148d
                                                (1 goal)
Last cap: 8 Apr 1899 v Scotland 2–1   aged 29yr 178d
England career: 4yr 30d – P2 W2 D0 L0 – 100%
Clubs: Sheffield United (1), Liverpool (1)

At 5ft 5¼in and 9st 8lb one of the smallest men to play for England, Rab Howell was a gypsy, thought to be the only one to have played for England. He's certainly the only one with at least five variations on his christian name: Rab, Raby, Rabbi, Rabbie – and Robert, which would make sense, but the source is unreliable.

ALAN
ANTHONY
HUDSON

b 21 Jun 1951   MIDFIELDER
Caps: 2   Goals: 0
First cap: 12 Mar 1975 v W Germany 2–0 aged 23yr 264d
Last cap: 16 Apr 1975 v Cyprus 5–0   aged 23yr 299d
England career: 0yr 35d – P2 W2 D0 L0 – 100%
Club: Stoke City

Interestingly, Alf RAMSEY included a very young Alan Hudson in the World Cup 40 for 1970 – but didn't take a chance with him. Don REVIE did, was rewarded with a fine, subtle performance against the Germans (and he could hardly have done much wrong against Cyprus) – then dropped him. Why? Because he didn't enjoy the squad bingo sessions? Who knows? A shambles.

JOHN
HUDSON

b 1860   d Nov 1941   HALF BACK
Caps: 1   Goals: 0   Captain: 1
Only cap: 24 Feb 1883 v Ireland 7–0   aged 22/23
England career: P1 W1 D0 L0 – 100%
Club: Sheffield Wednesday

Jack Hudson was brought in when the original captain NC BAILEY dropped out through injury. The revised Lamming book lists his club as the Sheffield Club, but also says he played for Wednesday 1880–83. The Complete History of the club also says Wednesday. He also played in Sheffield United's very first match. Help.

FRANCIS
CARR
HUDSPETH

b 20 Apr 1890   d 8 Feb 1963   LEFT BACK
Caps: 1   Goals: 0
Only cap: 24 Oct 1925 v Ireland 0–0 aged 35yr 187d
England career: P1 W0 D1 L0 – 50%
Club: Newcastle United

Possibly the oldest England debutant before COMPTON (but see MORTEN), Frank Hudspeth came into the team in Belfast only as third choice behind Sam WADSWORTH and Horace Cope of Notts County, who never did win a senior cap.

ARTHUR
EDWARD
HUFTON

b 25 Nov 1892/93   d 2 Feb 1967   GOALKEEPER
Caps: 6   Goals conceded: 14   Clean sheets: 0
First cap: 1 Nov 1923 v Belgium 2–2
                                     aged 28/29yr 341d
Last cap: 15 May 1929 v Spain 3–4   aged 35/36yr 171d
England career: 5yr 195d – P6 W2 D1 L3 – 41.66%
Club: West Ham United
Penalties: 1   Saved: 0

Ted Hufton was a highly respected goalkeeper whose international figures were ruined by Scotland in 1928 and Spain in 1929; they scored nine between them. He was beaten by Achille Schelstraete's penalty on his debut.

Above all, he had no luck. Wounded in the First World War, he broke a wrist playing against Ireland in 1927 and stayed on till half-time (when he was replaced by J BALL), by which time he'd conceded only HERBERT JONES' own goal. Long after he'd retired, he was badly injured in two road accidents in the same year.

EMLYN
WALTER
HUGHES

b 28 Aug 1947   LEFT BACK/CENTRAL DEFENDER
Caps: 62   Goals: 1   Captain: 23
First cap: 5 Nov 1969 v Holland 1–0   aged 22yr 69d
Last cap: 24 May 1980 v Scotland 2–0   aged 32yr 260d
                                              (sub 70min)
England career: 10yr 191d – P62 W32 D20 L10 – 67.74%
Clubs: Liverpool (59), Wolves (3)
Substitute: 3   Substituted: 1   Goals while captain: 0

Limited but intimidatingly confident (who else except himself – and RAMSEY – thought he had a good enough left foot to play at left back?), Emlyn Hughes was a favourite of four England managers: RAMSEY, MERCER, REVIE (in patches),

Greenwood. Like Stanley MATTHEWS he named his son after himself, but went one further by calling his daughter Emma.

LAWRENCE
HUGHES

b 2 Mar 1924   **CENTRE HALF**
Caps: 3   Goals: 0
First cap: 25 Jun 1950 v Chile 2–0   aged 26yr 115d
Last cap: 2 Jul   1950 v Spain 0–1   aged 26yr 122d
England career: 0yr 7d – P3 W1 D0 L2 – 33.33%
Club: Liverpool

Laurie Hughes won his caps, and did well, in the 1950 World Cup in Brazil. Injury in a Charity Shield match helped end his international career.

JOSEPH
HAROLD ANTHONY
HULME

b 26 Aug 1904   **OUTSIDE RIGHT**
Caps: 9   Goals: 4
First cap: 2 Apr   1927 v Scotland 2–1   aged 22yr 219d
Last cap: 1 Apr   1933 v Scotland 1–2   aged 28yr 218d
England career: 5yr 364d – P9 W5 D0 L4 – 55.55%
Club: Arsenal
2 Goals in a game: 1

The story may be apocryphal, but it illustrates – the Racing Club de Paris full back, substituted during a match against Arsenal, having only enough breath for three words: Hulme, *levrier* (hare), *fatigué*. Another version uses an *anguille* (eel) instead of the hare. Joe Hulme was quick and slippery, no doubt about it.

He played his first eight internationals almost consecutively, then had to wait more than four years for the ninth. His goals put England 2–0 up at half-time at the Vetch Field in 1928; they held on to win 3–2.

PERCY
HUMPHREYS

b 3 Dec 1880   d 13 Apr 1959   **INSIDE RIGHT**
Caps: 1   Goals: 0
Only cap: 4 Apr 1903 v Scotland 1–2   aged 22yr 122d
England career: P1 W0 D0 L1 – 0%
Club: Notts County

The *Glasgow Evening News* (but almost nobody else) credited the short, chunky Humphreys with WOODWARD's goal.

Right *George Hunt equalised at Hampden, but a goal at each end of the match by Jimmy McGrory won it for Scotland* (Lamming)

GEORGE
SAMUEL
HUNT

b 22 Feb 1910   CENTRE FORWARD
Caps: 3   **Goals:** 1
First cap: 1 Apr 1933 v Scotland 1–2   aged 23yr 40d
                                                 (1 goal)
Last cap: 20 May 1933 v Switzerland 4–0 aged 23yr 89d
England career: 0yr 49d – P3 W1 D1 L1 – 50%
Club: Tottenham Hotspur

Injury stopped a revival of George Hunt's international career; when Fred TILSON cried off, he was called up to play against Italy in 1934, only to drop out himself to let in Ted DRAKE for his first cap.

KENNETH
REGINALD GUNNERY
HUNT

b 24 Feb 1884 d 28 Apr 1949   LEFT HALF
Caps: 2   **Goals:** 0
First cap: 13 Mar 1911 v Wales 3–0   aged 27yr 17d
Last cap: 1 Apr 1911 v Scotland 1–1   aged 27yr 36d
England career: 0yr 19d – P2 W1 D1 L0 – 75%
Club: Leyton

Several England players went on to become clergymen; only hefty Kenneth Hunt was already ordained when he appeared in an international. He belonged to the amateur club that had nothing to do with Leyton Orient.

ROGER
HUNT

b 20 July 1938   FORWARD
Caps: 34   **Goals:** 18
First cap: 4 Apr 1962 v Austria 3–1   aged 23yr 258d
                                                (1 goal)
Last cap: 15 Jan 1969 v Romania 1–1   aged 30yr 149d
England career: 6yr 286d – P34 W25 D7 L2 – 83.82%
Club: Liverpool
4 Goals in a game: 1   **2 Goals in a game:** 2

Remembered as the workhorse who played in the World Cup Final while Jimmy GREAVES didn't, which is nowhere near the whole truth. He was once a very sharp goalscorer, and not just for Liverpool, with 15 in his first 16 internationals, including four in one match; also England's leading scorer in the season the World Cup was won, including three in the tournament itself (while Greaves didn't score). Played in 27 successive unbeaten games; a maligned player who had a very successful career – and the last laugh.

STEPHEN
KENNETH
HUNT

b 4 Aug 1956   MIDFIELDER
Caps: 2   **Goals:** 0
First cap: 26 May 1984 v Scotland 1–1   aged 27yr 296d
                                                (sub 75min)
Last cap: 2 Jun 1984 v USSR 0–2   aged 27yr 303d
                                                (sub 66min)
England career: 0yr 7d – P2 W0 D1 L1 – 25%
Club: West Bromwich Albion
Substitute: 2

An odd little experiment by Bobby ROBSON, if that's what it was, giving Steve Hunt a total of 49 minutes in international football (perhaps there was simply a shortage of covering players at the end of the season). Note that most sources give his date of birth as above, while Rothmans '83–84 and an American encyclopaedia say 8 July.

JOHN
HUNTER

b 1852 d 10 Apr 1903   HALF BACK
Caps: 7   **Goals:** 0   **Captain:** 1
First cap: 2 Mar 1878 v Scotland 2–7   aged 25/26
Last cap: 13 Mar 1882 v Wales 3–5   aged 29/30
England career: 4yr 11d – P7 W1 D0 L6 – 14.29%
Club: Sheffield Heeley (& possibly Providence,
             Sheffield Wednesday, Sheffield Albion)

Jack Hunter or JH FORREST may have been the first professional to play for England. But it was a grey, under-the-table area at the time. He played four times against Scotland because he was good and he was needed, but he couldn't do much to stem the tide. He was even on the losing side against Wales twice.

NORMAN
HUNTER

b 29 Oct 1943   MIDFIELDER
Caps: 28   **Goals:** 2
First cap: 8 Dec 1965 v Spain 2–0   aged 22yr 40d
                                                (sub 35min)
Last cap: 30 Oct 1974 v Czechoslovakia 3–0
                                            aged 31yr   1d
England career: 8yr 326d – P28 W16 D6 L6 – 67.86%
Club: Leeds United
Substitute: 4   **Substituted:** 2

The first player to make his England debut as a substitute, coming on for Joe BAKER v Spain in Madrid, he was on the winning side in his first seven internationals; after that, the record's more patchy. The way he played, the folkloristic reaction to it (Bites Yer Legs), the fact that he was the first Players' Player of the Year, says a lot about English football in the early seventies.

Right First to score in an FA Cup Final at Wembley, first to cost £10 000. DBN Jack, England's Number One (Lamming)

GEOFFREY
CHARLES
HURST

b 8 Dec 1941   STRIKER
Caps: 49   Goals: 24
First cap: 23 Feb 1966 v W Germany 1–0 aged 24yr 77d
Last cap: 29 Apr 1972 v W Germany 1–3 aged 30yr 143d
                                              (sub'd)
England career: 6yr 66d – P49 W31 D12 L6 – 75.51%
Club: West Ham United
Substitute: 2   Substituted: 2   3 Goals in a game: 2
2 Goals in a game: 2   Penalties: 4   Missed: 0

The only player to score a hat-trick in a World Cup Final (courtesy of an extra half-hour and a Soviet linesman), Geoff Hurst scored all four of his penalties in the same season (1968–69) in successive games, including two against France which contributed to his second hat-trick, the last for England before MACDONALD. A very powerful, relentless attacker (those puffed cheeks in the act of shooting said it all), defences were genuinely anxious when he was around. A French programme spelled his name Hurts. Exactly.

JAMES
IREMONGER

b 5 Mar 1876 d 25 Mar 1956   FULL BACK
Caps: 2   Goals: 0
First cap: 30 Mar 1901 v Scotland 2–2   aged 25yr 25d
Last cap: 22 Mar 1902 v Ireland 1–0   aged 26yr 17d
England career: 0yr 357d – P2 W1 D1 L0 – 75%
Club: Nottingham Forest

Jim Iremonger was tall. His brother Albert was taller, at 6ft 5in one of the loftiest League players of all time.

DAVID
BONE NIGHTINGALE
JACK

b 3 Apr 1899   d 10 Sep 1958   INSIDE RIGHT
Caps: 9   Goals: 3   Captain: 4
First cap: 3 Mar 1924 v Wales 1–2   aged 24yr 334d
Last cap: 7 Dec 1932 v Austria 4–3   aged 33yr 248d
England career: 8yr 281d – P9 W4 D4 L1 – 63.16%
Clubs: Bolton Wanderers (4), Arsenal (5)
2 Goals in a game: 0   Goals as captain: 2

Everyone knew how good David Jack was. Herbert Chapman broke the £10 000 transfer barrier to get him, and England recalled him at the age of 33. The mystery is how he came to win so few

caps. He was dropped for four years after 1924, made another comeback as captain in 1930, scoring a goal as Scotland were beaten 5–2, another on the European tour, and was left out again for another two years – the usual selectorial comings and goings. A great player, with names to match.

ELPHINSTONE
JACKSON

b 9 Oct 1868 d Dec 1945   FULL BACK
Caps: 1   Goals: 0
Only cap: 7 Mar 1891 v Wales 4–1   aged 22yr 149d
England career: P1 W1 D0 L0 – 100%
Club: Oxford University

Born in Calcutta, he was a founder member of the Indian FA in 1893.

BEAUMONT GRIFFITH
JARRETT

b 18 Jul 1855 d 11 Apr 1905   HALF BACK

Caps: 3 Goals: 0
First cap: 4 Mar 1876 v Scotland 0–3   aged 20yr 229d
Last cap: 2 Mar 1878 v Scotland 2–7   aged 22yr 227d
England career: 1yr 363d – P3 W0 D0 L3 – 0%
Club: Cambridge University (& Old Harrovians,
     and possibly Grantham FC)

It's hard to know whether BG was much of a player; he did little to stop the Scottish forwards scoring 13 goals in his three internationals, but there probably wasn't much he could have done: he was teamed with 22 other new caps in those three games, and the Scots swamped even the best of them.

FRANK

JEFFERIS

b 3 Jul 1884/88   d 21 May 1938   **INSIDE RIGHT**
Caps: 2 Goals: 0
First cap: 11 Mar 1912 v Wales 2–0 aged 23/27yr 252d
Last cap: 23 Mar 1912 v Scotland 1–1
                                aged 23/27yr 264d
England career: 0yr 12d – P2 W1 D1 L0 – 75%
Club: Everton

Slight and clever; a foil, as they say, to FREEMAN and HOLLEY in his two internationals.

BEDFORD AG
JEZZARD

b 19 Oct 1927   **CENTRE FORWARD**
Caps: 2 Goals: 0
First cap: 23 May 1954 v Hungary 1–7 aged 26yr 216d
Last cap: 2 Nov 1955 v N Ireland 3–0 aged 28yr 14d
England career: 1yr 163d – P2 W1 D0 L1 – 50%
Club: Fulham

Speedy Beddy went to Budapest as a kind of secret missile, but Lorant & Co weren't afraid of him; anyway it was the defence that needed the extra weaponry.

DAVID
EDWARD
JOHNSON

b 23 Oct 1951   **STRIKER**
Caps: 8 Goals: 6
First cap: 21 May 1975 v Wales 2–2   aged 23yr 210d
                                (2 goals)
Last cap: 12 June 1980 v Belgium 1–1 aged 28yr 232d
England career: 5yr 22d – P8 W5 D3 L0 – 81.25%
Club: Ipswich Town (3), Liverpool (5)
Substituted: 4
2 Goals in a game: 2

Never a fixture, David Johnson nevertheless had his moments in the England team, scoring after ten minutes of the start and six from the end of his debut, waiting more than four years for his fourth international, then scoring twice against

world champions Argentina in his fifth. In his sixth, against Northern Ireland, he was credited with what was very probably a Noel Brotherston own goal.

EDWARD
JOHNSON

b 1860   d 30 Jun 1901   **OUTSIDE RIGHT**
Caps: 2 Goals: 2
First cap: 15 Mar 1880 v Wales 2–3   aged 19/20
Last cap: 23 Feb 1884 v Ireland 8–1   aged 23/24
                                (2 goals)
England career: 3yr 344d – P2 W1 D0 L1 – 50%
Club: Saltley College & Stoke FC (1), Stoke alone (1)
2 Goals in a game: 1

He was once thought to have been born in 1862. Could that still be true? After all, no definite date of birth seems to have been found. If 1862 *is* correct, he may well have been only 17 when first capped, possibly even younger than PRINSEP.

JOSEPH
ALFRED

JOHNSON

b 4 Apr 1911   d 8 Aug 1983   **OUTSIDE LEFT**
Caps: 5 Goals: 2
First cap: 18 Nov 1936 v Ireland 3–1   aged 25yr 228d
Last cap: 20 May 1937 v Finland 8–0   aged 26yr 46d
                                (1 goal)
England career: 0yr 183d – P5 W4 D0 L1 – 80%
Club: Stoke City

Joe Johnson and clubmate Freddie STEELE scored seven goals between them in their last two internationals. His second name was once thought to be Arthur.

THOMAS
CLARK FISHER

JOHNSON

b 19 Aug 1900/01   d 28 Jan 1973   **INSIDE LEFT**
Caps: 5 Goals: 5
First cap: 24 May 1926 v Belgium 5–3
                          aged 24/25yr 272d (1 goal)
Last cap: 17 Oct 1932 v Ireland 1–0
                                aged 30/31yr 59d
England career: 6yr 146d – P5 W5 D0 L0 – 100 %
Clubs: Manchester City (2), Everton (3)
Hat-tricks: 0
2 Goals in a game: 2

The original 'Tosh' had an in-and-out but successful international career; five wins out of five, five goals. Between them, he and clubmate Dixie DEAN put three goals past the famous Zamora when England beat Spain 7–1 in 1931.

WILLIAM HARRISON JOHNSON

b 4 Jan 1876   d 17 Jul 1940   **HALF BACK**
Caps: 6   **Goals:** 1
First cap: 17 Mar 1900 v Ireland 2-0   aged 24yr 73d
(1 goal)
Last cap: 4 Apr 1903 v Scotland 1-2   aged 27yr 91d
England career: 3yr 18d – P6 W3 D1 L2 – 58.33%
Club: Sheffield United

Driving, respected all-rounder. It used to be thought that his second name was Harold. One or two sources refer to him as Bill, but the majority say Harry.

HENRY JOHNSTON

b 26 Sep 1919   d 12 Oct 1973   **LEFT/CENTRE HALF**
Caps: 10   **Goals:** 0
First cap: 27 Nov 1946 v Holland 8-2   aged 27yr 62d
Last cap: 25 Nov 1953 v Hungary 3-6   aged 34yr 60d
England career: 6yr 363d – P10 W5 D2 L3 – 60%
Club: Blackpool

Harry Johnston had to wait four years for his third cap, then two years for his fourth. Never quite at ease as a stopper, he was hardly the ideal counter to the deep-lying, hat-trick scoring Hidegkuti. There again, who was?

ALFRED JONES

b 1861   d unknown   **RIGHT/LEFT BACK**
Caps: 3   **Goals:** 0
First cap: 11 Mar 1882 v Scotland 1-5   aged 20/21
Last cap: 10 Mar 1883 v Scotland 2-3   aged 21/22
England career: 0yr 364d – P3 W0 D0 L3 – 0%
Clubs: Walsall Town Swifts (2), Great Lever (1)

Alf Jones, 'as good a back as has played for England for some time', and Doc GREENWOOD, 'one of the best of backs', played together at Hampden Park in 1882. Played well too, despite the scoreline. In the very next match, against Wales, AJ became the first player to score an own goal in an England match. But see FIELD.

HARRY JONES

b 24 May 1891   d ?   **LEFT BACK**
Caps: 1   **Goals:** 0
Only cap: 10 May 1923 v France 4-1   aged 31y 351d
England career: P1 W1 D0 L0 – 100%
Club: Nottingham Forest

Jules Dewaquez got away from Harry Jones to score in Paris, the first time an England team included professionals against France.

HERBERT JONES

b 3 Aug/Sep 1896   d 11 Sep 1973   **LEFT BACK**
Caps: 6   **Goals:** 0   **Own goals:** 1
First cap: 2 Apr 1927 v Scotland 2-1
aged 30yr 211/242d
Last cap: 31 Mar 1928 v Scotland 1-5
aged 31yr 210/241d
England career: 0yr 364d – P6 W4 D0 L2 – 66.66%
Club: Blackburn Rovers

Enjoyed his first four internationals, including an easy little trip to France and the Low Countries – then the roof fell in a bit. His own goal cost England the match against Ireland, then he came face-to-face with Alan Morton at Wembley.

MICHAEL DAVID JONES

b 24 Apr 1945   **CENTRE FORWARD**
Caps: 3   **Goals:** 0
First cap: 12 May 1965 v W Germany 1-0 aged 20yr 18d
Last cap: 14 Jan 1970 v Holland 0-0   aged 24yr 265d
(sub'd c.70min)
England career: 4yr 247d – P3 W2 D1 L0 – 83.33%
Clubs: Sheffield United (2), Leeds United (1)
Substituted: 1

Alf Ramsey gave Mick Jones a third cap four years after his second, then took him off and replaced him with HURST, who was similar but better.

WILLIAM JONES

b 6 Mar 1876   d c.1908   **HALF BACK**
Caps: 1   **Goals:** 0
Only cap: 9 Mar 1901 v Ireland 3-0   aged 25yr 03d
England career: P1 W1 D0 L0 – 100%
Club: Bristol City

England's half-back line read NEEDHAM, CRAWSHAW – and Bill Jones, who didn't quite belong in that company.

WILLIAM HENRY JONES

b 13 May 1921   **CENTRE HALF**
Caps: 2   **Goals:** 0
First cap: 14 May 1950 v Portugal 5-3   aged 29yr 1d
Last cap: 18 May 1950 v Belgium 4-1   aged 29yr 5d
England career: 0yr 4d – P2 W2 D0 L0 – 100%
Club: Liverpool

Bill Jones was the first attempt at a replacement for FRANKLIN, but both opposing centre forwards scored: Henrique Ben David (2) and Jef Mermans. He gave way to Laurie HUGHES.

BERNARD
JOY

b 29 Oct 1911   d 18 Jul 1984   CENTRE HALF
Caps: 1   Goals: 0
Only cap: 9 May 1936 v Belgium 2–3 aged 24yr 193d
England career: P1 W0 D0 L1 – 0%
Club: Arsenal (& Casuals & Corinthians)

Big, brainy, orthodox stopper, the last amateur
to play for England. Yearbooks and the revised
Lamming book show Casuals as his club, but he
was also on Arsenal's books at the time he was
capped. His own history of Arsenal confirms it.

EDGAR
ISAAC LEWIS
KAIL

b 26 Nov 1900   d 1976   INSIDE RIGHT
Caps: 3   Goals: 2
First cap: 9 May 1929 v France 4–1   aged 28yr 164d
                                          (2 goals)
Last cap: 15 May 1929 v Spain 3–4   aged 28yr 170d
England career: 0yr 6d – P3 W2 D0 L1 – 66.66%
Club: Dulwich Hamlet

Edgar Kail was the last to play for the senior England team while exclusively with an amateur
club. See JOY.

ANTHONY
HERBERT
KAY

b 13 May 1937   RIGHT HALF
Caps: 1   Goals: 1
Only cap: 5 June 1963 v Switzerland 8–1
                          aged 26yr 23d (1 goal)
England career: P1 W1 D0 L0 – 50%
Club: Everton

Classic red-haired midfield terrier. Sir Alf liked
him (he was reserve v Rest of the World in October 1963) but his career, like SWAN's, collapsed
after the sixties bribery scandal.

FREDERICK
WILLIAM
KEAN

b 10 Dec 1898?   d 28 Oct 1973   RIGHT/CENTRE HALF
Caps: 9   Goals: 0   Captain: 1
First cap: 19 Mar 1923 v Belgium 6–1 aged 24yr 99d?
Last cap: 15 May 1929 v Spain 3–4   aged 30yr 156d?
England career: 6yr 57d – P9 W5 D2 L2 – 66.66%
Clubs: Sheffield Wednesday (7), Bolton Wanderers (2)

Spain were the first foreign team to beat England.
The match in Madrid put an end to nine inter-
national careers: JH CARTER, JH HILL,
HUFTON, KAIL, J PEACOCK, BARRY, Fred
Kean – and Felix Quesada amd Mariano Yurrita.

JOSEPH
KEVIN
KEEGAN

b 14 Feb 1951   FORWARD
Caps: 63   Goals: 21   Captain: 29
First cap: 15 Nov 1972 v Wales 1–0   aged 21yr 274d
Last cap: 5 Jul 1982 v Spain 0–0   aged 31yr 141d
                                          (sub 63min)
England career: 9yr 242d – P63 W34 D17 L12 – 67.46%
Clubs: Liverpool (28), Hamburg (26), Southampton (9)
Substitute: 1   Substituted: 6   2 Goals in a game: 6
Goals while captain: 11   Penalties: 2   Missed: 1

You couldn't help wishing he'd fall off his wallet
sometimes, just to see the halo dislodged from
the perm – but Kevin Keegan was neverthelesss
one of the few reasons to be proud of English
football in the seventies, twice voted European
Footballer of the Year with Hamburg,
galvanising Liverpool, Southampton, Newcastle
and the England team, scoring in 9 successive
seasons (second only to R CHARLTON's slightly
dodgy 13), against 16 different countries, in
several matches as captain. There was a petulant
top and tail to his international career (he walked
out on REVIE, who took him back, and vowed
never to play for ROBSON, who didn't) but
Greenwood helped bring the best out of him.
Who knows what difference a fully-fit Keegan –
and BROOKING – might have made in Spain?

ERRINGTON
RIDLEY LIDDELL
KEEN
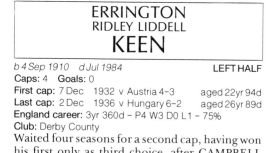

b 4 Sep 1910   d Jul 1984   LEFT HALF
Caps: 4   Goals: 0
First cap: 7 Dec 1932 v Austria 4–3   aged 22yr 94d
Last cap: 2 Dec 1936 v Hungary 6–2   aged 26yr 89d
England career: 3yr 360d – P4 W3 D0 L1 – 75%
Club: Derby County

Waited four seasons for a second cap, having won
his first only as third choice, after CAMPBELL
then TATE had to pull out. He was thankfully
known as Eric.

ROBERT
KELLY

b 16 Nov 1893   d 22 Sep 1969   INSIDE/OUTSIDE RIGHT
Caps: 14   Goals: 8
First cap: 10 Apr 1920 v Scotland 5–4   aged 26yr 146d
                                          (2 goals)
Last cap: 31 Mar 1928 v Scotland 1–5   aged 34yr 136d
                                          (1 goal)

England career: 7yr 355d – P14 W6 D2 L6 – 50%
Clubs: Burnley (11), Sunderland (1), Huddersfield Town (2)
Hat-tricks: 0   2 Goals in a game: 1

Skilful, angular, something like a shorter and faster Chris WADDLE who could score goals. Bob Kelly scored them in his first two and last two internationals, including a defiantly fierce last-minute free kick against the Wembley Wizards on his swansong. His mediocre statistics reflect England's record in the first half of the twenties.

ALAN
PHILIP
KENNEDY

b 31 Aug 1954   LEFT BACK
Caps: 2   Goals: 0
First cap: 4 Apr 1984 v N Ireland 1–0   aged 29yr 216d
Last cap: 2 May 1984 v Wales 0–1   aged 29yr 244d
England career: 0yr 28d – P2 W1 D0 L1 – 50%
Club: Liverpool

An attacking full back, Kennedy had apparently been a twinkle in REVIE's eye nine years before Bobby ROBSON drafted him. The second England team he played in wasn't one of the best ever.

RAYMOND
KENNEDY

b 28 Jul 1951   LEFT-SIDED MIDFIELDER
Caps: 17   Goals: 3
First cap: 24 Mar 1976 v Wales 2–1   aged 24yr 209d
                                                  (1 goal)
Last cap: 15 Jun 1980 v Italy 0–1   aged 28yr 292d
England career: 4yr 83d – P17 W8 D4 L5 – 58.82%
Club: Liverpool
Substitute: 3   Substituted: 1   2 Goals in a game: 0

Big and heavy (a converted striker) but good on the ball, Ray Kennedy scored on his debut, and in two matches against Luxembourg. After retirement, his face became more familiar on London Underground posters highlighting Parkinson's Disease.

WILLIAM
STANLEY
KENYON SLANEY

b 24 Aug 1847 d 24 Apr 1908   FORWARD
Caps: 1   Goals: 2
Only cap: 8 Mar 1873 v Scotland 4–2
                            aged 25yr 196d (2 goals)
England career: P1 W1 D0 L0 – 100%
Club: Wanderers (& Old Etonians)
2 Goals in a game: 1

An army captain at the time he was capped; indeed, some contemporary reports list his club as the Household Brigade. He scored England's first ever goal, after less than a minute of the second match, with 'almost the first run' of the game. England led 2–0, Scotland equalised, then he became the first to score twice for England, with a left-foot shot. The Scots appealed on the basis that the ball hadn't been thrown in legally (at right angles from touch), but the English referee Lloyd let the goal stand. No-one else scored more than two goals for England in total until EC BAMBRIDGE in 1880.

KS, later an MP, was the first England player born outside the country – in Rajkot, India.

DEREK
TENNYSON
KEVAN

b 6 Mar 1935   INSIDE LEFT/RIGHT/CENTRE FORWARD
Caps: 14   Goals: 8
First cap: 6 Apr 1957 v Scotland 2–1   aged 22yr 31d
(1 goal)
Last cap: 10 May 1961 v Mexico 8–0   aged 26yr 65d
England career: 4yr 34d – P14 W6 D4 L4 – 57.14 %
Club: West Bromwich Albion
2 Goals in a game: 1

Vittorio Pozzo, manager of the Italian teams that won the World Cup twice in the thirties, was a good judge of a player, especially a centre forward (he had Piola in 1938). When he described a goal as 'scored by Kevan with the outside of his head', it was cruel but probably fair enough. Big rawboned Derek, who kept Bobby SMITH and Brian CLOUGH out of the 1958 World Cup, scored twice in the tournament but was never an adequate replacement for Tommy TAYLOR.

BRIAN
KIDD

b 29 May 1949   STRIKER
Caps: 2   Goals: 1
First cap: 21 Apr 1970 v N Ireland 3–1   aged 20yr 327d
Last cap: 24 May 1970 v Ecuador 2–0   aged 20yr 360d
(sub'd c.70min, 1 goal)
England career: 0yr 33d – P2 W2 D0 L0 – 100%
Club: Manchester United
Substitute: 1

Brian Kidd had already been left out of the World Cup 22 when he scored within a few minutes of coming on in Quito.

ROBERT
STUART
KING

b 4 Apr 1862   d 4/6 Mar 1950   HALF BACK
Caps: 1   Goals: 0
Only cap: 18 Feb 1882 v Ireland 13–0   aged 19yr 320d
England career: P1 W1 D0 L0 – 100%

Club: Oxford University (& possibly Upton Park)

An ALCOCK's Annual listed CJS King in the team in Belfast, simple confusion with another player, a highly-rated full back who was at Hertford College Oxford at the same time (possibly a brother). RS is listed under K in yearbooks, and although Jon Silk has seen him 'double-barrelled on some occasions' in 'old Essex or university matches in *The Times*', several match reports and yearbooks disagree. He was ordained in 1887.

ROBERT KENNETT
KINSGFORD

b 23 Dec 1849   d 14 Oct 1895   FORWARD
Caps: 1   Goals: 1
Only cap: 7 Mar 1874 v Scotland 1–2
aged 24yr 74d (1 goal)
England career: P1 W0 D0 L1 – 0%
Club: Wanderers (& probably Old Malburians,
and possibly Crystal Palace)

Scored the first goal of the match in England's first ever defeat.

MATTHEW
KINGSLEY

b 1875/76   d 27 Mar 1960   GOALKEEPER
Caps: 1   Goals conceded: 0
Only cap: 18 Mar 1901 v Wales 6–0 aged 24–26
England career: P1 W1 D0 L0 – 100%
Club: Newcastle United

Matt Kingsley had very little to do while BLOOMER was scoring four at the other end.

GEORGE
KINSEY

b 1867   d 1911   LEFT HALF
Caps: 4   Goals: 0
First cap: 5 Mar 1892 v Wales 2–0   aged 24/25
Last cap: 16 Mar 1896 v Wales 9–1   aged 28/29
England career: 4yr 11d – P4 W4 D0 L0 – 100%
Club: Wolves (2), Derby County (2)

He and SANDILANDS started and finished their international careers in the same two matches. They were the only players never to play again after England's biggest win over Wales.

ALFRED
JOHN
KIRCHEN

b 26 Apr 1913   OUTSIDE RIGHT
Caps: 3   Goals: 2
First cap: 14 May 1937 v Norway 6–0   aged 24yr 18d
(1 goal)
Last cap: 20 May 1937 v Finland 8–0   aged 24yr 24d
(1 goal)

England career: 0yr 6d – P3 W3 D0 L0 – 100%
Club: Arsenal

Typical of the fast, direct wingers of his day, the 12th England player on Arsenal's books by the end of the season, big Alf Kirchen opened the scoring in both his first and last internationals.

ARNOLD
KIRKE SMITH

b 23 Apr 1850   d 8 Oct 1927   FORWARD
Caps: 1   **Goals:** 0
Only cap: 30 Nov 1872 v Scotland 0–0   aged 22yr 221d
England career: P1 W0 D1 L0 – 50%
Club: Oxford University

Usually found under Smith in yearbooks, but early books and contemporary reports list him as A Kirke-Smith. One magazine claims he was England's first ever captain, but all match reports, annuals, and histories are adamant about OTTAWAY.

WILLIAM
JOHN
KIRTON

b 2 Dec 1896   d 27 Dec 1970   INSIDE RIGHT
Caps: 1   **Goals:** 1
Only cap: 22 Oct 1921 v Ireland 1–1
                          aged 24yr 324d (1 goal)
England career: P1 W0 D1 L0 – 50%
Club: Aston Villa

When the North beat an England XI 6–1 in a trial match in 1920, four of the five forwards were then selected against Wales; Billy Kirton was the odd one out. He consoled himself with the only goal of the FA Cup Final a month later, and the equaliser in his only international.

ARTHUR
EGERTON
KNIGHT

b 7 Sep 1887   d 10 Mar 1956   LEFT BACK
Caps: 1   **Goals:** 0   **Captain:** 1
Only cap: 25 Oct 1919 v Ireland 1–1   aged 32yr 48d
England career: P1 W0 D1 L0 – 50%
Club: Portsmouth

Slow, past his best, lucky to be capped in place of PENNINGTON, Arthur Knight had won an Olympic gold medal with the United Kingdom team in 1912.

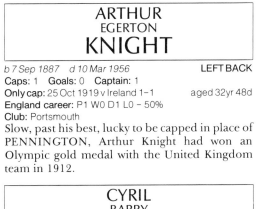

CYRIL
BARRY
KNOWLES

b 13 Jul 1944   RIGHT/LEFT BACK

Caps: 4   **Goals:** 0
First cap: 6 Dec 1967 v USSR 2–2   aged 23yr 146d
Last cap: 1 Jun 1968 v W Germany 0–1 aged 23yr 324d
England career: 0yr 178d – P4 W2 D1 L1 – 62.50%
Club: Tottenham Hotspur

First two caps on the right, last two on the left. Symmetrical one, Cyril.

BRIAN
LESLIE
LABONE

b 23 Jan 1940   CENTRE HALF
Caps: 26   **Goals:** 0
First cap: 20 Oct 1962 v N Ireland 3–1   aged 22yr 270d
Last cap: 14 Jun 1970 v W Germany 2–3 aged 30yr 142d
England career: 7yr 23d – P26 W14 D6 L6 – 65.38%
Club: Everton

After waiting four years for his fourth cap, Brian Labone settled in solidly if rather anonymously alongside Bobby MOORE. In 1968, he deflected the Beckenbauer shot that gave West Germany their first ever win over England.

FRANK
RICHARD G
LAMPARD

b 20 Sep 1948   LEFT BACK
Caps: 2   **Goals:** 0
First cap: 11 Oct 1972 v Yugoslavia 1–1 aged 24yr 21d
Last cap: 31 May 1980 v Australia 2–1   aged 31yr 234d
England career: 7yr 213d – P2 W1 D1 L0 – 75%
Club: West Ham United

Seven years after his first cap, Frank Lampard played in what was effectively a B international at the Sydney Cricket Ground just before the European Championship finals, a kind of long-service medal from his old club manager.

ERNEST
JAMES
LANGLEY

b 7 Feb 1929   LEFT BACK
Caps: 3   **Goals:** 0
First cap: 19 Apr 1958 v Scotland 4–0   aged 29yr 71d
Last cap: 11 May 1958 v Yugoslavia 0–5   aged 29yr 93d
England career: 0yr 22d – P3 W2 D0 L1 – 66.66%
Club: Fulham
Penalties: 1   **Missed:** 1

Jimmy Langley scored from a penalty in the first Fairs Cup Final, but missed one against Portugal in 1958 (R CHARLTON, who scored twice in that match, took them from then on). In Belgrade, the winger he was marking, Aleksandar Petakovic, scored a second-half hat-trick.

ROBERT

LANGTON

b 8 Sep 1918   **OUTSIDE LEFT**
Caps: 11   **Goals:** 1
First cap: 28 Sep 1946 v N Ireland 7–2   aged 28yr 20d
                                                (1 goal)
Last cap: 7 Oct 1950 v N Ireland 4–1   aged 32yr 29d
England career: 4yr 9d – P11 W8 D1 L2 – 77.27%
Club: Blackburn Rovers

Bobby Langton, who had a goal disallowed when Switzerland won 1–0 in 1947, was never really first choice for England He played when FINNEY was preferred to MATTHEWS on the other wing; when Matthews dropped out against Sweden in 1947; and when Peter Kippax of Burnley (who never did win an England cap) couldn't play against France in 1947.

ROBERT
DENNIS

LATCHFORD

b 18 Jan 1951   **CENTRE FORWARD**
Caps: 12   **Goals:** 4
First cap: 16 Nov 1977 v Italy 2–0   aged 26yr 302d
                                            (sub'd 75min)
Last cap: 13 Jun 1979 v Austria 3–4   aged 28yr 209d
                                            (sub'd HT)
England career: 1yr 146d – P12 W8 D3 L1 – 79.16%
Club: Everton
Substitute: 1   **Substituted:** 5
2 Goals in a game: 1

Big Bob got a lot of help from Kevin KEEGAN (to be fair, it was sometimes mutual) and kept Trevor FRANCIS out of the England team until his last match, when Francis replaced him at half-time and started his own short-lived run of success.

EDWIN
GLADSTONE
LATHERON

b 1887   d 14 Oct 1917   **INSIDE LEFT**
Caps: 2   **Goals:** 1
First cap: 17 Mar 1913 v Wales 4–3   aged 25/26
                                            (1 goal)
Last cap: 14 Feb 1914 v Ireland 0–3   aged 26/27
England career: 0yr 334d – P2 W1 D0 L1 – 50%
Club: Blackburn Rovers

Note that the 1990 Lamming book spells his surname Latherton: a simple misprint.

Seven new caps came in for the Wales match at Ashton Gate. Ted Latheron gave England a 2–1 lead they were never to lose, though it was a close thing.

CHRISTOPHER

LAWLER

b 20 Oct 1943   **RIGHT BACK**
Caps: 4   **Goals:** 1
First cap: 12 May 1971 v Malta 5–0   aged 27yr 204d
                                            (1 goal)
Last cap: 13 Oct 1971 v Switzerland 3–2 aged 27yr 358d
England career: 0yr 154d – P4 W3 D1 L0 – 87.50%
Club: Liverpool

If you had to back one player to be the only England defender to score on his international debut . . . Chris Lawler scored once in every nine games for Liverpool, and England's fifth against the Maltese at Wembley.

THOMAS
LAWTON

b 6 Oct 1919   **CENTRE FORWARD**
Caps: 23   **Goals:** 22
First cap: 22 Oct 1938 v Wales 2–4   aged 19yr 16d
                                            (1 pen)
Last cap: 26 Sep 1948 v Denmark 0–0   aged 28yr 355d
England career: 9yr 339d – P23 W16 D4 L3 – 78.26%
Clubs: Everton (8), Chelsea (11), Notts County (4)
4 Goals in a game: 2   **2 Goals in a game:** 1
Penalties: 2   **Missed:** 0

Every inch a star, England's answer to Silvio Piola, Tommy Lawton might still be England's record goalscorer but for the Second World War which cut seven years out of his international career; he scored 25 goals in wartime matches.

The first of only two players (see AJ CLARKE) to take a penalty on his England debut, the youngest player ever to score for England, he scored in his first six matches, then in another five in a row in 1948. He scored four against Holland in 1946; the next time he scored for England, he put another four past Portugal in 1947. A great goal machine and leader, probably the best header of the ball ever to play for England.

THOMAS

LEACH

b 23/27 Sep 1903   d 1970   **CENTRE HALF**
Caps: 2   **Goals:** 0
First cap: 20 Oct 1930 v Ireland 5–1   aged 27yr 23/27d
Last cap: 22 Nov 1930 v Wales 4–0   aged 27yr 56/60d
England career: 0yr 33d – P2 W2 D0 L0 – 100%
Club: Sheffield Wednesday

'Tony' Leach was one of several centre halves who did nothing very wrong while playing for England yet won only a few caps each (WEBSTER, GEE, O'DOWD, HART etc) between the reigns of JH HILL and JW BARKER.

ALEXANDER
LEAKE

b 11 Jul 1871/72   d 29 Mar 1938   **LEFT HALF**
Caps: 5   Goals: 0
First cap: 12 Mar 1904 v Ireland 3–1   aged 31/32yr 245d
Last cap: 1 Apr 1905 v Scotland 1–0
                                      aged 32/33yr 265d
England career: 1yr 20d – P5 W4 D1 L0 – 90%
Club: Aston Villa
Strong, even-tempered, capped surprisingly late, Alec Leake was the subject of the Billy Meredith bribery scandal.

ERNEST
ALBERT
LEE

b 1879   d 14 Jan 1958   **RIGHT HALF**
Caps: 1   Goals: 0
Only cap: 29 Feb 1904 v Wales 2–2   aged 24/25
England career: P1 W0 D1 L0 – 50%
Club: Southampton
None of the England team played particularly well at the Racecourse Ground; the pitch was icy and hard and they'd chosen the wrong studs. Bert Lee, at least, had other successes. He appeared in the FA Cup Final of 1902 and (with Dundee, as captain) the Scottish Cup Final of 1910.

FRANCIS
HENRY
LEE

b 29 Apr 1944   **FORWARD**
Caps: 27   Goals: 10
First cap: 11 Dec 1968 v Bulgaria 1–1   aged 24yr 226d
Last cap: 29 Apr 1972 v W Germany 1–3 aged 28yr 00d
                                           (1 goal)
England career: 3yr 140d – P27 W18 D6 L3 – 77.77%
Club: Manchester City
Substituted: 7   2 Goals in a game: 0
Penalties: 2   Missed: 2
Dynamic and strutting winger who galvanised a functional England team in his first season but had an anonymous World Cup, left alone up front with HURST, who also won his last cap in Netzer's Match; Franny's birthday equaliser was small consolation.

  Incredibly for someone who once put away a record 13 penalties in a League season, he shot wide each time for England, both in 1969 against Wales and Portugal.

JOHN
LEE

b 4 Nov 1920   **CENTRE FORWARD**

Caps: 1   Goals: 1
Only cap: 7 Oct 1950 v N Ireland 4–1
                                      aged 29yr 337d (1 goal)
England career: P1 W1 D0 L0 – 100%
Club: Derby County
A stop-gap but not a bad one, big Jackie put England 2–0 ahead after 65 minutes.

SAMUEL
LEE

b 7 Feb 1959   **MIDFIELDER**
Caps: 14   Goals: 2
First cap: 17 Nov 1982 v Greece 3–0   aged 23yr 283d
                                           (1 goal)
Last cap: 17 Jun 1984 v Chile 0–0   aged 25yr 130d
England career: 1yr 212d – P14 W8 D3 L3 – 67.86%
Club: Liverpool
Substitute: 1   Substituted: 2
In his first two years as manager, Bobby ROBSON picked a number of goodish club players who didn't step up in class: GREGORY, DUXBURY, SK HUNT, GP ROBERTS, BLISSETT, and cherubic Sammy, who had a big heart, a big engine, and one or two moments in the England team.

JOHN EDWARD
LEIGHTON

b 26 Mar 1865   d 15 Apr 1944   **OUTSIDE RIGHT**
Caps: 1   Goals: 0
Only cap: 13 Mar 1886 v Ireland 6–1   aged 20yr 352d
England career: P1 W1 D0 L0 – 100%
Club: Nottingham Forest (& Corinthians)
A slim right-winger who helped SPILSBURY to four goals against the Irish.

HENRY
EDWARD(?)
LILLEY

b 1873   d unknown   **LEFT BACK**
Caps: 1   Goals: 0
Only cap: 5 Mar 1892 v Wales 2–0   aged 18/19
England career: P1 W1 D0 L0 – 100%
Club: Sheffield United
While an all-professional England team was beating Ireland by the same score on the same day, Harry Lilley was one of eight new caps in a side made up entirely of amateurs.

JAMES
HENRY
LINACRE

b 1880/81   d 11 May 1957   **GOALKEEPER**
Caps: 2   Goals conceded: 1   Clean sheets: 1

First cap: 17 Mar 1905 v Wales 3–1   aged 23–25
Last cap: 1 Apr 1905 v Scotland 1–0   aged 23–25
England career: 0yr 5d – P2 W2 D0 L0 – 100%
Club: Nottingham Forest

The FORMANs were Harry Linacre's club colleagues and brothers-in-law. Excellent against the Scots, he was nonetheless one of six not to win another cap.

TINSLEY

LINDLEY

b 27 Oct 1865   *d 31 Mar 1940*   **CENTRE FORWARD**
Caps: 13   **Goals:** 14   **Captain:** 4 at least
First cap: 13 Mar 1886 v Ireland 6–1   aged 20yr 137d
                              (1 goal)
Last cap: 7 Mar 1891 v Ireland 6–1   aged 25yr 131d
                              (2 goals)
England career: 4yr 359d – P13 W9 D2 L2 – 76.92%
Clubs: Nottm Forest & Cambridge University (7), Nottm
       Forest alone (6); Corinthians throughout
3 Goals in a game: 1   **2 Goals in a game:** 2
Goals while captain: 5 at least

N Lane ('Pa') Jackson, founder of the Corinthians, wrote that he thought so highly of Tinsley Lindley that at a meeting of the international selection committee he nominated him for each of the five forward places in turn.

Certainly he set a number of early benchmarks. He was the first player to score 13 goals and play 9 consecutive games for England. He and F DEWHURST scored in 7 internationals together, still the England record (equalled by GREAVES with RA SMITH and R CHARLTON). He scored in 7 England matches without a break (probably not the 9 usually credited).

Very fast, a heavy scorer but an unselfish player, he may just possibly have been captain in his first international. This is unlikely but not out of the question, given that the regular captain NC BAILEY had cried off. Another source suggests SHUTT (who took Bailey's place in the team), which is just as improbable (it was his first cap too). At least three reports name PM WALTERS. If by some chance Lindley *was* captain, he was England's youngest ever (see RFC MOORE).

ALEC
LINDSAY

b 27 Feb 1948   **LEFT BACK**
Caps: 4   **Goals:** 0
First cap: 22 May 1974 v Argentina 2–2   aged 26yr 85d
Last cap: 5 Jun 1974 v Yugoslavia 2–2   aged 26yr 99d
England career: 0yr 14d – P4 W1 D3 L0 – 62.50%
Club: Liverpool

Did Uncle Joe Mercer really bring him into the team because Mike PEJIC didn't smile enough? Let's hope so.

WILLIAM
LINDSAY

b 3 Aug 1847   *d 15 Feb 1923*   **FULLBACK**
Caps: 1   **Goals:** 0
Only cap: 3 Mar 1877 v Scotland 1–3   aged 29yr 212d
England career: P1 W0 D0 L1 – 0%
Club: Wanderers (& Old Wykehamists)

A story that was to keep repeating itself: Scottish passing overcoming English dribbling. Both full backs (and five others) were new caps; England never really coped.

GARY
WINSTON

LINEKER

b 30 Nov 1960   **STRIKER**
Caps: 68   **Goals:** 45   **Captain:** 8
First cap: 26 May 1984 v Scotland 1–1   aged 23yr 178d
                            (sub 73min)
Last cap: 12 Jun 1991 v Malaysia 4–2   aged 30yr 194d
                            (4 goals)
England career: 7yr 17d – P68 W35 D23 L10 – 68.38%
Clubs: Leicester City (7), Everton (11), Barcelona (24),
       Tottenham (26)
Substitute: 4   **Substituted:** 16
4 Goals in a game: 2   **3 Goals in a game:** 3
2 Goals in a game: 5   **Goals as substitute:** 0
Goals as captain: 8   **Penalties:** 4   **Missed:** 0

The 1986 World Cup made Gary Lineker a world star – the first British player to be leading scorer in a finals tournament: six goals, including a hat-trick against Poland that saved everybody's bacon. In a run of six matches around that time, he scored 12 goals, including all four against Spain in Madrid while he was with Barcelona. In his first 25 internationals (four as substitute) he scored 23 goals; soon afterwards, he had an attack of jaundice and he and England have never been quite the same since (fair comment despite those four goals against Malaysia!). Though if he and HODDLE had scored instead of hitting the post against Holland in the European Championship finals . . .

Along the way, he's been among most of the records. The only player to twice (let alone thrice) score all three or more of England's goals in a match; England's leading scorer a record six seasons in succession; twice England's leading scorer in the World Cup (his 10 goals in the finals put him in very rarefied company); the first to score more than one hat-trick for England since HURST in 1969 (only GREAVES has scored more in total). The third player to score twice from the penalty spot in a match for England (after FINNEY and HURST), he sent the keeper the wrong way for each of his four penalties in all.

Gary Lineker wears an appropriate smile (and shirt) after scoring his first goal for England, the winner against the Republic of Ireland in 1985 (Bob Thomas)

First Division leading scorer with three different clubs, scorer in an FA Cup Final (*not* from the penalty spot!), hat-trick against Real Madrid – simply one of the best strikers in the world, possibly the best England have ever had, and certainly the most indispensable: 16 times the team's only scorer in a match, far and away the record.

EVELYN
HENRY
LINTOTT

b 2 Nov 1883   d 1 Jul 1916   LEFT HALF
Caps: 7   Goals: 0
First cap: 15 Feb 1908 v Ireland 3–1   aged 24yr 105d
Last cap: 31 May 1909 v Hungary 8–2   aged 25yr 210d
England career: 1yr 105d – P7 W6 D1 L0 – 92.86%
Club: QPR (3), Bradford City (4)

A relentless tackler, too much for the innocent Central Europeans on the summer tour.

HERBERT
BROUGHALL
LIPSHAM

b 29 Apr 1878   d 1932   OUTSIDE LEFT
Caps: 1   Goals: 0
Only cap: 3 Mar 1902 v Wales 0–0   aged 23yr 308d
England career: P1 W0 D1 L0 – 50%
Club: Sheffield United

Bert Lipsham was unlucky in later life. He lost a hand in a sawmill accident and died in a train crash, both in Canada.

BRIAN
LITTLE

b 25 Nov 1953   STRIKER
Caps: 1   Goals: 0
Only cap: 21 May 1975 v Wales 2–2
                    aged 21yr 177d (sub 71min)
England career: P1 W0 D1 L0 – 50%
Club: Aston Villa

Sharp little striker who might have put life into some of REVIE's desperate selections. Instead, given only enough time to cross for David JOHNSON to head a late equaliser at Wembley.

LAURENCE
VALENTINE
LLOYD

b 6 Oct 1948   CENTRE HALF
Caps: 4   Goals: 0
First cap: 19 May 1971 v Wales 0–0   aged 22yr 225d
Last cap: 17 May 1980 v Wales 1–4   aged 31yr 224d
                    (sub'd 80min)

England career: 8yr 364d – P4 W0 D2 L2 – 25%
Clubs: Liverpool (3), Nottingham Forest (1)
Substituted: 1

Recalled nearly eight years after Northern Ireland's last win over England, big (very big) Larry only had to stay on his feet to go to the European Championship finals as cover for Dave WATSON. Instead he had the worst comeback of all: booked, injured, substituted, generally run ragged, as well as scoring what looked like (but wasn't given as) an own goal at the end of Leighton James' run. No team has put four past England since.

ARTHUR
LOCKETT

b 1875   d 1957   OUTSIDE LEFT
Caps: 1   Goals: 0
Only cap: 14 Feb 1903 v Ireland 4–0   aged 27/28
England career: P1 W1 D0 L0 – 100%
Club: Stoke FC

Club colleague T HOLFORD also won only one cap, in the same game.

LEWIS
VAUGHAN
LODGE

b 21 Dec 1872   d 21 Oct 1916   FULL BACK
Caps: 5   Goals: 0   Captain: 0 (1?)
First cap: 12 Mar 1894 v Wales 5–1   aged 21yr 81d
Last cap: 4 Apr 1896 v Scotland 1–2   aged 23yr 105d
England career: 2yr 23d – P5 W3 D1 L1 – 70%
Clubs: Cambridge University & Corinthians (3),
              Corinthians alone (2)

Despite 'a tendency to rashness', Vaughan Lodge played in both full-back positions for England – and may just possibly have captained the team against Ireland in 1896 (see RAIKES and GO SMITH).

JOSEPH
MORRIS
LOFTHOUSE

b 14 Apr 1865   d 10 Jun 1919   OUTSIDE RIGHT
Caps: 7   Goals: 2
First cap: 28 Feb 1885 v Ireland 4–0   aged 19yr 320d
Last cap: 15 Mar 1890 v Ireland 9–1   aged 24yr 335d
                    (1 goal)

England career: 5yr 15d – P7 W4 D2 L1 – 71.43%
Clubs: Blackburn Rovers (6), Accrington FC (1)

A very quick, highly-rated winger, Joe Lofthouse scored both his international goals in his last two matches, including one (or so!) in the muddy mess at Ballynafeigh.

Nat Lofthouse in the shirt he wore while scoring both goals at Villa Park in 1951. The England attack often rested on his shoulders (Hulton)

NATHANIEL
LOFTHOUSE

b 27 Aug 1924 **CENTRE FORWARD**
Caps: 33 Goals: 30
First cap: 22 Nov 1950 v Yugoslavia 2–2 aged 26yr 87d
(2 goals)
Last cap: 26 Nov 1958 v Wales 2–2 aged 34yr 91d
England career: 8yr 04d – P33 W16 D12 L5 – 66.66%
Club: Bolton Wanderers
3 Goals in a game: 0 2 Goals in a game: 12
Substitute: 1 Substituted: 1

Lion of Vienna they called him, a title they might just as easily have given to Jozef Musil, the other half of that famous collision; Nat could hit a goalkeeper *hard.* Same with the back of the net – he equalled FINNEY's national record with his 30th goal, against the USSR in 1958; he was the first to score twice in a match 12 times (equalled only by R CHARLTON) and, against Finland in 1956, the first to score twice in a match as a substitute (matched only by T TAYLOR); he was England's leading scorer in four years out of five. The only surprise is that missing international hat-trick, which he nearly achieved in Vienna, hitting the woodwork as well as scoring twice.

EPHRAIM
LONGWORTH

b 2 Oct 1887 d 7 Jan 1968 **RIGHT BACK**
Caps: 5 Goals: 0 Captain: 1
First cap: 10 Apr 1920 v Scotland 5–4 aged 32yr 191d
Last cap: 14 Apr 1923 v Scotland 2–2 aged 35yr 195d
England career: 3yr 04d – P5 W3 D2 L0 – 80%
Club: Liverpool

Eph Longworth made his international debut in a team with an average age of over 30. He was England's captain in the first match against a foreign country after World War I, Belgium in 1921.

ARTHUR
LOWDER

b 1863 d 4 Jan 1926 **HALF BACK**
Caps: 1 Goals: 0
Only cap: 23 Feb 1889 v Wales 4–1 aged 25/26
England career: P1 W1 D0 L0 – 100%
Club: Wolves

Capped as late replacement for A SHELTON.

EDMUND
LOWE

b 11 Jul 1925 **LEFT HALF**
Caps: 3 Goals: 0
First cap: 3 May 1947 v France 3–0 aged 21yr 296d
Last cap: 25 May 1947 v Portugal 10–0 aged 21yr 318d
England career: 0yr 22d – P3 W2 D0 L1 – 66.66%
Club: Aston Villa

Eddie Lowe was one of several players tried out as Billy WRIGHT's half-back partner before DICKINSON arrived. The 1990 Lamming book calls him Edward; a printing error.

THOMAS
LUCAS

b 20 Sep 1895 d 11 Dec 1953 **LEFT/RIGHT BACK**
Caps: 3 Goals: 0 Captain: 1
First cap: 22 Oct 1921 v Ireland 1–1 aged 26yr 32d
Last cap: 24 May 1926 v Belgium 5–3 aged 30yr 246d
England career: 4yr 214d – P3 W2 D1 L0 – 83.33%
Club: Liverpool

Short, sharp in the tackle, captain in his last international.

EDWIN
LUNTLEY

b 1857 d 1 Aug 1921 **RIGHT BACK**
Caps: 2 Goals: 0
First cap: 13 Mar 1880 v Scotland 4–5 aged 22/23
Last cap: 15 Mar 1880 v Wales 3–1 aged 22/23
England career: 0yr 2d – P2 W1 D0 L1 – 50%
Club: Nottingham Forest

His last cap was also the end for his Forest clubmate, the goalkeeper SANDS.

ALFRED
LYTTLETON

b 7 Feb 1857   d 4 Jul 1913   FORWARD
Caps: 1   Goals: 1
Only cap: 3 Mar 1877 v Scotland 1–3
aged 20yr 24d (1 goal)
England career: P1 W0 D0 L1 – 0%
Club: Cambridge University (& Old Etonians)
Brother of E LYTTLETON, and the first England football international to play Test cricket (1880–84). He has a plaque in St Margaret's, the Parliament church next to Westminster Abbey.

EDWARD
LYTTLETON

b 23 Jul 1855   d 26 Jan 1942   FULL BACK
Caps: 1   Goals: 0
Only cap: 2 Mar 1878 v Scotland 2–7   aged 22yr 222d
England career: P1 W0 D0 L1 – 0%
Club: Cambridge University (& Old Etonians)
His brother was the Hon A LYTTLETON. Ed was an Hon and a Rev.

GARY
VINCENT
MABBUTT

b 23 Aug 1961
RIGHT BACK/CENTRAL DEFENDER/MIDFIELDER
Caps: 13   Goals: 1
First cap: 13 Oct 1982 v W Germany 1–2 aged 21yr 51d
Last cap: 9 Sep 1987 v W Germany 1–3 aged 26yr 17d
England career: 4yr 331d – P13 W8 D3 L2 – 73.08%
Club: Tottenham Hotspur
Substitute: 1   Substituted: 1
The matches v West Germany were the only statistical blots on Gary Mabbutt's international copybook. The prop of shaky Spurs defences throughout the eighties, he's a diabetic.

JOSEPH
McCALL

b 20 (6?) Jul 1886   d 3 Feb 1965   CENTRE HALF
Caps: 5   Goals: 1   Captain: 1
First cap: 17 Mar 1913 v Wales 4–3
aged 26yr 240 (254?)d (1 goal)
Last cap: 23 Oct 1920 v Ireland 2–0
aged 34yr 95 (109?) d
England career: 7yr 220d – P5 W4 D0 L1 – 80%
Club: Preston NE
A swarthy, old-fashioned centre half, hard in the tackle, quick with the long pass, Joe McCall was captain in his last international.

REGINALD
HEBER
MACAULAY

b 24 Aug 1858   d 15 Dec 1937   CENTRE FORWARD
Caps: 1   Goals: 0
Only cap: 12 Mar 1881 v Scotland 1–6   aged 22yr 200d
England career: P1 W0 D0 L1 – 0%
Club: Cambridge University (& Old Etonians)
A champion athlete, he and Clem MITCHELL constantly lost the ball to the Scots, and Reg was for the high jump.

TERENCE
McDERMOTT

b 8 Dec 1951   MIDFIELDER
Caps: 25   Goals: 3
First cap: 7 Sep 1977 v Switzerland 0–0 aged 25yr 273d
Last cap: 2 Jun 1982 v Iceland 1–1   aged 30yr 176d
England career: 4yr 266d – P25 W14 D7 L4 – 70%
Club: Liverpool
Substitute: 6   Substituted: 2   Goals as substitute: 1
2 Goals in a game: 1   Penalties: 1   Missed: 0
Sharp, reliable, hard-working, all-purpose (you get the picture), the kind of player that kept Glenn HODDLE out of many England teams, Terry McDermott came on as substitute in Basle and scored England's first goal in five matches, a record. It was his third of the season, including two (one penalty) against Norway in the opening game, making him England's top scorer for 1980–81.

COLIN
AGNEW
McDONALD

b 15 Oct 1930   GOALKEEPER
Caps: 8   Goals conceded: 11   Clean sheets: 2
First cap: 18 May 1958 v USSR 1–1   aged 27yr 185d
Last cap: 26 Nov 1958 v Wales 2–2   aged 28yr 42d
England career: 0yr 222d – P8 W1 D6 L1 – 50%
Club: Burnley
Colin McDonald played calmly and very well in the World Cup – then made the mistake that led to Anatoly Ilyin scoring the only goal of the play-off (see BRABROOK).

MALCOLM
IAN
MACDONALD

b 7 Jan 1950   STRIKER
Caps: 14   Goals: 6
First cap: 20 May 1972 v Wales 3–0   aged 22yr 134d
Last cap: 19 Nov 1975 v Portugal 1–1   aged 25yr 316d
(sub'd 74min)
England career: 3yr 183d – P14 W7 D4 L3 – 64.29%

Club: Newcastle United
Substitute: 5   Substituted: 4   5 Goals in a game: 1
Possibly the fastest player to play for England if not much else, Malcolm Macdonald's mind had only one track ('collect, turn, shoot') and he scored in only two internationals, but it was enough to set records. He scored the second against West Germany and all five against Cyprus, the only player to score six successive England goals and the last of four to score five in a match. His spree against the Cypriots was England's only hat-trick of the 1970s.

ROY
LESLIE
McFARLAND

b 5 Apr 1948   CENTRE HALF
Caps: 28   Goals: 0
First cap: 3 Feb 1971 v Malta 1-0   aged 22yr 304d
Last cap: 17 Nov 1976 v Italy 0-2   aged 28yr 227d
England career: 5yr 288d – P28 W17 D5 L6 – 69.64%
Club: Derby County
Substituted: 3

Before injuries broke him down, Roy McFarland looked set for a very long international career, which started promisingly (the first 7 games won, the first 16 unbeaten) and ended so-so (all his 6 defeats in the last 12 matches). Not especially tall but good in the air, and one of the best footballing centre halves.

WILLIAM
HARRY
McGARRY

b 10 Jun 1927   RIGHT HALF
Caps: 4   Goals: 0
First cap: 20 Jun 1954 v Switzerland 2-0 aged 27yr 10d
Last cap: 22 Oct 1955 v Wales 1-2   aged 28yr 134d
England career: 1yr 124d – P4 W2 D0 L2 – 50%
Club: Huddersfield Town
Later the spiky manager of Wolves, Bill McGarry came into the World Cup when Billy WRIGHT moved to centre half.

WILFRED
McGUINNESS

b 25 Oct 1937   LEFT HALF
Caps: 2   Goals: 0
First cap: 4 Oct 1958 v N Ireland 3-3   aged 20yr 344d
Last cap: 24 May 1959 v Mexico 1-2   aged 21yr 211d
                                              (sub'd 29min)
England career: 0yr 232d – P2 W0 D1 L1 – 25%
Club: Manchester United
Substituted: 1
Injuries ended what chance Wilf McGuiness had (and it wasn't much) of winning further caps.

ALBERT
McINROY

b 23 Apr 1901   d 7 Jan 1985   GOALKEEPER
Caps: 1   Goals conceded: 3
Only cap: 20 Oct 1926 v Ireland 3-3   aged 25yr 180d
England career: P1 W0 D1 L0 – 50%
Club: Sunderland
Gerontophilia ruled, OK? Only a handful of England keepers in the twenties were under 30; and only HIBBS was younger than McInroy when first capped.

STEPHEN
McMAHON

b 20 Aug 1961   MIDFIELDER
Caps: 17   Goals: 0
First cap: 17 Feb 1988 v Israel 0-0   aged 26yr 181d
Last cap: 14 Nov 1990 v Eire 1-1   aged 29yr 86d
England career: 2yr 270d – P17 W6 D9 L2 – 61.76%
Club: Liverpool
Substitute: 4   Substituted: 5
Supposedly the natural substitute for Bryan ROBSON, and certainly Steve McMahon hasn't lost England many games. Hasn't won many either.

ROBERT
McNAB

b 20 Jul 1943   LEFT BACK
Caps: 4   Goals: 0
First cap: 6 Nov 1968 v Romania 0-0   aged 25yr 109d
                                              (sub 10min)
Last cap: 3 May 1969 v N Ireland 3-1   aged 25yr 287d
England career: 0yr 178d – P4 W1 D3 L0 – 62.50%
Club: Arsenal
Substitute: 1
Bob McNab won his first cap as a right back, coming on for Tommy WRIGHT.

ROBERT
McNEAL

b 15 Jan 1891   d 15 May 1956   LEFT HALF
Caps: 2   Goals: 0
First cap: 16 Mar 1914 v Wales 2-0   aged 23yr 60d
Last cap: 4 Apr 1914 v Scotland 1-3   aged 23yr 79d
England career: 0yr 19d – P2 W1 D0 L1 – 50%
Club: West Bromwich Albion
The game at Ninian Park ended the international careers of six of the Welsh team and five of the English: BRITTLETON, COLCLOUGH, SHEA, SIMPSON and WEDLOCK. Bob McNeal survived till the next match, the last before the War.

MICHAEL
McNEIL

b 7 Feb 1940   **LEFT BACK**
Caps: 9   Goals: 0
First cap: 8 Oct 1960 v N Ireland 5-1   aged 20yr 244d
Last cap: 28 Sep 1961 v Luxembourg 4-1
                                       aged 21y 234d
England career: 0yr 355d – P9 W8 D1 L0 – 94.44%
Club: Middlesbrough

Young and tough, Mick McNeil came in when Ray WILSON was injured, and played throughout England's successful 1960–61 season before making way for Wilson's return.

STUART
MACRAE

b 1856   d 27 Jan 1927   **HALF BACK**
Caps: 5   Goals: 0
First cap: 3 Feb 1883 v Wales 5-0   aged 26/27
Last cap: 17 Mar 1884 v Wales 4-0   aged 27/28
England career: 1yr 33d – P5 W4 D0 L1 – 80%
Club: Notts County (Corinthians 1883-90)

He and Bruce Bremner RUSSELL were two of the four who took the total of England players to over 100. Born in Scotland, he played superbly against his homeland in 1883. Russell, despite the names, was born in London.

FB
MADDISON

See CHAPPELL.

PAUL
EDWARD
MADELEY

b 20 Sep 1944   **UTILITY DEFENDER**
Caps: 24   Goals: 0
First cap: 15 May 1971 v N Ireland 1-0   aged 26yr 237d
Last cap: 9 Feb 1977 v Holland 0-2   aged 32yr 142d
                                        (sub'd 62min)
England career: 5yr 270d – P24 W11 D7 L6 – 60.42%
Club: Leeds United
Substituted: 2

Sir Alf didn't hold it against Paul Madeley when he pulled out of the 1970 World Cup squad for family reasons; he was too useful. Tall and versatile, he filled in at right back in the years when England had a problem there.

THOMAS
PATRICK
MAGEE

b 12 May 1899   d 4 May 1974   **RIGHT HALF**

Caps: 5   Goals: 0
First cap: 5 Mar 1923 v Wales 2-2   aged 23yr 297d
Last cap: 21 May 1925 v France 3-2   aged 26yr 09d
England career: 2yr 77d – P5 W3 D1 L1 – 70%
Club: West Bromwich Albion

At 5ft 3in, Tommy Magee seems to have been easily the shortest half-back to play for England.

JOSEPH WILLIAM
HENRY
MAKEPEACE

b 22 Aug 1881   d 19 Dec 1952   **HALF BACK**
Caps: 4   Goals: 0
First cap: 7 Apr 1906 v Scotland 1-2   aged 24yr 228d
Last cap: 23 Mar 1912 v Scotland 1-1   aged 30yr 213d
England career: 5yr 350d – P4 W1 D1 L2 – 37.50%
Club: Everton

Waited four seasons before winning a second cap, then sat out the First World War before playing Test cricket. Made up for lost time with a century against Australia in 1921.

There's always been a problem with his christian names. Not the Henry (he was a Harry all right), but the rest. For years, he was listed as no more than H Makepeace (even in recent Wisdens). The *Wisden Book of Obituaries* and the original Farror–Lamming book call him Harry and nothing else. The *Wisden Book of Test Cricket* gives him the initials WHR. But Christopher Martin-Jenkins' *Who's Who of Test Cricketers* lists Joseph William Henry, and Bill Frindall's *England Test Cricketers* goes along with that, as does the revised Lamming Who's Who. No arguments here. Jim Creasy's research in Colindale unearthed John William Harry, but that may well be a newspaper's error.

GEORGE
CHARLES
MALE

b 8/9 May 1910   **RIGHT BACK**
Caps: 19   Goals: 0   Captain: 6
First cap: 14 Nov 1934 v Italy 3-2   aged 24y 189/190d
Last cap: 24 May 1939 v Romania 2-0 aged 29y 15/16d
England career: 4yr 191d – P19 W11 D2 L6 – 63.16%
Club: Arsenal

Both the Arsenal full backs captained England in the 1930s. Although HAPGOOD did it 21 times, in 1937 he had to play under modest, balding George Male, a converted wing-half, who was captain in six successive matches before being left out for two years in favour of Bert SPROSTON. His first international was HAPGOOD's first as captain.

Right *Even with them toecaps, wor Wilfie could pass you that ball with the laces facing the right way. Gazza? He's got it easy* (Lamming)

WILFRED
JAMES
MANNION

b 16 May 1918 INSIDE LEFT/RIGHT
Caps: 26 Goals: 11
First cap: 28 Sep 1946 v N Ireland 7–2 aged 28yr 135d
(3 goals)
Last cap: 3 Oct 1951 v France 2–2 aged 33yr 140d
England career: 5yr 05d – P26 W18 D4 L4 – 76.92%
Club: Middlesbrough
3 Goals in a game: 1 2 Goals in a game: 1
Penalties: 1 Missed: 1

Wilf Mannion's bright, often very bright, international career ended soon after a fractured cheekbone put him out of the match against Scotland in 1951. Often brilliant on the ball, a fine passer of it, he scored a hat-trick in England's first match after the War, and seven goals in his first five games. Ted Hinton of Northern Ireland saved his penalty at Goodison in 1947, a match drawn by Peter Doherty's last-minute diving header.

PAUL
MARINER

b 22 May 1953 CENTRE FORWARD
Caps: 35 Goals: 13
First cap: 30 Mar 1977 v Luxembourg 5–0
aged 23y 312d (sub HT)
Last cap: 1 May 1985 v Romania 0–0
aged 31y 344d (sub'd 83min)
England career: 8yr 32d – P35 W23 D5 L7 – 72.86%
Clubs: Ipswich Town (33), Arsenal (2)
Substitute: 5 Substituted: 8 2 Goals in a game: 1

Very good in the air (his goal from BROOKING's free kick against Switzerland was a fine piece of timing), not so very on the ground, he scored in five successive matches in 1982, including the clumsy little goal that took England to the World Cup finals. There, he tried to claim six in succession after Jozef Barmos had scored an own goal from his pass.

JOSEPH
THOMAS
MARSDEN

b 1868 d 18 Jan 1897 RIGHT BACK
Caps: 1 Goals: 0
Only cap: 7 Mar 1891 v Ireland 6–1 aged 22/23
England career: P1 W1 D0 L0 – 100%
Club: Darwen

With ROSE and UNDERWOOD, Joe Marsden made up a defence that was much too good for the Irish at Molineux.

WILLIAM MARSDEN

b 10 Nov 1901   d 1983   **LEFT HALF**
Caps: 3   Goals: 0
First cap: 20 Nov 1929 v Wales 6–0   aged 28yr 10d
Last cap: 10 May 1930 v Germany 3–3   aged 28yr 181d
England career: 0yr 171d – P3 W2 D1 L0 – 83.33%
Club: Sheffield Wednesday

In the first half in Berlin, Billy Marsden collided with Roy GOODALL and suffered a spinal injury that forced him to stay in the changing room at half-time. The following season, he turned out in five reserve matches for Wednesday, but never played first-team football again. Compensation of sorts was paid: £750 to him, £2000 to the club . . .

RODNEY WILLIAM MARSH

b 11 Oct 1944   **STRIKER**
Caps: 9   Goals: 1
First cap: 10 Nov 1971 v Switzerland 1–1 aged 27yr 30d
                                            (sub 60min)
Last cap: 24 Jan 1973 v Wales 1–1   aged 28yr 105d
England career: 1yr 75d – P9 W3 D4 L2 – 61.11%
Clubs: Queen's Park Rangers (1), Manchester City (8)
Substitute: 2   Substituted: 2

London champagne, seventies vintage: Ozzie, Big Martin, Alan Hudson, King Rodney. England managers never enjoyed the fizz for long.

THOMAS MARSHALL

b 12 Sep 1858   d 29 Apr 1917   **OUTSIDE RIGHT**
Caps: 2   Goals: 0
First cap: 15 Mar 1880 v Wales 3–2   aged 21yr 185d
Last cap: 26 Feb 1881 v Wales 0–1   aged 22yr 168d
England career: 0yr 348d – P2 W1 D0 L1 – 50%
Club: Darwen

Tom Marshall's last game saw Wales beat England for the first time.

ALVIN EDWARD MARTIN

b 29 Jul 1958   **CENTRE HALF**
Caps: 17   Goals: 0
First cap: 12 May 1981 v Brazil 0–1   aged 22yr 287d
Last cap: 10 Sep 1986 v Sweden 0–1   aged 28yr 43d
England career: 5yr 121d – P17 W11 D1 L5 – 67.65%
Club: West Ham United
Substitute: 1   Substituted: 1

Sometimes exposed for pace (by Reinaldo in his first international and Johnny Ekstrom in his last) but good in the air, big Alvin filled in well enough in the middle of the England defence. His date of birth in the revised Lamming Who's Who (19 July), may be a misprint: Rothmans, and *Rothmans Players' Records*, say 29 July.

HENRY MARTIN

b 5 Dec 1891   d unknown   **OUTSIDE LEFT**
Caps: 1   Goals: 0
Only cap: 14 Feb 1914 v Ireland 0–3   aged 22yr 71d
England career: P1 W0 D0 L1 – 0%
Club: Sunderland

The England team at Ayresome Park had won a grand total of five previous caps. A hotch-potch forward line featuring Harry Martin failed to spark.

BRIAN MARWOOD

b 5 Feb 1960   **OUTSIDE LEFT**
Caps: 1   Goals: 0
Only cap: 16 Nov 1988 v Saudi Arabia 1–1 aged 28yr 285d
                                            (sub 81min)
England career: P1 W0 D1 L0 – 50%
Club: Arsenal

Provided the left-sided width that made all the difference to Arsenal's championship win (Anders Limpar was bought to replace it), but may have been taken to Riyadh as cover rather than experiment. If not, it was a bizarre nine minutes. Only JW BARRETT and PD WARD had shorter England careers.

HARRY MART MASKREY

b 8 Oct 1880?   d 21 Apr 1927   **GOALKEEPER**
Caps: 1   Goals conceded: 1
Only cap: 15 Feb 1908 v Ireland 3–1   aged 27yr 130d?
England career: P1 W1 D0 L0 – 100%
Club: Derby County

Stood in capably for Sam HARDY before HP BAILEY was taken on the easy Continental tour.

CHARLES MASON

b 1 Apr 1863   d 3 Feb 1941   **LEFT BACK**
Caps: 3   Goals: 0
First cap: 5 Feb 1887 v Ireland 7–0   aged 23yr 310d
Last cap: 15 Mar 1890 v Ireland 9–1   aged 26yr 348d
England career: 3yr 38d – P3 W3 D0 L0 – 100%
Club: Wolves

There was a symmetry of sorts in Belfast: nine members of a team that scored nine goals never won another cap, including Charlie Mason who was Wolves' first international player.

REGINALD D
MATTHEWS

b 20 Dec 1933 **GOALKEEPER**
Caps: 5 **Goals conceded:** 5 **Clean sheets:** 1
First cap: 14 Apr 1956 v Scotland 1–1 aged 22yr 116d
Last cap: 6 Oct 1956 v N Ireland 1–1 aged 22yr 291d
England career: 0yr 175d – P5 W2 D3 L0 – 70%
Club: Coventry City

Reg Matthews' talent stood out in the lower reaches of the League; no other Third Division player won so many England caps. Note that the revised Lamming book (unlike Farror–Lamming in 1972 or the *Rothmans Players' Records*) says he was born in 1932.

STANLEY
MATTHEWS

b 1 Feb 1915 **OUTSIDE RIGHT**
Caps: 54 **Goals:** 11
First cap: 29 Sep 1934 v Wales 4–0 aged 19yr 240d
(1 goal)
Last cap: 15 May 1957 v Denmark 4–1 aged 42yr 103d
England career: 22yr 228d – P54 W32 D9 L13 – 67.59%
Clubs: Stoke City (18), Blackpool (36)
3 Goals in a game: 1 **2 Goals in a game:** 0

Sir Stan, the only footballer to be knighted for his services as a player as opposed to a manager or administrator, still holds the major England records for age and length of career; only SHILTON (and certainly no outfield player) comes close. He also spanned 22 years 7 days as a goalscorer in internationals, very nearly 10 years ahead of BLOOMER in second place.

Surely the greatest right-footed dribbler of all time, his one hat-trick for England was scored entirely with his left: three goals in a row, a genuine hat trick, against Czechoslovakia in 1937, including the winner (5–4) in off Josef Kostalek's shoulder. He made four of GW HALL's five against Ireland in 1938 (scoring the last himself), all five against Belgium in 1947, about the same in the 10–0 win over Portugal in the previous match. Etcetera etcetera.

Brilliant in the 1954 World Cup, he was listed as St Matthews in a match programme. The Swiss said it was a misprint. They weren't fooling anyone. England's greatest footballer.

VINCENT
MATTHEWS

b 15 Jan 1896 d 15 Nov 1950 **CENTRE HALF**
Caps: 2 **Goals:** 1

First cap: 17 May 1928 v France 5–1 aged 32yr 123d
Last cap: 19 May 1928 v Belgium 3–1 aged 32yr 125d
(1 goal)
England career: 0yr 2d – P2 W2 D0 L0 – 100%
Club: Sheffield United

One of the few centre halves to score for England before J CHARLTON, big Vince Matthews made the game safe after DEAN had put England 2–1 ahead.

WILLIAM
JOHN
MAYNARD

b 18 Mar 1853 d 2 Sep 1921
FORWARD/GOALKEEPER
Caps: 2 **Goals:** 0 **Goals conceded:** 3 **Clean sheets:** 1
First cap: 30 Nov 1872 v Scotland 0–0 aged 19yr 257d
Last cap: 4 Mar 1876 v Scotland 0–3 aged 22yr 351d
England career: 3yr 94d – P2 W0 D1 L1 – 33.33%
Club: 1st Surrey Rifles

Changed places with RC BARKER and played in goal during the second half of the first international match, played outfield throughout his second. He was the youngest player in England's first ever team (the first teenager to play international football) and England's youngest goalkeeper before MOON.

JAMES
MEADOWS

b 21 Jul 1931 **RIGHT BACK**
Caps: 1 **Goals:** 0
Only cap: 2 Apr 1955 v Scotland 7–2 aged 23yr 255d
England career: P1 W1 D0 L0 – 100%
Club: Manchester City

Later a Football League coach and manager, Jimmy Meadows might have won more caps if he hadn't been injured in the FA Cup Final a month after winning his first.

LESLIE
DENNIS
MEDLEY

b 3 Sep 1920 **OUTSIDE LEFT**
Caps: 6 **Goals:** 1
First cap: 15 Nov 1950 v Wales 4–2 aged 30yr 73d
Last cap: 28 Nov 1951 v Austria 2–2 aged 31yr 86d
England career: 1yr 13d – P6 W2 D4 L0 – 66.66%
Club: Tottenham Hotspur

Both wingers were dropped after Ocwirk & Co came to Wembley, namely MILTON and Les Medley, who was one of several Spurs players of the time who won caps at thirtysomething: RAMSEY, HA CLARKE, WILLIS, NICHOLSON, DITCHBURN.

THOMAS
MEEHAN

b 1896   d 18 Aug 1924   LEFT HALF
Caps: 1 **Goals:** 0
Only cap: 20 Oct 1923 v Ireland 1–2 aged 26/27
England career: P1 W0 D0 L1 – 0%
Club: Chelsea

Neither of the new wing halves, PANTLING or
little Tommy Meehan, was capped again after
both the Irish inside-forwards scored at Windsor
Park.

JAMES
MELIA

b 1 Nov 1937   INSIDE LEFT
Caps: 2 **Goals:** 1
First cap: 6 Apr 1963 v Scotland 1–2 aged 25yr 156d
Last cap: 5 Jun 1963 v Switzerland 8–1 aged 25yr 216d
England career: 0yr 60d – P2 W1 D0 L1 – 50%
Club: Liverpool

The three players winning their last England caps
all scored in the romp in Basle: DOUGLAS, KAY,
and Jimmy Melia, who was Brighton's manager,
white dancing shoes and all, in the 1983 FA Cup
Final.

DAVID
WILLIAM
MERCER

b 20 Mar 1893   d 4 Jun 1950   OUTSIDE RIGHT
Caps: 2 **Goals:** 1
First cap: 21 Oct 1922 v Ireland 2–0   aged 29yr 215d
Last cap: 19 Mar 1923 v Belgium 6–1   aged 29yr 364d
                                                (1 goal)
England career: 0yr 149d – P2 W2 D0 L0 – 100%
Club: Sheffield Wednesday

David Mercer, who scored England's fourth goal
in the first home match against a foreign team,
was the only player in the side not to win another
cap.

JOSEPH
MERCER

b 9 Aug 1914   d 9 Aug 1990   LEFT HALF
Caps: 5 **Goals:** 0
First cap: 16 Nov 1938 v Ireland 7–0   aged 24yr 99d
Last cap: 24 May 1939 v Romania 2–0   aged 24yr 288d
England career: 0yr 189d – P5 W3 D1 L1 – 70%
Club: Everton

No-one ever had a bad word for Joe Mercer,
whose famous spindleshanks appeared in England's last five matches before the War, and in 27
during it; the Mercer–CULLIS–BRITTON line
was famous. He was interim manager for seven
carefree matches ('Uncle' Joe) after RAMSEY.

GILBERT
HAROLD
MERRICK

b 26 Jan 1922   GOALKEEPER
Caps: 23 **Goals conceded:** 45
First cap: 14 Nov 1951 v N Ireland 2–0   aged 29yr 292d
Last cap: 26 Jun 1954 v Uruguay 4–2   aged 32yr 151d
England career: 2yr 224d – P23 W11 D7 L5 – 63.04%
Club: Birmingham City
Clean sheets: 5
Penalties: 3 **Saved:** 0

Gil Merrick's figures were savaged by a final season in which he let in 30 goals in 10 games,
including 13 in two against the rampant Hungarians; by the end of it he was a shadow of his former self, at fault with all four Uruguayan goals.

The former self had been beaten only 15 times
in its first 13 matches, the first 12 without defeat.

VICTOR
METCALFE

b 3 Feb 1922   OUTSIDE LEFT
Caps: 2 **Goals:** 0
First cap: 9 May 1951 v Argentina 2–1   aged 29yr 95d
Last cap: 19 May 1951 v Portugal 5–2   aged 29yr 105d
England career: 0yr 10d – P2 W2 D0 L0 – 100%
Club: Huddersfield Town

Vic Metcalfe took Sir Stan's place for the Festival
of Britain friendlies at the end of the season.

JOHN
WILLIAM
MEW

b 30 Mar 1889   d 1963   GOALKEEPER
Caps: 1 **Goals conceded:** 0
Only cap: 23 Oct 1920 v Ireland 2–0   aged 31yr 207d
England career: P1 W1 D0 L0 – 100%
Club: Manchester United

Despite not conceding a goal, Jack Mew was one
of six players who won their last caps in the same
game: F BULLOCK, DOWNS, DUCAT,
McCALL, F MORRIS.

BERNARD
MIDDLEDITCH

b 1871   d 3 Oct 1949   RIGHT HALF
Caps: 1 **Goals:** 0
Only cap: 20 Feb 1897 v Ireland 6–0   aged 25/26
England career: P1 W1 D0 L0 – 100%
Club: Corinthians

Not good enough to win a cap, lucky that he
could be hidden among the likes of
CRAWSHAW and NEEDHAM in the half back
line.

JOHN
EDWARD THOMPSON
MILBURN

b 11 May 1924   d 8 Oct 1988
CENTRE FORWARD/OUTSIDE RIGHT
Caps: 13   Goals: 10
First cap: 9 Oct 1948 v N Ireland 6–2   aged 24yr 151d
(1 goal)
Last cap: 2 Oct 1955 v Denmark 5–1   aged 31yr 144d
England career: 6yr 358d – P13 W10 D1 L2 – 80.77%
Club: Newcastle United
3 Goals in a game: 1   2 Goals in a game: 1
Substituted: 1

The most appropriate initials in football. Our Jackie was quick, very quick, probably better on the wing than through the middle (indeed, he won his last cap, almost four years to the day after his 12th, as a late replacement for Stanley MATTHEWS).

He scored in two of Newcastle's three FA Cup winning finals of the fifties – and got his share for England: three against Wales in 1949, two against Portugal in 1951, the winner against Argentina in

Jack (The Cat?) Mew (Lamming)

the previous match, preserving that pre-Puskas home record (some yearbooks credit MORTENSEN with both goals, but JET definitely scored the second, there's even a photo). His disallowed goal against Spain in 1950 may have cost England a place in the World Cup final pool.

GEORGE
BRIAN
MILLER

b 19 Jan 1937   **RIGHT HALF**
Caps: 1   Goals: 0
Only cap: 27 May 1961 v Australia 1–3   aged 24yr 128d
England career: P1 W0 D0 L1 – 0%
Club: Burnley
Brian Miller's clubmate John ANGUS also won his only cap in Vienna at the end of a hard European tour.

HAROLD
SYDNEY
MILLER

b 20 May 1902   d ?   **INSIDE LEFT**
Caps: 1   Goals: 1
Only cap: 24 May 1923 v Sweden 3–1   aged 21yr 04d
(1 goal)
England career: P1 W1 D0 L0 – 100%
Club: Charlton Athletic
Harold Miller followed his (Third Division) club colleague Seth PLUM into the England team.

GEORGE
ROBERT
MILLS

b 29 Dec 1908   d 15 Jul 1970   **CENTRE FORWARD**
Caps: 3   Goals: 3
First cap: 23 Oct 1937 v Ireland 5–1   aged 28yr 298d
(3 goals)
Last cap: 1 Dec 1937 v Czechoslovakia 5–4
aged 28yr 337d
England career: 0yr 39d – P3 W3 D0 L0 – 100%
Club: Chelsea
3 Goals in a game: 1
A classic thirties centre forward, big and unfussy, the first player to score a hat-trick on his England debut since F BRADSHAW in 1908, George Mills scored the first three goals of the match.

MICHAEL
DENIS
MILLS

b 4 Jan 1949   **FULL BACK/MIDFIELDER**
Caps: 42   Goals: 0   Captain: 8
First cap: 11 Oct 1972 v Yugoslavia 1–1 aged 23yr 280d

Last cap: 5 Jul 1982 v Spain 0–0   aged 33yr 182d
England career: 9yr 267d – P42 W28 D5 L9 – 72.62%
Club: Ipswich Town
Substitute: 2

A good club player often played out of position on the left (and once, none too cleverly, in midfield against Switzerland), Mick Mills had a rough time against Dragan Dzajic on his debut but was England's captain in the World Cup in Spain, his last five internationals.

GORDON MILNE

b 29 Mar 1937   RIGHT HALF
Caps: 14   Goals: 0
First cap: 8 May 1963 v Brazil 1–1   aged 26yr 40d
Last cap: 21 Oct 1964 v Belgium 2–2   aged 27yr 206d
England career: 1yr 166d – P14 W9 D2 L3 – 71.43%
Club: Liverpool

RAMSEY's first defensive midfielder; firm in the tackle, a good passer. But Alf was really looking for sterner stuff, and nobody's stuff was much sterner than Milne's successor, one Norbert P STILES.

CLEMENT ARTHUR MILTON

b 10 Mar 1928   OUTSIDE RIGHT
Caps: 1   Goals: 0
Only cap: 28 Nov 1951 v Austria 2–2   aged 23yr 263d
England career: P1 W0 D1 L0 – 50%
Club: Arsenal

The last player to be capped by England at cricket as well as football, Arthur Milton was anonymous against the Austrians at Wembley, lonely and underfed on the wing – but his game was built on self-confidence, and if his inside partner BROADIS had put away either of the early chances he made for him . . .

ALFRED WEATHERELL MILWARD

b 12 Sep 1870   d 10 Nov 1934   OUTSIDE LEFT
Caps: 4   Goals: 3
First cap: 7 Mar 1891 v Wales 4–1   aged 20yr 176d
                                        (1 goal)
Last cap: 3 Apr 1897 v Scotland 1–2   aged 26yr 203d
England career: 6yr 27d – P4 W3 D0 L1 – 75%
Club: Everton
2 Goals in a game: 0

Alf Milward and EW CHADWICK had a productive left-wing partnership for club and country. They won their first and last caps in exactly the same matches, scored on debut, and scored the same number of goals for England. Uncanny. Much the same kind of moustache, too.

CLEMENT MITCHELL

b 20 Feb 1862   d 6 Oct 1937   CENTRE FORWARD
Caps: 5   Goals: 5
First cap: 15 Mar 1880 v Wales 3–2   aged 18yr 23d
Last cap: 14 Mar 1885 v Wales 1–1   aged 23yr 22d
                                        (1 goal)
England career: 4yr 364d – P5 W2 D1 L2 – 50%
Club: Upton Park (& Corinthians)
3 Goals in a game: 1   2 Goals in a game: 0

An out-and-out striker, one of at least three players who were younger than D EDWARDS when first capped by England (see PRINSEP and ROSTRON), Clem Mitchell scored in his last three internationals.

JAMES FREDERICK MITCHELL

b 18 Nov 1897   d 30 May 1975   GOALKEEPER
Caps: 1   Goals conceded: 1
Only cap: 22 Oct 1924 v Ireland 3–1 aged 26yr 339d
England career: P1 W1 D0 L0 – 100%
Club: Manchester City

A 'speculative and spectacular' goalkeeper, and apparently the only man to play for England while wearing glasses, Jim Mitchell was beaten by WH SMITH's penalty for the only goal of the 1922 FA Cup Final. He was capped after Teddy TAYLOR dropped out with an injury.

HUGH MOFFAT

b Jan 1885   d 14 Nov 1952   RIGHT HALF
Caps: 1   Goals: 0
Only cap: 17 Mar 1913 v Wales 4–3   aged 28yr 45–75d
England career: P1 W1 D0 L0 – 100%
Club: Oldham Athletic

One of seven new caps called in for the match at Ashton Gate, after the record 3–0 defeat by Ireland.

GEORGE MOLYNEUX

b 1875   d 14 Apr 1942   LEFT BACK
Caps: 4   Goals: 0
First cap: 3 May 1902 v Scotland 2–2   aged 26/27
Last cap: 4 Apr 1903 v Scotland 1–2   aged 27/28
England career: 0yr 336d – P4 W2 D1 L1 – 62.50%
Club: Southampton

George won one of his caps at Molineux.

WILLIAM
ROBERT
MOON

b 27 Jun 1868   d 9 Jan 1943   GOALKEEPER
Caps: 7 **Goals conceded:** 8 **Clean sheets:** 1 **Captain:** 1
First cap: 4 Feb 1888 v Wales 5–1   aged 19yr 222d
Last cap: 4 Apr 1891 v Scotland 2–1   aged 22yr 281d
England career: 3yr 59d – P7 W5 D1 L1 – 78.57%
Club: Old Westminsters (& Corinthians)
In his first international, Billy Moon was the youngest England goalkeeper of all time. In his last, he was the second England goalkeeper-captain. See MORTEN for the first – and *The Times*, *The Football Annual*, *Lancashire Evening Express*, and *Athletic News* Annual for proof of the second.

HENRY THOMAS
MOORE

b 27 Jun 1861   d 24 Sep 1939   FULL BACK
Caps: 2 **Goals:** 0
First cap: 24 Feb 1883 v Ireland 7–0   aged 21yr 242d
Last cap: 14 Mar 1885 v Wales 1–1   aged 23yr 260d
England career: 2yr 18d – P2 W1 D1 L0 – 75%
Club: Notts County
Left back in his first international, right back in his second.

JAMES
MOORE

b 11 May 1889   d unknown   INSIDE RIGHT
Caps: 1 **Goals:** 1
Only cap: 21 May 1923 v Sweden 4–2   aged 34yr 10d
England career: P1 W1 D0 L0 – 100%
Club: Derby County
A statistician's nightmare. Two players, same surname, one cap each, scoring in different matches against the same country only three days apart. Yearbooks don't specify, contemporary newspapers barely mention the two matches, and the opposition didn't class the second game as a full international. Disaster.

Luckily, Swedish sources (including their version of Rothmans) say Jimmy Moore played in the first match, WGB MOORE in the second. The *Athletic News* Annual agrees. Phew.

ROBERT
FREDERICK CHELSEA
MOORE

b 12 Apr 1941   RIGHT HALF/CENTRAL DEFENDER
Caps: 108 **Goals:** 2 **Captain:** 90
First cap: 20 May 1962 v Peru 4–0   aged 21yr 38d
Last cap: 14 Nov 1973 v Italy 0–1   aged 32yr 216d
England career: 11yr 178d – P108 W67 D23 L18 – 72.69%
Club: West Ham United

2 Goals in a game: 0 **Goals as captain:** 2
Slow on the turn, average in the air, prone to fatal mistakes, especially in the twilight years: blueprint for one of the greatest defenders of all time. Positional sense and a severe tackle made him Player of the Tournament when he captained the World Cup winners (and made two of HURST's goals in the Final) and perhaps even better in Mexico. He overtook R CHARLTON as the most capped European player, and his 90 matches as captain is still a world record shared with WA WRIGHT. He played at least 10 times against each of the other Home countries, and in 27 consecutive games 1966–68. Significantly, he won exactly 100 caps under Sir Alf. And yes he really is called Chelsea; it's on the birth certificate.

WILLIAM
GREY BRUCE
MOORE

b 6 Oct 1894   d 26 Sep 1968   INSIDE RIGHT
Caps: 1 **Goals:** 2
Only cap: 24 May 1923 v Sweden 3–1   aged 28yr 230d
                                    (2 goals)
England career: P1 W1 D0 L0 – 100%
Club: West Ham United
Billy Moore scored the first and last goals of his only international.

JOHN
MORDUE

b 1887   d 14 Dec 1957   OUTSIDE LEFT/RIGHT
Caps: 2 **Goals:** 0
First cap: 10 Feb 1912 v Ireland 6–1   aged 24/25
Last cap: 15 Feb 1913 v Ireland 1–2   aged 25/26
England career: 1yr 05d – P2 W1 D0 L1 – 50%
Club: Sunderland
With CUGGY and BUCHAN, Jackie Mordue made up Sunderland's famous attacking triangle. They played together just once for England, in Belfast in 1913, when Mordue won his last cap and the other two their first as Ireland beat England for the first time.

CHARLES JOHN
MORICE

b 27 May 1850   d 17 Jun 1932   FORWARD
Caps: 1 **Goals:** 0
Only cap: 30 Nov 1872 v Scotland 0–0   aged 22yr 187d
England career: P1 W0 D1 L0 – 50%
Club: Barnes (& Harrow Chequers)
Made up a dribbling right wing with fellow CJs OTTAWAY and CHENERY in the first international.

ANTHONY
WILLIAM
MORLEY

b 26 Aug 1954   **OUTSIDE LEFT**
Caps: 6   **Goals:** 0
First cap: 18 Nov 1981 v Hungary 1-0   aged 27yr 84d
       (sub 65min)
Last cap: 17 Nov 1982 v Greece 3-0   aged 28yr 83d
England career: 0yr 364d – P6 W4 D2 L0 – 83.33%
Club: Aston Villa
Substitute: 1   **Substituted:** 2
Because Tony Morley was so often a match-winner in Villa's League and European Cup wins, more was expected of him in an England shirt; but he wasn't given much time to provide it.

HERBERT
MORLEY

b Oct 1882   d 15 Jul 1957   **RIGHT BACK**
Caps: 1   **Goals:** 0
Only cap: 12 Feb 1910 v Ireland 1-1 aged 27yr 104-34d
England career: P1 W0 D1 L0 – 50%
Club: Notts County
Tall and heavy and no prisoners taken. Some say he, and not Billy McCracken, patented the offside trap.

THOMAS
MORREN

b 1871/1875   d 31 Jan 1929   **CENTRE HALF**
Caps: 1   **Goals:** 1
Only cap: 5 Mar 1898 v Ireland 3-2   aged ?22-27 (1 goal)
England career: P1 W1 D0 L0 – 100%
Club: Sheffield United
With NEEDHAM and R HOWELL, Tommy Morren made up a complete United half-back line of England internationals who were all 5ft 5in or thereabouts. He scored England's first goal, an equaliser, in Belfast.

FREDERICK
MORRIS

b 27 Aug 1893   d 4 Jul 1962   **INSIDE LEFT**
Caps: 2   **Goals:** 1
First cap: 10 Apr 1920 v Scotland 5-4   aged 26yr 227d
       (1 goal)
Last cap: 23 Oct 1920 v Ireland 2-0   aged 27yr 58d
England career: 0yr 196d – P2 W2 D0 L0 – 100%
Club: West Bromwich Albion
Top scorer in the League that season, Fred Morris scored the equaliser after Scotland had led 4–2 at half-time.

JOHN
MORRIS

b 27 Sep 1923/24   **INSIDE RIGHT**
Caps: 3   **Goals:** 3
First cap: 18 May 1949 v Norway 4-1 aged 24/25yr 233d
       (1 goal)
Last cap: 21 Sep 1949 v Eire 0-2   aged 24/25yr 359d
England career: 0yr 126d – P3 W2 D0 L1 – 66.66%
Club: Derby County
Johnny Morris scored twice against France, including England's third (they won 3–1) in the last few minutes.

WILLIAM W
MORRIS

b 26 Mar 1913   **LEFT BACK**
Caps: 3   **Goals:** 0
First cap: 16 Nov 1938 v Ireland 7-0   aged 25yr 235d
Last cap: 24 May 1939 v Romania 2-0   aged 26yr 59d
England career: 0yr 189d – P3 W3 D0 L0 – 100%
Club: Wolves
Bill Morris won his last cap after HAPGOOD broke down in Belgrade. Sources are split as to whether his second name was Walter (which seems more likely) or Walker.

HAROLD
MORSE

b 1860?   d unknown   **LEFT BACK**
Caps: 1   **Goals:** 0
Only cap: 5 Apr 1879 v Scotland 5-4   aged 19?
England career: P1 W1 D0 L0 – 100%
Club: Notts County
May possibly have been the Harold Morse born in the first quarter of 1860. If so, he was 19 when capped.

THOMAS
MORT

b 1 Dec 1897   d 6 Jun 1967   **LEFT BACK**
Caps: 3   **Goals:** 0
First cap: 3 Mar 1924 v Wales 1-2   aged 26yr 93d
Last cap: 17 Apr 1926 v Scotland 0-1   aged 28yr 138d
England career: 2yr 45d – P3 W1 D0 L2 – 33.33%
Club: Aston Villa
Both full backs against Wales were Tommies from Villa: the well-known firm of SMART and Mort.

ALEXANDER
MORTEN

b 1831/32?   d 24 Feb 1900?   **GOALKEEPER**
Caps: 1   **Goals conceded:** 2   **Captain:** 1
Only cap: 8 Mar 1873 v Scotland 4-2 aged 40/42?

England career: P1 W1 D0 L0 – 100%
Club: Crystal Palace

It's a fact. Frank SWIFT wasn't the first goal-keeper to captain England; there were at least two others last century. Morten was the first, in only the second international ever played. He took over the captaincy when ALCOCK dropped out (not for the first or last time). Read *The Sporting Life* and *The Sportsman* for proof. He was probably made captain because (if his year of birth is correct) he was by far the oldest player in the team. If he really was over 40, he would still be England's oldest ever debutant, goalkeeper, and captain (see COMPTON and SHILTON). He played cricket as well as football for Palace, which was a different club from the one that exists today.

STANLEY
HARDING
MORTENSEN

b 26 May 1921   d 22 May 1991
INSIDE/CENTRE FORWARD

Caps: 25   Goals: 23
First cap: 25 May 1947 v Portugal 10–0   aged 25yr 364d
(4 goals)
Last cap: 25 Nov 1953 v Hungary 3–6   aged 32yr 183d
(1 goal)

England career: 6yr 184d – P25 W17 D2 L6 – 72%
Club: Blackpool
4 Goals in a game: 1   3 Goals in a game: 2
2 Goals in a game: 1

Pale, frail, and very quick, a poacher first and last, 'the other Stan' couldn't stop scoring. In his first two and last three internationals; in 15 in all; in five seasons in a row; even against the great Hungarians at the bitter end. He enjoyed his birthday the day after becoming the first player since VAUGHTON and A BROWN in 1882 to score four times on his England debut (he and LAWTON the first to score four together since the same pair); against Chile in 1950 he scored England's first ever goal in the World Cup finals; he was England's leading scorer three seasons in a row; he and FINNEY scored together in six matches, he and LAWTON in five.

He made an international debut of sorts by playing *against* England for Wales, coming on as substitute for Ivor Powell in the wartime match in 1943.

JOHN R
MORTON

b 26 Feb 1914   d 8 Mar 1986   OUTSIDE LEFT
Caps: 1   Goals: 1
Only cap: 1 Dec 1937 v Czechoslovakia 5–4
aged 23yr 278d (1 goal)
England career: P1 W1 D0 L0 – 100%

Jack Crayston, George Mills and (above) Jack Morton were all injured against Czechoslovakia and didn't play for England again (Lamming)

Club: West Ham United

Jack Morton was unlucky. He put England 2–1 ahead before he was injured and forced to take turns with CRAYSTON out on the right, effectively changing places with S MATTHEWS, who scored a hat-trick with his left foot.

WILLIAM
MOSFORTH

b 1858   d 11 Jul 1929   OUTSIDE LEFT
Caps: 9   Goals: 3
First cap: 3 Mar 1877 v Scotland 1–3   aged 18/19
Last cap: 13 Mar 1882 v Wales 3–5   aged 23/24
(1 goal)

England career: 5yr 10d – P9 W3 D0 L6 – 33.33%
Clubs: Sheffield Albion (5), Sheffield Wednesday (3)
2 Goals in a game: 0

Odd that Billy Mosforth's date of birth should be

proving so elusive. He was a famous footballer, the first to win six (let alone nine) England caps, the first to win five (let alone seven) in a row. An expert dribbler who sometimes held on too long, he had trouble with the Welsh as well as the Scots, but did have one crowded hour, when he and EC BAMBRIDGE scored three between them in the famous recovery from 4–1 down in 1879.

FRANK
MOSS

b 17 Apr 1895   d 15 Sep 1965   HALF BACK
Caps: 5 **Goals:** 0 **Captain:** 1
First cap: 22 Oct 1921 v Ireland 1–1   aged 26yr 188d
Last cap: 12 Apr 1924 v Scotland 1–1   aged 28yr 361d
England career: 2yr 173d – P5 W1 D3 L1 – 50%
Club: Aston Villa

Dominant midfielder with no weaknesses who should perhaps have captained England throughout the early twenties instead of just his last international, the first ever staged at Wembley.

FRANK
MOSS

b 5 Nov 1909   d 7 Feb 1970   GOALKEEPER
Caps: 4 **Goals conceded:** 6 **Clean sheets:** 1
First cap: 14 Apr 1934 v Scotland 3–0   aged 24yr 160d
Last cap: 14 Nov 1934 v Italy 3–2   aged 25yr 09d
England career: 0yr 114d – P4 W2 D0 L2 – 50%
Club: Arsenal

A short international career ended with some excellent second-half saves to preserve the win against Italy. Then HIBBS came back.

EDWIN
MOSSCROP

b 16 Jun 1892   d 14 Mar 1980   OUTSIDE LEFT
Caps: 2 **Goals:** 0
First cap: 16 Mar 1914 v Wales 2–0   aged 21yr 273d
Last cap: 4 Apr 1914 v Scotland 1–3   aged 21yr 292d
England career: 0yr 19d – P2 W1 D0 L1 – 50%
Club: Burnley

A frail winger, Eddie got very little change out of the experienced Alec McNair at Hampden.

BERTRAM
MOZLEY

b 21 Sep 1923   RIGHT BACK
Caps: 2 **Goals:** 0
First cap: 21 Sep 1949 v Eire 0–2   aged 26yr 00d
Last cap: 16 Nov 1949 v N Ireland 9–2   aged 26yr 56d
England career: 0yr 56d – P3 W2 D0 L1 – 66.66%
Club: Derby County

Seems to have been the first player to make his

England debut on his birthday, though Peter Desmond must have thought it was his when Bert fouled him to give away the penalty converted by Con Martin, the first goal of the match as the Republic became the first country from outside the Home Championship to win in England.

JAMES
MULLEN

b 6 Jan 1923   d Oct 1987   OUTSIDE LEFT
Caps: 12 **Goals:** 6
First cap: 12 Apr 1947 v Scotland 1–1   aged 24yr 96d
Last cap: 20 Jun 1954 v Switzerland 2–0 aged 31yr 165d
                                                                   (1 goal)
England career: 7yr 69d – P12 W8 D2 L2 – 75%
Club: Wolves
2 Goals in a game: 1 **Substitute:** 1

Jimmy Mullen had to fit his international career into the gaps left by FINNEY. After 10 minutes of the match against Belgium in 1950 he became the first substitute ever to come on for England, and the first goalscoring substitute when he equalised in the first minute of the second half. In his last match, against the World Cup hosts, he scored after dribbling past his full back and the goalkeeper.

ALAN
PATRICK
MULLERY

b 23 Nov 1941   MIDFIELDER
Caps: 35 **Goals:** 1 **Captain:** 1
First cap: 9 Dec 1964 v Holland 1–1   aged 23yr 17d
Last cap: 13 Oct 1971 v Switzerland 3–2 aged 29yr 324d
England career: 6yr 308d – P35 W22 D9 L4 – 75.71%
Club: Tottenham Hotspur
Substitute: 2 **Goals while captain:** 0

Alan Mullery waited nearly three years to become STILES' permanent replacement, which he did with a little more passing ability and less down-right ferocity. Well, usually. In the last minute of England's 424th match, a brutal European Championship semi-final against Yugoslavia in Florence, he became the first player to be sent off while playing for England. Of course, he was sorely provoked.

PHILIP
JOHN
NEAL

b 20 Feb 1951   RIGHT/LEFT BACK
Caps: 50 **Goals:** 4 **Captain:** 1
First cap: 24 Mar 1976 v Wales 2–1   aged 25yr 32d
Last cap: 21 Sep 1983 v Denmark 0–1   aged 32yr 273d
England career: 7yr 181d – P50 W28 D12 L10 – 68%

Club: Liverpool
Substitute: 1   **Substituted:** 5   **Own goals:** 1
2 Goals in a game: 0
Penalties: 2   **Missed:** 0

Phil Neal seems to have won an inordinate number of caps for someone who needed so much protection (often provided by COPPELL) from opposing wingers. When he didn't get it, he could be in trouble, witness Janito in Spain's win at Wembley in 1981. But a full back's duties changed some time ago, and he was usually given time and space to do good things going forward. Anyway, Bob Paisley and Ron Greenwood can't both have been wrong all the time.

He scored the winner from the penalty spot against Wales in 1983 very soon after missing one at Anfield that allowed Brighton to win an FA Cup tie. In his last match, his handball gave away the penalty that cost England a place in the European finals. In the previous game, he'd scored an own goal.

ERNEST
NEEDHAM

b 21 Jan 1873   d 8 Mar 1936   **LEFT HALF**
Caps: 16   **Goals:** 3   **Captain:** 1
First cap: 7 Apr   1894 v Scotland 2–2   aged 21yr 76d
Last cap: 3 Mar   1902 v Wales 0–0   aged 29yr 41d
England career: 7yr 330d – P16 W11 D3 L2 – 78.125%
Club: Sheffield United
Goals while captain: 1 (pen)

Short, hard and tireless, the Nudger had a long and successful international career that ran alongside CRABTREE's, beginning in the same season, ending in the same game, almost the same number of matches played.

Whereas Crabtree seems to have been the first player to take (and miss) a penalty for England, Needham was apparently the first to score from one, against Wales in 1901. In the two matches immediately after this, he became the first to take a penalty in each of three consecutive England matches (see FLOWERS and HURST) – and the first to miss two in all (see FINNEY, R BYRNE, F LEE), against Scotland in 1901 (when Harry Rennie came off his line to make the save) and Wales again in 1902.

KEITH
ROBERT
NEWTON

b 23 Jun 1941   **LEFT/RIGHT BACK**
Caps: 27   **Goals:** 0
First cap: 23 Feb 1966 v W Germany 1–0 aged 24yr 245d
                                                (sub'd 44min)
Last cap: 14 Jun 1970 v W Germany 2–3 aged 28yr 356d
England career: 4yr 111d – P27 W16 D7 L4 – 72.22%

Club: Blackburn Rovers
Substituted: 5

Terry COOPER's overlaps got the publicity in the 1970 World Cup, but Keith Newton made both England's goals against W Germany – and never played for England again. Tallish, toothy, good on either flank, he was substituted by Ray WILSON on his debut.

JOHN
NICHOLLS

b 3 Apr 1931   **INSIDE LEFT**
Caps: 2   **Goals:** 1
First cap: 3 Apr   1954 v Scotland 4–2   aged 23yr 00d
                                                (1 goal)
Last cap: 16 May 1954 v Yugoslavia 0–1   aged 23yr 43d
England career: 0yr 43d – P2 W1 D0 L1 – 50%
Club: West Bromwich Albion

Johnny Nicholls celebrated his 23rd birthday by putting England 2–1 ahead at Hampden.

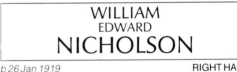

WILLIAM
EDWARD
NICHOLSON

b 26 Jan 1919   **RIGHT HALF**
Caps: 1   **Goals:** 1
Only cap: 19 May 1951 v Portugal 5–2   aged 32yr 113d
                                                (1 goal)
England career: P1 W1 D0 L0 – 100%
Club: Tottenham Hotspur

Bill Nick scored after only 30 seconds (some say 19) against Portugal, possibly the fastest debut goal in all international football (see COCK and Moreel). Solid but rather ordinary, he was selected as reserve any number of times, and actually to play more than once, but injury and Billy WRIGHT got in the way.

DAVID
JOHN
NISH

b 26 Sep 1947   **LEFT/RIGHT BACK**
Caps: 5   **Goals:** 0
First cap: 12 May 1973 v N Ireland 2–1   aged 25yr 228d
Last cap: 18 May 1974 v Scotland 0–2   aged 25yr 234d
England career: 1yr 06d – P5 W3 D1 L1 – 70%
Club: Derby County

Smooth, non-tackling full back. RAMSEY had a look at him, REVIE didn't, MERCER quite liked his style. CLOUGH (or rather Taylor) bought him.

MAURICE
NORMAN

b 8 May 1934   **CENTRE HALF**

Caps: 23 **Goals:** 0
First cap: 20 May 1962 v Peru 4–0 aged 28yr 12d
Last cap: 9 Dec 1964 v Holland 1–1 aged 30yr 215d
England career: 2yr 203d – P23 W11 D6 L6 – 60.87%
Club: Tottenham Hotspur

He had a Norfolk background, so the temptation to call him strong as an ox was never resisted very long. Apparently not especially good in the air, he was tall enough to do the job anyway.

HENRY
NUTTALL

b 9 Nov 1897 *d Apr 1969* RIGHT/LEFT HALF
Caps: 3 **Goals:** 0
First cap: 22 Oct 1927 v Ireland 0–2 aged 29yr 347d
Last cap: 13 Apr 1929 v Scotland 0–1 aged 31yr 155d
England career: 1yr 173d – P3 W0 D0 L3 – 0%
Club: Bolton Wanderers

Harry Nuttall played in all three of Bolton's FA Cup winning teams in the twenties, but was probably close to his sell-by date when he was finally capped. His other match was won 2–1 by Wales in 1927.

WILLIAM
JOHN
OAKLEY

b 27 Apr 1873 *d 20 Sep 1934* FULL BACK
Caps: 16 **Goals:** 0 **Captain:** 1
First cap: 18 Mar 1895 v Wales 1–1 aged 21yr 325d
Last cap: 30 Mar 1901 v Scotland 2–2 aged 27yr 337d
England career: 6yr 12d – P16 W10 D3 L3 – 71.88%
Clubs: Oxford University & Corinthians (5), Corinthians alone (11)

One of the all-amateur XI who did survive the match against Wales (see **RR BARKER, G DEWHURST, STANBROUGH**), he went on to have one of the longer international careers of his time. Very heavy towards the end ('slow in tackling'), light (and quick) enough to win the AAA long jump in 1894.

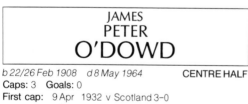

JAMES
PETER
O'DOWD

b 22/26 Feb 1908 *d 8 May 1964* CENTRE HALF
Caps: 3 **Goals:** 0
First cap: 9 Apr 1932 v Scotland 3–0
  aged 24yr 43/47d
Last cap: 20 May 1933 v Switzerland 4–0
  aged 25yr 84/88d
England career: 1yr 41d – P3 W3 D0 L0 – 100%
Club: Chelsea

No-one scored against England while Peter O'Dowd was in the team. Perhaps he had help. He was apparently the only Catholic in the tour party that met the Pope in 1933.

ROBERT ANDREW
MUTER MACINDOE
OGILVIE

b 1852 *d 5 Mar 1938* FULL BACK
Caps: 1 **Goals:** 0
Only cap: 7 Mar 1874 v Scotland 1–2 aged 21/22
England career: P1 W0 D0 L1 – 0%
Club: Clapham Rovers

Young and bulky, didn't look the part in England's first ever defeat. Contemporary reports list him as simply RA.

MICHAEL
O'GRADY

b 11 Oct 1942 OUTSIDE LEFT
Caps: 2 **Goals:** 3
First cap: 20 Oct 1962 v N Ireland 3–1 aged 20yr 09d
  (2 goals)
Last cap: 12 Mar 1969 v France 5–0 aged 26yr 152d
  (1 goal)
England career: 6yr 143d – P2 W2 D0 L0 – 100%
Clubs: Huddersfield Town (1), Leeds United (1)

A rather fleeting figure with Leeds, and of course with England, but fun while it lasted; goals in each match, over six years apart.

LEONARD
FREDERICK
OLIVER

b 1 Aug 1905 *d Aug 1967* RIGHT HALF
Caps: 1 **Goals:** 0
Only cap: 11 May 1929 v Belgium 5–1 aged 23yr 283d
England career: P1 W1 D0 L0 – 100%
Club: Fulham

Fulham were in the Third Division when Len Oliver was capped.

BENJAMIN
ALBERT
OLNEY

b 15/30 Mar 1899 *d Sep 1943* GOALKEEPER
Caps: 2 **Goals conceded:** 2 **Clean sheets:** 0
First cap: 17 May 1928 v France 5–1 aged 29yr 48/63d
Last cap: 19 May 1928 v Belgium 3–1 aged 29yr 50/65d
England career: 0yr 02d – P2 W2 D0 L0 – 100%
Club: Aston Villa
Penalties: 1 **Saved:** 0

Belgium went ahead after 22 minutes when Jacques Moeschal put a penalty past big Ben.

Only cap: 28 Nov 1927 v Wales 1–2   aged 28/29yr 128d
England career: P1 W0 D0 L1 – 0%
Club: Leicester City

Reg Osborne didn't feature in the missed penalty, two own goals or anything else in his only international.

PETER
LESLIE
OSGOOD

b 20 Feb 1947   **STRIKER**
Caps: 4   **Goals:** 0
First cap: 25 Feb 1970 v Belgium 3–1   aged 23yr 05d
Last cap: 14 Nov 1973 v Italy 0–1   aged 26yr 267d
England career: 3yr 262d – P4 W3 D0 L1 – 75%
Club: Chelsea
Substitute: 2

A very skilful, arrogant, potentially great striker denied a fistful of caps by a manager who worshipped work-rate – or just a dilettante? Alf may have been right, but he might have been seen to prove it by giving Peter Osgood more of a chance, especially when, at his peak, he was scoring the goals that helped win the 1970 FA Cup and 1971 European Cup Winners Cup. Was good, alright. Sometimes very.

RUSSELL
CHARLES
OSMAN

b 14 Feb 1959   **CENTRAL DEFENDER**
Caps: 11   **Goals:** 0
First cap: 31 May 1980 v Australia 2–1   aged 21yr 106d
Last cap: 21 Sep 1983 v Denmark 0–1   aged 24yr 219d
England career: 3yr 113d – P11 W2 D5 L4 – 40.90%
Club: Ipswich Town

Russell Osman played alongside Terry BUTCHER at the back for Ipswich; they made their England debuts in the same match and were clearly being groomed for a long international partnership. Then everything caved in for one of them: three defeats in a year, the 2–1 scorelines camouflaging very poor performances against Spain, Switzerland and Norway. Every part of the team played badly, but central defence looked the worst. Hard for any player to survive all that, or his last match, in which his old club manager did him no favours with some timid selections, including a midfield of WILKINS, GREGORY and Sammy LEE.

Belgium led 3–2 before Frank Osbourne (above) scored the last two goals of his England career (Lamming)

FRANK
RAYMOND
OSBORNE

b 14 Oct 1896   *d 8 Mar 1988*
         CENTRE FORWARD/OUTSIDE RIGHT
Caps: 4   **Goals:** 3
First cap: 21 Oct 1922 v Ireland 2–0   aged 26yr 07d
Last cap: 24 May 1926 v Belgium 5–3   aged 29yr 222d
                             (3 goals)
England career: 3yr 215d – P4 W4 D0 L0 – 100%
Clubs: Fulham (2), Tottenham Hotspur (2)

Frank Osborne admitted he 'was nowhere near ready' when he won his first cap. By 1926, he was good enough to become the last player to score a hat-trick in his last match for England. Reg OSBORNE was his brother.

REGINALD
OSBORNE

b 23 Jul 1898/99   *d 1977*   **LEFT BACK**
Caps: 1   **Goals:** 0

CUTHBERT
JOHN
OTTAWAY

b 20 Jul 1850   *d 2 Apr 1878*   **FORWARD**

Caps: 2   Goals: 0   Captain: 2
First cap: 30 Nov 1872 v Scotland 0–0   aged 22yr 133d
Last cap: 7 Mar 1874 v Scotland 1–2   aged 23yr 230d
England career: 1yr 97d – P2 W0 D1 L1 – 33.33%
Club: Oxford University (& Old Etonians)

Very much the public school sporting all-rounder (cricket, athletics, rackets, you name it), Cuthbert Ottaway was England's first ever captain, the first to be captain twice – and the youngest before Bobby MOORE in 1963 (but see LINDLEY).

JOHN ROBERT BLAYNEY
OWEN

b 1848   d 13 Jun 1921   FORWARD
Caps: 1   Goals: 0
Only cap: 7 Mar 1874 v Scotland 1–2   aged 25/26
England career: P1 W0 D0 L1 – 0%
Club: Sheffield Club

Ten others (including three Scots) won their last caps in England's first ever defeat.

SYDNEY
WILLIAM
OWEN

b 29 Sep 1922   CENTRE HALF
Caps: 3   Goals: 0
First cap: 16 May 1954 v Yugoslavia 0–1 aged 31yr 229d
Last cap: 17 Jun 1954 v Belgium 4–4   aged 31yr 261d
England career: 0yr 32d – P3 W0 D1 L2 – 16.66%
Club: Luton Town

Footballer of the Year as a result of taking Luton to the 1959 FA Cup Final at the age of 36, Syd Owen hadn't been the answer to England's problem at centre half. Pol Anoul scored twice against him in his last match, opening the way for the solution that had been there all the time: Billy WRIGHT moved over from right half.

LOUIS
ANTONIO
PAGE

b 27 Mar 1899   d 12 Oct 1959   OUTSIDE LEFT
Caps: 7   Goals: 1
First cap: 12 Feb 1927 v Wales 3–3   aged 27yr 322d
Last cap: 28 Nov 1927 v Wales 1–2   aged 28yr 289d
England career: 0yr 192d – P7 W4 D1 L2 – 64.29%
Club: Burnley

An unusual thing at the time, Louis Page's international appearances were all consecutive. A dashing, goalscoring winger who surprisingly did it only once for England, against Belgium.

TERENCE
LIONEL
PAINE

b 23 Mar 1939   OUTSIDE RIGHT
Caps: 19   Goals: 7
First cap: 29 May 1963 v Czechoslovakia 4–2
                                       aged 24y 67d
Last cap: 16 Jul 1966 v Mexico 2–0   aged 27yr 115d
England career: 3yr 48d – P19 W14 D3 L2 – 81.58%
Club: Southampton
3 Goals in a game: 1   2 Goals in a game: 1

A full-back himself, Sir Alf did believe in wingers, good wingers – and for a while Terry Paine was a fixture in a successful England team, linking especially well with GREAVES; they scored seven between them in the 8–3 win over Northern Ireland in 1963.

GARY A
PALLISTER

b 30 Jun 1965   CENTRAL DEFENDER
Caps: 4   Goals: 0
First cap: 27 Apr 1988 v Hungary 0–0   aged 22yr 305d
Last cap: 1 May 1991 v Turkey 1–0   aged 25yr 310d
                                        (sub 71min)
England career: 3yr 5d – P4 W2 D2 L0 – 75%
Clubs: Middlesbrough (2), Manchester United (2)
Substitute: 1

Very tall (6ft 4in), rawboned but getting better, first capped when still in the Second Division.

HARRY
HAROLD
PANTLING

b 1891   d 21 Dec 1952   RIGHT HALF
Caps: 1   Goals: 0
Only cap: 20 Oct 1923 v Ireland 1–2   aged 31/32
England career: P1 W0 D0 L1 – 0%
Club: Sheffield United

Obviously parents who believed in belt as well as braces. He was apparently known as Harold, but either way he seems to have been a Harry.

PAUL
ANDREW
PARKER

b 4 Apr 1964   RIGHT BACK/CENTRAL DEFENDER
Caps: 16   Goals: 0
First cap: 26 Apr 1989 v Albania 5–0   aged 25yr 22d
                                         (sub 76min)
Last cap: 3 Jun 1991 v N Zealand 1–0 aged 27yr 60d
England career: 2yr 38d – P16 W10 D4 L2 – 75%
Club: Queen's Park Rangers
Substitute: 1

Part of England's sudden and effective sweeper

system in Italia 90, a very quick little man-marker.

West Germany scored only one goal in each of their last three matches in Italia 90: two penalties, and (in a match decided on penalties) Paul Parker's huge, high deflection of Brehme's free kick which sent it over SHILTON and in. Someone had their *namen* written on the cup, alright.

THOMAS
ROBERT
PARKER

b 19 Nov 1897   d 1 Nov 1987   RIGHT BACK
Caps: 1   Goals: 0
Only cap: 21 May 1925 v France 3-2   aged 27yr 183d
England career: P1 W1 D0 L0 – 100%
Club: Southampton

Slow, and not a great distributor of the ball, Tom Parker had enough positional sense to make him Arsenal's veteran captain at the start of their successful run through the thirties.

PHILIP
BENJAMIN
PARKES

b 8 Aug 1950   GOALKEEPER
Caps: 1   Goals conceded: 0
Only cap: 3 Apr 1974 v Portugal 0-0   aged 23yr 238d
England career: P1 W1 D0 L0 – 100%
Club: Queen's Park Rangers

In what looks like an attempt to save his job by proving he *could* make changes (it didn't work, this was his last game in charge), Sir Alf picked six new caps in Lisbon: BOWLES, BROOKING, JM DOBSON, PEJIC, DV WATSON, and Phil Parkes, who, but for CLEMENCE/SHILTON/ CORRIGAN . . .

JOHN
PARKINSON

b Sep 1883   d 13 Sep 1942   CENTRE FORWARD
Caps: 2   Goals: 0
First cap: 14 Mar 1910 v Wales 1-0
                        aged 26yr 165-194d
Last cap: 2 Apr 1910 v Scotland 0-2
                        aged 26yr 184-213d
England career: 0yr 19d – P2 W1 D0 L1 – 50%
Club: Liverpool

A regular goalscorer at club level, Jack Parkinson wasn't selected again after England had managed only two goals throughout the Home Championship and failed to score against Scotland for the first time since 1884.

PERCIVAL
CHASE
PARR

b 2 Dec 1859   d 3 Sep 1912   INSIDE FORWARD
Caps: 1   Goals: 0
Only cap: 13 Mar 1882 v Wales 3-5   aged 22yr 101d
England career: P1 W0 D0 L1 – 0%
Club: Oxford University

The revised Lamming book says he scored against Wales, but there seems to be some confusion with EH PARRY, who's listed as one of the scorers by most yearbooks. *The Sporting Chronicle*'s match report confirms Parry. No great surprise, given that Parr played most of his club football as a goalkeeper.

EDWARD
HAGARTY
PARRY

b 24 Apr 1855   d 19 Jul 1931   FORWARD
Caps: 3   Goals: 1
First cap: 18 Jan 1879 v Wales 2-1   aged 23yr 269d
Last cap: 13 Mar 1882 v Wales 3-5   aged 26yr 323d
                        (1 goal)
England career: 3yr 54d – P3 W1 D0 L2 – 33.33%
Club: Old Carthusians (and possibly Swifts and Remnants)

Played in the first (abbreviated) match against Wales then put England 2-0 up at the Racecourse Ground before an own goal and two startling decisions from the Welsh referee turned the match.

RAYMOND
ALAN
PARRY

b 19 Jan 1936   INSIDE LEFT
Caps: 2   Goals: 1
First cap: 18 Nov 1959 v N Ireland 2-1   aged 23yr 303d
                        (1 goal)
Last cap: 9 Apr 1960 v Scotland 1-1   aged 24yr 81d
England career: 0yr 143d – P2 W1 D1 L0 – 75%
Club: Bolton Wanderers

Scored the winner in the last minute, just two minutes after Billy Bingham had equalised.

BASIL CLEMENT ALDERSON
PATCHITT

b 12 Aug 1900   d unknown
RIGHT/LEFT HALF
Caps: 2   Goals: 0   Captain: 2
First cap: 21 May 1923 v Sweden 4-2   aged 22yr 282d
Last cap: 24 May 1923 v Sweden 3-1   aged 22yr 285d
England career: 0yr 03d – P2 W2 D0 L0 – 100%
Club: Corinthians

One of the youngest players ever to captain England, not one of the best, he's often seen spelt Patchett.

FRANCIS WILLIAM (FRANK) PAWSON

b 6 Apr 1861   d 4 Jul 1921   OUTSIDE RIGHT/CENTRE FORWARD
Caps: 2   **Goals:** 1
First cap: 24 Feb 1883 v Ireland 7–0   aged 21yr 324d
                                                                (1 goal)
Last cap: 28 Feb 1885 v Ireland 4–0   aged 23yr 328d
England career: 2yr 04d – P2 W1 D1 L0 – 75%
Club: Cambridge University (and Swifts)
Won his first cap as late replacement for Clem MITCHELL. 'His' goal, typical of its time, came out of a ruck of players in the goalmouth. Some match reports don't credit it to a specific player.

JOSEPH PAYNE

b 17 Jan 1914   d 22 Apr 1975   CENTRE FORWARD
Caps: 1   **Goals:** 2
Only cap: 20 May 1937 v Finland 8–0   aged 23yr 123d
England career: P1 W1 D0 L0 – 100%
Club: Luton Town
Having set the current League record of 10 goals in his first match as a centre forward, Joe Payne (pictured left) played for England as a Third Division player (the last before the War) and scored the third and sixth goals in Helsinki.

ALAN PEACOCK

b 29 Oct 1937   CENTRE FORWARD
Caps: 6   **Goals:** 3
First cap: 2 Jun 1962 v Argentina 3–1   aged 24yr 216d
Last cap: 10 Nov 1965 v N Ireland 2–1   aged 28yr 12d
                                                                (1 goal)
England career: 3yr 161d – P6 W4 D2 L0 – 83.33%
Clubs: Middlesbrough (4), Leeds United (2)
2 Goals in a game: 1
Tall, straightforward centre forward who took a battering from Argentina's ruthless captain Ruben Navarro in his first international, and survived the rest pretty well.

JOHN PEACOCK

b 15 Mar 1897   d 4 Mar 1979   LEFT HALF
Caps: 3   **Goals:** 0
First cap: 9 May 1929 v France 4–1   aged 32yr 55d
Last cap: 15 May 1929 v Spain 3–4   aged 32yr 61d

England career: 0yr 06d – P3 W2 D0 L1 – 66.66%
Club: Middlesbrough

Gaspar Rubio got away from 'Joe' Peacock to score twice, as Spain recovered from 2–0 and 3–2 down.

STUART
PEARCE

b 24 Apr 1962   LEFT BACK
Caps: 41   Goals: 2   Captain: 1
First cap: 19 May 1987 v Brazil 1–1   aged 25yr 25d
Last cap: 12 Jun 1991 v Malaysia 4–2   aged 29yr 49d
England career: 4yr 24d – P41 W21 D18 L2 – 73.17%
Club: Nottingham Forest

Call 999, it's Psycho. Stuart Pearce, the last player before Neil Webb (1000) to be capped by England
(Allsport/David Cannon)

Substitute: 1   Substituted: 3
Goals as substitute: 0   Goals as captain: 1

The way was clear, post-SANSOM, for the man with the big thighs to hold off the more nimble DORIGO for the left-back berth, with 25 consecutive caps 1988–90. Like it or not (and most now like), England haven't lost many while he's been there. They've failed to win a few, though.

HAROLD
FREDERICK
PEARSON

b 7 May 1908   GOALKEEPER
Caps: 1   Goals conceded: 0
Only cap: 9 Apr 1932 v Scotland 3–0   aged 23yr 337d
England career: P1 W1 D0 L0 – 100%
Club: West Bromwich Albion

Harold Pearson's only cap was sandwiched in between two of his cousin Harry HIBBS' 25. His father Hubert had been picked to play in goal against France only nine years earlier.

JAMES
STUART
PEARSON

b 21 Jun 1949   CENTRE FORWARD
Caps: 15   Goals: 5
First cap: 8 May 1976 v Wales 1–0   aged 26yr 321d
Last cap: 16 May 1978 v N Ireland 1–0   aged 28yr 329d
England career: 2yr 08d – P15 W5 D4 L6 – 46.66%
Club: Manchester United
Substitute: 2   Substituted: 2   2 Goals in a game: 0

Stuart Pearson linked well at United with wingers COPPELL and HILL and fairly well with KEEGAN and CHANNON for England, but he always had more than his share of injuries.

JOHN HARGREAVES
(JACK)
PEARSON

b 25 Jan 1868   d 22 Jun 1931   INSIDE RIGHT
Caps: 1   Goals: 0
Only cap: 5 Mar 1892 v Ireland 2–0   aged 24yr 40d
England career: P1 W1 D0 L0 – 100%
Club: Crewe Alexandra

Crewe's only England international.

STANLEY C
PEARSON

b 15 Jan 1919   INSIDE FORWARD
Caps: 8   Goals: 5
First cap: 10 Apr 1948 v Scotland 2–0   aged 29yr 86d
Last cap: 18 May 1952 v Italy 1–1   aged 33yr 124d
England career: 4yr 38d – P8 W5 D2 L1 – 75%

Club: Manchester United
2 Goals in a game: 2
A touch player with an eye for goal, Stan Pearson scored the goals that beat Scotland 2–1 at Hampden in 1952, then won only one more cap.

WILLIAM
HAROLD
PEASE

b 30 Sep 1899   d 2 Oct 1955   OUTSIDE RIGHT
Caps: 1   **Goals:** 0
Only cap: 12 Feb 1927 v Wales 3–3   *aged 27yr 135d*
England career: P1 W0 D1 L0 – 50%
Club: Middlesbrough
Billy Whizz helped an inexperienced England attack (only Billy WALKER had more than one cap) score three times, then was dropped; not a piece of selectorial nonsense this time, he made way for Joe HULME.

DAVID
PEGG

b 20 Sep 1935   d 6 Feb 1958   OUTSIDE LEFT
Caps: 1   **Goals:** 0
Only cap: 19 May 1957 v Eire 1–1   *aged 21yr 180d*
England career: P1 W0 D1 L0 – 50%
Club: Manchester United
Capped as a replacement for the originally selected MATTHEWS. Among England players, only D EDWARDS was younger when he died (alongside him, RW BYRNE, SWIFT and T TAYLOR at Munich).

MICHAEL
PEJIC

b 25 Jan 1950   LEFT BACK
Caps: 4   **Goals:** 0
First cap: 3 Apr 1974 v Portugal 0–0   *aged 24yr 68d*
Last cap: 18 May 1974 v Scotland 0–2   *aged 24yr 113d*
                                   (1 own goal)
England career: 0yr 45d – P4 W2 D1 L1 – 62.50%
Club: Stoke City
A throwback to the hard old school of flat-nosed tacklers, Mike Pejic was the second player (see COMPTON) to score an own goal in his last international.

FREDERICK
RAYMOND
PELLY

b 11 Aug 1868   d 16 Oct 1940   LEFT BACK
Caps: 3   **Goals:** 0
First cap: 25 Feb 1893 v Ireland 6–1   *aged 24yr 198d*
Last cap: 7 Apr 1894 v Scotland 2–2   *aged 25yr 239d*

England career: 1yr 41d – P3 W2 D1 L0 – 83.33%
Club: Old Foresters (and Corinthians)
An *Athletic News* Annual described Fred Pelly as 'rather clumsy'. Hardly surprising, as he weighed 15 (or 16) stone, seemingly the heaviest England outfield player by far.
Note that the 1972 Farror–Lamming book lists the year of his birth as 1869 – and that the writer AE Whitcher called him Frank (see HARTLEY).

JESSE
PENNINGTON

b 23 Aug 1883/84   d 5 Sep 1970   LEFT BACK
Caps: 25   **Goals:** 0   **Captain:** 2
First cap: 18 Mar 1907 v Wales 1–1   *aged 22/23yr 207d*
Last cap: 10 Apr 1920 v Scotland 5–4
                              aged 35/36yr 230d
England career: 13yr 23d – P25 W16 D5 L4 – 74%
Club: West Bromwich Albion
Ivan Sharpe wrote that if Jesse Pennington 'had been rougher and tougher he would have been a better player. I played against him half-a-dozen times, and his very gentlemanliness gave me confidence.' Nevertheless . . .
Captain in his last two internationals, he was

What do you call a 15-stone full-back? Fred Pelly, Frank Pelly, or just plain Sir? (Lamming)

the oldest before Shilton in 1987 – whichever year he was born.

FREDERICK
BEACONSFIELD

PENTLAND

b 1883   d 16 Mar 1962   OUTSIDE RIGHT
Caps: 5   Goals: 0
First cap: 15 Mar 1909 v Wales 2–0   aged 25/26
Last cap: 1 Jun 1909 v Austria 8–1   aged 25/26
England career: 0yr 78d – P5 W5 D0 L0 – 100%
Club: Middlesbrough

Fred Pentland followed an unfortunate start (injured in the first minute of his first match) with five wins in five internationals – then did pretty well as a coach. He was in charge in 1929 when Spain became the first foreign country to beat England, and the first to do so at the first attempt.

CHARLES

PERRY

b Jan 1866   d 2 Jul 1927   CENTRE HALF
Caps: 3   Goals: 0
First cap: 15 Mar 1890 v Ireland 9–1   aged 24yr 43–73d
Last cap: 13 Mar 1893 v Wales 6–0   aged 27yr 41–71d
England career: 2yr 363d – P3 W3 D0 L0 – 100%
Club: West Bromwich Albion

England scored 21 goals and conceded two when Charlie Perry was in the side, which had something to do with his abilities in both defence and attack, and the weakness of Welsh and Irish football at the time. T PERRY was his brother.

THOMAS
PERRY

b 1871   d 18 Jul 1927   RIGHT HALF
Caps: 1   Goals: 0
Only cap: 28 Mar 1898 v Wales 3–0   aged 26/27
England career: P1 W1 D0 L0 – 100%
Club: West Bromwich Albion

A respected half back, Tom Perry didn't disgrace himself at Ninian Park but was replaced by the mighty NEEDHAM.

WILLIAM

PERRY

b 10 Sep 1930   OUTSIDE LEFT
Caps: 3   Goals: 2
First cap: 2 Nov 1955 v Ireland 3–0   aged 25yr 53d
Last cap: 14 Apr 1956 v Scotland 1–1   aged 25yr 217d
England career: 0yr 164d – P3 W2 D1 L0 – 83.33%
Club: Blackpool
2 Goals in a game: 1

Bill from Johannesburg scored twice against Spain in 1955 – and the much-televised winner in

the MATTHEWS Cup Final, before effectively taking the grand old man's place in three England teams.

STEPHEN
JOHN

PERRYMAN

b 21 Dec 1951   MIDFIELD
Caps: 1   Goals: 0
Only cap: 2 Jun 1982 v Iceland 1–1   aged 30yr 163d
                                          (sub 70min)
England career: P1 W0 D1 L0 – 50%
Club: Tottenham Hotspur

When England played Finland just before the World Cup, the team was on a run of five wins without conceding a goal. Another one in Helsinki would have sent them into their first group match with a record sequence behind them. As it was, Finland scored late on and the B match in Rekjavik the day before was upgraded. Just so that Steve Perryman could finally get his cap? If so (and Greenwood did have his sentimental streak), he owed it to a Kai Haaskivi penalty.

MARTIN
STANFORD

PETERS

b 8 Nov 1943   MIDFIELDER
Caps: 67   Goals: 20   Captain: 4
First cap: 4 May 1966 v Yugoslavia 2–0 aged 22yr 177d
Last cap: 18 May 1974 v Scotland 0–2   aged 30yr 191d
England career: 8yr 14d – P67 W42 D14 L11 – 73.13%
Clubs: West Ham United (32), Tottenham Hotspur (35)
Substitute: 3   Substituted: 3
2 Goals in a game: 2   Goals while captain: 0

An uncanny knack for arriving in the right place at the right time gave Martin Peters a high strike-rate for a midfielder; the goal which nearly won the World Cup Final said a lot about his sense of space and timing. Yet he always seemed to be either overrated or underrated, probably the most controversial of RAMSEY's favourites. He was captain in Sir Alf's last match, against Portugal in 1974.

MICHAEL

PHELAN

b 24 Sep 1962   MIDFIELDER
Caps: 1   Goals: 0
Only cap: 15 Nov 1989 v Italy 0–0   aged 27yr 52d (sub HT)
England career: P1 W0 D1 L0 – 50%
Club: Manchester United

Even in his very good last season with Norwich he was hardly dynamic. Hard to see him getting another cap.

LEONARD H
PHILLIPS

b 11 Sep 1922   **INSIDE LEFT/RIGHT HALF**
Caps: 3   **Goals: 0**
First cap: 14 Nov 1951 v N Ireland 2–0   aged 29yr 64d
Last cap: 1 Dec 1954 v W Germany 3–1   aged 32yr 81d
England career: 3yr 17d – P3 W3 D0 L0 – 100%
Club: Portsmouth
Cool, attacking midfielder who was injured in training for the next international, against Scotland, and never played first-class football again.

FREDERICK
PICKERING

b 19 Jan 1941   **CENTRE FORWARD**
Caps: 3   **Goals: 5**
First cap: 27 May 1964 v USA 10–0   aged 23yr 129d
                                        (3 goals)
Last cap: 21 Oct 1964 v Belgium 2–2   aged 23yr 276d
                                        (1 goal)
England career: 0yr 147d – P3 W2 D1 L0 – 83.33%
Club: Everton
Nothing subtle about Fred, but he carved out a remarkable little career in international football. One of the few to score in all his three games for England, and the last to score a hat-trick on his debut.

JOHN
PICKERING

b 18 Dec 1908   *d 10 May 1977*   **INSIDE LEFT**
Caps: 1   **Goals: 0**
Only cap: 1 Apr 1933 v Scotland 1–2   aged 24yr 104d
England career: P1 W0 D0 L1 – 0%
Club: Sheffield United
England took a raw team to Hampden and paid the price. Four of the forwards were winning their first caps: ARNOLD, GS HUNT, STARLING – and Jack Pickering, who was also (like ARNOLD, BLENKINSOP, HULME and WEAVER) winning his last.

NICHOLAS
PICKERING

b 4 Aug 1963   **LEFT BACK**
Caps: 1   **Goals: 0**
Only cap: 19 Jun 1983 v Australia 1–1   aged 19yr 309d
England career: P1 W0 D1 L0 – 50%
Club: Sunderland
If the tour to Australia was an experiment, none of the samples survived. Not one of the new caps were still playing for England 18 months later: BARHAM, GREGORY, SPINK, DJ THOMAS, WALSH, SC WILLIAMS, and Nick Pickering.

THELWELL MATHER
PIKE

b 17 Nov 1866 (1865?)   *d 21 Jul 1957*   **OUTSIDE LEFT**
Caps: 1   **Goals: 0**
Only cap: 13 Mar 1886 v Ireland 6–1   aged 19yr 146d
England career: P1 W1 D0 L0 – 100%
Clubs: Brentwood (and Cambridge University and Old Malvernians); and possibly Corinthians!
What *did* they call him on the pitch? Man on, Thelly. Easy ball, Mathe. Surely the only pseudonym to play for England.

BRIAN
PILKINGTON

b 12 Feb 1933   **OUTSIDE LEFT**
Caps: 1   **Goals: 0**
Only cap: 2 Oct 1954 v N Ireland 2–0   aged 21yr 232d
England career: P1 W1 D0 L0 – 100%
Club: Burnley
Called up to replace the injured FINNEY in Belfast.

JOHN
PLANT

b 1871/72   *d unknown*   **OUTSIDE LEFT**
Caps: 1   **Goals: 0**
Only cap: 7 Apr 1900 v Scotland 1–4   aged 27–29
England career: P1 W0 D0 L1 – 0%
Club: Bury
Scored in both of Bury's FA Cup Finals (1900 and 1903) but Celtic Park in 1900, with two team-mates injured and Bob McColl scoring a hat-trick before half-time, wasn't the place to make an international debut.

DAVID
ANDREW
PLATT

b 10 Jun 1966   **MIDFIELDER**
Caps: 22   **Goals: 7**
First cap: 15 Nov 1989 v Italy 0–0   aged 23yr 158d
                                     (sub 78min)
Last cap: 12 Jun 1991 v Malaysia 4–2   aged 25yr 2d
England career: 1yr 209d – P22 W14 D7 L1 – 79.54%
Club: Aston Villa
Substitute: 7   **Goals as sub: 1**   **2 Goals in a game: 1**
Penalties: 1   **Missed: 0**
With lungs like pumps, a knack (and the energy) for arriving late in the box to score, and his old club manager now in charge, the way looks clear for David Platt to do the same job (as captain?) that Bryan ROBSON did for England, perhaps for almost as long and just as invaluably. Only 107 minutes in his seven games as substitute, which puts his scoring rate into perspective.

SETH
LEWIS
PLUM

b 15 Jul 1899   d 29 Nov 1969   **RIGHT HALF**

Caps: 1   **Goals:** 0
Only cap: 10 May 1923 v France 4–1   aged 23yr 299d
England career: P1 W1 D0 L0 – 100%
Club: Charlton Athletic

Like his clubmate. HS MILLER two matches later, Seth Plum was capped as a Third Division player.

RAYMOND
POINTER

b 10 Oct 1936   **CENTRE FORWARD**

Caps: 3   **Goals:** 2
First cap: 28 Sep 1961 v Luxembourg 4–1
                  aged 24yr 353d (1 goal)
Last cap: 25 Oct 1961 v Portugal 2–0   aged 25yr 15d
                  (1 goal)

England career: 0yr 27d – P3 W2 D1 L0 – 83.33%
Club: Burnley

By the time Eusebio and Jose Aguas hit the woodwork three times between them, Ray Pointer had scored England's second after just ten minutes to clinch a place in the World Cup finals.

THOMAS
STODDARD
PORTEOUS

b 1865   d 23 Feb 1919   **RIGHT BACK**

Caps: 1   **Goals:** 0
Only cap: 7 Mar 1891 v Wales 4–1   aged 25/26
England career: P1 W1 D0 L0 – 100%
Club: Sunderland

Put the ball in the net from a free kick, only for the goal to be disallowed because it was indirect.

ALFRED
ERNEST
PRIEST

b 1875   d 5 May 1922   **LEFT-SIDED FORWARD**

Caps: 1   **Goals:** 0
Only cap: 17 Mar 1900 v Ireland 2–0   aged 24/25
England career: P1 W1 D0 L0 – 100%
Club: Sheffield United

The year before and the year after his only international, Fred Priest scored in the FA Cup Final.

David Platt scored three goals during Italia 90. Here he dots the I's and crosses the T's of a copybook Pearce cross to put England 1–0 ahead against Cameroon (Allsport)

JAMES FREDERICK McLEOD
PRINSEP

b 27 Jul 1861   d 22 Nov 1895   HALF BACK
Caps: 1   Goals: 0
Only cap: 5 Apr 1879 v Scotland 5–4   aged 17yr 252d
England career: P1 W1 D0 L0 – 100%
Club: Clapham Rovers

Farror and Lamming unearthed his date of birth as long ago as 1972, possibly earlier – yet he's generally remained one of the great statistical secrets. Time to shout from the rooftops a little: JFM Prinsep, not Duncan EDWARDS, was England's youngest ever player – and the youngest to win a last cap (!), though he was picked against Scotland in 1882, dropping out through injury.

Not just a young face, it seems. The writer W Unite Jones described him as 'one of the prettiest half-backs that ever did duty for the Rose'. He was born in India.

SYDNEY
CHARLES
PUDDEFOOT

b 17 Oct 1894   d 2 Oct 1972   INSIDE RIGHT
Caps: 2   Goals: 0
First cap: 24 Oct 1925 v Ireland 0–0   aged 31yr 07d
Last cap: 17 Apr 1926 v Scotland 0–1   aged 31yr 182d
England career: 0yr 175d – P2 W0 D1 L1 – 25%
Club: Blackburn Rovers

Past his best when he won official caps, Syd Puddefoot had appeared in Victory internationals in 1919.

JESSE
PYE

b 22 Dec 1918/19/21   d 1984   CENTRE FORWARD
Caps: 1   Goals: 0
Only cap: 21 Sep 1949 v Eire 0–2   aged 27–30yr 273d
England career: P1 W0 D0 L1 – 0%
Club: Wolves

A prolific scorer who paid the penalty for not doing it when the Republic became the first country from outside the Home Championship to win in England. Sources for year of birth are, respectively, Farror–Lamming, Lamming, and *Rothmans League Players' Records*.

RICHARD
HENRY
PYM

b 2 Feb 1893   d 27 Sep 1988   GOALKEEPER
Caps: 3   Goals conceded: 6   Clean sheets: 0
First cap: 28 Feb 1925 v Wales 2–1   aged 32yr 26d
Last cap: 1 Mar 1926 v Wales 1–3   aged 33yr 27d

England career: 1yr 01d – P3 W1 D0 L2 – 33.33%
Club: Bolton Wanderers

Aged 95yr 238d when he died, Dick Pym was the longest-lived of all England players, as far as records show. One or two of his seniors may still be alive.

ALFRED
EDWARD
QUANTRILL

b 22 Jan 1897   d 19 Apr 1968   OUTSIDE LEFT
Caps: 4   Goals: 1
First cap: 15 Mar 1920 v Wales 1–2   aged 23yr 53d
Last cap: 14 Mar 1921 v Wales 0–0   aged 24yr 52d
England career: 0yr 364d – P4 W2 D1 L1 – 62.50%
Club: Derby County

A sharp aggressive winger, Steve BLOOMER's son-in-law, Alf Quantrill was the youngest player in what was probably England's oldest team, against Scotland in his second match, when he scored in a 5–4 win.

ALBERT
QUIXALL

b 9 Aug 1933   INSIDE RIGHT/LEFT
Caps: 5   Goals: 0
First cap: 10 Oct 1953 v Wales 4–1   aged 20yr 62d
Last cap: 22 May 1955 v Portugal 1–3   aged 21yr 286d
                                                (sub 39min)
England career: 1yr 224d – P5 W2 D2 L1 – 60%
Club: Sheffield Wednesday
Substitute: 1

Lively, skilful little golden boy who never quite fitted Winterbottom's plans. The first player to win his last England cap as a substitute.

JOHN
RADFORD

b 22 Feb 1947   FORWARD
Caps: 2   Goals: 0
First cap: 15 Jan 1969 v Romania 1–1   aged 21yr 327d
Last cap: 13 Oct 1971 v Switzerland 3–2 aged 23yr 233d
                                                (sub 85min)
England career: 2yr 271d – P2 W1 D1 L0 – 75%
Club: Arsenal
Substitute: 1

Played alongside HURST and HUNT against Romania. Too many hard-working cooks.

GEORGE
BARKLEY
RAIKES

b 14 Mar 1873   d 18 Dec 1966   GOALKEEPER
Caps: 4   Goals conceded: 4   Captain: 1?
First cap: 18 Mar 1895 v Wales 1–1   aged 22yr 04d

Last cap: 4 Apr 1896 v Scotland 1–2 aged 23yr 21d
England career: 1yr 17d – P4 W2 D1 L1 – 62.50%
Club: Oxford University (and Corinthians)

Praised for his shot-stopping in match reports of all his four internationals, George Raikes was quite probably the last goalkeeper to captain England before SWIFT. At first it was hard to believe he'd been given the honour while GO SMITH was in the team, (v Ireland 1896 according to *Ireland's Saturday Night* and *The Irish Times*) but Smith hadn't captained England before, and this was the first match of the season, just four days after Raikes' birthday . . . (well, they were whimsical days) . . . *The Times*, however, does mention Smith as captain, which he certainly was against Scotland later in the year. Oh, and see LODGE.

Note that although the original Farror-Lamming book spells his second name Berkeley, the revised Lamming book confirms the spelling in *Wisden's Book of Obituaries*.

ALFRED
ERNEST
RAMSEY

b 22 Jan 1920 **RIGHT BACK**
Caps: 32 **Goals:** 3 **Captain:** 2
First cap: 2 Dec 1948 v Switzerland 6–0 aged 28yr 314d
Last cap: 25 Nov 1953 v Hungary 6–3 aged 33yr 307d
(1 pen)
England career: 4yr 358d – P32 W18 D9 L5 – 70.31%
Clubs: Southampton (1), Tottenham Hotspur (31)
Penalties: 3 **Missed:** 0

England's only really successful manager, Sir Alf was already known as The General in his playing days: not fast, but in charge, good enough to win his first cap as a Second Division player. His three successful penalties, all at Wembley, were the England record before FLOWERS. Exposed for speed (at last) by Czibor, he went the way of so many others against Hungary.

ARCHIBALD
RAWLINGS

b 2 Oct 1891 d 11 Jun 1952 **OUTSIDE RIGHT**
Caps: 1 **Goals:** 0
Only cap: 21 May 1921 v Belgium 2–0 aged 29yr 231d
England career: P1 W1 D0 L0 – 100%
Club: Preston NE

England took the Belgians lightly, but the Olympic champions made things difficult; Verbeeck marked Archie Rawlings out of the game and it took a late goal by CHAMBERS to settle things.

WILLIAM
ERNEST
RAWLINGS

b 3 Jan 1896 d 25 Sep 1972 **CENTRE FORWARD**
Caps: 2 **Goals:** 0
First cap: 13 Mar 1922 v Wales 1–0 aged 26yr 69d
Last cap: 8 Apr 1922 v Scotland 0–1 aged 26yr 95d
England career: 0yr 26d – P2 W1 D0 L1 – 50%
Club: Southampton

The second of two Third Division centre-forwards to play in consecutive England matches (see SIMMS), Bill Rawlings made his debut in the same match as clubmate Fred TITMUSS.

JOHN FREDERICK PEEL
RAWLINSON

b 21 Dec 1860 d 14 Jan 1926 **GOALKEEPER**
Caps: 1 **Goals conceded:** 0
Only cap: 18 Feb 1882 v Ireland 13–0 aged 21yr 59d
England career: P1 W1 D0 L0 – 100%
Club: Cambridge University (and Old Etonians)

'A capital goalkeeper', it was said, 'but rather too cool.' The Irish, in their first international, couldn't make it hot for him. He was later QC and MP.

HERBERT
EDWARD
RAWSON

b 3 Sep 1852 d 18 Oct 1924 **FORWARD**
Caps: 1 **Goals:** 0
Only cap: 6 Mar 1875 v Scotland 2–2 aged 22yr 184d
England career: P1 W0 D1 L0 – 50%
Club: Royal Engineers

Herbert and WS RAWSON were not only the first brothers to play together for England, but the first to win their first caps in the same match (see WALTERS).

WILLIAM
STEPNEY
RAWSON

b 14 Oct 1854 d 4 Nov 1932 **FULLBACK**
Caps: 2 **Goals:** 0 **Captain:** 1
First cap: 6 Mar 1875 v Scotland 2–2 aged 20yr 143d
Last cap: 3 Mar 1877 v Scotland 1–3 aged 22yr 140d
England career: 1yr 362d – P2 W0 D1 L1 – 25%
Club: Oxford University (and probably Wanderers and Old Westminsters)

A clogger in the style of the times, sometimes better than that. Captain in his last international, he was HE RAWSON's brother.

ALBERT
READ

b 1899 d ?   **RIGHT HALF**
Caps: 1 Goals: 0
Only cap: 21 May 1921 v Belgium 2–0   aged 21/22
England career: P1 W1 D0 L0 – 100%
Club: Tufnell Park
Note that a history of Reading FC calls him Arthur, and that he joined QPR in May 1921 (see FOX and his two clubs).

JOSEPH
READER

b 27 Feb 1866 d 8 Mar 1954   **GOALKEEPER**
Caps: 1 Goals conceded: 2
Only cap: 3 Mar 1894 v Ireland 2–2   aged 28yr 04d
England career: P1 W0 D1 L0 – 50%
Club: West Bromwich Albion
Joe Reader was in goal the first time Ireland avoided defeat against England, after 12 games going back to 1882.

The revised Lamming book calls him Josiah, while *The Book of Football* (1906) backs the Farror–Lamming original.

PAUL
REANEY

b 22 Oct 1944   **RIGHT BACK**
Caps: 3 Goals: 0
First cap: 11 Dec 1968 v Bulgaria 1–1   aged 24yr 50d
                                              (sub)
Last cap: 3 Feb 1971 v Malta 1–0   aged 26yr 104d
England career: 2yr 54d – P3 W2 D1 L0 – 83.33%
Club: Leeds United
Substitute: 1
Leeds mainstay who missed the 1970 World Cup with a broken leg after making his debut by coming on for Keith NEWTON.

KEVIN
PHILIP
REEVES

b 20 Oct 1957   **STRIKER**
Caps: 2 Goals: 0
First cap: 22 Nov 1979 v Bulgaria 2–0   aged 22yr 33d
Last cap: 20 May 1980 v N Ireland 1–1   aged 22yr 193d
                                      (sub'd 70min)
England career: 0yr 160d – P2 W1 D1 L0 – 75%
Club: Norwich City (1), Manchester City (1)
Substituted: 1
Man City (who else?) spent £1.25 million on Kevin Reeves, but it didn't work out – and the best thing to be said for him on the international front is that he made his debut in the same match as Glenn HODDLE.

CYRILLE
REGIS

b 9 Feb 1958   **CENTRE FORWARD**
Caps: 5 Goals: 0
First cap: 23 Feb 1982 v N Ireland 4–0   aged 24yr 14d
                                      (sub 65min)
Last cap: 14 Oct 1987 v Turkey 8–0   aged 29yr 247d
                                      (sub 72min)
England career: 5yr 233d – P5 W3 D1 L1 – 70%
Clubs: West Bromwich Albion (4), Coventry City (1)
Substitute: 3 **Substituted:** 2
Mobile, heavily muscled centre-forward who might have been expected to win more caps ahead of MARINER and WITHE but instead didn't complete 90 minutes for England and was recalled for less than 20, five years and a day after his fourth cap. His injury just before the 1982 World Cup finals probably saved Greenwood from having to explain why he wasn't taking him to Spain.

PETER
REID

b 20 Jun 1956   **MIDFIELDER**
Caps: 13 Goals: 0
First cap: 9 Jun 1985 v Mexico 0–1   aged 28yr 354d
                                      (sub 70min)
Last cap: 28 May 1988 v Switzerland 1–0 aged 31yr 343d
                                      (sub 78min)
England career: 2yr 354d – P13 W8 D2 L3 – 69.23%
Club: Everton
Substitute: 6 **Substituted:** 2
Helped fill the midfield after the first two matches in the Mexico World Cup, but more was needed against Argentina in the quarter-final.

DONALD
GEORGE
REVIE

b 10 Jul 1926 d 26 May 1989   **INSIDE RIGHT**
Caps: 6 Goals: 4
First cap: 2 Oct 1954 v N Ireland 2–0   aged 28yr 84d
                                      (1 goal)
Last cap: 6 Oct 1956 v N Ireland 1–1   aged 30yr 88d
England career: 2yr 04d – P6 W3 D1 L2 – 58.33%
Club: Manchester City
2 Goals in a game: 1 **Penalties:** 1 **Missed:** 0
The English attempt at a version of Hidegkuti, Don Revie scored twice against Denmark in 1955, including a first-half penalty. He was the only England manager to coach another country, the United Arab Emirates.

Right *DG Revie CBE, good international player turned great club manager* (Hulton)

JOHN
REYNOLDS

b 21 Feb 1869   d 12 Mar 1917   RIGHT HALF
Caps: 8   Goals: 3
First cap: 2 Apr 1892 v Scotland 4–1   aged 23yr 41d
Last cap: 3 Apr 1897 v Scotland 1–2   aged 28yr 42d
England career: 5yr 01d – P8 W5 D2 L1 – 75%
Clubs: West Bromwich Albion (3), Aston Villa (5)

After winning five caps for Ireland (1890–91) Jack Reynolds became the first of only two players (see RE EVANS) to appear for and against England, and the only one to score for and against (he'd scored his only goal for Ireland in the 1890 match, despite being picked out of position at centre forward and injured early on). Aggressive and highly regarded, he was one of the original little brick powerhouses: 5ft 5in, 12 stone.

CHARLES
HENRY
RICHARDS

b 9 Aug 1875   d unknown   INSIDE FORWARD
Caps: 1   Goals: 0
Only cap: 5 Mar 1898 v Ireland 3–2   aged 22yr 208d
England career: P1 W1 D0 L0 – 100%
Club: Nottingham Forest

Only one of four new caps survived. It wasn't Charlie.

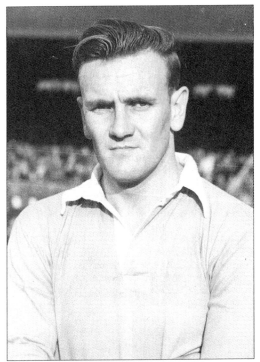

GEORGE
HENRY
RICHARDS

b 10 May 1880   d 1 Nov 1959   LEFT HALF
Caps: 1   Goals: 0
Only cap: 1 Jun 1909 v Austria 8–1   aged 29yr 22d
England career: P1 W1 D0 L0 – 100%
Club: Derby County

A free cap, an easy ride. His halfback partners were the mighty WARREN and WEDLOCK.

JOHN
PETER
RICHARDS

b 9 Nov 1950   STRIKER
Caps: 1   Goals: 0
Only cap: 12 May 1973 v N Ireland 2–1   aged 22yr 184d
England career: P1 W1 D0 L0 – 100%
Club: Wolves

A sharp, quick striker who fed off Derek Dougan at Wolves. Never likely to get the same service from CHIVERS, who took both goals for himself.

JAMES
ROBERT
RICHARDSON

b 8 Feb 1911   d 28 Aug 1964   INSIDE RIGHT
Caps: 2   Goals: 2
First cap: 13 May 1933 v Italy 1–1   aged 22yr 94d
Last cap: 20 May 1933 v Switzerland 4–0
                                          aged 22yr 101d (2 goals)
England career: 0yr 07d – P2 W1 D1 L0 – 75%
Club: Newcastle United

Jimmy Richardson, who provided the decisive 'over the line' cross in the 1932 FA Cup Final, scored twice in the second half in Berne.

WILLIAM
RICHARDSON

b 29 May 1909   CENTRE FORWARD
Caps: 1   Goals: 0
Only cap: 18 May 1935 v Holland 1–0   aged 25yr 354d
England career: P1 W1 D0 L0 – 100%
Club: West Bromwich Albion

Signed himself WG Richardson (G for 'Ginger') to avoid confusion with the other William Richardson playing for West Brom at the same time; in the 1931 FA Cup Final for instance, in which Billy G scored twice.

STANLEY
RICKABY

b 12 Mar 1924   RIGHT BACK

Caps: 1 Goals: 0
Only cap: 11 Nov 1953 v N Ireland 3–1   aged 29yr 244d
England career: P1 W1 D0 L0 – 100%
Club: West Bromwich Albion
Brief alternative to RAMSEY.

ARTHUR
RIGBY

b 7 Jun 1900   d 25 Mar 1960   INSIDE LEFT
Caps: 5 Goals: 3
First cap: 2 Apr 1927 v Scotland 2–1   aged 26yr 299d
Last cap: 28 Nov 1927 v Wales 1–2   aged 27yr 174d
England career: 0yr 240d – P5 W4 D0 L1 – 80%
Club: Blackburn Rovers
2 Goals in a game: 1

Went to Hampden as part of a very inexperienced team: Willis EDWARDS had won four
caps, the rest three or less. DEAN's goals
snatched unexpected victory and kept much the
same team together for the tour to Belgium, Luxembourg and France. Rigby scored twice in Brussels in a 9–1 win, and three minutes from time
against France (see G BROWN).

ELLIS
JAMES
RIMMER

b 2 Jan 1907   d 16 Mar 1965   OUTSIDE LEFT
Caps: 4 Goals: 2
First cap: 5 Apr 1930 v Scotland 5–2   aged 23yr 93d
                                         (2 goals)
Last cap: 9 Dec 1931 v Spain 7–1   aged 24yr 341d
England career: 1yr 248d – P4 W2 D2 L0 – 75%
Club: Sheffield Wednesday

Two new wingers came together for the match
against Scotland: Sammy CROOKS, who made
the first four goals, and tall powerful Ellis
Rimmer, who scored in each half (and twice in
the 1935 FA Cup Final).

JOHN
JAMES
RIMMER

b 10 Feb 1948   GOALKEEPER
Caps: 1 Goals conceded: 2
Only cap: 28 May 1976 v Italy 3–2
                                  aged 28yr 108d
                                        (sub'd HT)
England career: P1 W1 D0 L0 – 100%
Club: Arsenal
Started but didn't finish his only England match
as well as the 1982 European Cup final.

GRAHAM
RIX

b 23 Oct 1957   LEFT-SIDED MIDFIELDER
Caps: 17 Goals: 0
First cap: 10 Sep 1980 v Norway 4–0   aged 22yr 322d
Last cap: 4 Apr 1984 v N Ireland 1–0   aged 26yr 163d
England career: 3yr 207d – P17 W8 D5 L4 – 61.76%
Club: Arsenal
Substitute: 5 Substituted: 1

Played just the second half against Holland in
1982, and played it well enough to be preferred
to HODDLE by Greenwood (and Don HOWE
. . .) for the World Cup in Spain, but was never
influential for England.

GEORGE
ROBB

b 1 Jun 1926   OUTSIDE LEFT
Caps: 1 Goals: 0
Only cap: 25 Nov 1953 v Hungary 3–6   aged 27yr 177d
England career: P1 W0 D0 L1 – 0%
Club: Tottenham Hotspur

The London press wanted him in. They got him
in and got FINNEY out. The Hungarians got him
too.

CHARLES
ROBERTS

b 6 Apr 1883   d 7 Aug 1939   CENTRE HALF
Caps: 3 Goals: 0
First cap: 25 Feb 1905 v Ireland 1–1   aged 21yr 325d
Last cap: 1 Apr 1905 v Scotland 1–0   aged 21yr 360d
England career: 0yr 35d – P3 W2 D1 L0 – 83.33%
Club: Manchester United

Vittorio Pozzo coached Italy to two World Cup
wins in the 1930s with a style of play that hinged
on hard-tackling but essentially attacking centre-
halves (the South Americans Luisito Monti and
Miguel Andreolo), the result of admiration for
and conversations with Charlie Roberts, one of
the great Edwardian players. Nobody disputes
that he would have rivalled WEDLOCK for the
centre-half spot and CROMPTON for the England captaincy if his campaigning activities
hadn't counted against him (he was a founder
member of the Players' Union). One of the early
selectorial travesties.

FRANK
ROBERTS

b 3 Apr 1893/94   d 23 May 1961
                      INSIDE RIGHT/CENTRE FORWARD
Caps: 4 Goals: 2
First cap: 8 Dec 1924 v Belgium 4–0
                                  aged 30/31yr 249d

Last cap: 21 May 1925 v France 3-2 aged 31/32yr 48d
England career: 0yr 164d – P4 W3 D0 L1 – 75%
Club: Manchester City
2 Goals in a game: 1

Stocky, heavy, good in the air, his two first-half goals in his second international were just enough to beat Wales. According to one French source, he ended his international career in goal after Fred FOX was injured in Paris. All English sources name Billy WALKER (who was after all Aston Villa's reserve keeper) as Fox's replacement.

GRAHAM
PAUL
ROBERTS

b 3 Jul 1959   CENTRAL DEFENDER
Caps: 5   Goals: 0
First cap: 28 May 1983 v N Ireland 0-0   aged 23yr 329d
Last cap: 2 Jun 1984 v USSR 0-2   aged 24yr 333d
England career: 1yr 05d – P5 W2 D1 L2 – 50%
Club: Tottenham Hotspur
Ouch.

HENRY
ROBERTS

b 1 Sep 1907   d Oct 1984   INSIDE RIGHT
Caps: 1   Goals: 1
Only cap: 16 May 1931 v Belgium 4-1   aged 23yr 257d
(1 goal)
England career: P1 W1 D0 L0 – 100%
Club: Millwall

By the time Harry Roberts won his cap, Millwall had moved up into the Second Division (see FORT, FOX, RH HILL).

HERBERT
ROBERTS

b 19 Feb 1905   d 19 Jun 1944   CENTRE FORWARD
Caps: 1   Goals: 0
Only cap: 28 Mar 1931 v Scotland 0-2   aged 26yr 38d
England career: P1 W0 D0 L1 – 0%
Club: Arsenal

Not the first stopper centre half (not even the first for Arsenal: see JD BUTLER), Herbie Roberts was probably the first to be able to do the job and nothing else – but he had a hard time against the prolific Jimmy McGrory, who scored the second goal at Hampden.

ROBERT
JOHN
ROBERTS

b Apr 1859   d 28 Oct 1929   GOALKEEPER

Caps: 3   Goals conceded: 2   Clean sheets: 1
First cap: 5 Feb 1887 v Ireland 7-0
aged 27yr 281-310d
Last cap: 15 Mar 1890 v Ireland 9-1
aged 30yr 319-348d
England career: 3yr 38d – P3 W3 D0 L0 – 100%
Club: West Bromwich Albion

Despite the 9-1 win, the selectors must have agreed with the Irish press, who 'didn't think much' of Bob Roberts. There was much of him to think about: at 6ft 4in he was England's tallest goalkeeper before CORRIGAN.

WILLIAM
THOMAS
ROBERTS

b 29 Nov 1898/99   d 13 Oct 1965
CENTRE FORWARD
Caps: 2   Goals: 2
First cap: 1 Nov 1923 v Belgium 2-2
aged 23/24yr 337d (1 goal)
Last cap: 3 Mar 1924 v Wales 1-2
aged 24/25yr 95d (1 goal)
England career: 0yr 123d – P2 W0 D1 L1 – 25%
Club: Preston North End

Having scored a late equaliser in Antwerp, Tommy Roberts put England ahead against Wales – and never played international football again.

JOHN
ROBINSON

b 10 Aug 1917   d 1979   INSIDE RIGHT
Caps: 4   Goals: 3
First cap: 20 May 1937 v Finland 8-0   aged 19yr 283d
(1 goal)
Last cap: 22 Oct 1938 v Wales 2-4   aged 21yr 73d
England career: 1yr 156d – P4 W2 D0 L2 – 50%
Club: Sheffield Wednesday
2 Goals in a game: 1

It used to be thought that Jackie Robinson was probably the youngest player ever to be capped by England (17 years 9 months), but he'd cut two years off his age before his transfer to Sunderland (the transfer fee was later reduced!)

Skilful and confident, he scored twice when England won 6-3 in Berlin in the Nazi Salute match of 1938.

JOHN
WILLIAM
ROBINSON
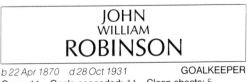

b 22 Apr 1870   d 28 Oct 1931   GOALKEEPER
Caps: 11   Goals conceded: 11   Clean sheets: 5
First cap: 20 Feb 1897 v Ireland 6-0   aged 26yr 304d
Last cap: 9 Mar 1901 v Ireland 3-0   aged 30yr 321d

England career: 4yr 17d – P11 W8 D1 L2 – 77.27%
Clubs: Derby County (2), New Brighton Tower (3),
   Southampton (6)
Penalties: 1   Missed: 1

Against Scotland in 1900, England were reduced to nine fit men and went 4–1 down before you could say Jack Robinson, who made save after save in a goalless second half. He was the first goalkeeper to win ten England caps and keep four clean sheets. Against Ireland in 1897 he came off his line when facing Bob Milne, who was duly distracted and missed the penalty 'by many yards'.

BRYAN
ROBSON

b 11 Jan 1957   MIDFIELDER
Caps: 89   Goals: 26   Captain: 65
First cap: 6 Feb 1980 v Eire 2–0   aged 23yr 26d
Last cap: 27 Mar 1991 v Eire 1–1   aged 34yr 75d
England career: 11yr 49d – P89 W45 D26 L18 – 65.17%
Clubs: West Bromwich Albion (13), Manchester United (76)
Substituted: 19   Goals while captain: 19
3 Goals in a game: 1   2 Goals in a game: 5
Penalties: 1   Missed: 0

First choice for England throughout the eighties (he was never a substitute) as captain as well as player (no-one else led the team out in his last 65 internationals), Bryan Robson's been one of the very best midfield players in the world for his tackling and above all his goals, an indecent total for a ball winner. Nineteen as captain (second only to WOODWARD), including two in Tel Aviv in his 50th international: goal of the season from HODDLE's cross and a very late winner from the penalty spot. His hat-trick in Istanbul in 1984 was the only one by an England captain between WOODWARD in 1909 and LINEKER in 1991.

Captain Marvel's injuries have always been the subject of ghoulish humour – he's suffered around 20 breaks or severe dislocations – but they cost England dear in two World Cups (the team reached the quarter-finals and semis without him, but can only have done better with). At his peak, probably as far back as the lead-up to the 1982 World Cup, he played in 19 consecutive matches, the first 16 without being substituted, scoring twice in each of two successive games, including those athletic goals against France in Bilbao. He scored three times in the first minute, including the fastest goal in the history of the World Cup finals (v France 1982) and the fastest in any senior match at Wembley (v Yugoslavia 1989).

Only WRIGHT and MOORE captained England more often; but for those famous injuries, their totals (and SHILTON's) would have come well within reach. A powerhouse.

ROBERT
WILLIAM
ROBSON

b 18 Feb 1933   INSIDE RIGHT/RIGHT HALF
Caps: 20   Goals: 4
First cap: 27 Nov 1957 v France 4–0   aged 24yr 302d
                                                      (2 goals)
Last cap: 9 May 1962 v Switzerland 3–1 aged 29yr 80d
England career: 4yr 202d – P20 W11 D7 L2 – 72.50%
Club: West Bromwich Albion
2 Goals in a game: 1

Having had two goals mysteriously disallowed in the 1958 World Cup in Sweden, Bobby Robson went to Chile in 1962, but his place had gone for ever to one RFC MOORE. The previous season, he'd been HAYNES' midfield partner in a team that averaged five goals a game. His eight years as England manager? The jury will probably always be out.

DAVID
ROCASTLE

b 2 May 1967   RIGHT-SIDED MIDFIELDER
Caps: 11   Goals: 0
First cap: 14 Sep 1988 v Denmark 1–0   aged 21yr 135d
Last cap: 15 May 1990 v Denmark 0–0   aged 23yr 13d
                                                      (sub 69min)
England career: 1yr 243d – P11 W7 D4 L0 – 81.82%
Club: Arsenal
Substitute: 4   Substituted: 2

Before being left out of the World Cup 22, he became only the third England player (see RUTHERFORD and BRIDGETT) to have an 11-match unbeaten career. He should come back, and the record should go.

WILLIAM CRISPIN
ROSE

b 1861   d 4 Feb 1937   GOALKEEPER
Caps: 5   Goals conceded: 4   Clean sheets: 1
First cap: 23 Feb 1884 v Ireland 8–1   aged 22/23
Last cap: 7 Mar 1891 v Ireland 6–1   aged 29/30
England career: 7yr 12d – P5 W4 D0 L1 – 80%
Clubs: Swifts (3), Preston NE (1), Wolves (1)

Didn't concede more than one goal in any of his England games, rare for the time. Had to wait 4 years 359 days for his last cap.

THURSTON
ROSTRON

b 21 Apr 1863   d 3 Jul 1891   FORWARD
Caps: 2   Goals: 0
First cap: 26 Feb 1881 v Wales 0–1   aged 17yr 311d
Last cap: 12 Mar 1881 v Scotland 1–6   aged 17yr 325d
England career: 0yr 14d – P2 W0 D0 L1 – 0%

Club: Darwen

If his date of birth is correct, Tot Rostron was one of two 17-year-olds to play for England (only PRINSEP was younger). He and J HARGREAVES appeared in the first defeat by Wales and the heaviest defeat at home. 'Tot' may be a diminutive of Thurston, or it may have something to do with size; he was 5ft 5in.

ARTHUR
SYDNEY
ROWE

b 1 Sep 1906   CENTRE HALF

Caps: 1   **Goals:** 0
Only cap: 6 Dec 1933 v France 4–1   aged 27yr 96d
England career: P1 W1 D0 L0 – 100%
Club: Tottenham Hotspur

Arthur Rowe, who managed the Spurs push-and-run Championship team of 1950–51, stopped the dangerous Jean Nicolas from scoring at White Hart Lane.

JOHN
FREDERICK
ROWLEY

b 7 Oct 1920   INSIDE RIGHT/LEFT/
CENTRE FORWARD/OUTSIDE LEFT

Caps: 6   **Goals:** 6
First cap: 2 Dec 1948 v Switzerland 6–0 aged 28yr 56d
                                              (1 goal)
Last cap: 5 Apr 1952 v Scotland 2–1   aged 31yr 181d
England career: 3yr 125d – P6 W5 D0 L1 – 83.33%
Club: Manchester United
4 Goals in a game: 1

Thrusting Jack Rowley, who played for England in four positions, was at centre forward when he scored four against N Ireland in 1949. All his goals came in his first three games.

WILLIAM
ROWLEY

b unknown   d unknown   GOALKEEPER

Caps: 2   **Goals conceded:** 1   **Clean sheets:** 1
First cap: 2 Mar 1889 v Ireland 6–1
Last cap: 5 Mar 1892 v Ireland 2–0
England career: 3yr 03d – P2 W2 D0 L0 – 100%
Club: Stoke FC
Penalties: 1   **Saved:** 1

In his last international, Bill Rowley played behind two full backs who were club colleagues (CLARE and UNDERWOOD) and saved the penalty Sam Torrans hit straight at him.

JOSEPH
(JOE)
ROYLE

b 8 Apr 1949   CENTRE FORWARD

Caps: 6   **Goals:** 2
First cap: 3 Feb 1971 v Malta 1–0   aged 21yr 301d
Last cap: 30 Mar 1977 v Luxembourg 5–0
                             aged 27yr 356d (sub'd HT)
England career: 6yr 55d – P6 W5 D1 L0 – 91.66%
Clubs: Everton (2), Manchester City (4)
Substitute: 1   **Substituted:** 1   **2 Goals in a game:** 0

Very strong in the air, folk hero at Everton then Oldham, not so for England.

HEROD
RUDDLESDIN

b 1876   d 26 Mar 1910   HALF BACK

Caps: 3   **Goals:** 0
First cap: 29 Feb 1904 v Wales 2–2   aged 27/28
Last cap: 1 Apr 1905 v Scotland 1–0   aged 28/29
England career: 1yr 32d – P3 W2 D1 L0 – 83.33%
Club: Sheffield Wednesday

Keith Farnsworth's *Sheffield Wednesday: A Complete Record* says he was sometimes known as Harry but also 'affectionally called Ruddy'. It also spells his christian name with two Rs, as does Richard Sparling's *Romance of the Wednesday* (1926). Whichever, name and christian name sit pretty well together.

JAMES
WILLIAM
RUFFELL

b 8 Aug 1900   d 5 (6?) Sep 1989   OUTSIDE LEFT

Caps: 6   **Goals:** 0
First cap: 17 Apr 1926 v Scotland 0–1   aged 25yr 252d
Last cap: 20 Nov 1929 v Wales 6–0   aged 29yr 104d
England career: 3yr 217d – P6 W3 D1 L2 – 58.33%
Club: West Ham United

Goals were expected from hard-shooting Jimmy Ruffell. None at all in a 6–0 win was probably the last straw.

BRUCE
BREMNER
RUSSELL

b 25 Aug 1859   d 13 May 1942   LEFT BACK

Caps: 1   **Goals:** 0
Only cap: 3 Feb 1883 v Wales 5–0   aged 23yr 162d
England career: P1 W1 D0 L0 – 100%
Club: Royal Engineers (and Corinthians)

Had little to do while Clem MITCHELL was scoring a hat-trick at the Oval.

JOHN
RUTHERFORD

b 12 Oct 1884   d 21 Apr 1963   OUTSIDE RIGHT
Caps: 11   Goals: 3
First cap: 9 Apr 1904 v Scotland 1–0   aged 19yr 179d
Last cap: 13 Jun 1908 v Bohemia 4–0   aged 23yr 244d
                                                              (1 goal)
England career: 4yr 65d – P11 W8 D3 L0 – 86.36%
Club: Newcastle United
2 Goals in a game: 0

Jock Rutherford had to wait three seasons for his second international, then played in the next ten. He went without a goal in his first eight games, then scored in the last three, all against European opposition. Of the players who never appeared in a losing England team, he (and later BRIDGETT and ROCASTLE) played in the most matches, for one of the most successful of all England careers. Playing seven times against weak continental teams helped.

DAVID
SADLER

b 5 Feb 1946   CENTRE HALF/MIDFIELD
Caps: 4   Goals: 0
First cap: 22 Nov 1967 v N Ireland 2–0   aged 21yr 290d
Last cap: 25 Nov 1970 v E Germany 3–1 aged 24yr 293d
England career: 3yr 03d – P4 W3 D1 L0 – 87.50%
Club: Manchester United
Substitute: 1

Versatile. Not great but not bad, especially at centre half.

CHARLES
SAGAR

b 28 Mar 1878   d 4 Dec 1919
                     INSIDE LEFT/CENTRE FORWARD
Caps: 2   Goals: 1
First cap: 17 Mar 1900 v Ireland 2–0   aged 21yr 355d
                                                              (1 goal)
Last cap: 3 Mar 1902 v Wales 0–0   aged 23yr 340d
England career: 1yr 351d – P2 W1 D1 L0 – 75%
Club: Bury

Charlie Sagar paid the price when England failed to score for the first time in 53 matches.

EDWARD
SAGAR

b 7 Feb 1910   d 16 Oct 1986   GOALKEEPER
Caps: 4   Goals conceded: 7   Clean sheets: 0
First cap: 19 Oct 1935 v Ireland 3–1   aged 25yr 254d
Last cap: 9 May 1936 v Belgium 2–3   aged 26yr 92d
England career: 0yr 203d – P4 W1 D1 L2 – 37.50%
Club: Everton
Penalties: 1   Saved: 0

Agile, long-serving Ted Sagar filled some of the gap between HIBBS and WOODLEY. Although he went the right way, Tommy Walker beat him with a famous equalising penalty at Wembley after the ball had twice been blown off the spot.

JOHN
SALAKO

b 11 Feb 1969   OUTSIDE LEFT
Caps: 4   Goals: 0
First cap: 1 Jun 1991 v Australia 1–0   aged 22yr 110d
                                                              (sub HT)
Last cap: 12 Jun 1991 v Malaysia 4–2   aged 22yr 121d
England career: 0yr 11d – P4 W4 D0 L0 – 100%
Club: Crystal Palace
Substitute: 2

Late addition to (and revelation of) England's summer tour: two goals created, the woodwork struck twice.

EDWARD A
SANDFORD

b 22 Oct 1910   INSIDE LEFT
Caps: 1   Goals: 0
Only cap: 16 Nov 1932 v Wales 0–0   aged 22yr 25d
England career: P1 W0 D1 L0 – 50%
Club: West Bromwich Albion

The entire centre-left of the England attack was dropped after the match at Wrexham.

RUPERT RENORDEN
SANDILANDS

b 7 Aug 1868   d 20 Apr 1946   OUTSIDE LEFT
Caps: 5   Goals: 3
First cap: 5 Mar 1892 v Wales 2–0   aged 23yr 211d
                                                              (1 goal)
Last cap: 16 Mar 1896 v Wales 9–1   aged 27yr 222d
England career: 4yr 11d – P5 W4 D1 L0 – 90%
Club: Old Westminsters (and Corinthians)
2 Goals in a game: 0

'The brilliant [but "in and out"] Old Westminster sprinter' won a single cap every year – and was dropped after being the only forward not to score against Wales, having been given very little of the ball.

JOHN
SANDS

b 1859   d 29 Feb 1924   GOALKEEPER
Caps: 1   Goals conceded: 2
Only cap: 15 Mar 1880 v Wales 3–2   aged 20/21
England career: P1 W1 D0 L0 – 100%
Club: Nottingham Forest

Wales pulled two goals back and ended the England careers of all three defenders.

KENNETH
GRAHAM
SANSOM

b 26 Sep 1958   LEFT BACK
Caps: 86   Goals: 1
First cap: 23 May 1979 v Wales 0–0   aged 20yr 239d
Last cap: 18 Jun 1988 v USSR 1–3   aged 29yr 265d
England career: 9yr 26d – P86 W44 D20 L22 – 62.79%
Clubs: Crystal Palace (9), Arsenal (77)
Substitute: 1   Substituted: 3
Short and stocky, very good coming forward, for a while one of the best in Europe, Kenny Sansom (*below*) had no real competition at home. England's most capped full back, he played in 37 consecutive internationals 1984–87.

FRANK
ETHERIDGE
SAUNDERS

b 26 Aug 1864   *d 14 May 1905*   HALF BACK

Caps: 1   Goals: 0
Only cap: 4 Feb 1888 v Wales 5–1   aged 23yr 162d
England career: P1 W1 D0 L0 – 100%
Club: Swifts (and Corinthians)
One of seven new caps in a match England were actually lucky to win.

AH
SAVAGE

b unknown   *d unknown*   GOALKEEPER
Caps: 1   Goals conceded: 3
Only cap: 4 Mar 1876 v Scotland 0–3
England career: P1 W0 D0 L1 – 0%
Club: Crystal Palace (and/or Rugby)
One of the most stubbornly obscure England players of all time (see **A HARVEY**). He may have been Arthur Harold Savage, or Arthur Henry Savage, or even the Arthur Henry Parick Savage born in Sydney 18 Oct 1850, died 15 Aug 1905. Since some reports apparently list his initials as AHP, the Australian's favourite. Whichever he was, he was big and red-bearded. The *Glasgow*

Evening News described him as 'a portly, Falstaff figure'.

JAMES
SAYER

b 1862   d 1 Feb 1922   OUTSIDE RIGHT
Caps: 1   **Goals:** 0
Only cap: 5 Feb 1887 v Ireland 7–0   *aged 24/25*
England career: P1 W1 D0 L0 – 100%
Club: Stoke FC

Clever and very quick, Jimmy Sayer might have won more caps but for the excellence of Joe LOFTHOUSE.

ERNALD
OAK
SCATTERGOOD

b 29 May 1887   d 2 Jul 1932   GOALKEEPER
Caps: 1   **Goals conceded:** 3
Only cap: 17 Mar 1913 v Wales 4–3   *aged 25yr 292d*
England career: P1 W1 D0 L0 – 100%
Club: Derby County

Short, well-respected, he was inevitably known as Ernie, but the full set of three makes a ripe mouthful.

JOSEPH
ALFRED
SCHOFIELD

b 1 Jan 1871   d 29 Sep 1929   LEFT-SIDED FORWARD
Caps: 3   **Goals:** 1
First cap: 5 Mar 1892 v Wales 2–0   *aged 21yr 64d*
Last cap: 9 Mar 1895 v Ireland 9–0   *aged 24yr 68d*
England career: 3yr 04d – P3 W3 D0 L0 – 100%
Club: Stoke FC

Like SANDILANDS the following year, Joe Schofield was dropped after being the only forward not to score in a nine-goal performance.

LAWRENCE
SCOTT

b 23/24 Apr 1917   RIGHT BACK
Caps: 17   **Goals:** 0
First cap: 28 Sep 1946 v N Ireland 7–2
        aged 29yr 157/158d
Last cap: 10 Nov 1948 v Wales 1–0
        aged 31yr 200/201d
England career: 2yr 43d – P17 W13 D3 L1 – 85.29%
Club: Arsenal

Smiling Laurie, a hard fast full back who played in England's first 17 matches after the War, lost his place after being injured early on against Wales.

WILLIAM
REED
SCOTT

b 6 Dec 1907   d 18 Oct 1969
INSIDE RIGHT
Caps: 1   **Goals:** 0
Only cap: 17 Oct 1936 v Wales 1–2   *aged 28yr 316d*
England career: P1 W0 D0 L1 – 0%
Club: Brentford

Brentford were in the First Division when Bill Scott was capped.

DAVID
ANDREW
SEAMAN

b 19 Sep 1963   GOALKEEPER
Caps: 7   **Goals conceded:** 5   **Clean sheets:** 3
First cap: 16 Nov 1988 v Saudi Arabia 1–1
        aged 25yr 58d
Last cap: 25 May 1991 v Argentina 2–2   *aged 27yr 248d*
England career: 2yr 190d – P7 W3 D4 L0 – 71.43%
Clubs: Queen's Park Rangers (3), Arsenal (4)
Substitute: 2

David Seaman won his third cap courtesy of his rival Chris WOODS, who cut a finger on a penknife while wrestling with the waistband of his tracksuit.

JAMES
SEDDON

b 20 May 1895   d 21 Oct 1971   CENTRE HALF
Caps: 6   **Goals:** 0
First cap: 10 May 1923 v France 4–1   *aged 27yr 355d*
Last cap: 13 Apr 1929 v Scotland 0–1   *aged 33yr 327d*
England career: 5yr 337d – P6 W3 D2 L1 – 66.66%
Club: Bolton Wanderers

Of the Bolton team that won the first Wembley FA Cup Final in 1923, one (Ted Vizard) was a Welsh international, and six played for England: W BUTLER, JACK, NUTTALL, PYM, J SMITH – and fearsomely strong Jimmy Seddon, who also played in the 1926 and 1929 Finals and was captain in the last.

JAMES
MARSHALL
SEED

b 25 Mar 1895   d 16 Jul 1966   INSIDE RIGHT
Caps: 5   **Goals:** 1
First cap: 21 May 1921 v Belgium 2–0   *aged 26yr 57d*
Last cap: 4 Apr 1925 v Scotland 0–2   *aged 30yr 10d*
England career: 3yr 318d – P5 W3 D1 L1 – 70%
Club: Tottenham Hotspur

Jimmy Seed came back from being gassed in the

First World War to play his fit, intelligent game and score in England's first home match against a foreign team (6–1 Belgium 1923). Later manager of Charlton, he died on the day England beat Mexico in the World Cup.

JAMES
SETTLE

b 1875/76   INSIDE LEFT
Caps: 6   Goals: 6
First cap: 18 Feb 1899 v Ireland 13–2   aged 22–24
                                                (3 goals)
Last cap: 14 Feb 1903 v Ireland 4–0   aged 26–28
England career: 3yr 361d – P6 W5 D1 L0 – 91.66%
Clubs: Bury (3), Everton (3)
3 Goals in a game: 1   2 Goals in a game: 0

Small, pushy and very quick, Jimmy Settle was the last player to score a hat-trick on his England debut till F BRADSHAW in 1908.

JOHN
SEWELL

b 24 Jan 1927   INSIDE RIGHT/LEFT
Caps: 6   Goals: 3
First cap: 14 Nov 1951 v N Ireland 2–0   aged 24yr 294d
Last cap: 23 May 1954 v Hungary 1–7   aged 27yr 119d
England career: 2yr 190d – P6 W3 D1 L2 – 58.33%
Club: Sheffield Wednesday
2 Goals in a game: 0

Jackie Sewell was having a nice little international career before the Hungarians came along. They were the opponents in his last two matches. Still, he managed an early equaliser against them at Wembley, a temporary finger in the dyke.

WALTER
RONALD
SEWELL

b 19 Jul 1890   d 4 Feb 1945   GOALKEEPER
Caps: 1   Goals conceded: 2
Only cap: 3 Mar 1924 v Wales 1–2   aged 33yr 228d
England career: P1 W0 D0 L1 – 0%
Club: Blackburn Rovers

Capped 10 years after winning an FA Cup medal with Burnley. In the 1972 Farror–Lamming book, his first name's William. Either way, he was certainly known as Ronnie.

LEONARD
FRANCIS
SHACKLETON

b 3 May 1922   INSIDE LEFT
Caps: 5   Goals: 1
First cap: 26 Sep 1948 v Denmark 0–0   aged 26yr 146d

Last cap: 1 Dec 1954 v W Germany 3–1 aged 32yr 182d
                                                (1 goal)
England career: 6yr 36d – P5 W4 D1 L0 – 90%
Club: Sunderland

Clown Prince Len had to wait five years for his fourth international, scored a dazzling goal against the world champions in his fifth, and was never picked again; another instalment of Selectors v Genius. Actually, the facts spoil a good story. The goal doesn't look so very remarkable on the screen – a straight run through on the 'keeper – and, for all the ball juggling and arrogance, how good a team player was he? Whose place would he have taken in an England team? Talent to burn, for sure, but how much up in smoke? Still, anyone who writes an autobiography that includes a blank page for a chapter on The Average Director's Knowledge of Football is one of the good guys in any fan's book. Flair on and off the pitch.

JOHN
SHARP

b 15 Feb 1878   d 27 Jan 1938 INSIDE/OUTSIDE RIGHT
Caps: 2   Goals: 1
First cap: 14 Feb 1903 v Ireland 4–0   aged 24yr 364d
                                                (1 goal)
Last cap: 1 Apr 1905 v Scotland 1–0   aged 27yr 45d
England career: 2yr 46d – P2 W2 D0 L0 – 100%
Club: Everton

Jack Sharp played Test cricket three times against Australia in 1909. He scored a goal in his first international and a century in his last.

LEE
STUART
SHARPE

b 27 May 1971   OUTSIDE LEFT
Caps: 1   Goals: 0
Only cap: 27 Mar 1991 v Eire 1–1 aged 19yr 304d (sub HT)
England career: P1 W0 D1 L0 – 50%
Club: Manchester United

Fair skills, youthful pace; Graham Taylor's first bright young thing.

GEORGE
EDWARD
SHAW

b 13 Oct 1899/1900   d Mar 1973   RIGHT BACK
Caps: 1   Goals: 0
Only cap: 9 Apr 1932 v Scotland 3–2   aged 31/32yr 179d
England career: P1 W1 D0 L0 – 100%
Club: West Bromwich Albion

If he *was* born in 1899, George Shaw, not JW

SMITH, was the last player born in the 19th century to play for England.

GRAHAM L

SHAW

b 9 Jul 1934   LEFT BACK
Caps: 5   Goals: 0
First cap: 22 Oct 1958 v USSR 5–0   aged 24yr 105d
Last cap: 21 Nov 1962 v Wales 4–0   aged 28yr 135d
England career: 4yr 30d – P5 W3 D2 L0 – 80%
Club: Sheffield United
Powerful full back who deserved the caps he won before (one after) the arrival of Ray WILSON and McNEIL.

DANIEL
SHEA

b 6 Nov 1887   d 25 Dec 1960   INSIDE RIGHT
Caps: 2   Goals: 0
First cap: 14 Feb 1914 v Ireland 0–3   aged 26yr 100d
Last cap: 16 Mar 1914 v Wales 2–0   aged 26yr 130d
England career: 0yr 30d – P2 W1 D0 L1 – 50%
Club: Blackburn Rovers
A quick, chunky, hard-shooting inside forward, Danny Shea had Irish parents and made his debut against Ireland when they scored their only three-goal win over England.

KENNETH J

SHELLITO

b 18 Apr 1940   RIGHT BACK
Caps: 1   Goals: 0
Only cap: 29 May 1963 v Czechoslovakia   aged 23yr 41d
England career: P1 W1 D0 L0 – 100%
Club: Chelsea
A bad injury in October 1963 stopped Ken Shellito from challenging COHEN for ARMFIELD's place.

ALFRED
SHELTON

b 11 Sep 1865   d 24 Jul 1923   HALF BACK
Caps: 6   Goals: 1
First cap: 2 Mar 1889 v Ireland 6–1   aged 23yr 172d
(1 goal)
Last cap: 2 Apr 1892 v Scotland 4–1   aged 26yr 203d
England career: 3yr 31d – P6 W5 D1 L0 – 91.66%
Club: Notts County
Charlie SHELTON's brother Alf was brought in as a replacement and stayed for the next three years.

CHARLES
SHELTON

b 22 Jan 1864   d 1899   HALF BACK
Caps: 1   Goals: 0
Only cap: 7 Apr 1888 v Ireland 5–1   aged 24yr 76d
England career: P1 W1 D0 L0 – 100%
Club: Notts Rangers
Came into a strong England team that scored five in each of three matches that season.

ALBERT
SHEPHERD

b 10 Sep 1885   d 8 Nov 1929   CENTRE FORWARD
Caps: 2   Goals: 2
First cap: 7 Apr 1906 v Scotland 1–2   aged 20yr 209d
(1 goal)
Last cap: 11 Feb 1911 v Ireland 2–1   aged 25yr 154d
(1 goal)
England career: 4yr 310d – P2 W1 D0 L1 – 50%
Clubs: Bolton Wanderers (1), Newcastle United (1)
The big gap between caps is explained by a poor game against Scotland (the goal came too late to matter), yet Charlie BUCHAN thought him the best centre forward before 1925: 'fast, fearless, and a born leader.'

PETER
LESLIE

SHILTON

b 18 Sep 1949   GOALKEEPER
Caps: 125   Goals conceded: 80   Clean sheets: 66
Captain: 15
First cap: 25 Nov 1970 v E Germany 3–1 aged 21yr 68d
Last cap: 7 Jul 1990 v Italy 1–2   aged 40yr 292d
England career: 19yr 224d – P125 W66 D35 L24 – 66.80%
Clubs: Leicester City (20), Stoke City (3), Nottingham
Forest (19), Southampton (49), Derby County (34)
Substituted: 15
Penalties: 15   Saved: 1   Missed: 1
They don't come any more ambitious – or much better. The Shilts set out to become the best of all time, and came as close as makes no difference, scooping up most of the England goalkeeping records on the way – most matches, clean sheets, captaincies – and coming second only to S MATTHEWS in terms of age and length of career.

He's Europe's most capped player. He played 11 times against N Ireland, 10 against Scotland. In the World Cup, he played 17 times in the final stages, a British record; kept 10 clean sheets, the record for any country; and went 499 (some say 500) minutes without conceding a goal, overtaken only by Italy's Zenga with the help of a Czech goal wrongly disallowed. Captain in his last match, he was England's oldest ever.

His figures would be even more impressive but for the number of penalties he had to face, far more than any other England goalkeeper. In 1985 he saved from Andreas Brehme (who had his revenge in the World Cup semi-final) and in 1986 Aleksandr Chivadze hit a post.

One of the few records he missed out on was BANKS' 7 consecutive matches without conceding a goal – but he came mightily close, twice reaching 6 in a row, once 5, twice 4. Oddly enough his best statistics came at a time when his form was beginning to ebb: only 4 goals conceded in 16 matches 1988–89, helped by playing less than a full match several times, often substituted by WOODS. But back in 1983, he deserved figures of only two goals in 9 games: an own goal and a penalty. And in his Forest days there were times when it was hard to believe anyone had ever kept goal better (above all his display against Czechoslovakia on a frozen Wembley pitch). But for REVIE, who only picked him three times, and Greenwood's oddball rotation of him and CLEMENCE, who knows how many caps it could have been? Should have been. One of the great, driven, players.

EDMUND
SHIMWELL

b 27 Feb 1920   d Oct 1988   **RIGHT BACK**
Caps: 1   **Goals:** 0
Only cap: 13 May 1949 v Sweden 1–3   aged 29yr 75d
England career: P1 W0 D0 L1 – 0%
Club: Blackpool

Eddie Shimwell was a little unlucky; the Swedes played with the sun behind them in the first half and took a 3–0 lead. ELLERINGTON then came in at right back for the two easier matches on the tour.

GEORGE
SHUTT

b 1861   d 1936   **HALF BACK**
Caps: 1   **Goals:** 0
Only cap: 13 Mar 1886 v Ireland 6–1   aged 24/25
England career: P1 W1 D0 L0 – 100%
Club: Stoke FC

Replaced NC Bailey in the team, *The Sportsman* says as captain as well as player Most say PM WALTERS.

JOHN
SILCOCK

b 15 Jan 1897/98   d 28 Jun 1966   **LEFT BACK**
Caps: 3   **Goals:** 0

First cap: 14 Mar 1921 v Wales 0–0   aged 23/24yr 57d
Last cap: 24 May 1923 v Sweden 3–1 aged 25/26yr 128d
England career: 2yr 71d – P3 W1 D1 L1 – 50%
Club: Manchester United

A gutsy full back, Jack Silcock was one of seven England debutants at Ninian Park.

RICHARD
PETER
SILLETT

b 1 Feb 1933   **RIGHT BACK**
Caps: 3   **Goals:** 0
First cap: 15 May 1955 v France 0–1   aged 22yr 103d
Last cap: 22 May 1955 v Portugal 1–3   aged 22yr 110d
England career: 0yr 07d – P3 W0 D1 L2 – 16.66%
Club: Chelsea

Big Peter's penalty, the only goal of the game against Wolves, won the League title. A month later in Paris, his foul on Jean Vincent resulted in the Raymond Kopa penalty that beat England.

ERNEST
SIMMS

b 23 Jun 1891/92   d late 1971   **CENTRE FORWARD**
Caps: 1   **Goals:** 0
Only cap: 22 Oct 1921 v Ireland 1–1   aged 29/30yr 121d
England career: P1 W0 D1 L0 – 50%
Club: Luton Town

Ernie Simms was the second in a spate of Third Division players who played for England in the early twenties.

JOHN
SIMPSON

b 25 Dec 1885   d 4 Jan 1959   **OUTSIDE RIGHT**
Caps: 8   **Goals:** 1
First cap: 11 Feb 1911 v Ireland 2–1   aged 25yr 48d
Last cap: 16 Mar 1914 v Wales 4–3   aged 28yr 81d
England career: 3yr 33d – P8 W6 D2 L0 – 87.50%
Club: Blackburn Rovers

Born of Scottish parents, Jock Simpson won all his caps with clubmate Bob CROMPTON as captain.

WILLIAM
JOHN
SLATER

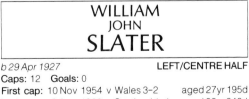

b 29 Apr 1927   **LEFT/CENTRE HALF**
Caps: 12   **Goals:** 0
First cap: 10 Nov 1954 v Wales 3–2   aged 27yr 195d
Last cap: 9 Apr 1960 v Scotland 1–1   aged 32yr 346d
England career: 5yr 151d – P12 W5 D5 L2 – 62.50%
Club: Wolves

Wolves provided the England half-back line in the 1958 World Cup: CLAMP, WA WRIGHT, and tall, clever Bill Slater, who was recalled at centre half for the match at Hampden.

TOM

SMALLEY

b 13 Jan 1912   d 12 Apr 1984   **RIGHT HALF**
Caps: 1   Goals: 0
Only cap: 17 Oct 1936 v Wales 1–2   *aged 24yr 278d*
England career: P1 W0 D0 L1 – 0%
Club: Wolves

Did well to win even one cap with the likes of CRAYSTON and BRITTON around.

THOMAS
SMART

b 20 Sep 1896/97   d Jun 1968   **RIGHT BACK**
Caps: 5   Goals: 0
First cap: 9 Apr   1921 v Scotland 0–3
                                      aged 23/24yr 201d
Last cap: 20 Nov 1929 v Wales 6–0   *aged 32/33yr ¨61d*
England career: 8yr 225d – P5 W1 D2 L2 – 40%
Club: Aston Villa

In true twenties fashion, big powerful Tommy Smart had to wait four years for his last cap.

ALAN
MARTIN

SMITH

b 21 Nov 1962   **CENTRE FORWARD**
Caps: 7   Goals: 1
First cap: 16 Nov 1988 v Saudi Arabia 1–1
                              aged 25yr 361d (sub 68min)
Last cap: 25 May 1991 v Argentina 2–2 *aged 28yr 185d*
England career: 2yr 190d – P7 W5 D2 L0 – 85.71%
Club: Arsenal
Substitute: 3   Substituted: 1

Brought back after another successful club season to resume his old Leicester partnership with LINEKER in Turkey, where he hit the bar and generally did some good things, then scored his first England goal three weeks later against the USSR.

ALBERT
SMITH

b 23 Jul 1869   d 18 Apr 1921   **RIGHT HALF**
Caps: 3   Goals: 0
First cap: 7 Mar 1891 v Wales 4–1   *aged 21yr 227d*
Last cap: 25 Feb 1893 v Ireland 6–1   *aged 23yr 217d*
England career: 1yr 355d – P3 W3 D0 L0 – 100%
Club: Nottingham Forest

Made up a strong half back line in his first two internationals with HOLT and Alf SHELTON.

BERT

SMITH

b 7 Mar 1892   d Sep 1969   **RIGHT HALF**
Caps: 2   Goals: 0
First cap: 9 Apr   1921 v Scotland 0–3   *aged 29yr 33d*
Last cap: 13 Mar 1922 v Wales 1–0   *aged 30yr 06d*
England career: 0yr 338d – P2 W1 D0 L1 – 50%
Club: Tottenham Hotspur

Had a bad time against a Scots left-wing triangle that scored a goal apiece.

CHARLES
EASTLAKE

SMITH

b 1850   d 10 Jan 1917   **FORWARD**
Caps: 1   Goals: 0
Only cap: 4 Mar 1876 v Scotland 0–3   *aged 25/26*
England career: P1 W0 D0 L1 – 0%
Club: Crystal Palace (and Wanderers)

Another who played for the old Crystal Palace, not the present club. GO SMITH was his cousin.

GILBERT OSWALD

SMITH

b 25 Nov 1872   d 6 Dec 1943   **CENTRE FORWARD**
Caps: 20   Goals: 11   Captain: 14 (16?)
First cap: 25 Feb 1893 v Ireland 6–1   *aged 20yr 92d*
                                                  (1 goal)
Last cap: 30 Mar 1901 v Scotland 2–2   *aged 28yr 125d*
England career: 8yr 33d – P20 W14 D3 L3 – 77.50%
Clubs: Oxford University and Old Carthusians (7),
        Old Carthusians alone (13); Corinthians throughout.
4 Goals in a game: 1   3 Goals in a game: 0
2 Goals in a game: 1   Goals while captain: 7

Thin, slowish, play-making centre forward with a good football brain behind a rather sour face, GO Smith was considered 'only a moderate performer' by the Scots but generally admired by selection committees as well as reporters and fellow players; the first to be capped 20 times by England, the first to play 10 consecutive matches, the first to captain England 10 times in a row. He was the first of only four players to score a hat-trick while captain (before WOODWARD, B ROBSON and LINEKER), though it was said that he needed 'to finish with a little more devil' and his shooting was even described (v Scotland 1896) as 'feeble'. Captain in his last 14 (or 16) internationals, he had a fine career for someone who suffered so badly from asthma.

HERBERT

SMITH

b 22 Nov 1879   d 6 Jan 1951   **LEFT BACK**

Caps: 4   **Goals:** 0
First cap: 27 Mar 1905 v Wales 3–1   aged 25yr 125d
Last cap: 19 Mar 1906 v Wales 1–0   aged 26yr 117d
England career: 0yr 357d – P4 W4 D0 L0 – 100%
Club: Reading

Big and good, a respected amateur. 'Smokes moderately', they said.

JAMES CHRISTOPHER
REGINALD
SMITH

b 20 Jan 1912   OUTSIDE LEFT
Caps: 2   **Goals:** 2
First cap: 9 Nov 1938 v Norway 4–0   aged 26yr 293d
          (2 goals)
Last cap: 16 Nov 1938 v Ireland 7–0   aged 26yr 300d
England career: 0yr 07d – P2 W2 D0 L0 – 100%
Club: Millwall

The left-wing pair of Smith and JE STEPHEN-SON hardly got a look in while Stanley MATTHEWS and Willie HALL were destroying the Irish at Old Trafford, but Reg had scored twice in the first half hour of his debut. His father was a South African called Schmidt; the name was changed when Germany were the opposition.

JOHN
WILLIAM
SMITH

b 28 Oct 1898   *d 19 Jan 1977*   INSIDE RIGHT
Caps: 3   **Goals:** 4
First cap: 17 Oct 1931 v Ireland 6–2   aged 32yr 354d
          (1 goal)
Last cap: 9 Dec 1931 v Spain 7–1   aged 33yr 42d
          (2 goals)
England career: 0yr 53d – P3 W3 D0 L0 – 100%
Club: Portsmouth
2 Goals in a game: 1

They let Jack Smith get hungry for a cap, fed him three in a row, and watched him gobble the goals: after just 10 minutes of his debut, after just three in his last match, at least one in every game; three easy wins out of three. His brother SC SMITH also played for England, but was never so voracious.

He may have been the last player born in the 19th century to play for England. See GE SHAW.

JOSEPH
SMITH

b 25 Jun 1889   *d 11 Aug 1971*   INSIDE LEFT
Caps: 5   **Goals:** 1
First cap: 15 Feb 1913 v Ireland 1–2   aged 23yr 235d
Last cap: 15 Mar 1920 v Wales 1–2   aged 30yr 264d
England career: 7yr 29d – P5 W1 D1 L3 – 30%
Club: Bolton Wanderers

By reputation one of the hardest shots of all time, Joe Smith lost 5 years 204 days of his international career to the First World War. His last match was the first Wales had won against England since 1882. He was Bolton's captain in 1923 when they won the first FA Cup Final staged at Wembley.

JOSEPH
SMITH

b 10 Apr 1890   *d 9 Jun 1956*   RIGHT BACK
Caps: 2   **Goals:** 2
First cap: 25 Oct 1919 v Ireland 1–1   aged 29yr 198d
Last cap: 21 Oct 1922 v Ireland 2–0   aged 32yr 194d
England career: 2yr 361d – P2 W1 D1 L0 – 75%
Club: West Bromwich Albion

Won his first cap alongside the other JOE SMITH.

LESLIE
GEORGE FREDERICK
SMITH

b 13 Mar 1918   OUTSIDE LEFT
Caps: 1   **Goals:** 0
Only cap: 24 May 1939 v Romania 2–0   aged 21yr 72d
England career: P1 W1 D0 L0 – 100%
Club: Brentford

Brentford were in the First Division when Leslie Smith was brought in, after an injury to Stanley MATTHEWS, as the only new cap in England's last match before the War.

LIONEL
SMITH

b 23 Aug 1920   LEFT BACK
Caps: 6   **Goals:** 0
First cap: 15 Nov 1950 v Wales 4–2   aged 30yr 84d
Last cap: 18 Apr 1953 v Scotland 2–2   aged 32yr 238d
England career: 2yr 154d – P6 W4 D2 L0 – 83.33%
Club: Arsenal

Lanky, long-legged centre half converted into full back late in life, with instant and surprising success. In internationals too.

ROBERT
ALFRED
SMITH

b 22 Feb 1933   CENTRE FORWARD
Caps: 15   **Goals:** 13
First cap: 8 Oct 1960 v N Ireland 5–2   aged 27yr 229d
          (1 goal)
Last cap: 20 Nov 1963 v N Ireland 8–3   aged 30yr 272d
          (1 goal)
England career: 3yr 43d – P15 W10 D2 L3 – 80%
Club: Tottenham Hotspur

Lionel Smith performs one of his last duties for England by kicking clear against the Scots at Wembley (Popperfoto)

2 Goals in a game: 4

Jimmy Greaves claimed Bobby Smith was more delicate and skilful than he looked. That's as may be – and one of his goals against Spain at Wembley was a clever lob – but it's hardly what goalkeepers will remember. A heavily-built man who enjoyed putting boot and head to ball, and shoulder to whatever got in the way of it, he scored in his first five internationals; he and GREAVES scored in seven together, giving them a share in the England record. He was on the winning side in his first five and last five matches.

SEPTIMUS
CHARLES
SMITH

b 13/15 Mar 1912   **RIGHT HALF**
Caps: 1   Goals: 0
Only cap: 19 Oct 1935 v Ireland 3–1   aged 23yr 218/220d
England career: P1 W1 D0 L0 – 100%
Club: Leicester City

JW SMITH was Sep's brother.

STEPHEN
SMITH

b 14 Jan 1874   d 19 May 1935   **OUTSIDE LEFT**
Caps: 1   Goals: 1
Only cap: 6 Apr 1895 v Scotland 3–0   aged 21yr 82d
England career: P1 W1 D0 L0 – 100%
Club: Aston Villa

One of Villa's best players while they won five League titles in seven seasons, Steve Smith sealed England's win over Scotland in the last minute of the first half. He was selected against Wales in 1901 (dropping out through injury) but was generally ignored by the selectors, a mystery to most professionals. It certainly wasn't because he was too old.

THOMAS
SMITH

b 5 Apr 1945   **MIDFIELDER**
Caps: 1   Goals: 0
Only cap: 19 May 1971 v Wales 0–0   aged 26yr 44d
England career: P1 W0 D1 L0 – 50%
Club: Liverpool

The French say there are two kinds of rugby player (three-quarters and forwards): those who play the piano, and those who shift it. RAMSEY hired some (STILES, STOREY, N HUNTER, even poor Tommy Smith) who kicked it to pieces.

TREVOR
SMITH

b 13 Apr 1936   **CENTRE HALF**
Caps: 2   Goals: 0
First cap: 17 Oct 1959 v Wales 1–1   aged 23yr 187d
Last cap: 28 Oct 1959 v Sweden 2–3   aged 23yr 198d
England career: 0yr 11d – P2 W0 D1 L1 – 25%
Club: Birmingham City

Played in the same two matches as Brian CLOUGH and had terrible trouble with Agne

Simonsson, a fine centre-forward who scored twice as Sweden became the second foreign country to win in England.

WILLIAM
HENRY

SMITH

b 23 May 1895   d 13 Apr 1951   **OUTSIDE LEFT**
Caps: 3   **Goals:** 0
First cap: 13 Mar 1922 v Wales 1–0   aged 26yr 294d
Last cap: 31 Mar 1928 v Scotland 1–5   aged 32yr 312d
England career: 6yr 18d – P3 W1 D0 L2 – 33.33%
Club: Huddersfield Town

Billy Smith, of the long legs and famous close control, had to wait 5 years 357 days for his last cap (par for the twenties course) then hit a post in the first few minutes. From the rebound, Scotland moved upfield, scored their first goal, and created the legend of the Wembley Wizards.

THOMAS HEATHCOTE
SORBY

b 16 Feb 1856   d 13 Dec 1930   **FORWARD**
Caps: 1   **Goals:** 1
Only cap: 18 Jan 1879 v Wales 2–1   aged 22yr 336d
(60min, 1 goal)

England career: P1 W1 D0 L0 – 100%
Club: Thursday Wanderers (Sheffield)

He and WHITFELD scored in their only international, England's first against Wales and the only England match to last only an hour because of snow.

JOHN
SOUTHWORTH

b Dec 1866   d 16 Oct 1956   **CENTRE FORWARD**
Caps: 3   **Goals:** 3
First cap: 23 Feb 1889 v Wales 4–1   aged 22yr 54–84d
(1 goal)
Last cap: 2 Apr 1892 v Scotland 4–1
aged 25yr 93–123d (1 goal)
England career: 3yr 39d – P3 W3 D0 L0 – 100%
Club: Blackburn Rovers

Jack Southworth, one of the leading strikers of his time, scored in each of his three internationals. He was selected to play at Celtic Park in 1894 but had to cry off, which probably suited the Scots: 'We have no centre within streets of Southworth.'

FRANCIS JOHN
SPARKS

b 4 Jul 1855   d 13 Feb 1934   **FORWARD**
Caps: 3   **Goals:** 3   **Captain:** 1

First cap: 5 Apr   1879 v Scotland 5–4   aged 23yr 275d
Last cap: 15 Mar   1880 v Wales 3–2   aged 24yr 254d
(2 goals)
England career: 0yr 344d – P3 W2 D0 L1 – 66.66%
Clubs: Hertfordshire Rangers (1), Clapham Rovers (2); possibly both at the same time.
2 Goals in a game: 1   **Goals while captain:** 2

After a goalless first half, he put England 2–0 and then 3–0 ahead before the Welsh pulled two goals back.

JOSEPH
WALTER

SPENCE

b 15 Dec 1895/98   d 31 Dec 1966   **OUTSIDE RIGHT**
Caps: 2   **Goals:** 1
First cap: 24 May 1926 v Belgium 5–3 aged 27/30yr 160d
Last cap: 20 Oct 1926 v Ireland 3–3   aged 27/30yr 309d
(1 goal)

England career: 0yr 149d – P2 W1 D1 L0 – 75%
Club: Manchester United

England equalised three times against the Irish at Anfield; Joe Spence scored the second. His cousin G BROWN played alongside him at inside right.

RICHARD
SPENCE

b 18 Jul 1908/13   d Mar 1983   **OUTSIDE RIGHT**
Caps: 2   **Goals:** 0
First cap: 6 May 1936 v Austria 1–2   aged 22/27yr 293d
Last cap: 9 May 1936 v Belgium 2–3 aged 22/27yr 296d
England career: 0yr 03d – P2 W0 D0 L2 – 0%
Club: Chelsea

Both wingers, HOBBIS and little Dicky Spence, played for England only on the 1936 summer tour.

CHARLES
WILLIAM

SPENCER

b 4 Dec 1899   d 9 Feb 1953   **CENTRE HALF**
Caps: 2   **Goals:** 0
First cap: 12 Apr 1924 v Scotland 1–1   aged 24yr 130d
Last cap: 28 Feb 1925 v Wales 2–1   aged 25yr 86d
England career: 0yr 322d – P2 W1 D1 L0 – 75%
Club: Newcastle United

Charlie Spencer and W BUTLER were the first players to make their England debuts at Wembley.

HOWARD

SPENCER

b 23 Aug 1875   d 14 Jan 1940   **LEFT/RIGHT BACK**
Caps: 6   **Goals:** 0   **Captain:** 3

First cap: 29 Mar 1897 v Wales 4–0 aged 21yr 218d
Last cap: 1 Apr 1905 v Scotland 1–0 aged 29yr 221d
England career: 8yr 03d – P6 W4 D1 L1 – 75%
Club: Aston Villa

Apparently the best full back in the country for a decade; fitter, more skilful, cleaner in the tackle than those of the WALTERS ilk and era. Captain in all three internationals in 1905.

FREDERICK
SPIKSLEY

b 25 Jan 1870 d 28 Jul 1948 **OUTSIDE LEFT**
Caps: 7 **Goals:** 5
First cap: 13 Mar 1893 v Wales 6–0 aged 23yr 47d
  (2 goals)
Last cap: 2 Apr 1898 v Scotland 3–1 aged 28yr 67d
England career: 5yr 20d – P7 W5 D2 L0 – 85.71%
Club: Sheffield Wednesday
2 Goals in a game: 2

Fred Spiksley was such a well-known player that it seems odd to find his name invariably spelt Spikesley in match reports (even in his own newspaper column). Both the Lamming books and the Sheffield Wednesday Complete Record leave out the first E, as did a leading amateur player RB Alaway, who apparently knew him personally.

However, Alaway also claims he saw him score three times 'in about ten minutes' against Scotland in 1893 – and certainly other sources also credit him with three (including the referee's report in the *Glasgow Evening News*). However, at least four contemporary match reports credit REYNOLDS with England's last goal, and *The Sportsman* says Spikesley 'very nearly' scored in the last minute, which is where the confusion may have taken root. He certainly scored two goals in two minutes in the same game.

Remarkably, one report credits him with three goals against Wales in the previous match, though *The Times* among others says only two. It's possible, then, that he was the first to score two hat-tricks in the same season and in successive matches for England, but probable that he didn't score even one!

Still, the point's been made: Fred Spiksley was an excellent finisher. He scored twice in each of his first two internationals, once in the third.

It seems he applied hot water to one of his knee joints then deliberately dislocated it so as to be certified unfit for active service in World War I. He was arrested in France in September 1914.

BENJAMIN
WARD
SPILSBURY

b 1 Aug 1864 d 15 Aug 1938 **INSIDE/OUTSIDE RIGHT**

Fred Spiksley – 5 goals in his first 3 internationals
(Lamming)

Caps: 3 **Goals:** 5
First cap: 28 Feb 1885 v Ireland 4–0 aged 20yr 211d
  (1 goal)
Last cap: 27 Mar 1886 v Scotland 1–1 aged 21yr 238d
England career: 1yr 27d – P3 W2 D1 L0 – 83.33%
Club: Cambridge University (and Derby County and Corinthians)
4 Goals in a game: 1

Scored four and had another disallowed against Ireland in 1886, but 'did not equal expectation' two weeks later at Hampden and was unavailable for the match against Wales after that.

NIGEL
PHILIP
SPINK

b 8 Aug 1958 **GOALKEEPER**
Caps: 1 **Goals conceded:** 0
Only cap: 19 Jun 1983 v Australia 1–1 aged 24yr 305d
England career: P1 W0 D1 L0 – 50% (sub HT)
Club: Aston Villa

Big and talented; SHILTON, and inconsistency, kept him out of the England team.

WILLIAM ALFRED SPOUNCER

b 1 Jul 1877   d 31 Aug 1962   OUTSIDE LEFT
Caps: 1   Goals: 0
Only cap: 26 Mar 1900 v Wales 1–1   aged 22yr 269d
England career: P1 W0 D1 L0 – 50%
Club: Nottingham Forest

Usually listed as A Spouncer, therefore probably known as Alf not Bill.

RONALD DERYK SPRINGETT

b 22 Jul 1935   GOALKEEPER
Caps: 33   Goals conceded: 48   Clean sheets: 7
First cap: 18 Nov 1959 v N Ireland 2–1   aged 24yr 119d
Last cap: 29 Jun 1966 v Norway 6–1   aged 30yr 342d
England career: 6yr 223d – P33 W17 D8 L8 – 63.63%
Club: Sheffield Wednesday
Penalties: 3   Saved: 2

Jimmy McIlroy gave the new goalkeeper a gift by hitting his penalty softly enough to save, after which England had an established No. 1 for the first time since MERRICK. Not that Big Ron had an easy time in internationals. Winterbottom's teams, designed to go forward, could have done with protecting their goalkeeper better, especially one who had a tendency to let in long-range goals that cost matches (v Hungary and Brazil in the 1962 World Cup, v Austria at Wembley in 1965). But he could stop them at close range: brilliantly from Vava in the same Brazil match, Oscar Montalvo's penalty in Lima (as far as records show, he was the only goalkeeper to save two penalties while playing for England). He even managed a few games – and saves – in the BANKS era.

BERT SPROSTON

b 22 Jun 1915   RIGHT BACK
Caps: 11   Goals: 0
First cap: 17 Oct 1936 v Wales 1–2   aged 21yr 117d
Last cap: 9 Nov 1938 v Norway 4–0   aged 23yr 140d
England career: 2yr 23d – P11 W7 D0 L4 – 63.63%
Clubs: Leeds United (8), Tottenham Hotspur (2), Manchester City (1)

Youthful speed and hardness made him one of the very best in his position just before the War, good enough to keep MALE out of the England team. It's possible that he was christened Albert, but the source is unreliable.

RALPH TYNDALL SQUIRE

b 10 Sep 1864   d 22 Aug 1944
     HALF BACK/RIGHT BACK
Caps: 3   Goals: 0
First cap: 13 Mar 1886 v Ireland 6–1   aged 21yr 184d
Last cap: 29 Mar 1886 v Wales 3–1   aged 21yr 200d
England career: 0yr 16d – P3 W2 D1 L0 – 83.33%
Club: Cambridge University and Old Westminsters
     (possibly already a member of the Corinthians)

Determined tackler, played in all three matches in 1886.

MAURICE HUGH STANBROUGH

b 2 Sep 1870   d 15 Dec 1904   OUTSIDE LEFT
Caps: 1   Goals: 0
Only cap: 18 Mar 1895 v Wales 1–1   aged 24yr 197d
England career: P1 W0 D1 L0 – 50%
Club: Old Carthusians (and Corinthians)

Classic dashing runner, his first name was originally thought to be spelt Morris, but in any case he was known by his second.

A walrus, not a carpenter. RT Squire esq, FA Committee member and Treasurer of the Corinthians
(Lamming)

RONALD
STANIFORTH

b 13 Apr 1924   **RIGHT BACK**
Caps: 8 **Goals:** 0
First cap: 3 Apr 1954 v Scotland 4–2   aged 29yr 355d
Last cap: 1 Dec 1954 v W Germany 3–1 aged 30yr 232d
England career: 0yr 242d – P8 W4 D1 L3 – 56.25%
Club: Huddersfield Town

A tall, smooth full-back, Ron Staniforth had the same trouble ('a blistered tongue') with Zoltan Czibor in Budapest as his predecessor RAMSEY had had at Wembley.

RONALD
WILLIAM
STARLING

b 11 Oct 1909   **INSIDE RIGHT/LEFT**
Caps: 2 **Goals:** 0
First cap: 1 Apr 1933 v Scotland 1–2   aged 23yr 172d
Last cap: 17 Apr 1937 v Scotland 1–3   aged 27yr 188d
England career: 4yr 16d – P2 W0 D0 L2 – 0%
Clubs: Sheffield Wednesday (1), Aston Villa (1)

Having won his first cap on the right, skilful Ronnie Starling was recalled four years later on the left. Same place, same result. Two very good Scotland teams.

DEREK
JAMES
STATHAM

b 24 Mar 1959   **LEFT BACK**
Caps: 3 **Goals:** 0
First cap: 23 Feb 1983 v Wales 2–1   aged 23yr 336d
Last cap: 15 Jun 1983 v Australia 1–0   aged 24yr 83d
                                          (sub'd 21min)
England career: 0yr 112d – P3 W2 D1 L0 – 83.33%
Club: West Bromwich Albion
Substituted: 2

Injuries stopped Derek Statham challenging more strongly for Kenny SANSOM's place.

FREDERICK
CHARLES
STEELE

b 6 May 1916   d 23 Apr 1976   **STRIKER**
Caps: 6 **Goals:** 8
First cap: 17 Oct 1936 v Wales 1–2   aged 20yr 164d
Last cap: 20 May 1937 v Finland 8–0   aged 21yr 14d
                                              (2 goals)
England career: 0yr 215d – P6 W4 D0 L2 – 66.66%
Club: Stoke City
3 Goals in a game: 1 **2 Goals in a game:** 2

A tour of Scandinavia gave fast Freddie his flattering figures: seven goals in three games including a hat-trick v Sweden, the best of a weak amateur

bunch. He was still very young, but the war and a bad injury prevented him challenging LAWTON for more caps. His date of birth appears as 6 September in one publication.

BRIAN
STEIN

b 19 Oct 1957   **STRIKER**
Caps: 1 **Goals:** 0
Only cap: 29 Feb 1984 v France 0–2   aged 26yr 133d
                                          (sub'd 78min)
England career: P1 W0 D0 L1 – 0%
Club: Luton Town

The Stein–WALSH partnership didn't transfer too well from Kenilworth Road to the Parc des Princes, where Platini scored twice, but Bobby ROBSON might have given it a little more than one incomplete match, against someone other than a French team which won all its matches that calendar year, including five in the European Championship.

CLEMENT
STEPHENSON

b 6 Feb 1890/91   d 24 Oct 1961   **INSIDE LEFT**
Caps: 1 **Goals:** 0
Only cap: 3 Mar 1924 v Wales 1–2   aged 33/34yr 26d
England career: P1 W0 D0 L1 – 0%
Club: Huddersfield Town

Of all the players who deserved more caps than they got, Clem Stephenson seems to come top of most experts' lists, although the truth is he lost his prime years to the First World War and was too old and slow (he'd never have been quick) when he was finally selected. Still, he was the midfield general of the Aston Villa side that won FA Cups in 1913 and 1920 and the Huddersfield team that won three consecutive League championships (1924–26), as well as still being good enough to play in the FA Cup Final in 1928. Go along with the consensus, then: that single cap does look a kind of insult.

GT STEPHENSON was his (less talented?) brother.

GEORGE
TERNENT
STEPHENSON

b 3 Sep 1900   d 18 Aug 1971   **INSIDE LEFT/RIGHT**
Caps: 3 **Goals:** 2
First cap: 17 May 1928 v France 5–1   aged 27yr 257d
                                              (2 goals)
Last cap: 14 May 1931 v France 2–5   aged 30yr 253d
England career: 2yr 362d – P3 W2 D0 L1 – 66.66%
Clubs: Derby County (2), Sheffield Wednesday (1)

2 Goals in a game: 1

Clem STEPHENSON's brother, he put England 2–1 and 4–1 ahead in Paris.

JOSEPH
ERIC
STEPHENSON

b Sep 1914   d 8 Sep 1944　　　　　INSIDE LEFT
Caps: 2   **Goals:** 0
First cap: 9 Apr   1938 v Scotland 0–1
　　　　　　　　　　　　　　 aged 23yr 191–220d
Last cap: 16 Nov 1938 v Ireland 7–0
　　　　　　　　　　　　　　 aged 24yr   47–76d
England career: 0yr 221d – P2 W1 D0 L1 – 50%
Club: Leeds United

Eric Stephenson couldn't get into the game against the Irish: the MATTHEWS and HALL show was going on away to the right.

ALEXANDER
CYRIL
STEPNEY

b 18 Sep 1944　　　　　　　GOALKEEPER
Caps: 1   **Goals conceded:** 1
Only cap: 22 May 1968 v Sweden 3–1　　aged 23yr 246d

Maestro Clem, the great orchestrator. Star of the club circuit, international one-night stand (Lamming)

England career: P1 W1 D0 L0 – 100%
Club: Manchester United

Sentiment's the last thing you'd accuse Sir Alf of, but it seems he gave Alex Stepney a cap to get him used to Wembley for the European Cup Final a week later. His day was spoiled slightly by substitute Rolf Andersson's goal in the last minute.

MELVYN
STERLAND

b 1 Oct 1961　　　　　　　RIGHT BACK
Caps: 1   **Goals:** 0
Only cap: 16 Nov 1988 v Saudi Arabia 1–1   aged 27yr 46d
England career: P1 W0 D1 L0 – 50%
Club: Sheffield Wednesday

A good attacking full back at club level, but looked a short-lived experiment from the start.

TREVOR
McGREGOR
STEVEN

b 21 Sep 1963　　　　　　　MIDFIELDER
Caps: 30   **Goals:** 3
First cap: 27 Feb 1985 v N Ireland 1–0   aged 21yr 159d
Last cap: 6 Feb 1991 v Cameroon 2–0 aged 27yr 138d
England career: 5yr 344d – P30 W19 D5 L6 – 71.67%
Clubs: Everton (25), Glasgow Rangers (5)
Substitute: 8   **Substituted:** 8
2 Goals in a game: 0

Just as COPPELL helped stabilise the right-hand side of Greenwood's midfield, so Trevor Steven tightened up ROBSON's team in Mexico after a miserable start (altogether, he played in seven successive clean-sheet wins before Maradona's hand came into play) and looked very impressive when he was allowed on in Italia 90. Very skilful as well as wholehearted, he's surely deserved more caps, though admittedly there have been injuries. All his goals were scored in his first eight internationals, including England's 1500th, against Egypt in 1986.

GARY
ANDREW
STEVENS

b 30 Mar 1962　　　　　　　MIDFIELDER
Caps: 7   **Goals:** 0
First cap: 17 Oct 1984 v Finland 5–0　　aged 22yr 202d
　　　　　　　　　　　　　　　　　　(sub HT)
Last cap: 18 Jun 1986 v Paraguay 3–0   aged 24yr 80d
　　　　　　　　　　　　　　　　　　(sub 57min)
England career: 1yr 244d – P7 W6 D1 L0 – 92.86%
Club: Tottenham Hotspur
Substitute: 6

Probably too versatile for his own good, a ball-playing central defender turned anonymous midfielder, Gary Stevens had impressive international match figures, but was a substitute in most, always in the second half.

MICHAEL
GARY
STEVENS

b 27 Mar 1963 **RIGHT BACK**
Caps: 42 Goals: 0
First cap: 6 Jun 1985 v Italy 1–2   aged 22yr 40d
Last cap: 21 May 1991 v USSR 3–1   aged 28yr 55d
England career: 5yr 349d – P42 W21 D14 L7 – 66.66%
Clubs: Everton (26), Glasgow Rangers (16)
Substitute: 1   Substituted: 1
Strong and rather crudely athletic, Gary Stevens could make mistakes and give the ball away coming forward, but also provide the crosses that brought goals: for LINEKER (v Poland and twice v Turkey), WADDLE (v Scotland), BARNES (v Poland).

JAMES
STEWART

b 1883   d 23 May 1957 **INSIDE LEFT**
Caps: 3 Goals: 2
First cap: 18 Mar 1907 v Wales 1–1   aged 23/24
                                                        (1 goal)
Last cap: 1 Apr 1911 v Scotland 1–1   aged 27/28
                                                        (1 goal)
England career: 4yr 14d – P3 W0 D3 L0 – 50%
Clubs: Sheffield Wednesday (2), Newcastle United (1)
All three of Jimmy Stewart's internationals were drawn 1–1. A famous touch player, he scored in the first and last. It's hard to know what he'd done to deserve a nickname like 'Tadger'.

NORBERT
PETER
STILES

b 18 May 1942 **HALF BACK**
Caps: 28 Goals: 1
First cap: 10 Apr 1965 v Scotland 2–2   aged 22yr 327d
Last cap: 25 Apr 1970 v Scotland 0–0   aged 27yr 342d
England career: 5yr 15d – P28 W18 D8 L2 – 78.57%
Club: Manchester United
Identikit for the common man as folk hero. Give him false teeth and glasses off the pitch, contact lenses on it. Make him short (on skill too), never-say-die bordering on (?) over-the-top. Call him Nobby. Pick him at number 9 to confuse the Germans in February 1966; have him score the only goal of the game. Last but not least, get him to dance a gap-toothed jig with the World Cup after the Final. Arise Sir Norbert.

LEWIS
STOKER

b 31 Mar 1910/11   d 1979 **RIGHT HALF**
Caps: 3 Goals: 0
First cap: 16 Nov 1932 v Wales 0–0   aged 21/22yr 230d
Last cap: 10 May 1934 v Hungary 1–2 aged 23/24yr 40d
England career: 1yr 175d – P3 W1 D1 L1 – 50%
Club: Birmingham FC
In between his first and last, the half-back line of Stoker–HART–COPPING was too good for Scotland, beaten 3–0 at Wembley.

HARRY
STORER

b 2 Feb 1898   d 1 Sep 1967 **INSIDE LEFT/LEFT HALF**
Caps: 2 Goals: 0
First cap: 17 May 1924 v France 3–1   aged 26yr 105d
Last cap: 22 Oct 1927 v Ireland 0–2   aged 29yr 263d
England career: 3yr 158d – P2 W1 D0 L1 – 50%
Club: Derby County
A hard man on and off the pitch, later Derby County manager and mentor of CLOUGH and Taylor, lantern-jawed Harry is sometimes credited with England's third goal in his first international, but all reports mention a deflection off a defender and most sources list it as an Edouard Baumann own goal.

PETER
EDWIN
STOREY

b 7 Sep 1945 **MIDFIELDER/RIGHT BACK**
Caps: 19 Goals: 0
First cap: 21 Apr 1971 v Greece 3–0   aged 25yr 226d
Last cap: 14 Jun 1973 v Italy 0–2   aged 27yr 280d
England career: 2yr 54d – P19 W11 D5 L3 – 71.05%
Club: Arsenal
When England arrived in West Berlin in 1972 needing to win by two goals, Ramsey picked Peter ('Leave Netzer to Me') Storey as well as Norman HUNTER in midfield. England escaped with a futile goalless draw, by dropping into the pits.

IAN
STOREY-MOORE

b 17 Jan 1945 **OUTSIDE LEFT**
Caps: 1 Goals: 0
Only cap: 14 Jan 1970 v Holland 0–0   aged 24yr 362d
England career: P1 W0 D1 L0 – 50%
Club: Nottingham Forest
Fired both barrels at Wembley without much luck, forcing a fine save from Jan van Beveren, having a headed goal very dubiously disallowed.

ALFRED
HENRY
STRANGE

b 2 Apr 1900   d Oct 1978 **RIGHT HALF**
Caps: 20   **Goals:** 0   **Captain:** 3
First cap: 5 Apr 1930 v Scotland 5–2   aged 30yr 03d
Last cap: 6 Dec 1933 v France 4–1   aged 33yr 248d
England career: 3yr 245d – P20 W13 D3 L4 – 72.50%
Club: Sheffield Wednesday

The thirties were a kind of golden age for half backs, too many good ones jostling for too few places in the England team. Alf Strange, with his quick tackle and accurate passing, was typical in everything except the relatively large number of caps he won.

ALFRED HUGH
STRATFORD

b 5 Sep 1853   d 2 May 1914 **FULL BACK**
Caps: 1   **Goals:** 0
Only cap: 7 Mar 1874 v Scotland 1–2   aged 20yr 183d
England career: P1 W0 D0 L1 – 0%
Club: Malvern College (and Wanderers)

Both backs, Stratford and OGILVIE, were winning their first caps – so was Harry McNiel, who gave them both trouble.

BERNARD R
STRETEN

b 14 Jan 1921 **GOALKEEPER**
Caps: 1   **Goals:** 0
Only cap: 16 Nov 1949 v N Ireland 9–2   aged 28yr 306d
England career: P1 W1 D0 L0 – 100%
Club: Luton Town

Essentially an England reserve, but good enough to be capped while in the Second Division.

ALBERT
STURGESS

b 21 Oct 1882   d 16 Jul 1957 **LEFT HALF/RIGHT HALF**
Caps: 2   **Goals:** 0
First cap: 11 Feb 1911 v Ireland 2–1   aged 28yr 113d
Last cap: 4 Apr 1914 v Scotland 1–3   aged 31yr 165d
England career: 3yr 52d – P2 W1 D0 L1 – 50%
Club: Sheffield United

Past his best, and not a first choice, in his last game.

MICHAEL
GEORGE
SUMMERBEE

b 15 Dec 1942 **FORWARD**
Caps: 8   **Goals:** 1

First cap: 24 Feb 1968 v Scotland 1–1   aged 25yr 71d
Last cap: 10 Jun 1973 v USSR 2–1   aged 30yr 177d
(sub 67min)
England career: 5yr 106d – P8 W4 D2 L2 – 62.50%
Club: Manchester City
Substitute: 2   **Substituted:** 1

Sly winger, one of City's stars in the MERCER–Allison glory days, sometimes there in the back of Sir Alf's mind.

ALAN
SUNDERLAND

b 1 Jul 1953 **STRIKER**
Caps: 1   **Goals:** 0
Only cap: 31 May 1980 v Australia 2–1   aged 26yr 335d
(sub'd 82 min)
England career: P1 W1 D0 L0 – 100%
Club: Arsenal

Substituted by another one-cap striker, Peter WARD.

JOHN WILLIAM
SUTCLIFFE

b 14 Apr 1868   d 7 Jul 1947 **GOALKEEPER**
Caps: 5   **Goals conceded:** 3   **Clean sheets:** 3
First cap: 13 Mar 1893 v Wales 6–0   aged 24yr 333d
Last cap: 2 Mar 1903 v Wales 2–1   aged 34yr 326d
England career: 9yr 354d – P5 W4 D1 L0 – 90%
Clubs: Bolton Wanderers (4), Millwall Athletic (1)

Very highly rated by contemporaries, a great shot-stopper, with the international figures to prove it, the last to play both football and rugby union for England (see RH BIRKETT and CP WILSON), John Willie was the oldest man to play for England before the First World War.

PETER
SWAN

b 8 Oct 1936 **CENTRE HALF**
Caps: 19   **Goals:** 0
First cap: 11 May 1960 v Yugoslavia 3–3 aged 23yr 216d
Last cap: 9 May 1962 v Switzerland 3–1 aged 25yr 213d
England career: 1yr 363d – P19 W11 D4 L4 – 68.42%
Club: Sheffield Wednesday

Confident, dominant stopper who didn't miss a game until it all went wrong: losing his place to the even heftier NORMAN just before the World Cup, falling very ill during it (England didn't take a doctor to Chile), being banned for life (with KAY) after a big bribery scandal. He played for Wednesday and Bury after an amnesty in the early seventies.

HARRY
ALBEMARLE
SWEPSTONE

b 1859   d 7 May 1907   **GOALKEEPER**
Caps: 6   **Goals conceded:** 18   **Clean sheets:** 2
First cap: 13 Mar 1880 v Scotland 4–5   *aged 20/21*
Last cap: 10 Mar 1883 v Scotland 2–3   *aged 23/24*
England career: 2yr 362d – P6 W2 D0 L4 – 33.3%
Club: Pilgrims (and Corinthians)

The first to play three (let alone six) times in goal for England, and the first to keep two clean sheets, Harry Swepstone was apparently a better keeper than the statistics show (having only two defenders in front of him and playing against Scotland three times didn't help); in fact he was chaired off the pitch 'for his brilliant play' although Scotland had won 5–1 in 1882.

FRANK
VICTOR
SWIFT

b 24 Dec 1913   d 6 Feb 1958   **GOALKEEPER**
Caps: 19   **Captain:** 2
Goals conceded: 18   **Clean sheets:** 9
First cap: 28 Sep 1946 v N Ireland 7–2   *aged 32yr 276d*
Last cap: 18 May 1949 v Norway 4–1   *aged 35yr 145d*
England career: 2yr 232d – P19 W14 D3 L2 – 81.58%
Club: Manchester City
Goals conceded while captain: 0
Penalties: 1   **Saved:** 0

Big cheerful Frank lost his best years to the Second World War but made a giant impression after it: huge hands, long reach, larger-than-life personality. The first to keep three successive clean sheets since S HARDY, he was the first keeper to captain England this century (v Italy, 1948). He died in the Munich air crash.

GEORGE
TAIT

b 1859   d 1882   **CENTRE FORWARD**
Caps: 1   **Goals:** 0
Only cap: 26 Feb 1881 v Wales 0–1   *aged 21/22*
England career: P1 W0 D0 L1 – 0%
Club: Birmingham Excelsior

Fondly remembered for his goals at club level, but played downright badly at Blackburn.

BRIAN
ERNEST
TALBOT

b 21 July 1953   **MIDFIELDER**
Caps: 6   **Goals:** 0
First cap: 28 May 1977 v N Ireland 2–1   *aged 23yr 311d*
                                              (sub 65min)

Last cap: 31 May 1980 v Australia 2–1   *aged 26yr 314d*
England career: 3yr 03d – P6 W2 D3 L1 – 58.33%
Clubs: Ipswich Town (5), Arsenal (1)
Substitute: 1

Part of Bobby ROBSON's hefty Ipswich team (BEATTIE, Burley, Hunter, WHYMARK), Brian Talbot hefted as much as anyone.

ROBERT
VICTOR
TAMBLING

b 18 Sep 1941   **STRIKER**
Caps: 3   **Goals:** 1
First cap: 21 Nov 1962 v Wales 4–0   *aged 21yr 64d*
Last cap: 4 May 1966 v Yugoslavia 2–0   *aged 24yr 228d*
England career: 3yr 164d – P3 W2 D0 L1 – 66.66%
Club: Chelsea

Bobby Tambling scored a record number of goals for Chelsea, and one for England as they pulled back from 3–0 down to 3–2 before losing 5–2 in Paris in 1963.

JOSEPH
THOMAS
TATE

b 4 Aug 1904   d 18 May 1973   **LEFT HALF**
Caps: 3   **Goals:** 0
First cap: 14 May 1931 v France 2–5   *aged 26yr 283d*
Last cap: 16 Nov 1932 v Wales 0–0   *aged 28yr 104d*
England career: 1yr 186d – P3 W1 D1 L1 – 50%
Club: Aston Villa

Tall and sometimes dominating – though not in Paris.

EDWARD
HALLOWS
TAYLOR

b 7 Mar 1891   d 5 Jul 1956   **GOALKEEPER**
Caps: 8   **Goals conceded:** 10   **Clean sheets:** 1
First cap: 21 Oct 1922 v Ireland 2–0   *aged 31yr 222d*
Last cap: 17 Apr 1927 v Scotland 0–1   *aged 35yr 41d*
England career: 3yr 178d – P8 W3 D3 L2 – 56.25%
Club: Huddersfield Town
Own goals: 1

Teddy Taylor is a problem. Just possibly two problems. The Football Encyclopaedia of 1934 gives him just the one initial, as do the early Rothmans. In 1972, Farror and Lamming introduced him as EH, which was taken up by the later Rothmans. Then in 1990, Douglas Lamming reverted to just the E – and changed the year of his birth to 1887. So what's been happening? Two E Taylors perhaps? If so, they were both born in Liverpool on 7 March, so it's unlikely. If he *was* born in 1887, he would have been 35 when he won his first cap and 39 at the time of his last.

Short and quick, simply a quality player, he kept his only clean sheet in his first international, and gave away the own goal that allowed Scotland to draw 1–1 at Wembley in 1924, the first international ever played there.

ERNEST
TAYLOR

b 2 Sep 1925   d 9 Apr 1985   **INSIDE RIGHT**
Caps: 1   Goals: 0
Only cap: 25 Nov 1953 v Hungary 3–6   aged 28yr 84d
England career: P1 W0 D0 L1 – 0%
Club: Blackpool

Little Ernie, who appeared for Blackpool and Manchester United in FA Cup Finals, was thrown to the Magic Magyars at Wembley and didn't come back.

JAMES
GUY
TAYLOR

b 5 Nov 1917   **CENTRE HALF**
Caps: 2   Goals: 0
First cap: 9 May 1951 v Argentina 2–1   aged 33yr 185d
Last cap: 19 May 1951 v Portugal 5–2   aged 33yr 195d

Teddy for short. Edward Hallows Taylor, every inch as good as Corrigan (Lamming)

England career: 0yr 10d – P2 W2 D0 L0 – 100%
Club: Fulham
Had trouble with both centre-forwards in the two Jubilee matches at Wembley.

PETER
JOHN
TAYLOR

b 3 Jan 1953   **OUTSIDE LEFT**
Caps: 4   Goals: 2
First cap: 24 May 1976 v Wales 2–1   aged 23yr 69d
                                     (sub HT, 1 goal)
Last cap: 15 May 1976 v Scotland 1–2 aged 23yr 121d
England career: 0yr 52d – P4 W3 D0 L1 – 75%
Club: Crystal Palace
Substitute: 1   Substituted: 1

A direct winger just short of international class, the first Third Division player to be capped by England since Johnny BYRNE, Peter Taylor was also the first player to score while making his debut as substitute.

PHILIP
HENRY
TAYLOR

b 18 Sep 1917   **RIGHT HALF**
Caps: 3   Goals: 0
First cap: 18 Oct 1947 v Wales 3–0   aged 30yr 30d
Last cap: 19 Nov 1947 v Sweden 4–2   aged 30yr 62d
England career: 0yr 32d – P3 W2 D1 L0 – 83.33%
Club: Liverpool

Phil Taylor's career was one of many that lost years to the Second World War.

THOMAS
TAYLOR

b 29 Jan 1932   d 6 Feb 1958
                        INSIDE LEFT/CENTRE FORWARD
Caps: 19   Goals: 16
First cap: 17 May 1953 v Argentina 0–0   aged 21yr 108d
Last cap: 27 Nov 1957 v France 4–0   aged 25yr 302d
                                          (2 goals)
England career: 4yr 194d – P19 W11 D6 L2 – 73.68%
Club: Manchester United
3 Goals in a game: 2   2 Goals in a game: 4
Substitute: 1   Substituted: 1   Goals as sub: 2 .

A class act in the air, good enough on the ground, successor to Lofthouse if not quite LAWTON, Tommy Taylor scored eight goals in the 1956–57 World Cup qualifying group, enjoying himself particularly against the Danes: a hat-trick at Wembley, two more (as well as hitting the bar twice) at the Idraetspark.

The match against France was England's last before the Munich air crash.

DEREK
WILLIAM

TEMPLE

b 13 Nov 1938   **OUTSIDE LEFT**
Caps: 1   **Goals:** 0
Only cap: 12 May 1965 v W Germany 1–0   aged 26yr 180d
England career: P1 W1 D0 L0 – 100%
Club: Everton
Laid on PAINE's 34th-minute winner in Nuremberg, but Sir Alf hadn't seen enough.

HENRY
THICKETT

b 1873   d 15 Nov 1920   **RIGHT BACK**
Caps: 2   **Goals:** 0
First cap: 20 Mar 1899 v Wales 4–0   aged 25/26
Last cap: 8 Apr 1899 v Scotland 2–1   aged 25/26
England career: 0yr 19d – P2 W2 D0 L0 – 100%
Club: Sheffield United
Aptly named, was Harry. If the figures are correct, he was under 5ft 9in but weighed 14st 7!

DANIEL
JOSEPH
THOMAS

b 12 Nov 1961   **RIGHT BACK**
Caps: 2   **Goals:** 0
First cap: 12 Jun 1983 v Australia 0–0   aged 21yr 212d
Last cap: 19 Jun 1983 v Australia 1–1   aged 21yr 219d
               (sub HT)
England career: 0yr 07d – P2 W0 D2 L0 – 50%
Club: Coventry City
Injury forced Danny Thomas to retire from football in late 1987.

DAVID
THOMAS

b 5 Oct 1950   **WIDE FORWARD**
Caps: 8   **Goals:** 0
First cap: 30 Oct 1974 v Czechoslovakia 3–0
            aged 24yr 25d (sub 62min)
Last cap: 19 Nov 1975 v Portugal 1–1
            aged 25yr 45d (sub 74min)
England career: 1yr 20d – P8 W4 D3 L1 – 68.75%
Club: Queen's Park Rangers
Substitute: 5
Important to a very good and attractive QPR team, and the first of REVIE's (half-hearted?) experiments with wingers.

GEOFFREY R
THOMAS

b 5 Aug 1964   **MIDFIELDER**

Caps: 7   **Goals:** 0
First cap: 1 May 1991 v Turkey 1–0   aged 26yr 269d
               (sub'd HT)
Last cap: 12 Jun 1991 v Malaysia 4–2   aged 26yr 335d
England career: 0y 66d – P7 W6 D1 L0 – 92.86%
Club: Crystal Palace
Substituted: 1
Captain and driving force of Palace's assault on League and Cup, Geoff Thomas formed with PLATT and WISE/BATTY the first England midfields without a single playmaker.

MICHAEL
LAURISTON

THOMAS

b 24 Aug 1967   **MIDFIELD**
Caps: 2   **Goals:** 0
First cap: 16 Nov 1988 v Saudi Arabia
            aged 21yr 84d (sub'd 80min)
Last cap: 13 Dec 1989 v Yugoslavia 2–1
            aged 22yr 111d (sub'd 67min)
England career: 1yr 27d – P2 W1 D1 L0 – 75%
Club: Arsenal
Five players made their England debuts in Riyadh: MARWOOD, SEAMAN, AM SMITH, STERLAND, and Michael Thomas, who seemed to catch stage fright (cue headline: Froze in Desert), and wasn't much better at Wembley. Yet he scored the perfect TV goal at Anfield, and should come again.

PETER
THOMPSON

b 27 Nov 1942   **OUTSIDE RIGHT/LEFT**
Caps: 16   **Goals:** 0
First cap: 17 May 1964 v Portugal 4–3   aged 21yr 172d
Last cap: 25 Apr 1970 v Scotland 0–0   aged 27yr 149d
England career: 5yr 343d – P16 W8 D5 L3 – 65.63%
Club: Liverpool
Substitute: 1   **Substituted:** 1
They say Sir Alf didn't want wingers, and point to Peter Thompson being left out of two World Cup squads. But look at the number of matches he (and PAINE and CONNELLY) played and remember what he did in them. No, nor can anyone else.

PHILIP
BERNARD

THOMPSON

b 21 Jan 1954   **CENTRAL DEFENDER**
Caps: 42   **Goals:** 1   **Own goals:** 1   **Captain:** 1
First cap: 24 Mar 1976 v Wales 2–1   aged 22yr 62d
Last cap: 17 Nov 1982 v Greece 3–0   aged 28yr 300d
England career: 6yr 238d – P42 W29 D5 L8 – 75%
Club: Liverpool

Substitute: 2   Goals while captain: 0

Phil Thompson tossed up for his legs with a sparrow and lost (Bill Shankly said that, so it must be true), but his partnership with DV WATSON was important to the Endland team. Gutsy, very sharp in the tackle, his only goal as captain was an own goal against Wales in 1980, but his header helped bring England back from a 2–0 half-time deficit against Italy in New York.

THOMAS
THOMPSON

b 10 Nov 1928   INSIDE RIGHT
Caps: 2   Goals: 0
First cap: 20 Oct 1951 v Wales 1–1   aged 22yr 344d
Last cap: 6 Apr 1957 v Scotland 2–1   aged 28yr 147d
England career: 5yr 168d – P2 W1 D1 L0 – 75%
Clubs: Aston Villa (1), Preston North End (1)

Very small, clever schemer, easily overlooked.

ROBERT
ANTHONY
THOMSON

b 5 Dec 1943   LEFT/RIGHT BACK
Caps: 8   Goals: 0
First cap: 20 Nov 1963 v N Ireland 8–3   aged 19yr 350d
Last cap: 9 Dec 1964 v Holland 1–1   aged 21yr 04d
England career: 1yr 19d – P8 W4 D3 L1 – 68.75%
Club: Wolves

A rather forgotten name now, but Bobby Thomson was an exciting prospect who covered for both COHEN and WILSON before their partnership was fully bedded down.

GEORGE
THORNEWELL

b 8 Jul 1898   d 6 Mar 1986   OUTSIDE RIGHT
Caps: 4   Goals: 0
First cap: 21 May 1923 v Sweden 4–2   aged 24yr 317d
Last cap: 21 May 1925 v France 3–2   aged 26yr 317d
England career: 2yr 0d – P4 W4 D0 L0 – 100%
Club: Derby County

Playing all four matches against Sweden and France brought about an unusually successful international career by 1920s standards.

IRVINE
THORNLEY

b 1883   d 24 Apr 1955   CENTRE FORWARD
Caps: 1   Goals: 0
Only cap: 18 Mar 1907 v Wales 1–1   aged 23/24
England career: P1 W0 D1 L0 – 50%
Club: Manchester City

Only player in the team not to win another cap.

SAMUEL
FREDERICK
TILSON

b 19 Apr 1903   d 21 Nov 1972   CENTRE FORWARD
Caps: 4   Goals: 5 (6?)
First cap: 10 May 1934 v Hungary 1–2   aged 31yr 21d
                                             (1 goal)
Last cap: 19 Oct 1935 v Ireland 3–1   aged 32yr 183d
                                            (1? goal)
England career: 1yr 162d – P4 W2 D0 L2 – 50%
Club: Manchester City
2 Goals in a game: 1(2?)

Of average height and build but very strong and direct, Fred Tilson was already a veteran by the time he was capped. Like JW SMITH, he made up for lost time, scoring in every international (of those who did the same, only CAMSELL played in more matches) including two against Wales in 1934. Most yearbooks credit him with another pair in his last international, but contemporary newspapers are divided: *Ireland's Saturday Night* and *The Sporting Life* say Ralph BIRKETT scored England's equaliser.

FREDERICK
TITMUSS

b 15 Feb 1898   2 Oct 1966   LEFT BACK
Caps: 2   Goals: 0
First cap: 13 Mar 1922 v Wales 1–0   aged 24yr 26d
Last cap: 5 Mar 1923 v Wales 2–2   aged 25yr 18d
England career: 0yr 357d – P2 W1 D1 L0 – 75%
Club: Southampton

Fred Titmuss made his debut in the same match as WE RAWLINGS, the first two Third Division players to appear together for England (see COOK and L GRAHAM) and the only two from the same club.

COLIN
TODD

b 12 Dec 1948   CENTRAL DEFENDER
Caps: 27   Goals: 0   Own goals: 1
First cap: 23 May 1972 v N Ireland 0–1   aged 23yr 148d
Last cap: 28 May 1977 v N Ireland 2–1   aged 28yr 153d
England career: 5yr 05d – P27 W12 D9 L6 – 61.11%
Club: Derby County
Substitute: 2

Kevin KEEGAN said, famously and rightly or wrongly, that Colin Todd (who had all the defensive talents) would rather have played a game of darts than play for England. If so, another 50 caps went begging.

His own goal at Hampden in 1974 is sometimes credited to Dalglish.

GEORGE

TOONE

b 10 Jun 1868   d 1 Sep 1943   GOALKEEPER
Caps: 2   Goals conceded: 1   Clean sheets: 1
First cap: 5 Mar 1892 v Wales 2–0   aged 23yr 93d
Last cap: 2 Apr 1892 v Scotland 4–1   aged 23yr 121d
England career: 0yr 28d – P2 W2 D0 L0 – 100%
Club: Notts County

An excellent goalkeeper in an age of very good ones. May possibly have been born on 6 September.

ARTHUR GEORGE
TOPHAM

b 19 Feb 1869   d 18 May 1931   HALF BACK
Caps: 1   Goals: 0
Only cap: 12 Mar 1894 v Wales 5–1   aged 25yr 23d
England career: P1 W1 D0 L0 – 100%
Club: Casuals (and Corinthians)

Played alongside his brother, R TOPHAM, who was winning his last cap.

ROBERT
TOPHAM

b 3 Nov 1867   d 31 Aug 1931 (1951?!)   OUTSIDE RIGHT
Caps: 2   Goals: 0
First cap: 25 Feb 1893 v Ireland 6–1   aged 25yr 114d
Last cap: 12 Mar 1894 v Wales 5–1   aged 26yr 129d
England career: 1yr 15d – P2 W2 D0 L0 – 100%
Club: Wolves (and Casuals); Corinthians 1894–98

Apparently declined an invitation to play for Wales against Scotland in 1885.

MARK
ANTHONY

TOWERS

b 13 Apr 1952   MIDFIELDER
Caps: 3   Goals: 0
First cap: 8 May 1976 v Wales 1–0   aged 24yr 26d
Last cap: 28 May 1976 v Italy 3–2   aged 24yr 46d
England career: 0yr 20d – P3 W3 D0 L0 – 100%
Club: Sunderland
Substitute: 1

A goodish club player, Tony Towers must have been as surprised as anyone else to find himself in some of REVIE's early teams.

WILLIAM J

TOWNLEY

b 14 Feb 1866   d 30 May 1950   OUTSIDE LEFT
Caps: 2   Goals: 2?
First cap: 23 Feb 1889 v Wales 4–1   aged 23yr 09d
Last cap: 15 Mar 1890 v Ireland 9–1   aged 24yr 29d
                                         (2? goals)

England career: 1yr 20d – P2 W2 D0 L0 – 100%
Club: Blackburn Rovers
2 (3?) Goals in a game: 1

Whether Bill Townley really was 'the fastest man we ever witnessed dribbling a ball', he was certainly quick, and could score goals, including the first FA Cup Final hat-trick two weeks after his last international, in which *The Field* and *The Northern Whig* credit him with another three goals, although other sources say he scored only twice. Or not at all (see GEARY). He also hit the bar once. Or twice.

His second name may have been John, but (yet again) the source isn't completely trustworthy.

JOHN
EDWARD (ERNEST?)

TOWNROW

b 28 Mar 1901   d 11 Apr 1969   CENTRE HALF
Caps: 2   Goals: 0
First cap: 4 Apr 1925 v Scotland 0–2   aged 24yr 07d
Last cap: 1 Mar 1926 v Wales 1–3   aged 24yr 338d
England career: 0yr 331d – P2 W0 D0 L2 – 0%
Club: Clapton Orient

Jack Townrow had trouble either side of the change in the offside law. Both the centre forwards he had to mark, Hughie Gallacher and Jack Fowler, scored twice.

RICHARD
DANIEL

TREMELLING

b 12 Nov 1897/99   d 1970   GOALKEEPER
Caps: 1   Goals conceded: 2
Only cap: 28 Nov 1927 v Wales 1–2   aged 28/30yr 16d
England career: P1 W0 D0 L1 – 0%
Club: Birmingham FC

The winner in Dan Tremelling's only international was an own goal by the England captain Jack HILL, in a match which ended four other international careers: A BAKER, R OSBORNE, PAGE and RIGBY.

JOHN

TRESADERN

b 26 Sep 1890/92   d 26 Sep 1959   LEFT HALF
Caps: 2   Goals: 0
First cap: 14 Apr 1923 v Scotland 2–2
                                         aged 30/32yr 200d
Last cap: 21 May 1923 v Sweden 4–2
                                         aged 30/32yr 237d
England career: 0yr 37d – P2 W1 D1 L0 – 75%
Club: West Ham United

A short, typically hard-working half back, Jack Tresadern did well alongside KEAN and George WILSON against Scotland.

DENNIS
TUEART

b 27 Nov 1949 **OUTSIDE LEFT**
Caps: 6 Goals: 2
First cap: 11 May 1975 v Cyprus 1–0 aged 25yr 165d
(sub 73min)
Last cap: 4 Jun 1977 v Scotland 1–2 aged 27yr 189d
(sub 67min)
England career: 2yr 24d – P6 W3 D1 L2 – 58.33%
Club: Manchester City
Substitute: 3 Substituted: 1 2 Goals in a game: 0
Winger with genuine flair who had one or two moments for England.

Three weeks after his last match for England, Fred Tunstall scored the only goal of the FA Cup Final
(Lamming)

FREDERICK
EDWARD
TUNSTALL

b 29 Mar 1900/01 d 18 Nov 1965 **OUTSIDE LEFT**
Caps: 7 Goals: 0
First cap: 14 Apr 1923 v Scotland 2–2 aged 22/23yr 16d
Last cap: 4 Apr 1925 v Scotland 0–2 aged 24/25yr 06d
England career: 1yr 355d – P7 W2 D2 L3 – 42.86%
Club: Sheffield United
Fred Tunstall, a quick, direct winger (were they ever slow and flexuous at the time?), appeared in three successive matches against Scotland without being on the winning side, a fair reflection of England's standing. They also lost several times

to Ireland and Wales in the twenties.

ROBERT
JOSEPH
TURNBULL

b 17 Dec 1895 d 18 Mar 1952 **OUTSIDE RIGHT**
Caps: 1 Goals: 0
Only cap: 25 Oct 1919 v Ireland 1–1 aged 23yr 312d
England career: P1 W0 D1 L0 – 50%
Club: Bradford FC (later Park Avenue)
Young Bob Turnbull came up against old Billy McCracken. No contest.

ARTHUR
TURNER

b 1877 d 4 Apr 1925 **OUTSIDE RIGHT**
Caps: 2 Goals: 0
First cap: 17 Mar 1900 v Ireland 2–0 aged 22/23
Last cap: 9 Mar 1901 v Ireland 3–0 aged 23/24
England career: 0yr 357d – P2 W2 D0 L0 – 100%
Club: Southampton
Injured in a collision with Peter Boyle and didn't come out for the second half of his last international.

HUGH
TURNER

b 6 Aug 1904 d ? **GOALKEEPER**
Caps: 2 Goals conceded: 6
First cap: 14 May 1931 v France 2–5 aged 26yr 281d
Last cap: 16 May 1931 v Belgium 4–1 aged 26yr 283d
England career: 0yr 02d – P2 W1 D0 L1 – 50%
Club: Huddersfield Town
France had beem threatening to do this to England. Things were calmer in Brussels for Harry HIBBS' stand-in.

GEORGE
JACOB
TWEEDY

b 6/8 Jan 1913 d 23 Apr 1987 **GOALKEEPER**
Caps: 1 Goals conceded: 2
Only cap: 2 Dec 1936 v Hungary 6–2
aged 23yr 327/329d
England career: P1 W1 D0 L0 – 100%
Club: Grimsby Town
Grimsby were in the First Division when George Tweedy was capped.

DEREK
GILBERT
UFTON

b 31 May 1928 **CENTRE HALF**

Caps: 1 **Goals:** 0
Only cap: 21 Oct 1953 v FIFA 4-4   aged 25yr 143d
England career: P1 W0 D1 L0 – 50%
Club: Charlton Athletic

Derek Ufton was the only England player not to appear against another country. He could say he stopped the great centre-forward Gunnar Nordahl from scoring, but in fact this was a forward line that constantly switched positions (heralding the Hungarians who arrived two matches later). Nordahl moved out to the wings, letting in Boniperti and Kubala, who scored two apiece. Apparently Bill ECKERSLEY did little to plug the gaps.

ALFRED
UNDERWOOD

b 1867/69   d 8 Oct 1928   LEFT/RIGHT BACK
Caps: 2 **Goals:** 0
First cap: 7 Mar 1891 v Ireland 6-1   aged 21-24
Last cap: 5 Mar 1892 v Ireland 2-0   aged 22-25
England career: 0yr 363d – P2 W2 D0 L0 – 100%
Club: Stoke FC

Had almost as bad a game as JD COX in Belfast 1892. Fouled Sam Torrans to give away the penalty that Bill ROWLEY saved.

THOMAS
URWIN

b 5 Feb 1896   d 7 May 1968   OUTSIDE LEFT/RIGHT
Caps: 4 **Goals:** 0
First cap: 21 May 1923 v Sweden 4-2   aged 27yr 105d
Last cap: 1 Mar 1926 v Wales 1-3   aged 30yr 24d
England career: 2yr 284d – P4 W2 D1 L1 – 62.50%
Clubs: Middlesbrough (2), Newcastle United (2)

A classic buzzing midget on either wing, Tommy Urwin had trouble with Swartenbroeks in Belgium in 1923. The whole team had problems against Wales.

GEORGE
UTLEY

b 1887   d 8 Jan 1966   LEFT HALF
Caps: 1 **Goals:** 0
Only cap: 15 Feb 1913 v Ireland 1-2   aged 25/26
England career: P1 W0 D0 L1 – 0%
Club: Barnsley

Ireland's first ever win over England ended the international careers of six other players: BENSON, BOYLE, MORDUE, WALL, RG WILLIAMSON, and Denis Hannon of Ireland.

OLIVER
HOWARD
VAUGHTON

b 9 Jan 1861   d 6 Jan 1937   FORWARD
Caps: 5 **Goals:** 6
First cap: 18 Feb 1882 v Ireland 13-0   aged 21yr 40d
                                                        (5 goals)
Last cap: 17 Mar 1884 v Wales 4-0   aged 23yr 68d
England career: 2yr 28d – P5 W2 D0 L3 – 40%
Club: Aston Villa
5 Goals in a game: 1

The Irish of 1882 were one of the very worst international teams of all time, so even Howard Vaughton, variously described as 'too light and outclassed for an international' and 'not a good shot on goal', was able to score five against them. In fact he scored England's first ever goal against Ireland, and one more than A BROWN in the match – so the chances are that he was the first to score a hat trick for England. Certainly he still holds the record for most goals in one international (shared by BLOOMER, GW HALL, MACDONALD and just possibly GO SMITH) – and no-one else has scored five on debut.

COLIN
CAMPBELL McKECHNIE
VEITCH

b 22 May 1881   d 26 Aug 1938   HALF BACK
Caps: 6 **Goals:** 0
First cap: 17 Feb 1906 v Ireland 5-0   aged 24yr 291d
Last cap: 15 Mar 1909 v Wales 2-0   aged 27yr 317d
England career: 3yr 26d – P6 W3 D2 L1 – 66.66%
Club: Newcastle United

Stocky, very strong, a fine passer, Colin Veitch was one of the most versatile players of his time. The half-back line of WARREN–WEDLOCK–Veitch was the best of its day, but only played for England three times.

JOHN
GOULD
VEITCH

b 19 Jul 1869   d 3 Oct 1914   FORWARD
Caps: 1 **Goals:** 3
Only cap: 12 Mar 1894 v Wales 5-1   aged 24yr 244d
                                                        (3 goals)
England career: P1 W1 D0 L0 – 100%
Club: Old Westminsters (and Corinthians)

Originally selected against Ireland four years earlier, John Veitch played in an all-amateur (in fact, all-Corinthian) team that was lucky to beat Wales at all, let alone by four goals, and became the fourth of five players who scored a hat-trick in their only match for England.

TERENCE
FREDERICK

VENABLES

b 6 Jan 1943   **INSIDE LEFT**
Caps: 2   **Goals:** 0
First cap: 21 Oct 1964 v Belgium 2–2   aged 21yr 289d
Last cap: 9 Dec 1964 v Holland 1–1   aged 21yr 338d
England career: 0yr 49d – P2 W0 D2 L0 – 50%
Club: Chelsea

Clever and confident, well known as the only player to be capped by England at 'all' levels (schoolboy, youth, amateur, under-23 and senior), Terry Venables became a manager of the highest class and a writer of the highest . . . well, co-author of the HAZEL series.

ROBERT
WALPOLE SEALY

VIDAL

b 3 Sep 1853   d 5 Nov 1914   **FORWARD**
Caps: 1   **Goals:** 0
Only cap: 8 Mar 1873 v Scotland 4–2   aged 19yr 186d
England career: P1 W1 D0 L0 – 100%
Club: Oxford University

Most famous of the very early dribblers, Robert Vidal took over from MAYNARD as England's youngest international (he'd played in an unofficial international at the age of 16) and later changed his name to RW Sealy.

COLIN
VILJOEN

b 20 Jun 1948   **MIDFIELDER**
Caps: 2   **Goals:** 0
First cap: 17 May 1975 v N Ireland 0–0   aged 26yr 325d
Last cap: 21 May 1975 v Wales 2–2   aged 26yr 329d
England career: 0yr 04d – P2 W0 D2 L0 – 50%
Club: Ipswich Town

Not to blame for everything against Wales, but he was all wrong alongside BALL and BELL.

DENNIS S

VIOLLET

b 20 Sep 1933   **INSIDE LEFT**
Caps: 2   **Goals:** 1
First cap: 22 May 1960 v Hungary 0–2   aged 26yr 245d
Last cap: 28 Sep 1961 v Luxembourg 4–1
                         aged 28yr 08d (1 goal)
England career: 1yr 128d – P2 W1 D0 L1 – 50%
Club: Manchester United

England had beaten Luxembourg 9–0 away but struggled at Highbury. Both inside forwards, Dennis Viollet, a slim sharp striker who survived Munich, and Johnny FANTHAM, paid the price.

PELHAM GEORGE

VON DONOP

b 28 Apr 1851   d 7 Nov 1921   **FORWARD**
Caps: 2   **Goals:** 0
First cap: 8 Mar 1873 v Scotland 4–2   aged 21yr 314d
Last cap: 6 Mar 1875 v Scotland 2–2   aged 23yr 312d
England career: 1yr 363d – P2 W1 D1 L0 – 75%
Club: Royal Engineers

There was a deluge at the Oval in 1875 and the pitch was a sea of mud; not ideal for the English dribbling game, and PG found it hard going.

HENRY
WACE

b 21 Sep 1853   d 5 Nov 1947   **FORWARD**
Caps: 3   **Goals:** 0   **Captain:** 2?
First cap: 2 Mar 1878 v Scotland 2–7   aged 24yr 162d
Last cap: 5 Apr 1879 v Scotland 5–4   aged 25yr 196d
England career: 1yr 34d – P3 W2 D0 L1 – 66.66%
Club: Wanderers (and probably Clapham Rovers)

Possibly captain in his last two internationals. At least two match reports say he led England out against Wales in 1879, but at least one other says AW CURSHAM, who had been captain in the previous match. Wace was definitely captain in the following game, but perhaps only because Cursham wasn't playing. He took over from FAIRCLOUGH as the longest-lived England player: 94 years 45 days (since outlived by HOWARD BAKER, then PYM).

CHRISTOPHER
ROLAND

WADDLE

b 14 Dec 1960   **OUTSIDE LEFT/RIGHT**
Caps: 61   **Goals:** 6
First cap: 26 Mar 1985 v Eire 2–1   aged 24yr 112d
Last cap: 17 Oct 1990 v Poland 2–0   aged 29yr 307d
                                    (sub 57min)
England career: 5yr 205d – P61 W28 D22 L11 – 63.93%
Clubs: Newcastle United (8), Tottenham Hotspur (35), Marseille (18)
Substitute: 14   **Substituted:** 20
2 Goals in a game: 0

Hunched, gangling, wibbly-wobbly, man-beater extraordinary – and opinion-splitter in the HODDLE and John BARNES class; but the possibilities have always been exciting when Chris Waddle's in the team. Or in reserve; no-one's been substitute (or substituted) more often in England matches.

SAMUEL JOHN WADSWORTH

b 13 Sep 1896 d 1 Sep 1961 **LEFT BACK**
Caps: 9 **Goals:** 0 **Captain:** 4
First cap: 8 Apr 1922 v Scotland 0–1 aged 25yr 207d
Last cap: 20 Oct 1926 v Ireland 3–3 aged 30yr 37d
England career: 4yr 195d – P9 W2 D3 L4 – 38.88%
Club: Huddersfield Town (9)

Captain in his last four internationals, yet Sam Wadsworth's caps were handed out almost randomly – one this year, two (or none) the next – in the style of the times. Players of class and selectors with whims.

WILLIAM RUSSELL WAINSCOAT

b 28 Jul 1897/98 **INSIDE LEFT**
Caps: 1 **Goals:** 0
Only cap: 13 Apr 1929 v Scotland 0–1 aged 30/31yr 259d
England career: P1 W0 D0 L1 – 0%
Club: Leeds United

England, and especially Russell Wainscoat, had no luck at Hampden in 1929. He was involved

Russell Wainscoat played in only a single, unlucky, controversial match for England (Lamming)

when an indirect free-kick was illegally charged down close to the Scottish goal-line, then had to watch while Alex Cheyne's last-minute corner sailed straight in.

ANTHONY KEITH WAITERS

b 1 Feb 1937 **GOALKEEPER**
Caps: 5 **Goals conceded:** 10 **Clean sheets:** 0
First cap: 24 May 1964 v Eire 1–1 aged 27yr 113d
Last cap: 9 Dec 1964 v Holland 1–1 aged 27yr 312d
England career: 0yr 199d – P5 W2 D2 L1 – 60%
Club: Blackpool

In 1964 Alf Ramsey dropped Gordon Banks for the match in the Maracana. Pele was dominant, Brazil won 5–1, Tony Waiters was the last England goalkeeper to concede more than four goals in a game, in the last match England lost by more than three. He later coached Canada in England's last match before the 1986 World Cup.

FREDERICK INGRAM WALDEN

b 1 Mar 1888 d 3 May 1949 **OUTSIDE RIGHT**
Caps: 2 **Goals:** 0
First cap: 4 Apr 1914 v Scotland 1–3 aged 26yr 34d
Last cap: 13 Mar 1922 v Wales 1–0 aged 34yr 12d
England career: 7yr 343d – P2 W1 D0 L1 – 50%
Club: Tottenham Hotspur

Believed to have been the smallest man ever to play for England (but see JF CRAWFORD) and one of the tiniest county cricketers, the mighty Fanny weighed 8st 9 and stood 5ft 2⅛in (his own claim was '5ft 2in, but only after a haircut'). The gap between his caps is one of the longest among England players.

DESMOND SINCLAIR WALKER

b 26 Nov 1965 **CENTRAL DEFENDER**
Caps: 36 **Goals:** 0
First cap: 14 Sep 1988 v Denmark 1–0 aged 22yr 292d
(sub 65min)
Last cap: 12 Jun 1991 v Malaysia 4–2 aged 25yr 198d
England career: 2yr 271d – P36 W21 D13 L2 – 76.39%
Club: Nottingham Forest
Substitute: 3 **Substituted:** 1

In the first match after the European Championships fiasco, Bobby ROBSON introduced the most important element in the 17-match unbeaten run towards the World Cup finals. Juventus offered £8 million for Des Walker, no robbery for probably the best and certainly the fastest man-marker England have ever had, his speed covering the holes that kept threatening to appear in the flat back-four. Already a world class player, already indispensable: 29 consecutive caps before being rested, five more since.

WILLIAM
HENRY

WALKER

b 29 Oct 1897   d 28 Nov 1964
INSIDE LEFT/GOALKEEPER
Caps: 18   Goals: 9   Goals conceded: 0   Captain: 3
First cap: 23 Oct 1920 v Ireland 2–0   aged 22yr 359d
(1 goal)
Last cap: 7 Dec 1932 v Austria 4–3   aged 35yr 39d
England career: 12yr 45d – P18 W9 D5 L4 – 63.88%
Club: Aston Villa
3 Goals in a game: 0   2 Goals in a game: 2
Goals while captain: 0

No-one played more times for England in the 1920s than Billy Walker's meagre 17, as good a comment as any on selectorial thinking at the time. Well built, commanding, as good on the ground as in the air, he was recalled after a gap of 5 years 298 days to captain a veteran side against the Austrian *Wunderteam*. He was also captain against France in 1925, when he took over in goal from the injured FOX after 76 minutes. He kept a clean little sheet as England held on to win 3–2; the last goalkeeper to captain England before SWIFT!

His miss from the penalty spot against Belgium in 1924 made him the first of only two England players (see BROOK) to miss a hat-trick by missing a penalty.

CHARLES
WILLIAM

WALLACE

b 20 Jan 1885   d 7 Jan 1970   OUTSIDE RIGHT
Caps: 3   Goals: 0
First cap: 17 Mar 1913 v Wales 4–3   aged 28yr 56d
Last cap: 10 Apr 1920 v Scotland 5–4   aged 35yr 80d
England career: 7yr 24d – P3 W2 D0 L1 – 66.66%
Club: Aston Villa

After a gap of 6 years 56 days caused mainly by the First World War, Charlie Wallace was recalled to the Dad's Army XI who beat Scotland after being 4–2 down at half-time. PENNINGTON and S HARDY (who were even older) were also winning their last caps, as was COCK.

Back in 1913, Wallace was apparently the first player to miss a penalty in an FA Cup Final, the last before John Aldridge in 1988.

DAVID L

WALLACE

b 21 Jan 1964   OUTSIDE LEFT
Caps: 1   Goals: 1
Only cap: 29 Jan 1986 v Egypt 4–0   aged 22yr 8d (1 goal)
England career: P1 W1 D0 L0 – 100%
Club: Southampton

One of the smallest players ever capped by England, 'Danny' Wallace volleyed England's third goal in Cairo.

PAUL
ANTHONY

WALSH

b 1 Oct 1962   STRIKER
Caps: 5   Goals: 1
First cap: 12 Jun 1983 v Australia 0–0   aged 20yr 254d
(sub 59min)
Last cap: 2 May 1984 v Wales 0–1   aged 21yr 184d
England career: 0yr 325d – P5 W1 D2 L2 – 40%
Club: Luton Town
Substitute: 1   Substituted: 1

A sharp young striker for Luton (less so at Liverpool and Tottenham), Paul Walsh may or may not have been England material, but there was no chance to find out. He played in some dreadful England teams, against Australia, France, Wales . . .

ARTHUR
MELMOTH
WALTERS

b 26 Jan 1865   d 2 May 1941   RIGHT/LEFT BACK
Caps: 9   Goals: 0   Captain: 1
First cap: 28 Feb 1885 v Ireland 4–0   aged 20yr 33d
Last cap: 5 Apr 1890 v Scotland 1–1   aged 25yr 69d
England career: 5yr 36d – P9 W4 D3 L2 – 61.11%
Clubs: Old Carthusians and Cambridge University (5),
Old Carthusians alone (4); Corinthians 1885–93

Like his brother, a big rough erratic full back of the old school. There's a little confusion as to whether he or PM WALTERS captained England against Scotland 1889 (most sources say PM), and the possibility that he was captain against Wales the year before. Neither's very likely. Note, however, that *The Athletic News*, *The Field* and *The Accrington Times* list him as captain (albeit all a little ambiguously) against Scotland in 1890. If he was, he and PM were the only brothers to both captain England. They were certainly the only brothers to win their first and last caps in exactly the same matches. Both were persuaded by their parents to give up the game after their brother HM was killed playing it in November 1890.

MARK
WALTERS

b 12 Jan 1961   OUTSIDE LEFT
Caps: 1 **Goals:** 0
Only cap: 3 Jun 1991 v N Zealand 1-0
                    aged 30yr 142d (sub'd 70min)
England career: P1 W1 D0 L0 – 100%
Club: Glasgow Rangers

Very skilful but labelled 'promising' for too long (surprising to see how old he was when finally capped). On the fringes for several years, but there was BARNES and now there's SHARPE and SALAKO.

PERCY
MELMOTH
WALTERS

b 30 Sep 1863 d 6 Oct 1936   LEFT/RIGHT BACK
Caps: 13 **Goals:** 0 **Captain:** 4 (6?)
First cap: 28 Feb 1885 v Ireland 4-0   aged 21yr 151d
Last cap: 5 Apr 1890 v Scotland 1-1   aged 26yr 187d
England career: 5yr 36d – P13 W8 D3 L2 – 73.08%
Clubs: Old Carthusians and Oxford University (2),
      Old Carthusians alone (11); Corinthians 1885–92

As good as his brother when it came to shoulder charging (and it came a great deal), his kicking apparently 'huge', he may have been captain in his last international (he was captain in his other match for England that season, but possibly allowed AM WALTERS to lead the team out just this once) and, most probably, against Wales in 1889.

NATHANIEL
WALTON

b 1867 d 3 Mar 1930   FORWARD
Caps: 1 **Goals:** 0–3
Only cap: 15 Mar 1890 v Ireland 9-1   aged 22/23
England career: P1 W1 D0 L0 – 100%
Club: Blackburn Rovers

Nat Walton won his only cap while another England side were beating Wales on the same day, a situation repeated in 1891 and 1892. *The Field* credits him with England's second goal, *The Times* and *Sporting Life* with the first *and* second, *The Sporting Chronicle* with the first, second, and eighth! But see GEARY.

JAMES
THOMAS
WARD

b 28 Mar 1865   d apparently prior to 1900
                                        LEFT BACK

Caps: 1 **Goals:** 0

Only cap: 14 Mar 1885 v Wales 1-1   aged 19yr 351d
England career: P1 W0 D1 L0 – 50%
Club: Blackburn Olympic

One of England's youngest ever defenders, Jimmy Ward was one of five players with local clubs in the match at Blackburn.

PETER
DAVID
WARD

b 27 Jul 1955   STRIKER
Caps: 1 **Goals:** 0
Only cap: 31 May 1980 v Australia 2-1   aged 24yr 309d
                                        (sub 82min)
England career: P1 W1 D0 L0 – 100%
Club: Brighton & Hove Albion

Those eight minutes equalled J BARRETT's record for the shortest ever England career.

TIMOTHY
VICTOR
WARD

b 17 Oct 1917/18   RIGHT HALF
Caps: 2 **Goals:** 0
First cap: 21 Sep 1947 v Belgium 5-2
                          aged 28/29yr 339d
Last cap: 10 Nov 1948 v Wales 1-0 aged 30/31yr 24d
England career: 1yr 50d – P2 W2 D0 L0 – 100%
Club: Derby County

When Laurie SCOTT was injured after 25 minutes against Wales, Tim Ward moved to right back, and (surprise, surprise) neither played for England again.

THOMAS
WARING

b 12 Oct 1906   d 20 Dec 1980   CENTRE FORWARD
Caps: 5 **Goals:** 4
First cap: 14 May 1931 v France 2-5   aged 24yr 214d
                                          (1 goal)
Last cap: 9 Apr 1932 v Scotland 3-0   aged 25yr 179d
                                          (1 goal)
England career: 0yr 330d – P5 W4 D0 L1 – 80%
Club: Aston Villa
2 Goals in a game: 1

'Pongo', who was nicknamed after a cartoon dog and never stopped chasing goals even at international level – in his first match, in his last, and twice against Ireland – was as good a centre forward as any of the others who took over: GS HUNT, BOWERS, TILSON, the declining DEAN. It's said that Herbert Chapman wanted him when he already had Ted DRAKE ('You'd like to buy me wouldn't you, Herbert? I'm better than any of your lot.'). No lack of confidence, or height, or all-round centre-forward talent.

CONRAD

WARNER

b 19 Apr 1852   d 10 Apr 1890   **GOALKEEPER**
Caps: 1   **Goals conceded:** 7
Only cap: 2 Mar 1878 v Scotland 2–7   aged 25yr 317d
England career: P1 W0 D0 L1 – 0%
Club: Upton Park

Debuts don't come much worse than this. Well actually they do: J Hamilton was in goal when England won 13–0 in the first international Ireland ever played, and another Irishman Hugh Kelly conceded nine against England on his debut in 1949 – but Warner's was the worst for any England keeper, the first of only two to concede seven in a single match. Like MERRICK, it wasn't all his fault (he was quite highly rated), this was just the most glaring example of several years of domination for the Scottish passing game over English individualism. At one stage the Scots led 6–0.

BENJAMIN
WARREN

b 1879   d 15 Jan 1917   **RIGHT HALF**
Caps: 22   **Goals:** 2
First cap: 17 Feb 1906 v Ireland 5–0   aged 26/27
Last cap: 1 Apr 1911 v Scotland 1–1   aged 31/32
England career: 5yr 43d – P22 W17 D4 L1 – 86.36%
Clubs: Derby County (13), Chelsea (9)
2 Goals in a game: 0

Ben Warren's remarkable career statistics owe something to two summer tours against inferior continental opposition, but his consistency over five years was never in question: 'yet to play a bad game for his country' said *The Sporting Life* after his 15th international. Would probably have been capped right up to World War I if he hadn't suddenly been certified insane in 1912 and sent to Derby Lunatic Asylum, dying soon after his release.

GEORGE
SMITH

WATERFIELD

b 2 Jun 1901   d ?   **LEFT BACK**
Caps: 1   **Goals:** 0
Only cap: 12 Feb 1927 v Wales 3–3   aged 25yr 255d
England career: P1 W0 D1 L0 – 50%
Club: Burnley

England were twice ahead, but needed DEAN's second goal to save the game. The defence was never comfortable, and neither fullback won another cap.

DAVID
WATSON

b 20 Nov 1961   **CENTRE HALF**
Caps: 12   **Goals:** 0
First cap: 10 Jun 1984 v Brazil 2–0   aged 22yr 202d
Last cap: 2 Jun 1988 v USSR 1–3   aged 26yr 194d
England career: 3yr 358d – P12 W6 D3 L3 – 62.50%
Clubs: Norwich City (6), Everton (6)
Substitute: 2   **Substituted:** 1

A standard stopper, like his namesake but less dominating, Dave Watson won a surprising number of caps without ever being a fixture.

DAVID
VERNON

WATSON

b 5 Oct 1946   **CENTRE HALF**
Caps: 65   **Goals:** 4   **Captain:** 3
First cap: 3 Apr 1974 v Portugal 0–0   aged 27yr 180d
Last cap: 2 Jun 1982 v Iceland 1–1   aged 35yr 240d
England career: 8yr 60d – P65 W33 D21 L11 – 66.92%
Clubs: Sunderland (14), Manchester City (30), Werder Bremen (1), Southampton (18), Stoke (2)
Substitute: 2   **Substituted:** 6
2 Goals in a game: 0   **Goals while captain:** 0

Among defenders, only Big Jack scored more often for England than Big Dave, a late developer and a slowish old-fashioned but muscular and effective fixture in Greenwood's teams, with 33 consecutive caps 1977–80.

VICTOR
MARTIN

WATSON

b 10 Nov 1897/98   d 3 Aug 1988   **CENTRE FORWARD**
Caps: 5   **Goals:** 4
First cap: 5 Mar 1923 v Wales 2–2   aged 24/25yr 115d (1 goal)
Last cap: 14 May 1930 v Austria 0–0   aged 31/32yr 185d
England career: 7yr 70d – P5 W1 D4 L0 – 60%
Club: West Ham United
Hat-tricks: 0   **2 Goals in a game:** 1

Quick and direct, the only centre forward to play for England before and after the change in the offside law in 1925, Vic Watson had to wait 6 years 356 days between his second and third caps, both against Scotland. He made up for lost time with two goals in a 5–2 revenge for the Wembley Wizards of two years earlier.

WILLIAM

WATSON

b 11 Sep 1890   d 1 Sep 1955   **LEFT HALF**
Caps: 3   **Goals:** 0

First cap: 5 Apr 1913 v Scotland 1–0 aged 22yr 206d
Last cap: 25 Oct 1919 v Ireland 1–1 aged 29yr 44d
England career: 6yr 203d – P3 W1 D1 L1 – 50%
Club: Burnley

Bill Watson was another of those whose England careers were interrupted by the First World War, missing 6 years 56 days in all.

WILLIAM
WATSON

b 7 Mar 1920   **RIGHT HALF**
Caps: 4 **Goals:** 0
First cap: 16 Nov 1949 v N Ireland 9–2 aged 29yr 254d
Last cap: 22 Nov 1950 v Yugoslavia 2–2 aged 30yr 260d
England career: 1yr 06d – P4 W3 D1 L0 – 87.50%
Club: Sunderland

Willie Watson, later a Test cricket selector, shared a match-saving partnership with Trevor Bailey against Australia at Lord's in one of his 23 Tests. He and another county cricketer, COMPTON, were dropped along with HANCOCKS after Yugoslavia recovered from 2–0 down.

SAMUEL
WEAVER

b 8 Feb 1909   d 15 Apr 1985   **LEFT HALF**
Caps: 3 **Goals:** 0
First cap: 9 Apr 1932 v Scotland 3–0 aged 23yr 61d
Last cap: 1 Apr 1933 v Scotland 1–2 aged 24yr 52d
England career: 0yr 357d – P3 W2 D0 L1 – 66.66%
Club: Newcastle United

Sam Weaver and Tommy GARDNER seem to have been the first players to be better known for long throws than anything else.

GEORGE
WILLIAM
WEBB

b 1887/88   d. 28 Mar 1915   **CENTRE FORWARD**
Caps: 2 **Goals:** 1
First cap: 13 Mar 1911 v Wales 3–0 aged 22–24
(1 goal)
Last cap: 1 Apr 1911 v Scotland 1–1 aged 22–24
England career: 0yr 45d – P2 W1 D1 L0 – 75%
Club: West Ham United

George Webb made his debut as partner to another amateur, WOODWARD, who scored the other two goals.

NEIL
JOHN
WEBB

b 30 Jul 1963   **MIDFIELDER**
Caps: 20 **Goals:** 2

First cap: 9 Sep 1987 v W Germany 1–3 aged 24yr 41d
(sub 64min)
Last cap: 7 Jul 1990 v Italy 1–2 aged 26yr 342d
(sub 72min)
England career: 2yr 301d – P20 W10 D6 L4 – 65%
Clubs: Nottingham Forest (18), Manchester United (2)
Substitute: 3 **Substituted:** 5
2 Goals in a game: 0 **Goals as substitute:** 0

Neil Webb was just beginning if not to control then to do some good things in England's midfield before a snapped Achilles in the qualifying match in Sweden kept him out of the World Cup until the very gentle third-place match, a setback from which his form still hasn't recovered. Without it, he might have gone on to be remembered for something more than being the 1000th player to be capped by England.

MAURICE
WEBSTER

b 13 Nov 1899   d Feb 1978   **CENTRE HALF**
Caps: 3 **Goals:** 0
First cap: 5 Apr 1930 v Scotland 5–2 aged 30yr 143d
Last cap: 14 May 1930 v Austria 0–0 aged 30yr 182d
England career: 0yr 39d – P3 W1 D2 L0 – 66.66%
Club: Middlesbrough

The STRANGE–Webster–MARSDEN line played in three successive matches in 1930.

WILLIAM
JOHN
WEDLOCK

b 28 Oct 1880   d 24 Jan 1965   **CENTRE HALF**
Caps: 26 **Goals:** 2
First cap: 16 Feb 1907 v Ireland 1–0 aged 26yr 111d
Last cap: 16 Mar 1914 v Wales 2–0 aged 33yr 139d
(1 goal)
England career: 7yr 28d – P26 W19 D6 L1 – 84.62%
Club: Bristol City

Along with Johnny Holt probably England's shortest ever centre-half, Billy the Rubberman had a long and very successful career during which he set a new record for the most successive caps: 25. The first match he missed was the first in which Ireland beat England. He was out for the rest of that 1913 season and celebrated his comeback with a goal in his last international. No-one else played in 25 consecutive matches for England until BLENKINSOP in 1933.

One of the first centre halves to score for England, he was the first to do it twice.

DAVID
WEIR

b 1862/63   d Nov 1933   **CENTRE HALF/INSIDE LEFT**

Caps: 2   Goals: 1?
First cap: 2 Mar 1889 v Ireland 6-1   aged c.26
Last cap: 13 Apr 1889 v Scotland 2-3   aged c.26
                                    (1 goal?)
England career: 0yr 42d – P2 W1 D0 L1 – 50%
Club: Bolton Wanderers

It's hard to know, now, why he was ever credited with England's second goal against Scotland. One match report offers it to BRODIE, but it was yet another of those goalmouth scrimmages, and most sources (*Glasgow Herald*, *The Field*, *North British Daily Mail*) don't specify an actual scorer. It's unlikely that anyone saw exactly who it was.

REGINALD
DE COURTENAY
WELCH

b 1851   d 4 Jun 1939   DEFENDER/GOALKEEPER
Caps: 2   Goals: 0   Goals conceded: 2
First cap: 30 Nov 1872 v Scotland 0-0   aged 20/21
Last cap: 8 Mar 1873 v Scotland 4-2   aged 21/22
England career: 0yr 98d – P2 W1 D1 L0 – 75%
Club: Harrow Chequers (and Wanderers, and possibly Remnants)

He and CHENERY were the first players to play for England twice. He was a back in the first ever international and goalkeeper in the second.

KEITH
WELLER

b 11 Jun 1946   MIDFIELDER
Caps: 4   Goals: 1
First cap: 11 May 1974 v Wales 2-0   aged 27yr 334d
Last cap: 22 May 1974 v Argentina 2-2   aged 27yr 345d
England career: 0yr 11d – P4 W2 D1 L1 – 62.50%
Club: Leicester City

Attacking midfielder who headed the only goal of the game against Northern Ireland at Wembley.

DONALD
WELSH

b 25 Feb 1911   d 2 Feb 1990   LEFT HALF/INSIDE LEFT
Caps: 3   Goals: 1
First cap: 14 May 1938 v Germany 6-3   aged 27yr 78d
Last cap: 24 May 1939 v Romania 2-0   aged 28yr 88d
                                    (1 goal)
England career: 1yr 10d – P3 W2 D0 L1 – 66.66%
Club: Charlton Athletic

Don Welsh scored England's last goal before (and had a successful international career during) the Second World War.

GORDON
WEST

b 24 April 1943   GOALKEEPER

Caps: 3   Goals conceded: 2   Clean sheets: 1
First cap: 11 Dec 1968 v Bulgaria 1-1   aged 25yr 231d
Last cap: 1 Jun 1969 v Mexico 0-0   aged 26yr 38d
England career: 0yr 172d – P3 W1 D2 L0 – 66.66%
Club: Everton

Bulky and erratic ('tumbling bear') but talented. Did nothing wrong as BANKS' stand-in.

WILLIAM
RAYMOND
WESTWOOD

b 14 Apr 1912   d Jan 1982   INSIDE LEFT
Caps: 6   Goals: 0
First cap: 29 Sep 1934 v Wales 4-0   aged 22yr 168d
Last cap: 17 Oct 1936 v Wales 1-2   aged 24yr 186d
England career: 2yr 18d – P6 W4 D0 L2 – 66.66%
Club: Bolton Wanderers

Not big but always ready with the shoulder charge, Ray Westwood made his international debut in very good company. Five others were winning their first caps: JW BARKER, BOWDEN, BRAY, BRITTON and Stanley MATTHEWS. Quite a little pantheon.

OLIVER
WHATELEY

b 1862   d Oct 1926   INSIDE RIGHT/LEFT
Caps: 2   Goals: 2
First cap: 24 Feb 1883 v Ireland 7-0   aged 20/21
                                    (2 goals)
Last cap: 10 Mar 1883 v Scotland 2-3   aged 20/21
England career: 0yr 14d – P2 W1 D0 L1 – 50%
Club: Aston Villa
2 Goals in a game: 1

Listed at numbers 6 and 11 in his two international line-ups, Olly Whateley was essentially a striker. Some yearbooks include him in all three England line-ups for 1883, but contemporary newspapers say he was originally chosen against Wales but replaced by AL BAMBRIDGE, who's mentioned in all match reports.

JOHN E
WHEELER

b 26 Jul 1928   RIGHT HALF
Caps: 1   Goals: 0
Only cap: 2 Oct 1954 v N Ireland 2-0   aged 26yr 68d
England career: P1 W1 D0 L0 – 100%
Club: Bolton Wanderers

Well-built and hard with it, Johnny Wheeler kept Jimmy McIlroy quiet at Windsor Park.

GEORGE FREDERICK

WHELDON

b 1 Nov 1869/71   d 13 Jan 1924   **INSIDE FORWARD**
Caps: 4   **Goals:** 6
First cap: 20 Feb 1897 v Ireland 6-0
aged 25/27yr 111d (3 goals)
Last cap: 2 Apr 1898 v Scotland 3-1
aged 26/28yr 152d (1 goal)
England career: 1yr 41d - P4 W4 D0 L0 - 100%
Club: Aston Villa
3 Goals in a game: 1   2 Goals in a game: 1

The figures do Fred Wheldon justice: he was one of the sharpest strikers of the day, Villa's leading scorer in the League when they won the Double in 1897. On his England debut he put an end to some over-elaboration from the other forwards (the ball was 'pedipalated from toe to toe') by smashing in the shot that gave him his hat-trick.

THOMAS
ANGUS

WHITE

b 29 Jul 1908   d 13 Aug 1967   **CENTRE HALF**
Caps: 1   **Goals:** 0
Only cap: 13 May 1933 v Italy 1-1   aged 24yr 288d
England career: P1 W0 D1 L0 - 50%
Club: Everton

Like FOX and JW BARRETT, Tommy White was unlucky. He pulled a thigh muscle in Rome but stayed in defence.

JAMES

WHITEHEAD

b 1870/71   d Aug 1929   **INSIDE RIGHT**
Caps: 2   **Goals:** 0
First cap: 13 Mar 1893 v Wales 6-0   aged 21-23
Last cap: 3 Mar 1894 v Ireland 2-2   aged 22-24
England career: 0yr 355d - P2 W1 D1 L0 - 75%
Clubs: Accrington FC (1), Blackburn Rovers (1)

Skilful and cocky, Jimmy Whitehead was good enough to have won more caps. But there was wholesale panic after the Irish had stolen a draw.

HERBERT

WHITFELD

b 25 Nov 1858   d 6 May 1909   **FORWARD**
Caps: 1   **Goals:** 1
Only cap: 18 Jan 1879 v Wales 2-1   aged 20yr 54d
(60 min, 1 goal)
England career: P1 W1 D0 L0 - 100%
Club: Old Etonians

Scored England's first ever goal against Wales.

MICHAEL
WHITHAM

b 6 Nov 1867   d 6 May 1924   **LEFT HALF**
Caps: 1   **Goals:** 0
Only cap: 5 Mar 1892 v Ireland 2-0   aged 24yr 150d
England career: P1 W1 D0 L0 - 100%
Club: Sheffield United

Almost without exception, contemporary match reports spell his name Whittam (or Whittem, or Whittame!), which is probably a mistake (or mistakes).

STEPHEN
WHITWORTH

b 20 Mar 1952   **RIGHT BACK**
Caps: 7   **Goals:** 0
First cap: 12 Mar 1975 v W Germany 2-0 aged 22yr 357d
Last cap: 19 Nov 1975 v Portugal 1-1   aged 23yr 244d
England career: 0yr 252d - P7 W4 D3 L0 - 78.57%
Club: Leicester City

Four players won their last caps in the match that cost England any real chance of a European Championship quarter-final: CLARKE, MAC-DONALD, David THOMAS – and Steve Whitworth, who (despite the good statistics) had formed an eyebrow-raising partnership with GILLARD.

TREVOR
JOHN
WHYMARK

b 4 May 1950   **CENTRE FORWARD**
Caps: 1   **Goals:** 0
Only cap: 12 Oct 1977 v Luxembourg 2-0
aged 27yr 161d (sub 64min)
England career: P1 W1 D0 L0 - 200%
Club: Ipswich Town

The tired old theory about small countries being frightened of big centre-forwards was still alive and kicking. The fact that he was given less than half an hour, and that he didn't score, showed that it wasn't kicking too hard.

SAM
WELLER
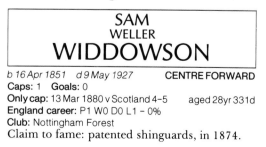
WIDDOWSON

b 16 Apr 1851   d 9 May 1927   **CENTRE FORWARD**
Caps: 1   **Goals:** 0
Only cap: 13 Mar 1880 v Scotland 4-5   aged 28yr 331d
England career: P1 W0 D0 L1 - 0%
Club: Nottingham Forest

Claim to fame: patented shinguards, in 1874.

FRANK

WIGNALL

b 21 Aug 1939   CENTRE FORWARD
Caps: 2   **Goals:** 2
First cap: 18 Nov 1964 v Wales 2–1   aged 25yr 89d
                                         (2 goals)
Last cap: 9 Dec 1964 v Holland 1–1   aged 25yr 110d
England career: 0yr 21d – P2 W1 D1 L0 – 75%
Club: Nottingham Forest

Sir Alf picked some blunt instruments at centre forward in his early years: SMITH, PICKERING, BRIDGES, and arguably Mick JONES. They didn't come much blunter than big Frank, who nevertheless put England 2–0 up after an hour against Wales.

ALBERT

WILKES

b 1874   d 9 Dec 1936   HALF BACK
Caps: 5   **Goals:** 1
First cap: 18 Mar 1901 v Wales 6–0   aged 26/27
Last cap: 3 May 1902 v Scotland 2–2   aged 27/28
                                         (1 goal)
England career: 1yr 46d – P5 W2 D3 L0 – 70%
Club: Aston Villa

Even though his goal helped pull England back from a two-goal deficit, he (along with BEATS, W GEORGE and HOGG) never played international football again.

RAYMOND
COLIN

WILKINS

b 14 Sep 1956   MIDFIELDER
Caps: 84   **Goals:** 3   **Captain:** 10
First cap: 28 May 1976 v Italy 3–2   aged 19yr 256d
Last cap: 12 Nov 1986 v Yugoslavia 2–0 aged 30yr 59d
                                         (sub 83min)
England career: 10yr 168d – P84 W45 D21 L18 – 66.07%
Clubs: Chelsea (24), Manchester United (38), Milan (22)
Substitute: 6   **Substituted:** 6
2 Goals in a game: 0   **Goals while captain:** 0

Ray Wilkins started out as a great attacking young talent, teenage captain of Chelsea, then won too many caps for someone who played so many square passes. Managers, both club and international, seem to have liked him for it, in England, Italy, France and Scotland. Never mind that he scored too few goals: none before his 24th international, none in his last 41. He was the fourth and last England player to be sent off (the first for England in the World Cup), against Morocco in Mexico.

BERNARD
WILKINSON

b 12 Sep 1879   d 28 May 1949   CENTRE HALF
Caps: 1   **Goals:** 0
Only cap: 9 Apr 1904 v Scotland 1–0   aged 24yr 210d
England career: P1 W1 D0 L0 – 100%
Club: Sheffield United

England scored early and tackled hard at Celtic Park, especially the new centre half, who 'like CROMPTON is none too particular in the manner in which he meets his opponents'. The selectors seem to have been rather more so after that.

LEONARD RODWELL

WILKINSON

b 15 Oct 1868   d 9 Feb 1913   GOALKEEPER
Caps: 1   **Goals conceded:** 1
Only cap: 7 Mar 1891 v Wales 4–1   aged 22yr 143d
England career: P1 W1 D0 L0 – 100%
Club: Oxford University (and Corinthians)

Just the one cap – and he'd hardly broken sweat: England were 4–0 up by half-time.

BERT
FREDERICK
WILLIAMS

b 31 Jan 1920   GOALKEEPER
Caps: 24   **Goals conceded:** 34   **Clean sheets:** 3
First cap: 22 May 1949 v France 3–1   aged 29yr 111d
Last cap: 22 Oct 1955 v Wales 1–2   aged 35yr 264d
England career: 6yr 153d – P24 W13 D4 L7 – 62.50%
Club: Wolves
Penalties: 2   **Saved:** 0

An original Cat, Bert Williams was spectacular and could be brilliant (he made save after save as England somehow beat Italy 2–0 in 1949), but he wasn't always safe and he let in a few goals too many while playing for England. The first arrived within 28 seconds (scored by another new cap, Georges Moreel) but after that he was a regular choice, despite appearing in quite a high percentage of losing England teams. The USA's goal in the 1950 World Cup was at least partly his fault.

OWEN

WILLIAMS

b 23 Sep 1895/96   d 9 Dec 1960   OUTSIDE LEFT
Caps: 2   **Goals:** 0
First cap: 21 Oct 1922 v Ireland 2–0   aged 26/27yr 28d
Last cap: 5 Mar 1923 v Wales 2–2   aged 26/27yr 163d
England career: 0yr 135d – P2 W1 D1 L0 – 75%
Club: Clapton Orient

One of the fastest players of his time, some say of all time.

STEVEN CHARLES WILLIAMS

b 12 Jul 1958 **MIDFIELDER**
Caps: 6 **Goals:** 0
First cap: 12 Jun 1983 v Australia 0–0 aged 24yr 335d
Last cap: 14 Nov 1984 v Turkey 8–0 aged 26yr 125d
  (sub'd 67min)
England career: 1yr 155d – P6 W4 D1 L1 – 75%
Club: Southampton
Substitute: 1 **Substituted:** 1
Often unnecessarily aggressive in club matches, in the end unnecessary for England, Steve Williams promised a lot.

WILLIAM WILLIAMS

b 20 Jan 1876 d 22 Jan 1929 **FULL BACK**
Caps: 6 **Goals:** 0
First cap: 20 Feb 1897 v Ireland 6–0 aged 21yr 31d
Last cap: 20 Mar 1899 v Wales 4–0 aged 23yr 59d
England career: 2yr 28d – P6 W6 D0 L0 – 100%
Club: West Bromwich Albion
Despite 'his habit of reckless jumping', Bill Williams' record of Played 6, Won 6 is the England best, equalled by HINE.

ERNEST CLARKE WILLIAMSON

b 24 May 1890 d 30 Apr 1964 **GOALKEEPER**
Caps: 2 **Goals conceded:** 3
First cap: 21 May 1923 v Sweden 4–2 aged 32yr 362d
Last cap: 24 May 1923 v Sweden 3–1 aged 33yr 00d
England career: 0yr 03d – P2 W2 D0 L0 – 100%
Club: Arsenal
Ernie Williamson was nicknamed 'Tim' after the other goalkeeper called WILLIAMSON who played for England. All three goals conceded by Ernie Tim in internationals were scored by Harry Dahl, who was the first foreign player to score twice, let alone three times, against England.

REGINALD GARNET WILLIAMSON

b 6 Jun 1884 d 1 Aug 1943 **GOALKEEPER**
Caps: 7 **Goals conceded:** 6 **Clean sheets:** 2
First cap: 25 Feb 1905 v Ireland 1–1 aged 20yr 264d
  (own goal)
Last cap: 15 Feb 1913 v Ireland 1–2 aged 28yr 254d
England career: 7yr 355d – P7 W3 D3 L1 – 64.29%
Club: Middlesbrough
'Tim' Williamson had to wait 5 years 351 days for a second cap – perhaps not too surprisingly since he was the only player to score an own goal on his England debut. After that, things looked up: it wasn't until his last match that he conceded more than one goal in any international.

CHARLES KENNETH WILLINGHAM

b 1 Dec 1912 d May 1975 **RIGHT HALF**
Caps: 12 **Goals:** 1
First cap: 20 May 1937 v Finland 8–0 aged 24yr 170d
  (1 goal)
Last cap: 18 May 1939 v Yugoslavia 1–2 aged 26yr 168d
England career: 1yr 363d – P12 W7 D1 L4 – 62.50%
Club: Huddersfield Town
An aggressive little midfielder, Ken Willingham played in 11 consecutive internationals, then missed the last before the Second World War.

ARTHUR WILLIS

b 2 Feb 1920 **LEFT BACK**
Caps: 1 **Goals:** 0
Only cap: 3 Oct 1951 v France 2–2 aged 31yr 243d
England career: P1 W0 D1 L0 – 50%
Club: Tottenham Hotspur
England struggled throughout, and four weren't capped again.

DENNIS JAMES (JOHN?) WILSHAW

b 11 Mar 1926 **INSIDE LEFT**
Caps: 12 **Goals:** 10
First cap: 10 Oct 1953 v Wales 4–1 aged 27yr 213d
  (2 goals)
Last cap: 6 Oct 1956 v N Ireland 1–1 aged 30yr 209d
England career: 2yr 362d – P12 W6 D2 L4 – 58.33%
Club: Wolves
4 Goals in a game: 1 **2 Goals in a game:** 2
In 1955, in the 72nd match between the two countries, Dennis Wilshaw scored England's first hat-trick against Scotland, the only player to score four in a match for either side. He scored regularly for England (including once in the 1954 World Cup finals) without ever quite being a fixture.

CHARLES PLUMPTON WILSON

b 12 May 1859 d 9 Mar 1938 **HALF BACK**
Caps: 2 **Goals:** 0

First cap: 15 Mar 1884 v Scotland 0–1   aged 24yr 307d
Last cap: 17 Mar 1884 v Wales 4–0   aged 24yr 309d
England career: 0yr 02d – P2 W1 D0 L1 – 50%
Club: Hendon (and Corinthians)

Nineteen years older than his brother GP WILSON, Charles P also played rugby union for England.

CLAUDE
WILLIAM
WILSON

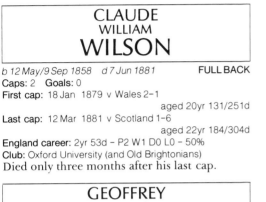

b 12 May/9 Sep 1858   d 7 Jun 1881   **FULL BACK**
Caps: 2   **Goals:** 0
First cap: 18 Jan 1879 v Wales 2–1
                              aged 20yr 131/251d
Last cap: 12 Mar 1881 v Scotland 1–6
                              aged 22yr 184/304d
England career: 2yr 53d – P2 W1 D0 L0 – 50%
Club: Oxford University (and Old Brightonians)

Died only three months after his last cap.

GEOFFREY
PLUMPTON
WILSON

b 21 Feb 1878   d 30 Jul 1934   **INSIDE LEFT**
Caps: 2   **Goals:** 1
First cap: 26 Mar 1900 v Wales 1–1   aged 22yr 34d
                                            (1 goal)
Last cap: 7 Apr 1900 v Scotland 1–4   aged 22yr 46d
England career: 0yr 12d – P2 W0 D1 L1 – 25%
Club: Corinthians

His brother and fellow Corinthian CP WILSON also played for England – at two different sports.

GEORGE
WILSON

b 14 Jan 1892   d 25 Nov 1961   **CENTRE HALF**
Caps: 12   **Goals:** 0   **Captain:** 7
First cap: 14 Mar 1921 v Wales 0–0   aged 29yr 59d
Last cap: 17 May 1924 v France 3–1   aged 32yr 123d
England career: 3yr 64d – P12 W4 D4 L4 – 50%
Club: Sheffield Wednesday

George Wilson wasn't tall, but he could head a ball – and lead a team: he was captain in his last five internationals.

RAMON
WILSON

b 17 Dec 1934   **LEFT BACK**
Caps: 63   **Goals:** 0
First cap: 9 Apr 1960 v Scotland 1–1   aged 25yr 114d
Last cap: 8 Jun 1968 v USSR 2–0   aged 33yr 174d
England career: 8yr 60d – P63 W36 D16 L11 – 69.84%
Clubs: Huddersfield Town (30), Everton (33)
Substitute: 1

The oldest player in the 1966 World Cup Final, now an undertaker with the attendant sense of humour ('here's my card'), Ray Wilson overtook CROMPTON as England's most capped full back before SANSOM; his last match was the European Championships third-place match in Rome. The mistimed header that set up Haller's goal in the Wembley final was commonly acknowledged as his first mistake of the tournament. Good coming forward, exceptional staying back: England's best.

THOMAS
WILSON

b 16 Apr 1896   d 2 Feb 1948   **CENTRE HALF**
Caps: 1   **Goals:** 0
Only cap: 31 Mar 1928 v Scotland 1–5   aged 31yr 349d
England career: P1 W0 D0 L1 – 0%
Club: Huddersfield Town

A dominating figure in the Huddersfield teams that won three successive League titles and reached four FA Cup Finals, Tom Wilson was unlucky to be capped just once, very late, against the Wembley Wizards; although he did stop the great Hughie Gallacher from scoring.

WILLIAM
NORMAN
WINCKWORTH

b 9 Feb 1870   d 9 Nov 1941   **CENTRE HALF**
Caps: 2   **Goals:** 1
First cap: 5 Mar 1892 v Wales 2–0   aged 22yr 25d
Last cap: 25 Feb 1893 v Ireland 6–1   aged 23yr 16d
                                            (1 goal)
England career: 0yr 357d – P2 W2 D0 L0 – 100%
Club: Old Westminsters (and Corinthians)

Norman Winckworth scored England's fifth goal against Ireland at a time when half backs were essentially auxiliary forwards.

JAMES
EDWIN (EDWARD?)
WINDRIDGE

b 21 Oct 1882/83   d 23 Sep 1939   **INSIDE LEFT**
Caps: 8   **Goals:** 7
First cap: 15 Feb 1908 v Ireland 3–1   aged 24/25yr 117d
Last cap: 13 Feb 1909 v Ireland 4–0   aged 25/26yr 115d
England career: 0yr 363d – P7 W6 D1 L0 – 92.86%
Club: Chelsea
Hat-tricks: 0   **2 Goals in a game:** 1

In his year of international football, Jimmy Windridge enjoyed himself in Europe, scoring in six successive matches.

CECIL VERNON
WINFIELD-STRATFORD

b 7 Oct 1853   d 5 Feb 1939   OUTSIDE LEFT
Caps: 1   **Goals:** 0
Only cap: 3 Mar 1877 v Scotland 1-3   aged 23yr 147d
England career: P1 W0 D0 L1 – 0%
Club: Royal Engineers

Retired as Brigadier Cecil Vernon Wingfield-Stratford, CMG, CB. They don't name 'em like that any more.

NIGEL
WINTERBURN

b 11 Dec 1963   LEFT BACK
Caps: 1   **Goals:** 0
Only cap: 15 Nov 1989 v Italy 0-0   aged 25yr 339d
                                              (sub 67min)
England career: P1 W0 D1 L0 – 50%
Club: Arsenal

Arsenal provided both England full backs in the eighties – Viv ANDERSON and Kenny SANSOM – and might still do the same in the nineties with Lee DIXON and Winterburn, who so far has jumped the queue behind PEARCE for just 23 minutes.

DENNIS F
WISE

b 15 Dec 1966   WIDE MIDFIELDER
Caps: 5   **Goals:** 1
First cap: 1 May 1991 v Turkey 1-0   aged 24yr 137d
                                              (1 goal)
Last cap: 8 Jun 1991 v N Zealand 2-0   aged 24yr 175d
England career: 0yr 38d – P5 W5 D0 L0 – 100%
Club: Chelsea
Substitute: 1   **Substituted:** 1

Graham Taylor's first I Told You So? Capped despite a poor spell with his club, he scrambled (handled?) a goal in Izmir.

PETER
WITHE

b 30 Aug 1951   CENTRE FORWARD
Caps: 11   **Goals:** 1
First cap: 12 May 1981 v Brazil 0-1   aged 29yr 255d
Last cap: 14 Nov 1984 v Turkey 8-0   aged 33yr 76d
England career: 3yr 186d – P1 W5 D3 L3 – 59.09%
Club: Aston Villa
Substitute: 2   **Substituted:** 2

Big Withey did score goals but somehow wasn't quite (just?) a goalscorer – even his winner in the European Cup Final went in off the post from just a few yards out.

CHARLES
HENRY REYNOLDS
WOLLASTON

b 31 Jul 1849   d 22 Jun 1926   FORWARD
Caps: 4   **Goals:** 1   **Captain:** 1
First cap: 7 Mar 1874 v Scotland 1-2   aged 24yr 219d
Last cap: 13 Mar 1880 v Scotland 4-5   aged 30yr 225d
England career: 6yr 06d – P4 W0 D1 L3 – 12.50%
Club: Wanderers (and Lancing Old Boys, and perhaps
        Clapham Rovers)

Handicapped by a damaged knee throughout his first international, captain in his last, Charles Wollaston had the longest England career up to that time.

SAMUEL
WOLSTENHOLME

b 1876/78   d unknown   RIGHT HALF
Caps: 3   **Goals:** 0
First cap: 9 Apr 1904 v Scotland 1-0   aged 25-28?
Last cap: 27 Mar 1905 v Wales 3-1   aged 26-29?
England career: 0yr 352d – P3 W2 D1 L0 – 83.33%
Clubs: Everton (1), Blackburn Rovers (2)

Formed a raw but aggressive half-back line in Glasgow with LEAKE and Bernard WILKINSON.

HARRY
WOOD

b 26 Jun 1868   d 5 Jul 1951   INSIDE FORWARD
Caps: 3   **Goals:** 1
First cap: 15 Mar 1890 v Wales 3-1   aged 21yr 262d
Last cap: 4 Apr 1896 v Scotland 1-2   aged 27yr 282d
England career: 6yr 20d – P3 W1 D1 L1 – 50%
Club: Wolves

In 1890 he was England's 'best inside left for many years', but then had to wait almost exactly six years between his second and third caps, and was only 'a real good worker, though nothing brilliant' when recalled in place of the irreplaceable BLOOMER: it meant an end to England's six-year run of 20 matches without defeat.

RAYMOND E
WOOD

b 11 Jun 1931   GOALKEEPER
Caps: 3   **Goals conceded:** 3   **Clean sheets:** 1
First cap: 2 Oct 1954 v N Ireland 2-0   aged 23yr 113d
Last cap: 20 May 1956 v Finland 5-1   aged 24yr 344d
England career: 1yr 231d – P3 W3 D0 L0 – 100%
Club: Manchester United

One of seven new caps who played in England's first match after the World Cup.

ANTHONY STEWART
WOODCOCK

b 6 Dec 1955   STRIKER
Caps: 42   Goals: 16
First cap: 16 May 1978 v N Ireland 1–0   aged 22yr 161d
Last cap: 26 Feb 1986 v Israel 2–1   aged 30yr 82d
(sub 54min)
England career: 7yr 286d – P42 W25 D10 L7 – 71.43%
Clubs: Nottingham Forest (6), Cologne (33), Arsenal (3)
Substitute: 12   Substituted: 10
2 Goals in a game: 3   Goals as substitute: 1

Tony Woodcock's scoring rate was pretty good for someone who played only 20 complete matches. His partnership with Trevor FRANCIS was promising great things for the 1980 European Championship finals before Francis was injured. Even then, Woodcock's disallowed goal against Belgium may have made all the difference. In his next match, against Italy, he was on the losing side for the first time. Twice he scored in three consecutive internationals. Generally a tale of what might have been.

GEORGE
WOODGER

b 3 Sep 1883/84   3 1961   OUTSIDE LEFT
Caps: 1   Goals: 0
Only cap: 11 Feb 1911 v Ireland 2–1   aged 26/27yr 161d
England career: P1 W1 D0 L0 – 100%
Club: Oldham Athletic

His style of play earned him the nickname 'Lady'.

GEORGE
WOODHALL

b 5 Sep 1863   d 29 Sep 1924   OUTSIDE RIGHT
Caps: 2   Goals: 1
First cap: 4 Feb 1888 v Wales 5–1   aged 24yr 152d
(1 goal)
Last cap: 17 Mar 1888 v Scotland 5–0   aged 24yr 194d
England career: 0yr 42d – P2 W2 D0 L0 – 100%
Club: West Bromwich Albion

'Spry' Woodhall's goal against Wales was the 100th scored by England.

VICTOR ROBERT
WOODLEY

b 26 Feb 1910/11   d 23 Oct 1978   GOALKEEPER
Caps: 19   Goals conceded: 26   Clean sheets: 7
First cap: 17 Apr 1937 v Scotland 1–3 aged 26/27yr 50d
Last cap: 24 May 1939 v Romania 2–0 aged 28/29yr 87d
England career: 2yr 37d – P19 W13 D1 L5 – 71.05%
Club: Chelsea
Penalties: 1   Saved: 0

Very much HIBBS' successor and one of the first English goalkeepers to come off his line for crosses, Vic Woodley's run of 19 consecutive internationals was ended only by the Second World War.

CHRISTOPHER CHARLES ERIC
WOODS

b 14 Nov 1959   GOALKEEPER
Caps: 24   Goals conceded: 8   Clean sheets: 19
First cap: 16 Jun 1985 v USA 5–0   aged 25yr 214d
Last cap: 12 Jun 1991 v Malaysia 4–2   aged 31yr 206d
England career: 5yr 361d – P24 W17 D6 L1 – 83.33%
Clubs: Norwich City (4), Glasgow Rangers (20)
Substitute: 9

Peter SHILTON generally kept Chris Woods out of the England team – yet helped him to some remarkable statistics. Partly as a result of playing a total of only 70 minutes in three of his early matches (replacing Shilts each time), Woods didn't concede a goal until the closing minutes of his sixth international, a record for any England goalkeeper. He then kept another six clean sheets (five in complete matches) before meeting the USSR in Frankfurt (1–3). Another five followed before he received a Tony Cascarino header as an unwelcome 31st birthday present in Dublin.

VIVIAN JOHN
WOODWARD

b 3 Jun 1879   d 31 Jan 1954   CENTRE FORWARD
Caps: 23   Goals: 29   Captain: 13
First cap: 14 Feb 1903 v Ireland 4–0   aged 23yr 225d
(2 goals)
Last cap: 13 Mar 1911 v Wales 3–0   aged 31yr 252d
(2 goals)
England career: 8yr 27d – P23 W18 D4 L1 – 86.96%
Clubs: Tottenham Hotspur (21), Chelsea (2)
4 Goals in a game: 2   3 Goals in a game: 2
2 Goals in a game: 5   Goals while captain: 21

Vivian Woodward scored more goals for England than anyone else before 1958 – but it was achieved rather cheaply, even a little dubiously.

No fewer than 15 of his goals were scored against Austria and Hungary, weak emergent amateur teams at the time. Against the only other strong country, Scotland, he scored just once – unlike BLOOMER, who scored eight, including two with Woodward alongside him. There's also a doubt as to whether he did score 29 in all, or only equalled Bloomer's record: one of his goals against Hungary in 1909 is listed as an own goal by *The Sporting Life* and in official Hungarian records.

Reservations apart, his list of England records sounds impressive. He scored at least two goals in the game nine times, the record until N LOFTHOUSE in 1955. The total of goals he scored while captain is still the England record (see B ROBSON) and he's still the only England captain to score two, let alone three, hat-tricks – and it might well have been four if he hadn't allowed HILSDON to take a penalty against Ireland in 1909 after he'd scored twice himself. He scored a hat-trick in each of two successive games (v Hungary, Austria, 1909), matched by only DEAN and T TAYLOR. He scored eight goals in all against Austria and seven against Hungary, records against non-British countries. He put six past Hungary's Ferenc Bihari alone, the record for one England player against any one goalkeeper (equalled only by GREAVES against Harry Gregg). He was captain in England's 100th international, against Wales in 1909.

In 67 internationals, amateur and professional, he scored 86 goals, still a world record of sorts (some of Pele's 97 were scored against club teams and regional selections). He and A BERRY were the only two full internationals to win two Olympic gold medals (1908 and 1912).

Selected to play against Ireland in 1908, he cried off with an injury.

MAXWELL
WOOSNAM

b 6 Sep 1892   d 14 Jul 1965   **CENTRE HALF**
Caps: 1   Goals: 0   Captain: 1
Only cap: 13 Mar 1922 v Wales 1–0   aged 29yr 188d
England career: P1 W1 D0 L0 – 100%
Club: Manchester City
One of a spate of 1920s amateurs who captained England in their only internationals (KNIGHT, PATCHITT (2), DOGGART, ASHTON), Max Woosnam was much better at tennis, winning the Wimbledon men's doubles in 1921, reaching the final of the mixed a year later, and playing in the 1920 and 1924 Olympics.

FREDERICK
WORRALL

b 8 Sep 1910/11   d 13 Apr 1979   **OUTSIDE RIGHT**
Caps: 2   Goals: 2
First cap: 18 May 1935 v Holland 1–0
aged 23/24yr 252d (1 goal)
Last cap: 18 Nov 1936 v Ireland 3–1
aged 25/26yr 71d (1 goal)
England career: 1yr 184d – P2 W2 D0 L0 – 100%
Club: Portsmouth
Fred Worrall, a fast straightforward winger typical of the thirties (BIRKETT, BROOK, HULME,

KIRCHEN etc) did well to be capped at all in the era of CROOKS and S MATTHEWS.

FRANK
STUART
WORTHINGTON

b 23 Nov 1948   **STRIKER**
Caps: 8   Goals: 2
First cap: 15 May 1974 v N Ireland 1–0   aged 25yr 174d
(sub 65min)
Last cap: 20 Nov 1974 v Portugal 0–0   aged 26yr 07d
(sub 70min)
England career: 0yr 187d – P8 W3 D4 L1 – 62.50%
Club: Leicester City
Substitute: 2   Substituted: 3   2 Goals in a game: 0
Skilful and seriously smooth, very much a MERCER not a REVIE player (the story goes that he once combed his hair on the pitch), Frank Worthington scored the only goal of England's game against Bulgaria in Sofia.

CHARLES
WREFORD-BROWN

b 9 Oct 1866   d 26 Nov 1951   **HALF BACK**
Caps: 4   Goals: 0   Captain: 1
First cap: 2 Mar 1889 v Ireland 6–1   aged 22yr 116d
Last cap: 2 Apr 1898 v Scotland 3–1   aged 31yr 147d
England career: 9yr 31d – P4 W3 D1 L0 – 87.50%
Clubs: Oxford University and Old Carthusians (1),
Old Carthusians alone (3); Corinthians throughout
A half back all-rounder typical of his day, his England appearances were scattered about: 1889, 1894, 1895, 1898, including a gap of 5 years 9 days between the first two. May have been captain against Wales in 1894.

EDWARD
GORDON
DUNDAS
WRIGHT

b 3 Oct 1884   d 5 Jun 1947   **OUTSIDE LEFT**
Caps: 1   Goals: 0
Only cap: 19 Mar 1906 v Wales 1–0   aged 21yr 167d
England career: P1 W1 D0 L0 – 100%
Club: Cambridge University (and Corinthians)
Gordon Wright won an Olympic gold medal with the 1912 United Kingdom team.

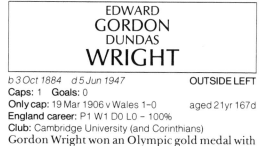

Right *On top of the world (well, getting there). After winning his 100th cap in the win over Scotland in 1959, Billy Wright climbs into a chair manufactured by Messrs Clayton and Howe* (Colorsport)

IAN
WRIGHT

b 3 Nov 1963 **STRIKER**
Caps: 4 **Goals:** 0
First cap: 6 Feb 1991 v Cameroon 2–0 aged 27yr 92d
Last cap: 8 Jun 1991 v N Zealand 2–0 aged 27yr 217d
England career: 0yr 122d – P4 W3 D1 L0 – 87.50%
Club: Crystal Palace
Substitute: 1 **Substituted:** 1

Late developer fron non-League. Ability to twist and turn and beat a man. Exciting possibilities, but time and LINEKER stand in the way and a goal wouldn't go amiss.

JOHN
DOUGLAS
WRIGHT

b 29 Apr 1917 **LEFT HALF**
Caps: 1 **Goals:** 0
Only cap: 9 Nov 1938 v Norway 4–0 aged 21yr 194d
England career: P1 W1 D0 L0 – 100%
Club: Newcastle United

Easy for England at St James's Park, a cushy number for Doug Wright.

MARK
WRIGHT

b 1 Aug 1963 **CENTRAL DEFENDER**
Caps: 40 **Goals:** 1 **Captain:** 1
First cap: 2 May 1984 v Wales 0–1 aged 20yr 274d
Last cap: 12 Jun 1991 v Malaysia 4–2 aged 27yr 315d
England career: 7yr 41d – P40 W22 D13 L5 – 71.25%
Clubs: Southampton (16), Derby County (24)
Substitute: 1 **Substituted:** 2

A ball-playing centre half who made mistakes in the first phase of his England career (Mark Hughes heading the only goal of their mutual debut; Ray Houghton heading the only goal of the match in Stuttgart after Wright went for a ball that wasn't his) and was kept out of the 1986 World Cup finals by a broken leg, he was recalled just before Italia 90, where he looked one of the very best defenders in the tournament and headed the only goal of the game against Egypt.

THOMAS
JOHN
WRIGHT

b 21 Oct 1944 **RIGHT BACK**
Caps: 11 **Goals:** 0
First cap: 8 Jun 1968 v USSR 2–0 aged 23yr 231d

Last cap: 7 Jun 1970 v Brazil 0–1   aged 25yr 230d
England career: 1yr 364d – P11 W5 D4 L2 – 63.63%
Club: Everton
Substitute: 2 **Substituted:** 1

A chunky all-round full back who didn't look out of place in the England team, Tommy Wright played against Brazil without having completely recovered from the previous match, in which Romania's Mihai Mocanu fouled NEWTON and Francis LEE so badly they had to be substituted; Tommy Wright came on for Newton and was kicked by the same player, who escaped without so much as a booking.

WILLIAM
AMBROSE
WRIGHT

b 6 Feb 1924   RIGHT/LEFT/CENTRE HALF
Caps: 105 **Goals:** 3 **Captain:** 90
First cap: 28 Sep 1946 v N Ireland 7–2 aged 22yr 234d
Last cap: 28 May 1959 v USA 8–1   aged 35yr 111d
England career: 12yr 242d – P105 W60 D25 L20 – 69.05%
Club: Wolves
2 Goals in a game: 0 **Goals while captain:** 3

After 59 caps as a mediocre wing-half, Billy Wright moved into the middle during the 1954 World Cup – and settled in for life. Lucky that manager Winterbottom thought so much of him, the fact remains that he was a success in central defence with his tackling and ability in the air. His appearance records might not have been achieved under another manager but were still remarkable for his time; some still stand.

Against Scotland in 1959 he became the first footballer, from any country, to win 100 caps; the last 70 were consecutive, still the world record (all as captain, another world best), as is his total number of games as captain (equalled by Bobby MOORE).

He overtook CROMPTON's record number of England caps in 1952, Billy Meredith's British record in 1953; he and FRANKLIN overhauled BLENKINSOP's total of 26 consecutive caps in 1950; he reached 33 before missing an international for the first time, then reached 34 in 1955 on his way to that record 70. He was also England's oldest captain between PENNINGTON and SHILTON.

JOHN GEORGE
WYLIE

b 1854   d 30 Jul 1924   FORWARD
Caps: 1 **Goals:** 1
Only cap: 2 Mar 1878 v Scotland 2–7   aged 23/24
England career: P1 W0 D0 L1 – 0%
Club: Wanderers (and probably Sheffield FC)

Scored England's first goal with the score already 6–0. Was once listed as having played against Scotland in 1874. See HAWLEY EDWARDS.

JOHN
YATES

b 1861   d 1 Jun 1917   OUTSIDE LEFT
Caps: 1 **Goals:** 3
Only cap: 2 Mar 1889 v Ireland 6–1 aged 27–28 (3 goals)
England career: P1 W1 D0 L0 – 100%
Club: Burnley

An England team with nine new caps went to Anfield, 'chosen with the object of giving several players who might not otherwise have a chance of attaining International honours, an opportunity of distinction.' Jack Yates grasped it firmly.

RICHARD
ERNEST
YORK

b 25 Apr 1899   d 9 Dec 1969   OUTSIDE RIGHT
Caps: 2 **Goals:** 0
First cap: 8 Apr 1922 v Scotland 0–1 aged 22yr 348d
Last cap: 17 Apr 1926 v Scotland 0–1 aged 26yr 357d
England career: 4yr 09d – P2 W0 D0 L2 – 0%
Club: Aston Villa

Tricky Dicky's international career was neat if nothing else: both matches against the same country, both at home, both 1–0 defeats.

ALFRED
YOUNG

b 4 Nov 1905/07   d 30 Aug 1977   CENTRE HALF
Caps: 9 **Goals:** 0
First cap: 16 Nov 1932 v Wales 0–0 aged 25/27yr 12d
Last cap: 22 Oct 1938 v Wales 2–4 aged 30/32yr 341d
England career: 5yr 329d – P9 W5 D1 L3 – 61.11%
Club: Huddersfield Town

Classic overpowering stopper who had to wait four seasons for a second cap, then more or less established himself despite competition from CULLIS.

GERALD
MORTON
YOUNG

b 1 Oct 1936   LEFT-HALF
Caps: 1 **Goals:** 0
Only cap: 18 Nov 1964 v Wales 2–1   aged 28yr 48d
England career: P1 W1 D0 L0 – 100%
Club: Sheffield Wednesday

Won his cap as a stand-in for Bobby MOORE, and coped well enough.